THE LIVING LIGHT DIALOGUE

Volume 3

THE LIVING LIGHT DIALOGUE

Volume 3

※

Through the mediumship of
Richard P. Goodwin

Living Light Books

The Living Light Dialogue Volume 3
Copyright © 2010 Serenity Association

Through the mediumship of Richard P. Goodwin.

All rights reserved. Printed in the United States of America. No portion of this book may be reproduced—electronically, mechanically, or via internet transmission—without advance, express written permission of the publisher except in the case of brief quotations embodied in critical articles and reviews. No derivative work—games supplemental material, video—may be created without advance, express written permission of the publisher. For information address Living Light Books, P.O. Box 4187, San Rafael, CA 94913-4187.

Cover design copyright © 2010 by Serenity Association
Cover photograph by Serenity Association, 2010; copyright © 2010 by Serenity Association.

www.livinglight.org

Library of Congress Control Number 2007929762

FIRST EDITION

This volume of teachings is dedicated to the spirit friends who brought to Earth the Living Light philosophy. With eternal gratitude, we pray that we may demonstrate these principles and continue to bring to publication these teachings.

CONTENTS

Acknowledgement ix
Preface xi
Consciousness Class 45 3
Consciousness Class 46 20
Consciousness Class 47 37
Consciousness Class 48 55
Consciousness Class 49 73
Consciousness Class 50 88
Consciousness Class 51 102
Consciousness Class 52 119
Consciousness Class 53 138
Consciousness Class 54 158
Consciousness Class 55 174
Consciousness Class 56 190
Consciousness Class 57 212
Consciousness Class 58 230
Consciousness Class 59 253
Consciousness Class 60 270
Consciousness Class 61 294
Consciousness Class 62 317
Consciousness Class 63 335
Consciousness Class 64 358
Consciousness Class 65 375
Consciousness Class 66 393
Consciousness Class 67 413
Consciousness Class 68 429
Appendix 455

ACKNOWLEDGMENT

Grateful acknowledgement is made to the many friends and associates for invaluable aid in compiling this book, for their helpful suggestions, for their loyal interest and encouragement.

Special acknowledgement is due to those who painstakingly and selflessly transcribed and proofread the text.

PREFACE

This book, Volume 3 of *The Living Light Dialogue*, brought forth from the realms of Light, is a guide and teacher. Through application of these teachings, we are led into the inner being where all experiences are created, thus giving us the opportunity to make changes which we may find useful in our lives.

"Whatever you are seeking is also seeking you, and like the hands of the clock, opportunity meets every so often." This is not just a saying which, incidentally, appeared in Volume 2 of *The Living Light Dialogue*. It is a universal law which is emphasized, discussed, and demonstrated in a philosophy known as the Living Light. The philosophy was brought to Earth over a twenty-five-year period through the mediumship of Richard P. Goodwin, founder of the Serenity Association, teacher, and friend to those who chose to learn from his example and apply his teachings.

While Mr. Goodwin had been consciously aware of angels since he was fourteen, it was on January 6, 1964, that he became a trance medium and it is the first recorded instance of his spirit teacher expressing. In trance mediumship, the consciousness of the channel is removed from the channel's physical form and another being is then free to express through that form. The proper owner of the physical form is generally unaware of what is being said through their form. In the early discourses, Mr. Goodwin was completely unaware of what was being said.

Under the guidance of angels, on August 20, 1968, Mr. Goodwin and four other individuals founded Camp Serenity. The *Serenity Sentinel*, the monthly magazine of Serenity, states the following in its July 1969 issue:

The specific and primary purpose of Camp Serenity is to teach and to sponsor classes, symposiums, seminars and conferences, representing the science, philosophy, and religion of spiritualism, as these concepts concern the nature of man, the universe, and of God and the relationship between them, leading to a sense of unity in people's consciousness and promoting brotherhood among all races, creeds, and persons.

Mr. Goodwin concentrated his efforts to bring forth these teachings as described in the above dedication. As students, we have continued to discover that, through daily study and conscious effort of application of the laws discussed, we are aware and reveal to ourselves our own inner being. With the understanding of the Living Light philosophy, its demonstrable laws, affirmations, prayers, and student-teacher dialogue, we begin to piece together an awareness of our own inner being which is made up of our subconscious, conscious, and superconscious. The self discovery is parallel to the revelation that Mr. Goodwin demonstrated and offered to his students.

When Mr. Goodwin became aware of angels, it was in essence the beginning of the Living Light philosophy classes. In these teacher-and-student dialogue classes are many definitions of laws, soul faculties, and self-healing exercises. "How to" examples are given throughout each class. In conveying the teachings through his mediumship, Mr. Goodwin furthered his own understanding of the teachings and was able to observe the laws being demonstrated by himself and his students on a daily basis.

Mr. Goodwin demonstrated affirming the good in all situations, the teaching that by losing your concern over yourself—through selfless service—you could serve on a much higher level of consciousness and serve for the greater good of humanity.

Now, transcribed for your benefit, these spiritual teachings and affirmations can be experienced on a personal level. You can discover for yourself the beauty, peace, and love of your own inner being and demonstrate for yourself how to control and change your experiences right now, for a more fuller and abundant life.

CONSCIOUSNESS CLASSES

CONSCIOUSNESS CLASS 45

Good evening, students, and welcome to our forty-fifth class of the spiritual awareness course.

We open our classes by one of the students reading one of the discourses from *The Living Light*. And then, that will be followed by what is known as our "Total Consideration" affirmation.

Now I know that the students who are new this evening do not yet know that affirmation. However, I'm confident that with a little effort and application we all, of course, will know it by next Thursday. We speak in unison this affirmation. You are free at the question time to ask any questions that you have concerning the course, the study book [*The Living Light*], the affirmations that are given, or any questions of a spiritual nature.

Now, there is no reason to be timid by the words *spiritual nature*. We mean that questions of a personal nature, such as "Where will I be next year?" are not a part of the study course. The purpose of the spiritual awareness classes is to help you to become aware, through your own application of the knowledge and the understanding that you gain from these classes; to help you to make the necessary changes inside of yourselves, so that you may experience a more beautiful, a more practical, a more fulfilling life.

Now, no one is going to tell you what is fulfilling for your life, because it would be rather silly, since, in truth, we all know what is right for us and we all know, in truth, what it is we are really seeking.

Now, following the reading of the discourse, we will turn off the lights and we will, in unison, speak the "Total Consideration" affirmation. And that will be followed by a short concentration and meditation period. Now, our understanding of concentration is placing the mind, pointedly and fixedly, upon the object of your choice, until only its essence remains. After a very brief concentration—a minute or two—that will be followed by what we call a meditation. Meditation is when no thought is entertaining your mind, no thought of anything. At the concentration time, we do recommend to our students to concentrate upon peace. And, of course, *peace* means different things to different people at different times. Because what is meant by *peace* to one person in a certain level of consciousness in the next moment that does not represent peace to them. But we strive to go beyond that mental level of consciousness and to go into the perfect peace that passeth all understanding.

When you attain that degree of meditation and you experience that great peace, it is not something that words can describe, but you will know it. And this is a part of the study of these classes: to reach that level of consciousness, so that you may enjoy in this life a greater happiness and a greater fulfillment.

[A student reads Discourse 38 aloud. The class speaks the "Total Consideration" affirmation aloud, which is followed by a short period of meditation. See the appendix for the text of the affirmation.]

As I had explained earlier, these classes, based upon this understanding, are more of an open-forum, question-and-answer type of class. And we do not follow any strict or rigid rules, because it is not our purpose here to teach some new dogma to the world. The world seems to have a sufficient amount already. Our purposes, here, are to help you to learn initiative thinking: to be able to think, perhaps for many, for the first time in your lives from a level of consciousness known as reason.

Now I know that we all like to think that we are thinking from that level of consciousness, but when we look over our lives, we see that it has been rare that we have expressed or thought from a level of consciousness known as reason. And let us analyze that, perhaps for a few moments, that we may gain a greater understanding.

We know that reason is total consideration, for man cannot express reason unless he has considered all things involved before expressing on any subject or any thought. So the question must arise within our minds, How often do we consider all these things when we speak and act and think? No, my friends, if we are honest with ourselves and if we will make the effort to look inside of ourselves, we will find that we are thinking and we are acting from levels of consciousness known as a programmed, patterned computer.

How do we go beyond these patterns of our own subconscious? Well, of course, we cannot go beyond them until we can understand them, at least to some extent. And so that is one of the many purposes of these classes: to help you to become aware of yourself. Not the way we think we are, but the way we really are. This happens, my friends, when you make the effort to look inside, not once a day in a morning meditation, but to look *inside* every time you find yourself emotionally disturbed or you find things in your life not going the way that you want them to go. Then, stop in that moment. Be a little peaceful with yourself and ask yourself the honest question, "What am I, in truth, expressing that is bringing me this experience that is distasteful to me at this moment?" Because it is these teachings which are demonstrable: that man, indeed, is a law unto himself and that all experiences in our life are the direct effect of a level of consciousness that, for some reason or other, we insist upon entertaining in mind and expressing in life.

I am aware that that type of a teaching is not very acceptable to what we call the king brain. But our purposes here are not to satisfy the functions of man, but to share with those who are seeking a path to freedom for our own soul.

Now, we have all come to class with motives that are as varied as the flowers of the meadows, but we all have one thing in common: we are all here this moment. And so let us start upon the path of freedom and let us ask whatever questions are important to our own mind. Now you are free, my friends, to ask any questions that you have, if you will just be so kind as to raise your hands. Yes.

In tonight's discourse, "And though responsibility ofttimes seems to be a heavy cross, it is never beyond your capacity to endure." I'm wondering if a person attempts suicide or, in fact, does commit suicide, does that contradict this statement?

No, it doesn't. Thank you very much. The lady is referring to a statement in *The Living Light* that though the cross may seem heavy, it is never beyond your own endurance. And is it contradictory that a person would take their own life or commit suicide when our crosses to bear are not beyond our capacity and our ability to bear them? No, it is not contradictory. We all have a choice. At every moment in our lives we have choice. We are in a constant process of making decisions. Many times in life, although the seeming difficulties or so-called crosses are burdens, we may choose not to bear. That is still our divine right: not to bear them. However, that does not, in any sense, mean that we are going to escape from anything that we have set into motion. Therefore, when a person decides that this life here on Earth is beyond their abilities to endure and they commit suicide, as they call it, they still face in another dimension—because our mind goes with us, my friends. It's made of mental substance. It is not composed of the elements of this planet and, therefore, does not return to this planet (the mind). So our mind, our mental body, goes with us. The problem, whatever it may or may not have been, goes on with us in mind, because it is a mental problem. Therefore, in truth, though we have chosen to try to escape what we do not care to face in life, we find, leaving this physical dimension, that we have taken the very thing that we chose to escape along with us.

Now, that does not mean that in time, as we make the effort inside of ourselves, that we do not grow through it, because in time we do. I hope that's helped with your question.

If the light is within and we are to be bearers of the light, how can we ever be the observer and not the observed? When we draw people to the light, we draw people to ourselves, don't we, to the light within us? That's my question, sir. How can we be the observer and not the observed?

Thank you very much. It is not ourselves that are drawing people to the Light. We are simply the vehicle through which the Light is expressing itself. It may express itself in a great, luminous way or a very small, minute way. That is entirely dependent upon man and his receptivity to being universal in thought, act, and deed.

One of the very basic teachings of this philosophy is selfless service. Now, so many people seem to misunderstand what *selfless service* really means. If we are serving anything, no matter what it is, selflessly, then we have no thought and no emotion of the effects of our efforts. If we have any concern about what is being done with the energy or the work that we are doing and we think it is selfless, then we should take another view at our motive. Because, my friends, if you are serving selflessly anyplace in the universes, then you have no interest and no concern what comes out of the energy that you have spent. Now, selfless service is a very basic teaching.

It is taught here, the Law of Disassociation is what illumines us; it is what transforms us. Can man in any way disassociate himself from himself as long as he entertains thoughts of self-concern? It is impossible. We must learn to lose ourselves before we can find ourselves, and by that I mean the layers of consciousness, the levels of awareness, that we have given so much thought and feeling to that we have lost our own divinity. That's the reason we don't experience the peace that passeth all understanding. How is it possible to experience freedom or peace when our minds are filled with what somebody else is doing or not doing? And the more that our minds are filled with concern, the more we are bound and chained to the form known as self.

It is in our own best interest, my good friends. If you think God is out there, then it's a long journey on an endless chain. But if you entertain the thought that God is expressing through you, as well as the plants, the trees, the dogs, and the cats, if you entertain that kind of feeling, then you are on the first step to universal consciousness. And sooner or later, you're going to get there, as we all will in time.

Now remember, that which we give thought to, we give power to. Again and again and again, the teaching remains the same. You see, friends, truth may be individually perceived, but truth is one. It wears many garments and many forms, but there's only one truth, because there's only one Light. There's only one Life, in truth, and there's only one God.

*Yes, sir. In a previous class, we discussed the solar plexus or the father aspect of our universe. Here [*The Living Light*] it says, it makes a statement, that the heart is the mother aspect of our universe, but it doesn't go further to clarify why the heart is the mother aspect of the universe. I wonder if you could elaborate on that.*

What is your understanding of that statement?

Well, it says, "We shall speak now of the heart, the mother aspect of the universe. It is life, light, and love." That would be my understanding of the mother aspect: loving kindness.

Thank you. Now I have a question to ask you. What causes the heart to beat?

The life within. It's just life that causes the heart to beat. Without life, you don't have any heartbeat.

When you give it some more thought, we will discuss it at a future class. Thank you very much. Someone else have a question? Yes, please.

On the forming and deforming of the body, is this referring to the spiritual body? Or do we form and deform our body here with our thinking and our speaking—our thinking, mainly?

Thank you very much. In reference to the forming and deforming of the body, what the passage is referring to is the mental and astral bodies. You cannot deform that which is spiritual. Now, I know that many people think that they will worry or concern themselves with the hereafter when they reach the hereafter. But let us think for a moment, friends. The hereafter is here and now, this moment. We have a physical body, we have a mental body, and we have an astral body. We are in process, hopefully, of building or creating our spiritual body, through our soul faculties.

Now, when we express and entertain thoughts which are discordant (attitudes of mind which are not harmonious), what takes place is a deforming of what is known as our mental body. That deforming also affects our astral body. Now, because we cannot see with our physical sight our so-called mental body or astral body with physical eyes is, in and of itself, absolutely no proof that it does not exist. You see physical substance with physical sight and you see mental substance with mental sight and astral substance with astral sight. However, this deforming and forming is taking place every moment here and now. I do hope that's helped with your question.

You mentioned earlier a brief discussion on self. And there is a discussion in The Living Light *on what is known as the higher self and lower self and also the mention of inner self. Could you discuss this?*

Thank you very much. In mentioning the various selves or levels of consciousness in our book [*The Living Light*], the student has asked for perhaps a discussion on the lower self, the higher self, and the inner self. Man's aspirations constitute what is referred to in this book as his higher self. His emotions, his functions create what is known as his lower self. His awareness and awakening to his life eternal and the multitudes of experiences that he has already encountered as his journey travels through these many incarnations throughout the universes composes what is termed his inner self.

Now, we have discussed before that when the soul incarnates into form, prior to its incarnation it has a review and a preview. It reviews all of its experiences that it has already passed through and it has a preview of what is yet to come. This inner self is this universal consciousness, that man may know beyond a shadow of any doubt, without being told or without asking anyone. He knows. There is a level of consciousness within our being that knows. It is the inner self. It knows where we have been. It knows how we got there. It knows why we're here. It knows what we have to do. And it knows where we're going. That is our inner self. I hope that's helped with your question.

Thank you.

You're welcome.

I've had a word that has been running around my head for three or four days, and that's the word confession. *And I looked it up in the dictionary and it isn't what I had in mind for an answer. I think it has to do with an "acceptance within" or something like that. Could you help me with that?*

With the word *confession?* Thank you very much. Our understanding of the word *confession* is "to become aware on a level of consciousness that has not accepted an act that we have done inside of ourselves." To become aware and to accept that and, in accepting it, to be free from the bondage and the disturbance on that level of consciousness.

Now, my friends, we have eighty-one levels of consciousness. You know, we think things on one level and they're not acceptable to the other levels of consciousness. However, through *confession,* which means "to free"—which means confession inside of ourselves, you understand—then we gain acceptance on the other levels of consciousness. And I do hope that's helped with your question. Remember, friends, it also frees us from what is commonly referred to in psychology as a guilt complex. And guilt complexes are extremely destructive to any human soul. So remember, to forgive is to free. And so confession, indeed, is good for our soul, because it frees it. But we confess to our own levels of consciousness.

You see, acceptance *is* the divine will. After all, my friends, have you ever found anything or anyone that God, the Divine Intelligence, has not accepted? So is not acceptance, indeed, the divine will? Now if the divine will is acceptance, who are we as men (humanity) not to accept? Does that mean that we are greater than God, the divine Infinite Intelligence? Think about that, friends, every time you reject something in your mind. Think about it. Because what you're doing to yourself is declaring that you are greater than God, the greatest of all intelligence. You see, my friends, it's been said before: Until man expresses his soul faculty of humility, he will never find what is known as God. And it takes a bowing to a greater authority to accept God. But until we do that, we're not going to find our God.

Now remember, we understand that God is equal to our understanding. So a little understanding: a little God. A great understanding: a great God. But it's up to us, you see. It's entirely up to us.

Faith, poise, and humility is the second soul faculty. And it takes a little humility to bow to greater authority than, of course, our own brain. Thank you.

I want to know more about the areas of intelligence known to some of us, or known to me a little bit, such as mineral, vegetable, animal, and human. Is there more, being soul, going back to past incarnations? Would it be of the same nature as we would experience something labeled as Earth?

Thank you very much for your question. Thank you. I believe from your question that you are referring to the forms and the intelligence that expresses through them. For example, if the Divine Intelligence at one time is expressing through a blade of grass, does it always express through a blade of grass or does that blade of grass become transformed and become something else in the evolutionary path? Is that what you're referring to?

Yes.

Yes. Well, my friends, all things evolve. What was yesterday a blade of grass returns to Mother Nature, from whence she came, and she may come up tomorrow as a weed. She may come up the next year as a tree. Now, we are talking not about the seed of the tree, but we're talking about the elements which compose the seed. And so it is, you see, that man—the Divine Intelligence is expressing through man. And we perhaps are entertaining the question, "Well, I'm expressing in this form today. Will I always express in the form similar to what I look like at this time?" Is that correct? No, you will not, and neither will anyone else.

For example, you don't look the same as you did forty years ago. You've changed quite a bit. And so have all of us. And so it is, my friends, as this Divine Intelligence expresses through form, form is in a constant state of change. It's in a constant process of evolution. Now, think of the importance of the statement, Be ever ready and willing to change.

Don't you see? My friends, you're bucking the divine law. You are trying to stand in the way of Divinity herself. When you refuse to make changes, you put yourself out of the harmony and the flow of God, the Divine Intelligence itself. Be ever ready and willing to change. All forms are in a constant process of changing. The mind is form and it, too, is in a constant process of changing. The physical body is form and it, too, is in a constant process of changing. Think about that when you hold fast to a thought or an opinion. Think about it deeply. And think about it thoroughly. What you are doing, my friends, is trying to stop your own progression.

Now, the reason that we seemingly have such great difficulty in making changes in ourselves is because we have found—and we insist upon it—a false security in the things with which we are familiar. But that is stagnation, my friends. That is not progression. So let us be receptive to the possibility that there is something greater. Every moment that you have a difficulty in making a change of thought or feeling, entertain the thought, "There is something greater waiting if I will only let go."

Now, it doesn't mean to let go of your shoes or your cars or your houses or your radios or your television sets. Those are effects of your holdings, of your mental holdings. It means to let go of an attitude of mind, to let go of a thought, to learn to release the things that disturb you. Then, you see, my friends, you will let the doors open to a broader horizon, to a greater life, to one filled with purpose and meaning. I do hope that's helped with your question.

On the same subject of change, "be ever willing," many people try to change our thinking. Many people who are spiritual try to have you come their way. How do you know if you're having spiritual guidance from within to make that change? Or if you are unwilling to make the change because of your own inner levels. Specifically, in the workaday world, you find people trying to sell you this or sell you that and buy this and buy that, and you're not willing to do this. So what I want to know is, How does one know that the change has been made for the progression?

Thank you very much. And especially in reference to when others try to get you to change your ways spiritually, etc. Now remember, friends, the only time that anyone gets us to change our ways, the only time that that is possible, is when that way is our way. Otherwise, it is not accepted by our own mind. Now, because we are not aware of these levels of consciousness and because we are not aware that that, in truth, is our way—but we are not aware *consciously* that it is our way—then, you see, we accept that, because it is, in truth, our way. We just haven't awakened to it yet! And if everything goes right, then that's a wonderful friend. But you let one thing go wrong and you're their worst enemy. But what I'm trying to say, my good students, is that the moment we accepted it is a revelation that it is our way on a certain level of consciousness. We just hadn't brought it to the fore, not just yet.

Now, in reference to people selling us this or selling us that, well, should we accept or should we not accept? That, of course, is what we're here for in this world: to make decisions. But, my friends, when these decisions are based upon our faculty of reason, they are wise decisions for us. After all, acceptance is the divine will. When man accepts something here, he accepts the divine right of another individual to be on the street corner selling pencils. He accepts the divine right of the individual, when someone passes by, to ask them if they want to purchase it. That does not mean that he goes home with a warehouse filled with pencils. No. Our way, my friends, is constantly being revealed to us.

Now, how is our way constantly being revealed to us? Well, it's very simple. Each person, in each experience, throughout our days and nights, is a mirror telling us where we are at any given moment. Now, for example, we come into contact with someone and they disturb us terribly. What does that mean to us? What does it really mean to us? It means that their expression is something we cannot tolerate, because we never made the effort to consider it in the first place. And by not making the effort to consider it, we can't possibly understand it, because we cannot understand anything that we do not consider. So the prophets have always said, O man, know thyself and ye shall know the truth and the truth shall set ye free. But how, my good students, can we possibly know ourselves, when we spend so much of the hours of our days trying to know everyone else's business? Don't you see, friends, we need to spend more time—God forbid, I don't mean to be judging—but perhaps it would behoove us to spend more time to find out what *our* business is, the business of our own life. "How is it I feel this way one minute? How is it that I feel another way another minute? What is causing this inside of my head? Why am I experiencing a good life one week and a terrible one the next one? What is the cause of this?" This is the business and the divine right of each individual soul.

But we've got to spend some time on it. We've got to start thinking. This is what I'm talking about, friends: initiative thinking. Ask yourself the question—if it's necessary, a thousand times a day—"Why do I always seem to merit this? Or why do I always seem to merit that?" Well, let's ask the level inside of our head that's causing it. See? Let's ask this thing up here. And let us be humble and let us be sincere, like a little child, and then we will find out. Take a little while, because, you see, we've spent such a lifetime not asking, that when we start to ask, we're going to have to be patient. And we're going to have to have a little humility. And we're going to have to have a little directed faith and a little bit of confidence—confidence in the Divine Intelligence that we will get there. It's just going to take us a little while.

Now, I do hope that's helped with that question. I'm so grateful that student brought that question up, because it's very important. This is a class of self-awareness: to become aware of ourselves. And we can't become aware of ourselves if we don't start thinking. My friends, please do yourself an eternal favor and start to think. See?

Don't look out and blame the world. Don't look out and blame the government. Don't look out and blame your husbands, nor your wives, nor your girlfriends, nor your brothers, nor your sisters. Don't do that to yourself. This is why there's such a seeming hodgepodge of problems—seeming—in our world today. Because we have spent generations upon generations of blaming everything out there.

You know, it isn't a popular thing to teach, or try to teach, to share self-awareness, because none of us want to look at ourselves unless we're feeling great. Now, when we're feeling great, we don't mind looking at ourselves. We don't even mind talking about ourselves. But, you see, when we're down there, you know—and, you know, we want to put up a good front. Of course, we want to. Because the truth of the matter is that God wants to express through us more fully, naturally. And it's that goodness inside of us that wants to come out and shine like the sunshine. It really is striving to do that.

So why keep the rain and the clouds in your life? It isn't necessary. It isn't necessary at all. You know, if you only spent one day in a year telling everyone you met what a beautiful day it was and how grateful you were to be alive, you'd begin to transform your lives. Thank you very much. Does someone else have a question? Yes.

I've got a question that I would like your understanding on. I know that it's been Serenity's understanding of incarnation that we may only incarnate, maybe once or twice on this particular planet Earth—

I don't believe that's ever been stated. Thank you very much.

Well, OK. But anyway, in reading some other spiritual books, which say our soul is like a tree: it has branches that it forms. Is this possibly why some people say that they have been incarnated many times on this particular planet or if we have experiences or flashbacks? Could it possibly be that our soul has been everywhere and seen everything?

Thank you very much. Now in reference to your question of some people feeling that they have been everywhere and seen everything, well, of course, that's a very true statement to the people who have reached a level of consciousness known as the cosmic, the illumination within their own being. Because then we will become aware that there is no past; there is no future; there is only the eternal now. Now when we truly become aware of that, then we're in communion with all intelligence, because we are, then, a truly unobstructed vehicle of the expression of that Divine Intelligence. And that Divine Intelligence is expressing everywhere at all time. But it is a rare experience that a person truly reaches this illuminating state, and it's only for fleeting moments. Then, we are aware that the part of us that is formless and free, known as God, Spirit—whatever you care to call it—is an inseparable part of the divine whole. So you see the great responsibility that man truly has.

The responsibility, my friends—this is why we should consider, when we are bogged down with a little mundane universe of problems and things of that nature, let us think about our true responsibility. We're a part of everything, everywhere, have always been, will always be. So just give that some thought. Our world is not as small as we like to think it is at times. I do hope that has helped with your question. Thank you.

In the back of The Living Light, *there are quotations, and I would like a little explanation on the saying, "Patience is the only path to Truth." And the word* only *is what I'm questioning.*

The statement is made in the book that "Patience is the only path to Truth." And the student is questioning the word *only*. And by your question, do I understand that you are implying that the statement means there are no other paths to truth? Is that what your question is? You had questioned the word *only*. I would like clarification on the questioning of the word.

Well, we've heard that there are so many paths to Truth, so many ways that wind and wind. And kindness was a way to Truth, and all these different faculties are the way to truth. And—

May I ask you a question? Do all of the ways to truth take patience?

I would think so.

Thank you very much. You have your answer.

Are states of consciousness and levels of understanding one and the same?

States of consciousness and levels of awareness are one and the same. Yes. States of consciousness and levels of awareness, yes. Thank you.

Thank you. I have two questions. First, would you clarify the difference between confession and courage? And the second question is on ego. Is ego a separate entity or is it a composite of a number of functions? I was thinking in terms of ego and pride, for example.

Thank you very much. In reference to your last question concerning the word *ego*, by our use of that word, we mean to say the house of the functions, and it's commonly referred to as ego. Now, in reference to your first question, for perhaps some clarification or sharing on the words *courage* and *confession*. Courage and confession are inseparably united in all their expression.

Now, you might ask the question, "I have a great deal of courage and I'm not using a bit of confession." My good students, anytime you express courage, you are confessing to yourselves—though you may not be aware of that level of consciousness—you are confessing to yourselves the weaknesses on each and every level. And therefore to the extent and degree that you make that confession is your courage expressed, and no greater and no lesser.

Now, that may seem a little difficult for some of the new students to perhaps understand, but if you wish a further discussion, I will be happy to share with you. However, we're running over time. Someone else have a question? *[After a brief pause in which no questions are asked, the Teacher continues.]* Now, remember, friends, this is what these classes are all about. You're here to question. It's your class. But if you don't question, then I won't have to work so hard. You see? And if I don't have to work so hard, I'm sure—if not tonight, maybe tomorrow—some of you will think you paid too much. But that's up to you, you see. Yes.

You were just mentioning, a little while ago, about releasing your thoughts or releasing it to God or to the Divine Intelligence. And we do this subconsciously and yet we don't get the results that we really would like to have. Is that from conditioning in our past lives? What can we do to overcome this? What can we do to get out of these levels of consciousness?

Thank you very much. And the student has brought up a very good point and we've discussed it many times before. The conscious mind is electrical. The subconscious mind is magnetic. And it is the subconscious that pulls all these experiences into our life by its magnetic pull. Now, a student has asked, then, I have released these things consciously, but how do I release them subconsciously, because I keep experiencing them? Isn't that your basic question? Yes. Well, my friends, first we must bridge the gap between the conscious and the subconscious, and that's known as self-awareness. So we must make the effort, you see, to sit down each day and have our meditations. It takes a little more than that. Sit down and ask yourself the question, "Who am I really?" Be patient. Because the old subconscious will tell you who you are. And it will tell you from different levels of consciousness and you'll be surprised who you are. You'll be surprised what your subconscious thinks you are. That will depend on whatever level of consciousness that you're tapping back here at any given moment.

So, you see, friends, it certainly behooves us to make some effort to sit down and talk to ourselves. But, you see, it seems to be the problem of what they call the ego. It doesn't want to have people aware that it's talking to itself. Well, my friends, you're talking to another part that you're hardly even familiar with, you see. It's almost like talking to a stranger. It depends on which level you're talking to. But at least, if you'll make the effort, slowly but surely, you'll not only start to understand, you'll start changing some of these people back here that you weren't aware that you were.

Now, everyone knows that some bring out the good in us and some bring out the worst. Well, how does that happen? We all know how it happens. Some people appeal to certain levels of consciousness that are in our head and the good comes out of us. Some people appeal to those lower levels—if you want to call them lower—those other levels of consciousness and the so-called bad comes out of us. So if you're not getting along with someone, don't blame the someone. Sit down and say, "Well, now, let me see, if I appeal to that level of consciousness in his head, he's a very fine person." Well, isn't it worth appealing to that level of consciousness? It depends, of course, my friends, what you want in life. You see, it's really quite that simple.

Now thank you all very much. We ran a little over time. And I am sure—and I especially want to speak, if I may, for a moment to the new students—I'm aware that some of this may seem to you a bit Greek—I think they call it—but be patient and give yourself a chance. Because you'll be surprised—and it won't be long—when you'll ask your own questions. And it will be a lot more simple than your mind, at present, may think.

Thank you very much. Let us go have refreshments.

MAY 2, 1974

CONSCIOUSNESS CLASS 46

I know that most of you have become familiar with our little affirmation. And before we get into our concentration and our meditation, many students have asked—that have not had private class work—concerning meditation. Now, it seems that one of the difficulties in meditation is the seeming inability to concentrate upon one thing and to keep the mind upon that one thing. As we spoke last week, we use in this Association for our meditation the word *peace*.

Now, what happens when we think of a word? What really happens when we think any word is it goes through our mind and through our subconscious, and it attracts, like a magnet, everything that is associated with it. Now this is the importance of the spoken word. You learn in these classes that the spoken word is life-giving energy. But there have been so few questions on why the spoken word is life-giving energy. What happens when we speak a word, any word? Through the Law of Association, through all of our experiences here in this earth realm, and even prior, we are directly in rapport and connected to what that word means to us.

Now a person may use the word *action* and they may think that that word is only associated with their present act. But that is not true, friends. You're totally disregarding the Law of Association of your own mind. So choose your word or words wisely, because they put you into rapport with that that you have been associated with, therefore giving life to the experiences in the universe that you have been in rapport and associated with at some time in your life's expression.

Now, because over the centuries man has lost the true meaning of words—because we use them so freely—we don't stop to think what we're doing when we're speaking. When we speak words, we attract into our life all of those experiences. Now, because we cannot consciously see those living experiences does not in any way exempt us from the effect that they have upon us. Therefore, in your concentration, become aware. Become aware when you're concentrating upon peace, become aware of your feelings. Become aware of what type of thoughts are passing through your mind. Become aware of yourself. Now when that happens, there will be many thoughts that pass through your mind: there will be different experiences. And then, you will have a greater understanding of what words really mean to you. Because the word *peace* means one thing to one mind, and it means something else to another mind. So we have to go through those experiences until we can rise to a level of consciousness, which we call the superconscious, where you can experience, truly experience, the peace that transforms your being and that makes life truly more beautiful.

Now, if you'll catch the lights, please. And we'll say our "Total Consideration" affirmation and we'll go into our concentration and our meditation. Remember, friends, don't try too hard to concentrate. You see, we try too hard and we put the mind ahead of our spirit. And then, we have what some people call a bummer meditation. That's because we're trying too hard with the wrong vehicle.

Thank you very much.

[The class speaks the "Total Consideration" affirmation aloud. After this, the class meditates.]

I should like to speak this evening for a few moments, before getting into our regular question-and-answer period of our class, on what man commonly refers to as boredom. I do believe that it is a rare mind that truly understands what motivates—what is computed by our brain as boredom. Usually, a person feels, when they say that they're bored with anything, usually what it is that they are saying is that the experience no longer appeals to them.

Now, we must be honest with ourselves and ask ourselves the question, "Why, in life, at some time in our life, does a thought or an experience appeal to us and at another time in our life it no longer appeals to us?" Well, my friends, we must go deeper than the surface of our conscious mind and ask ourselves the honest question, "What was I seeking in the first place?"

Now we're speaking on boredom because—believe it or not—in this world today, with all of the fancy frills and things, man still entertains a level of consciousness known as boredom. So, my friends, we find that what we were seeking—for example, if it's with spiritual matters—was not spiritual things at the moment that we first were seeking. What we were, in truth, seeking was a change from the patterns that we were at that moment experiencing. Any change would have served the purpose. But change for the sake of change is not progression, nor is it growth. So let us give thought for a few moments this evening on what it is we really want.

Now, we can say, "Well, I want this and I want that. And I want something else." And those are all things. Well, if that is what we want, then let us prepare ourselves to stay on the merry-go-round of creation and be entertained by its constant panorama. But if we want to seek a way through this duality known as creation, if we want to experience it and not be affected by it, then we must learn, friends, some degree of self-control. Because if we don't learn some degree of self-control, then we're going to be washed from shore to shore by our own emotions. We do not find happiness in the realm known as emotion. We may find temporary moments of excitement or pleasure, but it is never where we find happiness.

We have the constant experience of feeling high one moment, only guaranteeing to feel low the next moment, because we have attached ourselves, our mind, to creation. Now, that is not where we're going to find truth. It is not where we're going to find freedom. Until we learn to separate the true inner being, called, in this philosophy, spirit, from the form known as creation, we will not reach that peace and that joy.

However, what does that all have to do with boredom? Whenever the mind seeks creation, it guarantees, as sure as the night follows the day, it absolutely guarantees what the mind calls boredom. Because the senses are entertained only for so long in repetition without becoming bored. It is the very nature of form itself. Therefore, my friends, if you seek the Light, your Light— call it God or Infinite Intelligence, it makes no difference—if you are truly seeking that, then recognize, realize, and accept the truth that on the path of Light, many, many things will distract you.

For example, it is interesting to note how the seasons of the weather affect us. Don't you see, my friends, when the sun is shining and if we have a pattern to be here or there when the sun is shining, that pattern of mind, locked in the depths of our own being, will demand that we be there. And if we do not bow to that demand from the depths of our own being, we will be unhappy. Now is that, I ask you, in truth, is that freedom?

That doesn't mean that when the sun is shining we shouldn't be at the beach, if that is where we want to be. It doesn't mean when the sun is shining, we shouldn't be out sailing or something else. Because that, in truth, is our divine right. But it does mean, my friends, if we do not recognize what is controlling us, how can we ever have discipline and self-control in our lives, if we don't become aware of these eighty-one levels of consciousness through which our soul is expressing at different moments and different levels at different times? At least, become aware of what is controlling your life.

It's nice to take a moment each day and to organize and to tell yourself from your own soul faculty of reason, "This is what I will do." And then have the courage of your conviction and do it. But that is not the way most of us spend our days, nor our nights. So let's give some thought on that, my friends. And I assure you, when you become aware of the things that are controlling your life—for awareness is the first step in control. You see, my friends, without control, you cannot have truth.

Truth is not a limited thing. It is a limitless thing. But until you learn control, you cannot have truth. Because we must learn control: control of ignorance and control of error. But that is something that we must learn inside of ourselves. Here we are at this little class, the second one of this semester. And I do hope that it may be in divine order that someone, if only one, before this semester finishes, will not only become aware of the things that are controlling their soul, but will have the courage to do something about it.

Thank you very much. Now you're free to ask your questions, if you will be so kind as to just raise your hands.

I have some confusion between the idea of control and the idea of being receptive and the feeling of letting go. The spiritual literature seems to be just about evenly balanced. I'm not sure if they're saying the same thing or saying something different.

Thank you very, very much for that question. It's a very important question, friends. The lady is asking in reference to the word *control* and the word *receptive*. All people are being controlled by something at every moment of their lives. Now what they're being controlled by is dependent on what they're receptive to. For example, if we are receptive to a level of consciousness here in our mind that is dictating that life is ever as we make it and just the way we take it, then we will start to awaken to the truth that man is a law unto himself.

Now, first, we must work on, or at least consider working on, awareness. Because, you see, we are all receptive and, being receptive, we are controlled by what we are receptive to. So the first step is self-awareness or spiritual awareness: awareness of one's own birthright, awareness of one's own spirit, awareness of one's own soul. When that awareness starts to dawn, then the individual knows. They know why they have come to Earth. They know the lessons they have to learn. They not only know the lessons that they have to learn, they know the ones that they flunked in the experience prior to this one. Now that deals with awareness, what we call spiritual or self-awareness.

When that awareness dawns in a person's life—now, how does that awareness dawn? That's a good question. Well, it dawns by controlling the things that you are presently aware of. Because, my friends, we cannot control something that we're not yet aware of. So where control begins is controlling our feelings, our emotions. For example, if you're walking down the street and somebody looks at you sideways and you are so sensitive that your feelings are hurt, then that means that you have given that individual power over you. Because you have permitted them—you have given to them the power to rob you of your own self-control. Do you understand? All right. So the first thing we start working on is controlling the things in life—our life—that we are aware of.

If we feel, for example, that the financial situation of the country is in such dire straits that we become miserable and emotionally upset, that means that we have given control to the financial condition of the country. Therefore, when the financial condition of the country goes up or down, our emotions, our life goes up or down. We have lost control. We've lost control of ourselves. We've given it to a country. Do you understand?

Now, if a man and his wife have problems and the wife or the husband is upset because the other partner is upset, then he or she has given power to that individual. What we start to do: we learn to control those things. In other words, we don't let our business, our job, the country, the government, and all these things outside of us, our automobiles, our television sets, the money we have in the bank or we don't have in the bank—that's where we start on control. Because, you see, obviously, we are already receptive to those levels of consciousness or they would not be affecting us. Does that help with your question?

Thank you very much.

You're more than welcome. Yes.

Thank you. When we talk about loyalty and we talk also about these levels of consciousness and self-control, there comes a time in all countries when there is time for voting on certain issues and for certain people. Now, when we do that, are we not giving our strength to this issue? We don't know if they're right or wrong. How are we affected spiritually by all this belief for people and belief for issues? I hope I've made myself clear.

You certainly did. And I thank you very, very much. And the lady wants to know how we're affected when we go to vote at the polls, etc. And, of course, my friends, that's very individual.

It depends on the person that's doing the voting. Now, if you are voting for anything and you are voting from a level of consciousness that is known as principle, then, my friends, you will not be affected by whether or not that person gets in office or doesn't get in office. However, if you are voting for someone and you're voting from a level of personality, which is from your magnetic or your emotional field, then, indeed, will you be affected by it.

This is why we teach to give what you have to give in the universe and to care less what happens to it. Because, you see, my friends, whenever you give—you give of your thought; you give of your time; you give of your energy; you give of your supply—whenever you give and you have any thought with what is done with your givingness, with whatever is done with the thought that you have given or the supply or the object, then what that is revealing to you is that you are attached to its effect. So that doesn't really make very much sense for an individual to give somebody a coat and then, when the person doesn't wear the coat, the person who gave him the coat is all emotionally upset. To me, that seems most impractical. Well, my friends, this is what we're talking about, you see.

You see, that is giving. That is true. But it is giving from the level of the magnetic field of emotion, personality, and self. And so you're going to be affected according to what the person does with what you have given.

There is a better way to give. And that givingness frees your spirit and it frees your soul. You give because that is what you want to do. You give of your suggestion. You give of your ideas. You give of your thoughts. You give of your objects. And when you give, the joy is in the act of giving. Do not let the effect, the person, be your joy. Because if you let that happen to you, you have sold your soul in that moment.

Now, some of us sell a little bit of our soul and some of us sell a great big part of our soul. But, of course, that's up to us. Now, how much of our soul are we selling? How can we find out how much of our soul we have sold in any area? It's the simplest thing in the world, my friends. Sit back and take stock: watch the panorama of life and see how much it affects you. Does your bank account affect your emotions? Does your house affect your emotions? Does your car affect your emotions? Do your children affect your emotions? Does your husband or your wife affect your emotions? To the extent that those things—and they're personal to each person, of course—to the extent that we are affected by them, that's how much of our soul we have sold. Because, you see, we sold our freedom. We sold our spirit. We sold our divine right.

This is why, my friends, it's so important: Give, in life, whatever it is you have to give. Be sure to care less what anybody does with it. Because, don't you see, my friends, you may give of your years in life to another person. You never know when that person is going to express through a level of consciousness that you have not yet seen them express through, and it may very well be the level of consciousness that you cannot tolerate.

Now, we teach here that duty, gratitude, and tolerance is the first soul faculty; that the foundation stone of all soul faculties is understanding. Now, when we understand something, we're on the step to being free. That's why, in all our getting, we seek to get understanding. Not understanding out there: understanding of ourselves. How many of us understand ourselves? We may say, "Well, I understand myself." There's a possibility we might understand that one level of ourselves, but we've got eighty more to go through.

You know, ofttimes in life, friends, there are moments when we feel that we never could be so good; life is so wonderful. And then, the next day, we never realized that we could be so bad. So, don't you see, what exists in one exists in everyone. If we can't tolerate it, it's because we don't yet understand it. We haven't yet permitted ourselves to express that level and therefore we have no tolerance towards it. What we mean, of course, is we have no tolerance to that level inside of ourselves that we're seeing somebody out there expressing. That's what it really means.

Now, let us not, please, delude ourselves to think that we are unique as a human being. We are part of a whole human race. And we have the same tendencies, the same potentialities of every other human being that is in the human race. Now that alone, my friends, ought to help us to have some degree of tolerance. I do hope that's helped with your question.

Speaking along the same lines, I've been doing a lot of thinking about anger, credulity, and, and . . .

Suspicion, perhaps.

Suspicion and logic. And I found in myself that I have a kind of purist attitude that if I am going to be spiritual or spiritual in orientation, then I ought not to express any anger or recognize that I have it. And what happens is that I take it out on myself somatically and end up with knots in my neck and shoulders. And I've been trying to do a lot of thinking about it. I see a relationship between my own frustrations and my tendency to either totally believe something or totally suspect it, but I don't see the balance of it. And I feel like I'm just beginning to give myself permission to express anger. As you were talking about, I am human and I will experience anger now and again. Though the part of me that wants to be very spiritual says, "Oh no, I don't ever feel anger." And I would like to hear from you anything that you can share with me that would help me.

Yes, thank you very much. The lady is speaking on the function known as anger. Now we understand that anger, of course, is simply an expression from our magnetic or emotional field. Now, it's a release of energy. You know, there's an old saying that before you get angry, count to ten and you won't be angry anymore. Well, what it simply means is that you are making the effort to rise that energy to, of course, a different level of consciousness.

Now, if a person, for some reason or other, finds some enjoyment or pleasure in expressing anger, then, of course, there is for them a need to express it. However, what does it bring to us? Now, many people like to express anger or temper or whatever you want to call it. What does it gain us to express it? Well, for one thing, after we've expressed anger, we're usually pretty relaxed. Some people think it's peaceful. I don't, myself, think it is, but, at least, they say they feel better. Well, of course, we *feel* better, because we've got the energy locked into that level of consciousness and once it finally gets expressed, then, of course, we do feel better, even though we're exhausted, usually, afterward.

Now, we also know that it is merely and purely energy; that it can be directed by the power of our own will or self-control. However, when a person gets to release their energy through that level of consciousness known as anger and they feel so depleted of energy afterward, what it usually brings them, of course, is attention from someone. And when it brings some attention, they're getting their energy back, because, you see, energy follows attention. That is a demonstrable law of the universe. Therefore, if we as individuals give attention to people who express their anger and their emotional outbursts, then, of course, the only thing we're doing is to guarantee the continuity of it. Because, you see, they're depleted of energy when they have finished. And so, like a sponge, they're trying to absorb it back up again. And naturally, they're going to get it from any person, place, or thing that they can. So we must face within ourselves, "What is it within me that enjoys expressing my anger?"

Now, we all know that it is not beneficial to our soul and to our mind to entertain thoughts of guilt. Now, when we think that it is not spiritual to express the functions, when we entertain that kind of thinking, we're no longer spiritual. My good friends, our Spirit, God, the Divine, is expressing through a physical form, a mental form, an astral form, and several other forms here, this moment. And if we think that we are only spiritual when we no longer express our sense functions, then we have lost the true meaning of spirituality. If that were the case, surely the Divine Intelligence would not be expressing through sense functions. What we are trying to teach here is a balance between our sense functions, of course, and our soul faculties. Because that is just a direction of the energy.

You see, now we're speaking here, of course, I understand, on anger. Why does a person express anger? What is it that truly motivates them? Let us think for a moment. Is it because things in our life are not going our way or the way that we think is best? Or is it because someone that we are associated with in some way isn't doing what *we* think they should be doing? You see, my friends, it goes right back to the one basic teaching: self-awareness, self-control. Because, my friends, the reason that we express energy through the function known as anger is because we are expressing our soul consciousness through a level of consciousness known as judgment. *We* have decided how things should be in our life! *We* have decided how people associated with us should think, should act, and even how they should dress. That, my friends, is where we get these emotional outbursts. We get them because we have judged in here and we have decided not only what is best for ourselves, but what is best for the world.

Remember, friends, the moment that you or I or anyone else decides what's best for our life, that guarantees the day, the moment, when we will decide what is best for somebody else's life. And when we get onto that treadmill, believe me, we become absolutely miserable, because we're in a constant state of turmoil. A constant state of turmoil.

Now, we've spoken in these classes before on self-will and divine will. Well, what's the difference? What is the difference? Well, it's really quite simple, I think, myself—it's my own understanding, but I'll share it with you. Knowledge knows much—and that's called the brain—but wisdom knows better—and that's called the Spirit, God, the Divine.

Now, when we look through life and we see that we've put our efforts here, we've put our energy there, and it hasn't turned out just the way that we think it should have—but, don't you see, my friends, we're not a brand new soul that came direct from God and that came to this old earth realm. We are an evolving, expanding, individualized soul that has stumbled along the way through untold centuries, that has merited this life, this experience, this moment. So man decides he wants this and he wants that. Man decides what's best in his life and he makes all of those decisions. He *thinks* he's making those decisions. The truth of the matter is, he isn't. What is truly making those decisions are the patterns of mind that we have become addicted to. That's the great sadness.

Now, when we try to make the effort to release what *we* decide is best in life, when we really make that effort and become receptive to an infinite intelligence, then our ship will sail serene on the sea of time. It doesn't mean that we won't have some experiences, because we've already set those laws into motion. But if we will stick with it long enough, then we will see the change and the transformation, because we have let God move into our lives. But that takes, my friends, a little bit of faith, poise, and humility. And that is the second soul faculty.

In one of the discourses, it mentions procrastination and grounding. We understand that God is an intelligence, which is neutral, and that which it comes in contact with, it neutralizes. When we procrastinate and we are grounded, to what degree are we completely grounded? Do we have any kind of flow that flows through while we are being grounded? Are we completely grounded or do we have any spiritual flow or any balance in our lives?

Thank you very much for your question, in reference to grounding and procrastination and when we are grounded, do we have any spiritual flow in our lives? Yes, my friends, we still have some spiritual flow, because without the Spirit, we wouldn't be able to stay grounded. The only thing we have done—we have directed the energy or the Spirit into our own grounding. That's what we have done. But the energy, of course, is still flowing.

You see, it deals with the teaching to nip it in the bud. When you have a feeling or a thought that is not pleasant to you and you don't care to entertain it, well, get rid of it as quickly as possible, because the longer you hold something in thought, the more difficult it is to get out of it. Because you, the individual, are directing the Infinite Energy, the Divine Intelligence, to that thing, whatever it may be. And therefore you become a part of it. You see, the things in life that we put our attention on, we have a tendency to become. But remember, friends, the things that we believe in—the things that we have faith in, we are. We truly are.

Now, if we're having difficulty with procrastination, which is, in truth, the theft of all time, in a dimension of time, and we are having any difficulty with what we call grounding—and by grounding, I believe you are referring to a negative state of consciousness. Is that correct?

I imagine it would be negative.

Yes, the grounding means it's not beneficial to you. Yes, that's my understanding. Well, when we find ourselves grounded, the longer that we think about being grounded, the longer we're going to stay grounded. Because, you see, energy is following our thought. That is the law. Do you understand? So what is the wisest thing to do? If the person says, "Thank you, God. I recognize I'm grounded. Now let me direct my attention, let me direct my thought to something else." Don't direct your thought into the level of consciousness to get ungrounded, because that just keeps you right where you are. Direct your thought to something that is pleasing to your mind. That's the easiest way to come out of any level of consciousness.

For example, say a man has a fight with his wife. Well, if he likes to go to the corner bar and have a beer, all he's got to do is think about it and he feels better. And he's gone! So, you see, it's the same principle. Don't you see? I hope that's helped with your question.

Due to our prior incarnations, my question is, How strong is the hereditary factor against the environmental factor that we try to recognize and correct?

Thank you very much for your question. The gentleman is referring to the influences in our life of what is known as the hereditary factor and the environmental factor. Well, in reference to this hereditary factor—that is an effect, of course, of what our soul has merited for its lessons in life. In other words, one soul enters a certain family and certain hereditary tendencies, and another soul enters a different family with different hereditary tendencies. That is a part of the lessons in life that we are passing, hopefully. Because, you see, when you look at your parents and you look at your family, and then you will know, if you look clearly, that you have merited that particular situation. Your soul entered into that. Look at them and see what they have to offer you, because they're revealing to you the lessons that you have to learn.

Now, you have the environmental factor. Well, the environmental factor is a secondary factor and it also deals with the lessons that have been earned through our soul's evolution through forms. However, it is a secondary factor. And it is, in truth, easier to learn than the primary factor of the hereditary. I hope that's helped with your question.

In this study, I understand that we always have a choice. Would you share your knowledge of choice and responsibility? Do you have the two working at the same time?

Thank you very, very, very much. My friends, choice and responsibility are inseparable. Now, one person may decide that staying in a certain situation is their responsibility. However, the moment that they had made that decision, they exercised their divine right of choice. You see, you cannot have choice without responsibility, and you cannot have responsibility without choice, because they are inseparable.

Now, the question is, "In making the decision or the choice, am I being governed by factors outside of myself? What decisions have I reached before this moment that dictate that such and such and such *is* my responsibility?" And when we make a choice, how long a duration is that responsibility? Friends, don't look outside. Don't look outside to find responsibility. Don't look outside to find choice. Come right back inside and ask yourself the question, "I find myself in this situation. The situation itself must not govern my soul." Because, don't you see, unless we use reason, we, the dreamer, become the dream that we have dreamed. In other words, we no longer have, or can express, the divine right known as choice.

You see, when we make a decision, which is choice, and it places us in a situation in life, we made a choice and a decision from that level of consciousness at that time. However, the years may have passed and we must make a reassessment within ourselves of our own values. And then, we must make another choice. And the moment you make choice, you open the door of responsibility. And man is doing that a hundred times a day.

You see, my friends, each part of our anatomy has a certain representation of a sense function and a soul faculty. We spoke at our last semester on the mouth. It represents truth. It represents the door. And the tongue is the key. So you see what we're doing constantly: we're speaking forth the life-giving energy—that's the key—and we're opening up doors. And the sadness is, because we're not thinking before we're speaking, we're opening up all kinds of doors. And one day, all of a sudden, we feel that we're totally burdened with responsibility. And then, we pull back and we try to close all of those doors. That's not the way, my friends. Because the closed doors, not having fulfilled the purpose that we set into motion, will open again with another experience, the same experience in principle, but different in form. That's the only difference.

So one must say to oneself, "I opened a door. I made a choice. I find my responsibility. How long is that to last? Did I make that decision when I opened the door? What other qualifications did I make inside of my own mind when I opened the door of responsibility through choice?" Then, my friend, only you as an individual soul and your God—remember that God is ever equal to our understanding at any given moment. God is no greater and God is no lesser than our understanding. As our understanding expands, through the soul faculties of duty, gratitude, and tolerance; faith, poise, and humility, as our understanding expands, our God gets greater, our God gets bigger. Because that's what God is: equal to our understanding. So if we have a little, small mind, a little, narrow understanding, no tolerance, no duty to our soul, no gratitude, no faith, no poise, no humility, then that god is so small that life, surely, isn't even worth being here. I do hope that that has helped with your question. Are there any other questions?

I have two questions. One is, Would you expand a little bit more on the level of consciousness that is called principle? And the second is, In The Living Light, *it says something about the five steps towards creation. I don't know what creation is. What do you mean by "creation"?*

Thank you very much. By using the word *creation*, we mean to say "all things brought into form in all universes everywhere." That that we call creation is the effect of two opposite poles brought together through the cohesive–adhesive principle of what we know as the Divine Spirit. It is our understanding that the Divine Spirit, known as God or Infinite Intelligence, holds all things in space and expresses through the smallest molecule, through the rock, the tree, the blade of grass, and the human being. It is also our understanding that the Divine Intelligence is expressing divine intelligence through all forms of life everywhere; that the intelligence is only limited by the form through which it is expressing. For example, the plant expresses its feelings to the degree and limitation of the type of plant it is. If it's a tree, it grows according to its species. And it expresses in its own way. And so does the rock. And so does the dog. And so does the human. But that divine Infinite Intelligence is everywhere, everywhere present, never absent or away.

Now, creation, those negative and positive poles that are brought together by this Divine Principle, known as God, those, you understand, are not lasting and enduring. Anything and everything that has form has beginning. And anything and everything that has beginning guarantees its own ending by the Law of Beginning. So surely a wise man does not spend a lifetime on things that are so temporary, because they come and go. And you never know when they're going to go. So doesn't it behoove us to rely upon something that is permanent, that is guaranteed, that is eternal, that will always be with us if we choose to be with it?

Now, I do hope that's helped with your question. I see we're running over time. Thank you, friends, very much. I'll see you Sunday and next Thursday.

MAY 9, 1974

CONSCIOUSNESS CLASS 47

This evening I should like to take a few moments to speak to you on the topic of self-control. Now, we have discussed, somewhat, about self-will and divine will. And this evening let us spend a few moments in discussing the benefits of self-control. At our last class, the statement was made that knowledge knows much, but wisdom knows better. Now the question must arise in our minds, "What is the difference, if any, between knowledge and wisdom?" Well, my friends, the moment that you apply knowledge, you express wisdom.

Many of us are knowledgeable in many things in this life. But it is a fact, if we will look at ourselves, that it is not frequent that we apply the knowledge that we have. For example, we are most knowledgeable about the traffic laws governing the community in which we live, but we do not always apply that knowledge, and therefore we and we alone pay the penalties of our acts, our thoughts, of course, and our deeds. And so it is with spiritual knowledge, knowledge of spiritual matters. We may know many laws that govern the universes and we may know many laws that govern our own life, but how often do we express wisdom? How often do we apply the knowledge that we already have? Now the question arises in the mind, If we have all of this knowledge, then why don't we apply the knowledge that we already have? Well, my friends, I believe if you will listen to our last class, you will remember that we discussed, to a great extent, the patterns of mind, the levels of consciousness that control our lives.

You know, it's like the story of the little children. They're willing to play the game with another as long as the game is played by their rules and their way. And so it is that we find ourselves here in this world, in adult bodies, playing the games the way *we* think they should be played—or we won't play at all. Now this is known, in this understanding, as rejection, which guarantees retaliation. And so it was when we were little, small children, if things didn't go the way we wanted, we felt rejected. And when we feel rejected, we guarantee ourselves to retaliate.

My friends, the moment that you feel or sense a rejection, you may be rest assured that you are in a level of consciousness known as personality; you are expressing through your emotional, magnetic field of expression, through which principle does not flow. For there is no reason in that level of consciousness. There is only personality or what is commonly referred to as self-interest and self-pity.

So what is it, my friends, that we look about within our own universe and find most beneficial to us? And, of course, that word is *self-control*: to be able to control ourselves when we have experiences in this life that we find distasteful to us. If we will express some degree of self-control, then we will free ourselves, our soul, from the magnetic field of emotion and personality and we will go on in this life with principle.

We all know, in our inner being, that we are seeking something in this great universe, and that something, when it comes right down to it, may be termed spiritual freedom. But what is spiritual freedom? How do we experience it? What is it in life that will guarantee an expression of this so-called spiritual freedom? Well, my good friends, spiritual freedom is nothing more and nothing less than the direct effect of self-control. When we control ourselves, we experience what we call spiritual freedom.

We discussed in the last class how cheaply so many of us sell our soul. We sell our soul to our emotions and to the patterns that we have become addicted to. We sell our soul to the circumstances that we have placed ourselves in. That's not the purpose of these classes, friends. It is not our purpose to give you platitudes. It is our purpose to share with you an understanding, once applied, which will free us from all of these entrapments, from all of these emotional realms, from all of these experiences of rejection where we have to express retaliation. Now, when we feel rejected and we automatically, so to speak, retaliate, who, in truth, are we harming? Who, in truth—whose soul is being placed into the bondage and the prison house of that level of consciousness? Not someone else's soul, unless the other individual is so weak and so lacking in self-control that they sell their soul to the person who retaliates. So let us give that some thought this evening. What are we truly working for in life, and what are we truly doing with our life?

Where is God in our universe, if God is not in our thought, in our attitude of mind, in our feelings, in our faith, in our consideration, and in our spoken word, act, and deed? On this path to what some call illumination—and I personally prefer to call awakening or awareness—there are many, many, many things that will distract us. For there are many, many, many things that we have given power to. So let us consider more deeply and more thoughtfully what it is we truly want in life. Then, let us go about our business and let us attain it.

It takes a constant effort, my good students, to maintain and to sustain any degree of freedom. As we walk upon the spiritual path, as we unfold our soul faculties, we find things magnified in our lives—magnified because we are becoming more sensitive. Now when we become more sensitive to these higher rates of vibration, known as spiritual vibratory waves, we also become more sensitive to the gross and to the mundane. We find that our feelings are more easily hurt. We more quickly take a slight for an injury. But that is part, my friends, of the payment of growth.

Nothing in the universe grows without its struggle, because, my friends, the struggle is in the changing. Stop and think. Whenever you've had a struggle—or if you are presently experiencing one—what, in truth, are you really doing? You are in the process of changing a pattern, an attitude of mind. The struggle, my friend, is in the unwillingness to let go of a way of thinking, of a way of living. That is where the struggle is. It's in the process of letting go and changing. Now, none of us are greater than the Divine Intelligence. None of us are greater than the laws of creation. And the laws of creation guarantee, for all form, change. And this is what we call struggle and suffering. Let us accept willingly, in our mind, the process of change that we are growing through. For if we will accept that, within our thinking, it will no longer be as difficult for us as it has been before.

Now, my friends, I know that it's much easier to believe and to have faith in the things that we can see and hear and touch with our physical senses. Of course, it is easier. It's not easy to have faith in something that we cannot see, hear, and feel with our senses. No, that takes an awakening deep within ourselves.

Now, we have come on our journey, seeking spiritual things in our life, seeking a greater freedom, and seeking a greater peace. But did you ever know of anything or anyone that attains one ounce of anything that they do not release an equal ounce of something else? Nothing rises higher to the Light without letting go of the darkness that it's been in.

It is said that it is the sleep of satisfaction—and that it is irritation that wakes the soul. And indeed, my friends, it is. When we truly get irritated with anything or anyone sufficiently, we will start to make some changes in our attitude of mind. We will start to make some changes in our own way of thinking and, in making those changes, we will rise to another level of consciousness.

There are many experiences in life, and ofttimes we call those "hurt feelings." But if we're honest with ourselves, we can say to ourselves, "Interesting that I should merit this experience at this moment." My good students, if you want to help yourselves, ask yourselves one question whenever you have an experience that has any import to you: "Why this and why now?" If you will do that with all of life's experiences, you will start on the inward journey, through your own mind, to find what laws you have set into motion. And, having found those laws that you've set into motion, you are then in a position to change them.

Now, my good students, you're free to ask any questions that you have.

Would you please speak about commitment and the principle involved in commitment?

Thank you very much. The lady is asking the question on commitment and the principle involved in commitment. It's, indeed, an important question, because many of us make commitments and the next moment, the next day, the next week, or the next year, we no longer want to fulfill those commitments. Well, what this really means is at the time the commitment was made by the individual, that person set a law into motion. However, a day later, a moment later, or even a year later, their soul, expressing through another level of consciousness, does not want to fulfill that commitment, because the commitment was not made on that other level of consciousness. This is why it is so very important that we not only recognize and realize, but that we accept the truth, that there are, indeed, eighty-one levels of consciousness.

Now, one of the great sadnesses in the world, in our world, as individuals, is in making commitments and not fulfilling them. Well, a person may say, "I have a change of mind, a change of attitude, and I no longer see that the way I saw it at the time that I made the commitment." My friends, when you make a commitment, you commit your soul, your spirit, your mind, your being. Now, if you do not fulfill that commitment, the principle of the commitment—the principle of a thing is the essence of a thing—the principle of that commitment will come back to you in another day, in another way, at another time. Not necessarily in the same form that you originally established the commitment, but it will always return to you until such time as you awaken and make wise commitments, fulfill the commitment, and go on to your next expression. I do hope that that has helped with your question.

Last week you discussed anger in relation to judgment and self-will. Would you make some connection with anger in—well, The Living Light *states that we express anger when credulity and suspicion are out of balance with logic* [Discourse 11]. *I wondered if that's what you were really saying last week or is that a different path to anger?*

No. That is absolutely correct. Whenever the circle of logic is pierced by an imbalance between either suspicion or credulity, then we will express anger. Now, the lady has brought up an important point. The circle of logic—remember that logic is a function and that reason is a soul faculty. There is a difference. Now whenever this function, the circle known as logic, is pierced, either by suspicion or credulity, we do express anger. What pierces it is our own judgment of what is right or wrong. Now, we have stated before that our conscience is a spiritual sensibility with a dual capacity, knowing right or wrong for ourselves. When we are receptive to our conscience, then no judgment is made in the circle of logic; it is not pierced, either by suspicion or credulity, and we cannot express anger. I do hope that's helped with your question.

Where does frustration fit into this circle and the piercing?

Yes. Thank you very much. I'm sure we will all agree that frustration is simply an expression of suppressed, unfulfilled desires. One of the basic teachings of this philosophy is never suppress desire, ever. It is energy. And energy must be released through our being. Either fulfill the desire that your mind entertains or educate the desire, but release the energy, for frustration is the effect of suppressed desire.

I would like to ask—last week you mentioned that when one expresses anger, that one might feel better because the energy is locked into a level. How is this energy dissipated?

Thank you very much. When a person expresses anger, they are releasing this energy. That is not the most beneficial way to release the energy. It means that the energy is blocked in the individual's own universe or aura. Now, through some degree of self-control, they may rise their level of consciousness and permit the energy to be expressed in a more beneficial way for themselves. However, we must learn to talk to ourselves at the moment that we feel this need to express this energy through the level of consciousness known as anger. Does that help with your question?

I'm interested in what law or laws that set in the particular incarnation, if only the earth incarnation, of positive and negative. What really constituted that that made us realize this being, so to speak?

Thank you very much. You're referring to the laws governing creation, known as the positive and negative. Is that correct?

Yes.

Yes. Thank you very much. I believe we have discussed, at one of our other classes, the principle of adhesion and cohesion. And perhaps it would be of some benefit to discuss it a bit further this evening. It is stated in this philosophy that like attracts like and becomes the Law of Attachment. Now, are there any students present who have any understanding they would care to share on what is cohesion and what is adhesion? I'm sure that some of my students know the difference between cohesion and adhesion. Thank you very much. Would you rise, please?

Well, as I think on that, I would think that adhesion is adhering. It would be more, in a sense, continuity of an individual and his efforts, his path. Whereas cohesion is like a binding force, where there would be a duality of purposes. Sorry, I'm getting lost.

Thank you very much. Would you agree, class, that that is cohesive is in harmony?

Yes. [Many students respond.]

Thank you very much. Now, my friends, the statement has been made that like attracts like and becomes the Law of Attachment. The like that attracts like is the divine principle controlling creation, known as cohesion, and becomes the Law of Attachment, which is known as adhesion. So we find that like attracts like, but opposites attach, and so is the principle that governs creation or form. I do hope that's helped with your question.

Tonight's class is on self-control and you said that when you apply knowledge, you express wisdom.

Yes.

Are wisdom and knowledge on different levels of consciousness? Do we have wisdom as the overall power, over all these levels? Or does wisdom follow each bit of knowledge as we go through the eighty-one levels?

Perhaps this would help you, class, in expressing it this way. We stated, I believe, last Thursday that knowledge was a function of our brain and that wisdom is an expression of our soul faculties. Now, knowledge, when applied—the application of it—constitutes what is known as wisdom. Therefore, do you not see that when a sense function is properly applied, according to the laws governing functions, it becomes a soul faculty? I do hope that's helped with your question. Thank you very much. This is why we teach, Don't annihilate the sense functions. You're not going to be spiritualized that way. We're trying to bring them into balance: 50 percent there and 50 percent over there.

Would you please explain the principle of guilt, where it comes from, and how it is related to conscience?

Thank you very much. And the lady is asking for an explanation of the principle of guilt. Well, first of all, friends, you cannot feel, sense, or think guilt until you have made a judgment. And so we find that guilt is the effect of a judgment that we have made at some time in our life and are unable to release. Now, when we make the judgment—you understand, our mind makes the judgment—and then we are not able to apply what we have judged, we experience this so-called feeling known as guilt. It simply is a matter of a lack of self-control. We judge this, which is right for us, and, of course, therefore guarantees what is to be right for our family, our friends, and the world. And then, on another level of consciousness, we find that we are unable to apply what we have judged for ourselves. You see, man is a law unto himself. And therefore, we feel guilty. We feel guilty because we know that we have made the judgment. We do not use sufficient self-control to apply it, and we feel what is known as guilt. I do hope that's helped with your question.

I have a question that seems self-explanatory, but it isn't immediately. "Be ever the observer and not the observed [Discourse 28]." Would you give us your understanding of this?

Thank you very much. And the lady is asking a question in reference to the statement that is made, "Be ever the observer and never the observed." May I ask you a question, student, please? What does it mean to you to be observed?

Well, it means that I'm being noticed.

Thank you very much. That's most helpful in explaining what we have to explain. When a person is in self-control—in control of themselves—when they are the captain of their ship, they become the masters of their destiny, for they are at that point of consciousness the observer. Now, when we feel a need for energy, commonly referred to as attention, we set certain laws into motion, that we may become the observed. For, you see, my friends, it is the observed that receive the energy, not the observer. Now I do hope that has helped with your question.

Thank you.

The observer is a spiritual level and the observed is a level of form or creation. Thank you.

With reference to being the observer, rather than the observed, I have gotten confused in the area where it says—it seems like— say a person has a job to do: public speaking or teaching or something like that. Perhaps I'm too literal. I don't know. But by nature he's observed and frequently a person who is in that position gets a lot of feeding from being observed in that way. And yet it seems to be something that is his talent to do at the same time. I don't understand how that fits in with the explanation you just gave.

Thank you very much. And perhaps we can clarify that for you. Number one: If the person is a public speaker or anything else or in any position in life that they are observed, then they, and they alone, have set the law into motion to merit that expression or that soul talent, if you care to refer to it as that. Now let us not misunderstand, friends: we are all observed. And if, for a moment, we think we're not, we set laws into motion to make sure that we are. And, of course, we set all kinds of laws into motion to become observed. I mean, after all, the ladies go to the beauty shop. What do you think they go there for? It's very sensible. And the men get their hair cut a certain way, etc. We commonly refer to that as pride. Well, that's being observed, would you not agree? And so I'm sure we will all agree that we're all being observed at some time during the course of a day. And if we're not being observed, we become very unhappy. Would you not agree? Fine. So it only goes to prove, my friends, that we don't annihilate the sense functions. Because if we try that, you know, we become most unhappy, you see. My friends, everything is inseparably united. But what we're trying to do is to bring a balance between the observer and the observed. After all, there is a time in life and in our day when it behooves us to keep our mouth shut. Would you not agree? I do hope that's helped with your question. Thank you so much.

At various times in the past you have spoken about the conscious, the superconscious mind, soul mates, clairsentience, and intuition. I wonder if you could give us some further clarification of the relationship between or among these things.

Thank you very much. Perhaps we could begin with the conscious mind. We've discussed it before: that is what we are consciously aware of and it is our electrical field. The subconscious mind, which is, of course, our magnetic field—the feeling of our emotions, etc.—and where all of the experiences are stored in that so-called memory par excellence in our subconscious mind. And the superconscious, we understand to be the neutral and also through which the Divine expresses. Now, it is our understanding that the Divine Intelligence expresses through the superconscious to the conscious and our subconscious reacts or expresses itself.

In reference to soul mates or guardian angels, that is known as the so-called better half of ourselves. Now, the Law of Creation is the Law of Duality. And so our soul is the covering of the formless, free Spirit. Being the covering, it has form. Now, anything that comes into form has its own counterpart: it has its equal half. For example, the soul has form: it has a covering. We are, to some extent, consciously aware of it—some of us. And it also has that other part of us known as our guardian angel. Some people refer to it as our soul mate. Now, our so-called soul mate or guardian angel is not a separate personality or entity. It is that better half of ourselves. For example, when the divine, formless Spirit expresses into creation, it splits, according to the Law of Creation. And when it splits, you have the soul expressing in the physical form and you have a soul expressing in the spiritual form. Do you understand? However, now please don't misunderstand and think, "Well, I'm only half a soul." Well, a half a soul with God is better than no soul at all. I do hope that's helped with your question.

It has been said of certain persons that when they speak, they speak from the soul level. I'm a little confused. I want to keep this down to a point of asking a question. I'm a little confused of what that would be. Would that be when you're speaking spiritually only or would it be in all parts, if the principle is in the speaking?

Thank you very much for your question. And to the best of my understanding and awareness, it would take a person on a level known as receptive to soul in order to reach a decision whether or not the individual speaking to them was speaking from a soul level. Therefore, this, of course, would be a very personal thing. And, however, let us not get confused. I have heard some students, where another student agrees with them, say, "You know, that's a beautiful person. They speak on a soul level." Well, let's not confuse a soul level, friends, with one that fulfills the desire and what we are trying to attain. This is very important.

Now, how do we know if a person is speaking on a soul level? Well, we don't necessarily. There's no guarantee that we know that—because it pleases us—the person that is speaking to us or agreeing with us. That doesn't guarantee it's a soul level. It simply means that there is some degree of rapport and harmony with that level of consciousness. It certainly could be a far, far climb from what we call a soul level. Now, we all know that truth is individually perceived. Fine. So if we have a true inner feeling that someone is speaking from a soul level, and we listen to that individual and we apply what they have to say and in that application we find our life better for so doing, then, of course, for us, that is most beneficial. I do hope that's helped with your question.

I'd like to understand the Declaration of Principles. Would you explain to me what nature's physical and spiritual laws are? [During the church service the Declaration of Principles of the National Spiritualist Association of Churches was read aloud by the congregation.]

Thank you very much. The lady has asked in reference to this Association's Declaration of Principles, What are the physical and spiritual laws governing life? They are as numbered, my good students, as the hairs upon your head, and then some. However, let us be practical, perhaps to find a simple example. You will accept there is such a thing in the physical world known as the Law of Gravity, won't you? That is known as a *physical* law. Will you accept a spiritual law that states that like attracts like and becomes the Law of Attachment? Has that been proven to your satisfaction by your own mind? That's a spiritual law. Now, from that point, friends, we must expand. It is a spiritual law that forgiveness frees our soul; it frees our thought. That is a spiritual law. And so it is that as we spend a little time to ponder and to think—Will you accept the spiritual law that says that man is a law unto himself, that all of our experiences are the effect and never the cause? Those are spiritual laws. I hoped that's helped.

Thank you. What is a body?

Thank you very much. When we refer to a body, we are referring to the effect of a negative and positive pole, which are brought together by the principle of cohesion and adhesion, by a divine principle. Now, our understanding of this divine principle—the best we're able to express it, because the moment you define something, you limit it; and the moment you limit it, you no longer have it. However, throughout all universes, there is this adhesion and cohesion principle that is at work. A body is the effect of the laws that are set into motion.

Now, let us take perhaps even a more simple example. Anything that has form is a body. A thought *is* a body. A physical being *is* a body. However, most of us, not having opened our vision to the realm of thought, are not aware. And, indeed, it is more difficult for us to believe—it's difficult to believe what we do not see with our physical eyes—that when you think, if you think the word *beauty*, in a realm of thought, a beautiful thing is created. Now that creation, that body, will last as long as you direct energy to it. The most beautiful things that are created by the human being are from the soul faculties. When you express duty to your spirit, and faith and poise and humility and appreciation and understanding, those create beautiful forms in the atmosphere.

Now the question may well arise, in reference to bodies, the question may well arise, What is it that governs the shape that this thought will take? My friends, the law governing creation governs that: man's law. And you've got to go back throughout the centuries and untold ages. Man had a feeling and we, today, call that feeling beauty. That feeling expressed out into the atmosphere and a beautiful thing was created. He looked at the sunrise and he had a feeling and we call that beauty. And so that's what those bodies are. Therefore, do we not see the great importance of controlling our thought?

Now, we may say, "Now that's one level of consciousness." We may say, "When I think the word *beauty*, I see a serene lake, because that's always meant beauty to me." That is another level. That is another body of creation. But the greatest body of creation is what is known as the level of mass thinking: creation throughout the ages. It is the primitive mind. You see, my friends, we all have a primitive mind. We have it here and now. It is in the elements that have composed our physical being. They call it the primitive mind.

When you're unfolding—what we call spiritual unfoldment— you start to descend. You start to descend into your levels of consciousness, through your own subconscious, through your own suppressions, through your own aggressions, through your own desires, etc. All right. So you start to act emotionally like a little child. The truth of the matter is, you don't start to act like a little child: you become aware that you've always acted like a little child. Because we're controlled by those emotional feelings of a little child, because we're still a little child. What it is in the unfoldment process—and we're still talking about bodies—what it is in the unfoldment process, is that we start to awaken. We start to see that somebody didn't play the game our way and we're going to not play the game at all. Well, that's the little child. But we've been doing that all along. We just start to become aware of it. And when we start to become consciously aware of it, we're infuriated! Our ego, our pride, and all of those functions don't like it at all.

Then, gradually but surely, we get through that level of consciousness—ever on guard and alert, because we can always go back to that level—and we start going through what is known as the primitive mind. And there, friends, are what is commonly referred to as the elementals and all those things. Well, let us ask ourselves the question, "Shall we get through them here and now or at least make the attempt? Or shall we wait until we lose this dense physical body and we find ourselves in an astral realm and we see all those thought forms, the children of our own creation, and we don't like their looks at all?" In fact, we find it most distasteful. Now, that's what the religions of the world have been talking about when they're talking about Satan and all of his army, and when they're talking about the devil and all of those demons. Well, my friends, they're talking about the demons that man—ourselves—we have created.

You see, when you have a feeling of jealousy, you've just created a demon. Well, of course, you did. You don't have to say he's got one eye and twenty teeth. You don't have to say that at all. That's created according to a natural law. However—see, it pays to be good, friends—just at least try, because, my gosh, when you see some of those things, the so-called DTs *[delirium tremens]* are a pleasure. Well, it's a terrible nightmare. But it's a nightmare of our own creation.

This is why religion tries to get you to think of God, to worship something outside your brains, you see? Look, it doesn't matter whether it's Buddha or the Virgin Mary or it's Jesus or it's Mazda or it's any of those figureheads. What matters, my friends, is that you are bowing in humility to some power, to some intelligence, greater than your brain. That's where it really is. See, God, the true God, is a humble God. He's the greatest servant of all servants. He serves and sends the rain on everybody, whether he likes that person or not. Whether that person is a so-called bad person or a good person, when the law is set into motion, the rain falls on all of us. When the next law is set into motion, the sun shines on all of us. See how impartial God, the greatest servant of all servants, really is.

So if religion, in its way, is trying—all religions—to get you to bow this thing called the ego to a greater authority—and when you do that, you feel better, you live better. You don't have all of these problems. You don't try to decide to do God's work for him, to run the whole universes, and tell him that he's done a lousy job. That he made a microscopic mistake along the way: he should have given us nine days to the week instead of seven and all these foolish things. Do you see what I mean? Now, which is the best way, really, which is the best? To tell God he's making all kinds of mistakes in life because he's permitted some of these people to get away with so many different things or to say, "Well, now that's their merit system. Don't let me judge them—because if I judge them, then I'm going to find myself in the same situation—in order that I may be granted understanding."

My friends, who amongst us, *who* is so illumined that we know what is best for everyone in the universe? Who amongst us is so illumined that we even know what is best for ourselves, when we are not even aware of how we really got here, let alone all those schools of expression that we were in before? We have merited this experience because we flunked those lessons the last time. Well, my gosh, let us stop and think. Let us give a little thought to an intelligence that holds all things in space. Why, we can't even do that ourselves. Just take a ball and throw it out there and expect it to stay suspended in midair. I know darn well you can't do it. But you could, if you understood the laws that govern gravity. Don't you see what I mean? Knowledge knows much, but wisdom knows better. Now to understand the laws that govern gravity, we got to have consideration for all of the component parts, not just what this thing is willing to accept.

Think, my friends. What is our greatest difficulty in life? And don't tell me we don't have difficulties. I never met a human being that didn't have one or two, at least. But what is it? What is it that's causing it? Well, it's our acceptance. We don't want to accept change. Now, we say here, "Gosh, look at all the changes I'm making." Well, the moment we say that, we can be rest assured that we haven't really even started. But we have been thinking about it. Now that is a step. We have been thinking about it, don't you see?

You see, my friends, what does it matter, what does it really matter, how something works, as long as it works, as long as the fruit is of benefit in our lives? I mean, what does it matter how it works? What really matters is that it does work. Now, for example, let us say, I want to know the principle by which the tree produces its fruit. I want to know the principle by which the ear of corn grows in the ground. OK, so we start searching and we get to a certain point and that's as much as we can get to. OK. Does that benefit, in any way, shape, or form, our appetite? My goodness, when you're hungry, you want to eat. Is that not true? And so what do you do? You eat.

Now I'm not saying we should try to demonstrate blind faith, because we're doing that all the time, you see? We're demonstrating blind faith all the time. Stop and think. We have faith. We turn the light switch on, the light goes on. We have faith that the ground is going to produce food. Well, is that knowledgeable faith or is that blind faith? Well, of course, that's blind faith. It's blind faith. We have accepted that it's always done it, so it's always going to do it. That's blind faith. So we're all expressing blind faith in something, see? OK, we go to school and we learn so much. All right. That's the way it works, because that's what we've learned from the book. OK? Fine. We've accepted that. Therefore, it can't work any other way. It's impossible. Well, what we are doing in that moment is demonstrating blind faith. We are demonstrating total blindness, through faith, of what the book says and we can't go a step further. That, my friends, to me at least, is blind faith. And I am sure that you will all agree.

Let us go have refreshments and thank you all very, very much.

MAY 16, 1974

CONSCIOUSNESS CLASS 48

Good evening, class. We have spoken in our classes—and many times—of selfless service, of faculties and functions, of attitudes of mind, of levels of consciousness, of broadening our horizons, and many, many, many different ways to find the peace and the light within ourselves. And so the question, of course, must arise: With so many different ways shown to the student to free themselves, what is the seeming difficulty with many to find this great peace, this harmony, this joy, and this awareness?

Well, my friends, we must stop and we must pause and think. How much that we receive are we, in truth, applying? Now *application* means many different things to different people. To some people, it simply means applying what they have received in thought. That means to give it some mental consideration. However, my friends, no matter what it is that we are learning in life—and we are learning many things every day—application must apply in each dimension of our soul's expression. And, of course, I know we will all agree that our soul not only expresses through a mental body, but it also expresses through a physical body.

Now, these seeming difficulties that some of us seem to have in application should be considered more often. If we, in truth, are seeking to free ourselves—to free ourselves from certain levels of consciousness and disturbances—if we are truly seeking that, if that is our true motivation—not our apparent one, but our true motivation—then it is evident that we will make greater effort, more often to apply, of course, what we are learning. For to learn anything in life, my friends, without the benefit of application, of course, is no value to anyone. And so the question arises, "Do I truly know within my being what it is I really want?"

Now, there is a statement, made some time ago, that man always gets what he really wants. And, my friends, though that's rather a blunt statement, it is a very accurate and a very true one. So if we'll give some consideration to that statement—man always gets what he really wants—then we can look at our lives and we can see what it is that we are receiving. We can see whether we like it or we don't like it. And if there is something in what we're receiving, known as effect, that we don't like, then wisdom dictates to go inside and find out what it is that we're doing inside, in our own attitude, in our own mind, that is guaranteeing these distasteful experiences in our lives. That, my friends, is known as application. To make the effort more often to find out, in truth, what our attitudes are, what our motives are, what our true values are—not perhaps what we *think* they are, but let us consider what they really are. For life is constantly revealing to us exactly—no more and no less—it is revealing to us exactly what we truly want. Because we do, indeed, get what we really want, according to the laws that we alone are setting into motion.

This type of an awareness class is not popular in a world that is not willing to find the cause of all feelings, the cause of all experiences, the cause of all circumstances inside of their own being. Of course, it cannot be popular until such time as man is willing to bow in humility to the truth. And so it is our teachings, If the light is too bright, it is best they see it not now.

On the spiritual path of awakening, we reach a crossroad. Some of us reach many small crossroads. But we all reach that crossroad, and that crossroad is known as decision. And the decision that all people on the path will make someday—and some are making today—is very simple: "Do I want to face the truth inside of myself or do I want to continue in my slumber and in my sleep of satisfaction?" This crossroad must be reached by all souls someday. If we truly have made up our mind to face whatever it is that we have to face, if we have made that decision, then, my friends, we will be strong enough and we will remain on the spiritual path throughout this incarnation. But that is a decision that no one can make for us.

It is a decision that each student, that each soul, must make for himself. I can only say this: It is, indeed, worthwhile to give up a little self-motivation in order to receive divine inspiration. It's worth it to all of us. And, believe me, it is a path that is inevitable.

So when we have something to face, is it not sensible that we face it when we become aware of it? Procrastination is not only the theft of all time, but it is more difficult to face a lesson in life the second time or the third time. Only a fool puts off till tomorrow what can be accomplished today.

I do hope, my friends, that that will help to stimulate your thinking, because I know if it will do that, that you will at least make the effort to apply whatever is necessary to change the attitudes of mind that have proven themselves already to be not beneficial in your lives.

Now you're free to ask any questions that you have.

Tying in with this talk of yours, will you please give us a discussion on acceptance, the divine will? So that we will have a better understanding of acceptance and what we are accepting.

Thank you very much. I think we have spoken on that subject a bit at one of our other classes, but perhaps we can approach it from a little different perspective. We have stated that God, of course, is ever equal to our understanding. And as we look out at nature, we see that God, or the Divine, is the perfect example of acceptance. The Divine accepts all creation and cares for all creation. The Divine has no rejection, whether it's the blade of grass or it's the human being. Now, the lesson that nature has to offer to us is a total acceptance of all things, of all people, of all form, of all attitudes of mind: of the believer and the disbeliever. All are accepted by the Divine.

Now, when man decides that he will accept this and he will reject that, then man has become greater than the Divine itself, because man has become partial. Man has decided what is best for himself. It is true that the Law of Creation is the Law of Duality, which guarantees choice and variety. When we are speaking on acceptance, the divine will, we are speaking on the acceptance of all things everywhere, at all times.

So many of us, when speaking to another human soul or having an experience, seemingly automatically reject it according to what we have accepted at some other time in our life. Therefore, we are no longer free. We are now controlled by the patterns of acceptance, and we cannot broaden our horizons or expand our consciousness. Because, my friends—don't you see?—we have become greater in our thinking than God, the Divine.

Now a person might say, "Someone expresses certain levels of consciousness and I refuse to accept that. I tune them out." I've heard that phrase so many times. And while speaking on acceptance, I would also like to speak on this phrase that I have heard from some of my students, of "tuning out" this or "tuning out" that. If you would study more deeply your study book [*The Living Light*], you would not only find that the ears represent ego, but they also represent something else. And if you'll refer to a certain little allegory given here in that book, "And the ears of ego heard not, for the door was locked by the key of fear." My friends, the ears not only represent ego: the ears represent perception.

Now, if we decide that we're going to tune out this and tune out that, we will guarantee the day, my friends, when we will have difficulty in hearing at all. Don't you see what we do to ourselves? At first, it is consciously selective: we are consciously aware that we have closed our ears to this or that, which we have found distasteful. The natural process of the mind, of our own subconscious, is to accept what is consciously fed into it by the conscious mind through repetition. And so it is, my friends: you now know the cause of hearing problems.

And what does this have to do with acceptance? It has everything to do with acceptance. We accept the divine right of every human soul to think the way that they feel best for them. Now in that acceptance, we do not guarantee license, which means to do what you want to do, when you want to do it, and how you want to do it, with total disregard for responsibility.

Now, my friends, when we accept anything, we set a law into motion. So the question arises: "Then must I be more selective in my accepting?" No, my friends, accept from a level of spirituality. If this person you don't like—accept their right to express themselves. If that situation you don't like, accept it as an effect and not as a cause. If God—and it has become demonstrable—is the total epitome of acceptance, then who is man to reject, when God, the Divine itself, accepts all and rejects nothing? I do hope that's helped with your question. Thank you. Yes.

I believe this question ties in with that. Would you discuss self-will and the soul faculty of initiative?

Thank you very much. And the lady has asked a most important question, dealing with self-will and the soul faculty of initiative. Initiative, being a soul faculty and not a sense function, is guided by the Law of Consideration, or the foundation of reason. Self-will, being a function, does not have consideration (total), nor does it have the foundation of reason. Therefore, if a person feels an initiative within themselves to do something, they may be rest assured—if it is, in truth, the soul faculty of initiative that is impressing them—then they will demonstrate consideration, reason, and responsibility, which is another soul faculty. I do hope that's helped with your question. Thank you.

Would you give me your understanding of the words meekness *and* weakness? *I have observed that some people look upon meekness as weakness.*

Thank you very, very much. And that statement, that question that you have asked—the difference, if any, between meekness and weakness—is indeed a most important one, considering that many seem to mistake kindness for weakness. And so it is meekness is the art of being kind. It has total consideration. It has an expression of divine love and its guiding hand is humility, in comparison to what man refers to as weakness.

Now, what do we really mean by *weakness*? By whose standard is it judged? Is it the standard of the Divine? Well, we don't believe in a God that's a judge; so we cannot get the standard from that level of consciousness at all. Man has decided and man has judged what is weak and what is strong. And so, when we're speaking of weakness, we're speaking of man's judgment. Does that help with your question? You're more than welcome.

Yes, sir. It seems many times—at least I can speak for myself and say that I find myself doing the right thing for the wrong reason, and the wrong thing for the right reason. And I think we've seen quite a bit of that in the news of late. I wonder if you would speak on this application of trying to get the two together?

Thank you very much. And that's a very good question. The gentleman has stated about doing the right thing for the wrong reason, and the wrong thing for the right reason. My friends, that seems to be a contradiction and certainly does open the door to confusion. So we must go deeper beyond the appearance and the apparent reason.

A person says that, "Well, I'm doing the right thing. I'm doing the right thing, but it's for the wrong purpose." Now, we must realize, my good friends, if we are doing the *right* thing—if it is the *right* thing—then the effect is ever equal to the motivation. So, in truth, it is not possible to do the *right* thing for the wrong purpose, or to do the wrong thing for the right purpose.

Don't you see, my friends, the law is very clear: like attracts like and becomes the Law of Attachment. So if man's motivation is right, then the effect can only be right. But it is the duality of our mind—this so-called great decision maker—that says, "I've spent all my time doing that. I had a pure motive and look what came out of it." No, my friends. No person, no group, no country, no world can do the right thing for the wrong purpose or do the wrong thing for the right purpose. It is our own perspective that sees that contradiction, because we do not see beyond appearance.

Now ofttimes a person—I've heard people say, "Well, I expected to find more spiritual people when I attend a church." Well, what are we thinking? Are we thinking because a person enters into a house of God that they're automatically transformed into an angel? I haven't seen it happen yet. I haven't even seen it happen after a lifetime of attendance. No! So where is the perspective? Did we enter the church doors with a true motive of seeking spirituality? Or did we enter the church doors with the true motive of finding the sawdust in another's eye while the plank is blinding our own?

Now let us think, friends. We cannot have a true motive, a pure motive, a right motive and have a wrong effect. It is contrary to the natural law, which is demonstrable. I do hope that's helped with your question.

I have two questions. One is, I'd like to know where in the center of the body is the air located. Second—and this is of great importance to me—is an understanding of having, let's say, of going over a conversation before it happens physically—and it could be hours or days later—going over that same conversation, almost to the word, that you've already gone over before it even happens on the physical level, knowing that such a thing was going to take place. Just knowing that that type of conversation was going to happen. I would certainly enjoy learning more how this function works.

Thank you very much for your questions. In reference to your first one, dealing with the occult anatomy and the centers, that is covered in my private classes and not in the public ones. However, in reference to your question of perceiving or becoming aware of a conversation before it takes place in the physical world, that's most understandable. When we understand that there is no time and space, and when our soul level of consciousness rises to that level where all past and all seeming future is the eternal moment, then it is most understandable that we would become aware of conversations taking place in a physical world a week, a day, an hour, or even a year later. And I do hope that's helped with your question. Thank you very much.

Sort of on that same topic, I've been wondering about meditation. In meditation, do we seek to learn or to receive messages from spirits on another level or plane? And if we do, are these spirits still progressing towards perfection so that they, in fact, are not perfect? And how do we trust, as truth for us, what we hear?

Thank you very much for that question. It's a most important one. The purpose for meditation, for concentration and the daily sitting, is not—*is not*—for the purpose of communication with other dimensions. That is not its true purpose. Its true purpose—and always has been with this Association—is to find God. To find God inside of yourself.

Now, in the finding of that God—of that Light within—we will have many experiences. Some of those experiences will, of course, be communion with the so-called departed, with those who have gone on before us. However, they will not be on a higher level of consciousness than our own soul aspiration.

Now anyone, anything that is in form is under the Law of Creation, known as duality, and therefore they are not infallible. I have never communicated with what is known as an infallible spirit in my thirty-four years of communication. Now, that doesn't mean that the percentages are not satisfactory to me or I would not continue on with communication. Do you understand?

Now, one of the most wonderful and beautiful things of communion with this other dimension is that it's like a mirror: we get to find out where we really are. For example, some time ago, when there was so much talk concerning the seeming earthquake that was to befall San Francisco a number of years ago, we wrote an article in our little magazine about the prophets of doom. The prophets, you understand—their inspirers, their guides, and teachers—are no higher nor lower than the soul aspiration of the person that they work through. And so it is, my friends, that if you are in communion with these other dimensions and you are not satisfied with the results that you are receiving, if the accuracy doesn't come up to your standards, then stop for a few moments and reflect. It is only the mirror that is revealing your level of consciousness at the time of communication.

You see, like attracts like and becomes the Law of Attachment. Your guides and teachers cannot be more accurate, they cannot be more honest, they cannot be more awakened, they cannot be more deceptive, they cannot be more illumined than your own basic soul. Does that help with your question? And so it is in communication that we seek to commune with God. And remember that God has given his angels charge over us lest we dash our foot against the stone of ignorance.

But it is a very dangerous thing, my friends, to seek communication with another dimension for the purpose of communication. Do not seek that! Do not do such a grave injustice to your soul. If that is what is meant for you, by the divine laws, it shall come to pass. Do not seek the psychic. Do not seek mediumship. But seek God. And then, all things will be harmoniously arranged around you. We're not all meant to be pianists. We're not all meant to be plumbers. We're not all meant to be carpenters. And we're not all meant to be mediums. But we can all find God in those few moments of meditation. I hope that has helped you. Thank you very much. Yes.

It was mentioned in our previous semester that understanding is the foundation for all of the soul faculties. It was also mentioned this evening of keeping a foundation of reason.

That's correct.

Can you speak on those?

Yes. We spoke in one of our classes that understanding is the foundation of all the soul faculties and we spoke this evening on a foundation of reason. My friends, without understanding, there is no reason. And so the first thing that we seek is to understand something; then we can express reason concerning it. But we can't even get to the foundation block of understanding without total consideration. Because we can't understand something that we don't consider, and we can't use reason concerning anything that we don't understand. And so we find that total consideration, understanding, and reason are an inseparable foundation upon which the soul faculties are built, beginning with the first one—that you all well know—of duty, gratitude, and tolerance.

Now do you see, my friends, until you unfold duty, gratitude, and tolerance; faith, poise and humility, you can't have total consideration? And if you can't have total consideration, you can't have understanding. And if you can't have understanding, you certainly cannot express reason. Remember that reason is a soul faculty. It is logic that is a sense function. Thank you very much.

What is the best way to get rid of a feeling of being impoverished mentally? So many people, when asked to give, feel impoverished. No matter how much they have, they still feel poor. I sometimes have gone through this—not very much of it—but I have gone through it, and I'd like to know how to free my mind from that feeling, if you could help me?

Thank you. I'm glad you mentioned the mind in reference to that statement because, my friends, of course, wealth or poverty or whatever you want to call it is an attitude of mind. Now, you can feel very poor with six million dollars in the bank, if that is what you choose to feel. And you can feel very wealthy with two dollars in the bank. I speak for myself and I feel extremely wealthy.

So, my dear friends, don't you see, it's only an attitude of mind. It has nothing whatsoever to do with how many dollars you have in your bank account. It has absolutely nothing to do with how many clothes you wear on your back. It has absolutely nothing to do with how many automobiles you drive and what make they are. It has nothing to do with all those things. It's an attitude of mind.

Now sometimes—you know, it's so interesting: the lady's brought up a beautiful point—sometimes a person is asked perhaps for a dollar or two and she says, well, they feel impoverished, they feel very poor. Well, you know, there's an old saying: You can always get money if you don't ask for too much and you don't ask too often. Now, you can always get it, but you've got to know how.

Now, if a person feels a charge of energy by giving you a dollar bill, then to them it's well worth the giving. After all, let us not forget, my dear friends, that we're all in physical forms and we all have functions and the house of the functions is known as the ego. Now, if you ask a person the right way and you ask him on the right level of consciousness and perhaps that will give him an extra charge of energy at that time and they feel the need of that extra charge of energy, you'll probably get the dollar that you're asking for. But it depends, you see—look, my friends, if you have problems asking for a dollar bill for a good cause, don't look at the person you're asking the dollar from. Don't do that to yourself. Don't delude yourself. Say to yourself, "Now, let me see, every time I ask this person they say no or get all frustrated. Now, what level inside of me triggers that level inside of them?" Now, *that's* the question to ask. Ask it inside, see? Say, "Now, what level inside of me causes me to open my mouth to that person at that time and I always get the same reaction? Is it because I wasn't thinking the first time I asked them, and that's the way they reacted, and I accepted in my mind that so-and-so was that way, and so every time I ask them, they react that way?" See, my friends, it's inside. A thousand million times: It's all inside. You see?

Now some people respond out of embarrassment. And so if that's the way to get it, then you embarrass them. Now some people respond out of encouragement. And if that's the way to get it, then you encourage them. Don't you see, my good friends, the end justifies the means. If the end is an eternal spiritual verity, the end justifies the means. The form it comes and the form it goes. But remember, we do unto others as we desire others should do unto us. We don't want to take bread out of their mouth. That's not the purpose. That certainly isn't spirituality. But let's get rid of this so-called money hang-up.

You know, every time that word is mentioned, somebody gets all emotional. You know, just because you people might not be able to see it physically—I see all that tightness and all that emotional upset. My goodness' sakes, look what it does to us! Look at all the diseases we have that are directly attributed to money. Either too much of it or we think we've got too little of it. See? Why do we make it such a bad word? A medium of exchange. Why do we give it such power over our lives?

My friends, it comes and goes. Only this day I looked in the paper and saw there was a shortage of pennies. I thought it was just beautiful. Wonderful. Maybe we will have aluminum ones. But stop and think. Why do we spend so much of our energy, so much of our thought, so much of our feelings about money? Is it because, perhaps, that's the way we found of getting attention? Because—you know something?—you'll have plenty of ears if you're talking about money. You'll have all the ears in the world listening to you. Now is it because we have found that we can get energy that way—attention, you know—when we can't get it any other way? I hope that's helped with your question, student. And remember, it's an attitude of mind and that's all that it is.

And remember one thing more, friends: You don't need money—and neither do I—but money needs me. And it also needs you. Because what value is it without us? We're the ones that created it. We're the ones that made it. What good is it without us? Just remember that. Stop running around and saying you need money. It needs you. And don't forget it. I hope that's helped you all. Thank you very much.

[There is a brief pause, and then the Teacher continues.] I didn't really want to end on that seeming material vibration—and besides you're ten minutes early—but if there are no more questions, I'll be happy to. Yes.

There's a question I'd like to have answered about concentration. I've heard about meditation and contemplation. Can you give us an explanation of contemplation and if this follows meditation?

Thank you very much. That is not the teachings that we offer. We offer concentration, meditation, and manifestation. Now I know that you are all well versed, as you have had private class work in concentration and in meditation and manifestation. But for the benefit of those who have not yet had private class work, I'll be happy to share a little with you.

Concentration: The first part of our meditation period is set aside, placing the mind pointedly and fixedly upon the object of your choice, and that object that we have chosen here, in this Association, is peace. That is followed by a meditation: The meditation is when there is no thought in the mind. Some people seem to have a little difficulty in that area. And then it's followed by what we call manifestation. And manifestation is when you're receptive and you become the receiving set to receive these vibrations and impressions from these other dimensions.

Now remember, friends, that when you concentrate, you set a law into motion. You rise your soul to the highest possible level that you're able to rise to at that time, and then you maintain and sustain that by a perfect, *total* void. That's when the gray matter is still, in those few moments. Then, what you receive is coming along your own vibratory wave. That's where you've tuned in and that's where your soul is. So what you receive, then, friends—you know, don't tell them, don't say, "I don't like you. You go away." Because you're talking to a part of yourself. That person that has entered has entered according to the law, and you are on that level of consciousness—though you might not consciously think so—you are on that level of consciousness and they're revealing to you that that's a level that's inside of you. I hope that's helped you. Yes.

In referring to your previous question about money needs us, I know that other students, as well as myself, have experienced a shortage in the past, and we still encounter the same problem. As a matter of fact, probably the church does also—

I totally disagree. Thank you very much. But you go right ahead, that is, with the church's problem. It doesn't exist. Because we keep making sure that it doesn't. Thank you.

But anyway, we find ourselves in this mundane world of existing and our obligations and we are in need of this so-called money, some more so than others. Therefore, some of our energies are greater than the other person's, but yet, with this particular understanding—and to try to get away from that same old habit pattern and levels of consciousness or why we merited this shortage. And we try to overcome this thing. I realize that through understanding and also, say—patience is another way that we can also overcome this. Can you give me your understanding on that, please?

Thank you very much. And I knew, when that door opened, we would have much discussion concerning that word. [*The Teacher coughs.*] Excuse me. It seems that all our minds have accepted that we have a need. We have accepted, of course, this in our thought and in our mind. And the more we entertain it, the more life demonstrates, for us, anyway, the continuity thereof.

I do disagree that your church *needs* money. It doesn't *need* money. I am not saying that those who have chosen to support it should not. Because if they don't, we wouldn't be here. But I assure you, my friends, we would be someplace else.

Now, what is this need, so-called, inside of us that says that when we have what is called money, everything is beautiful; and when we don't have it, everything is miserable? Why is it that way? Now I question anyone to tell me that they didn't have emotion when they accept they're short of cash. Is there anyone present who doesn't have any emotion when they're short of cash? Now I know everyone present, and I can well recall—I have an excellent memory to remind them of the time they were emotional when they said they were short. All right, so we'll all agree that we all have emotion when we've accepted that we're short of cash. Now what does that really reveal? What does it reveal? Tell me where it is. I can tell you where it is very easily. Anybody know? Where is it? Yes, thank you.

It's lack of the spirit.

Certainly it's lack of the spirit.

Lack of faith.

Lack of faith. It goes even beyond. Yes, thank you.

Lack of gratitude.

Lack of gratitude. Lack of gratitude! Yes.

Ego.

Ego. Now think, friends. What happens to us when we decide that we're short of cash? The moment we decide that we're short of cash, we have all kinds of desires. All kinds of desires come up in our head. We haven't had a new pair of boots for years. We haven't eaten out for weeks, maybe months. Every kind of desire you can think of starts to scream for attention the very moment we say we're short of cash. Why does that do that? Why does that do that? Does anybody know? Does anybody know why the moment we say we're short of cash all of our desires start screaming in our subconscious and they all want expression and attention that very moment? Does anybody know that? Why? Why do all those desires scream at that time? Why don't they scream at some other time?

Because we've gone into a self-motivation.

Thank you very, very much. We've gone into a self-motivation, or, as one of the other students says, a lack of the spirit. We have become grounded. The moment we say we're short of cash, see, we deny our divinity. That's what we do. And the student that asked the question, please don't feel sensitive, because we all do it. We have denied our divinity the moment that we say we're short of anything. And the moment we say we're short of anything, we deny our divinity, we ground ourselves in the magnetic field, and all of our little creatures, all of our creations, known as desires, they all scream for attention. And then, we have an emotional problem.

And this is why, as we discussed earlier—the lady was asking, Why do people seem impoverished when they're asked to donate a dollar bill—well, don't you see what you're triggering? You're triggering that level of consciousness and all those little entities come up in their head and start screaming. And then, they get kind of emotional. You know, friends, there's one way of getting a person emotional: just discuss money that's not going to them. I guarantee you, it'll work 99.9 percent of the time. Now they might not show it too much: it depends on what they've computed as pride and dignity. But be rest assured, it works. It works every time. Why does it work? Because, all of a sudden, friends, we no longer have any reason. We have no understanding. We have no consideration. All we have is that magnetic field of suppressed desires. That's all we have. Don't you see?

So what is it? Look, God has given us everything. But he's not going to come down and control our minds and say, "You stupid fool, take a look: here it is in front of you!" See?

Look, man's the one that decides he's short or he's flush, according to his values and the standards that he has established for himself. Now some people are very flush with ten dollars a week or two dollars a week. And some people are terribly short if they have no less than a thousand. So now what kind of standard is that? It varies with each individual. Don't you see what I mean?

Now, look what happens to a person. All right, they go to the city and they look and see all those beautiful clothes and this and that, and they say, "Oh, I'd like to have that," and then the thought arises in the mind, "Oh, let's see, I'd better not spend that, because if I spend that I won't have it for another desire I have over here or I won't have it for a responsibility that I have over there." Now that brings up a very important question: responsibility. What is responsibility? What causes responsibility? Anybody know what causes responsibility? What is responsibility the effect of?

Duty.

Duty.

I'm tempted to say expression.

Thank you. Anyone else?

Commitment.

Commitment.

Choices.

Choices.

Desire! Responsibility is the direct effect of desire. You have to desire it before you get to be responsible for it. Would you not agree? First came desire. So man desires this and then, he becomes responsible for it. Man desires an automobile; he gets his automobile. And then, he has the blessed opportunity of the responsibility of caring for it. And if he doesn't care for it and he shirks his responsibility, his desire gets upset because it breaks down.

Think, friends. Responsibility is the direct effect of desire. So when you go to express another desire, think of the doors that you're opening. So man says he's short. What he means to say is, "I've had so many desires in my life; I've got so many responsibilities that I'm short." That's what we mean to say. It's like a man who has three automobiles, six houses, and two yachts. He's got all kinds of responsibility, because he had all kinds of desire and he fulfilled them. Now that's what we're really talking about. When we say we're short, we simply mean that our responsibilities, you understand, have become a heavy burden. Now remember, friends, don't let your responsibilities, and the burden thereof, exceed your love of God.

Is responsibility—in an earlier class one time you spoke of the plane of adaptability—

Yes?

And the Law of Creation. And that when we have a desire for anything—whatever it may be—that oftentimes the reason why something will not come into fruition in our lives is because we're stuck in the plane of adaptability. Is this tied to—in other words, when we have a desire, we have the responsibility to adapt, to bring it into fruition. Is this what you're saying?

What I'm saying is, the responsibility is the direct effect of desire. Now, we have a statement, "When of naught desire is, in vain shall sorrow speak." Because, of course, when man has no desire, he has no sorrow. You understand?

Now, it is the nature of form to desire. You see, it is a part of the creative principle. Now, it is also most important that man educate or fulfill his desires. Now many people seem to have problems—seeming problems—in what we call educating a desire. You see, my friends, there is a way of releasing the energy which you have directed to a desire. It deals with the creative principle. For example, say that you desire a new car. You may fulfill that desire in a dimension that is not of the physical realm. Do you understand? The energy is therefore dissipated through the creative principle and you're not burdened down with a multitude of responsibilities. Does that help with your question?

Thank you, friends. I see the hour is passed. Thank you all very much.

MAY 23, 1974

CONSCIOUSNESS CLASS 49

Good evening, class. This evening we're going to take a few moments in discussing something that is of great import to all of us, all inhabitants of this planet—and all planets—and that is the process commonly referred to as death or transition.

Now I know that many students have their own preconceived thoughts concerning what actually takes place at that important moment, but we would like to share with you our understanding of what does take place. First of all, we all have a mind and what is known as a mental body; and this astral, so-called, body is the effect of that mental body. And so it's critically important—our attitude of mind and our thought patterns. When we leave this physical body, at that time, that moment of transition, our soul is taken to another dimension encased in this mental, astral body.

Many things, during the time of this transition process, will distract us. These distractions are planes of consciousness which have been created by our own attitude of mind and our own thoughts during our lifetime. When we are actually in the process of transition, if we permit ourselves to be distracted by the panorama of events that we see taking place as we're leaving the physical body, if we do not keep our mind, our attention, our thought, and our feeling upon the Divine Light itself, we will find ourselves in an astral world, on the level of consciousness that we have been distracted by. Now, these distractions are most compelling, because, my friends, we have already become familiar with them and we know them as levels of consciousness or attitudes of mind. And so it is that many, in their transition, arrive at a plane of consciousness that is not particularly satisfactory to them.

And so it goes back to a very ancient teaching: to nip it in the bud, so to speak, whenever you have a thought or an attitude that you find is not beneficial to you. The longer that the soul expresses on a level of consciousness, the more difficult it is for the soul to rise from that level of consciousness. And so what you are learning here and now is not only for your day-to-day benefit, but it is also your preparation.

When I'm speaking on your preparation, I'm not speaking of just the moment when you leave the physical body. I'm speaking also on your day-to-day and moment-to-moment preparation. You see, my friends, every moment we die and every moment we are born, because our soul continuously and constantly expresses on these different levels of consciousness. Unless you learn some degree of concentration—the ability to hold your mind fixedly and pointedly upon the object of your choice—when your day comes to leave this physical dimension, you will not be able to keep your mind upon the Light, the path of freedom itself, and you will find yourselves on whatever level of consciousness that has been the strongest in your Earth expression.

Now that does not mean that simply by the process of concentration that we are going to override, so to speak, all of the laws that we have set into motion, because that would be contrary to the law itself. However, we're all familiar with the ways that we feel in the course of a day or a week. And we all know which feelings we care to express and which ones we do not. Therefore, we are discussing the importance of transition to you at this time. If you find a difficulty here and now in controlling an attitude of mind, that simply reveals to you, that when your astral, mental body leaves the physical dimension, that you will not be able to rise your soul above that level of consciousness and that plane of expression. And so, my friends, the practice of self-control is critical in this great eternity.

Now you're free to raise your hands and ask any questions that you may have.

Would you clarify the difference between perception and awareness? And I have two other questions that are related to that. May I ask them now?

Yes, you may.

The second one is, Could you offer some rationale of why the ego is headquartered, so to speak, in the ears, rather than the eyes? And third, why is it so important to unfold our awareness before we unfold clairsentience or intuition?

Thank you very much. And the lady has brought up a most important point on perception and awareness. I'm sure that most students present are aware that our understanding is the eyes in the physical anatomy are representative of awareness and the ears, perception.

Now, what is the difference, if any, between perception and awareness? Well, number one: We can only perceive what we are receptive to. And so we find that our perception, at any moment, is governed and controlled by our willingness to accept or be receptive to. Now, awareness is not just what we are, ourselves, receptive to, but true awareness is an awareness of all things: it is the Light itself. Now, awareness is a soul faculty.

The lady has asked, Why is perception—or the ears—and what is their relationship to the ego? It is the ego that determines for most of us, most of the time what we will accept, which is contrary to the divine will, for the divine will *is* acceptance. Now man, his so-called ego, according to the patterns and the things that he has accepted—not only when he was a child, but according to the things that he was willing and able to accept in the prior expression of life—merited a form that would limit his soul in its perception and in its acceptance. So the lesson, you see, my friends, is not just a lesson of this particular soul incarnation at this time, but goes far beyond that.

Now, many people absolutely refuse to accept anything that they do not first send through the brain computer. Now the reason for this, obviously, is whether or not the computed patterns are harmonious with that which is waiting to be accepted. And, of course, this *is* our own limitation. Now, through awareness, man would see and accept—you see, we discussed before the difference between acceptance and expression. When man accepts, all things are possible. Then, man is accepting a God that is limitless, formless, free, and all-powerful. However, as we have stated before, that God is ever equal to our understanding. It is our limited understanding that does not permit an encompassing of this divine God. I hope that's helped with your question.

Yes. Thank you.

You're more than welcome.

On the subject of faith, I have always understood faith to be a supernatural virtue of God. I would like to know, in this study, if it is a God-given virtue or a manmade principle. And I see many, many degrees of faith and, in some cases, no faith at all. And I'm wondering if a person has not been educated in the spiritual values, how do they learn faith? I understand from Discourse 46 in your book [The Living Light], *that the Earth is the planet of faith and we should learn it while we're here in this form. So if you have no beginning or instruction, how do you learn that while you are here?*

Thank you very much for your question concerning faith. Number one: Faith is a divine principle. Although it appears that many people on this earth realm do not have faith, there is no soul expressing on the earth realm that isn't expressing faith. Now, we must realize, or try to realize, friends, that we have our own conception of what faith really is. And when we say *faith,* then our conceived thoughts are faith in a divine power and faith in God, etc. Well, faith and fear are one and the same thing. When this power, known as faith, is directed in a positive way, we say that we have faith. And when it's directed into a negative way, we say that we have fear. So everyone is expressing faith.

Now many people, I will admit, are expressing faith in the negative. Otherwise, we would not have so much fear expressing itself in our world today. However, we're here to learn the true principle of faith. A man goes into his car and he turns the key and expects the ignition to go on. Well, man has faith that that will happen. Now, the reason that he has faith that that will happen is because he has accepted that for himself. Having accepted it, he has faith that it will happen. And when it doesn't happen, he usually gets a bit emotional, you see. And it's the same way when you turn the light switch on: you have faith that the room will be illumined by the light glow. However, when it doesn't, you express through your magnetic field and have a bit of emotion. Now, that is because, my friends, you have accepted. What you have accepted, you have faith in.

So don't you see the wisdom of the divine will of acceptance? All things are possible. A person has faith there's going to be a great shortage in the world. And if his faith is sufficiently demonstrated in his world, there will be a great shortage. Another person has faith that God will take care of all of their needs. If they truly have faith, then all of their needs will be taken care of. Not that a God comes down and takes care of them. God, the Divine Intelligence, is everywhere present and therefore will take care of anything that we are receptive to, have faith in, and truly believe. You see, faith is a complete conviction, not only of the conscious mind, but of the subconscious mind. And when the subconscious and the conscious mind are in total rapport and in harmony on anything, the Divine, moving through the superconscious within us, brings it into manifestation, you see. And so it is that everyone is expressing faith in some way here and now.

However, are we selective with the expressing of this faith? Do we believe that the world is this way or that way and have faith that it is and find that's the way our world is? This is why this world, and all worlds, are so different to so many different people: it is entirely dependent upon what they accept. Does that help with your question?

I would like to ask if promise is a spiritual faculty, on what trinity is it. And if, at any time, a promise we've given, our commitment—not so much a commitment to a big thing, but a small promise—if it can't be fulfilled, how can we fulfill it? Can we fulfill it mentally or do something in another way so that we are not breaking a law of our being?

Thank you very much for your question. And I noticed that you have associated the word *promise* with the word *commitment*. Do you understand them to be one and the same thing?

In a way, yes.

Yes. Well, perhaps we can shed a little of our understanding over that. There is a statement that hell herself is paved with good intentions and broken promises. Fine. The word *commitment*, as used in this understanding, is when we commit our spirit, our soul, our mind, and our body. Then, we have made a spiritual commitment. The word *promise*, we find in this world, is not only greatly used but greatly abused. Ofttimes a person makes a promise so that they do not have to give an explanation that they do not feel like giving at that particular time. And so the word, in our language today, of *promise* has become, for so many, a device. Now device is not something that is in our teachings. We do teach method. If the motive is pure, then the method, for that individual, is legal. Promise is, however, a spiritual faculty, but its use in this world is hardly recognizable. I do hope that's helped with your question.

Thank you.

You're welcome.

Upon the soul review before incarnation, working in the Law of Merit, my question is, Is it the consciousness or the will that determines the meriting of the form that it is conceived into?

Thank you very much. It is the will. Our consciousness is God. It is the will, man's will.

Could you speak a bit upon the vital body?

Thank you very much. Yes, we have mentioned a bit before on the vital body. And the vital body, in our understanding, is what is known as our energy body. It's where we get, of course—the vital body—all of our vitality. Now when the electric and magnetic fields are out of balance, that is, there is an imbalance between our conscious expression and our subconscious desires, then we have what is known as an imbalance in the electric and magnetic fields. Now, when that takes place, we have a depletion of vitality. Because the energy in the vital body is kept in its finest possible expression of vitality or energy by a harmonious balance between our conscious and our subconscious mind. And this is the great importance, my friends, of self-awareness, of learning a little something about the self. Because we've become so busy learning about the world outside, we've spent so little time on the inward journey, which is the eternal journey. I do hope that's helped with your question.

I was wondering if you could share with us what teeth symbolize?

Yes, in our understanding, they represent determination.

Could you speak on perhaps the difference, if there is one, between determination and will?

Yes, thank you very much. And there is quite a difference. The gentleman has asked for perhaps a sharing of understanding on the word *determination* and the word *will*. Now man wills many things in his life. It is his will to live a better life. It is his will to have this. It is his will to do that. However, if man does not express sufficient courage to put that will into action, then he's not expressing what is known as his determination. Now, many people—all of us have will, but it takes courage to get determination. Thank you.

Could you please give us your—or Serenity's—understanding on growth or progression? A slow growth is a healthy growth. Because so many people that I have talked to have felt that they are not progressing. And what progression means to you. Thank you.

Thank you very much. The lady is referring to a statement that is made in this Association that a slow growth is *usually* a healthy growth. Now, you see, I have noticed for some time that many of my students leave out that critical word. You see, the statement was never made that a slow growth *is* a healthy growth. The statement was made some time ago that a slow growth is usually—*usually*—a healthy growth. You see, my friends, by going slow, that doesn't mean that we're going to have a healthy growth in any sense of the word. And ofttimes, you know, if there's something that we don't want to do, it's very easy to say, "No, I'm not going to do that. A slow growth is a healthy growth, and I'm growing." Well, that's not what the statement is all about at all, and I'm sorry to see that it's been abused, let alone used.

Progression is very individual, of course, to each and every soul. Now, many times when a person reaches the crossroads in their life—and many crossroads there are. Many times, when things don't seem to go their way in any particular situation, and then, they say to themselves in order to satisfy their feelings, "Well, a slow growth is a healthy growth. I'm just going to back off for now." You see. Well, that may or may not serve a good purpose for that individual, because just think what happens the next time that they face a decision in their life. The next time that it is difficult to make a growth step and they use the same statement again. Well, you see, my friends, whatever is repeated by the conscious mind becomes the law of the subconscious mind. And so let us choose wisely what words we use, what we mean by those words, how we use them, because that is the thing—the spoken word, which is life-giving energy—that is the thing that makes a law unto ourselves. And once having established that law, you see—choice, once having been made, becomes destiny. That is the law.

So we find ourselves in circumstances and conditions that we're not happy with. But we're the ones that made the choice and set the law into motion. Now that doesn't mean that once we've gotten onto that path, that destiny, having established that law for ourselves, that we cannot make another choice and decision and go onto another path. However, we must put an equal amount of energy into the change and that, my friends, takes some effort and some application. Thank you very much. Yes.

I feel that every problem that we have is due to a lack of the Spirit and I'd like to have you elaborate on that for us.

Thank you very much. The lady has spoken on all of our problems are a lack of the Spirit. Well, certainly, if we mean by the "Spirit"—and I'm sure the lady means by the "Spirit," the divine Infinite Intelligence. Now if we, at all times, were receptive to divine, infinite, Eternal Intelligence and applied it in all of our acts, thoughts, and activities, why, of course, no problem could exist, because the Divine Intelligence—you see, the Wisdom of Wisdom—would be what is expressing. However, the Divine Intelligence is expressing through creation, which is duality. And so as long as you have form, you're going to have experience. You see, the Divine Formless has no experience—the great void—until it enters the principle of duality. That's where experience is. And if you don't have duality, you don't have experience.

Now, one of the most important things in your daily meditation is that you have that great peace and you have that great God and you have no thoughts: you're in the void. That's the

Divinity itself. And so it is that our problems surely are a lack of *receptivity* to the Divine Intelligence, known as the Spirit. However, that takes education of the senses. That takes a willingness to accept that that the eyes cannot see—the physical eyes—and that that the ears—the physical ears—cannot hear.

Man's greatest problem is his refusal to accept an intelligence that is greater than his brain. That is where our problem—and problems—truly lie. Now, when a person has what they call a problem, their attention and their energy are directed to it, usually in hopes of a solution. However, if man would direct that energy and attention to releasing that so-called problem to a Divine Intelligence and let the Divine move in, the problem would disappear. But that, my friends, goes right back to that soul faculty of acceptance: our unwillingness to accept an intelligence guiding our life, greater than our own mind. Thank you very much.

Yes, sir. When I meditate, I've made an effort to always face north. But yet I find that it seems like it's sort of conflicting here with the sun rising from the east. And it usually rises from my right, to my right ear. Now, is there a geographical location or a difference?

Yes, our teaching has been, and remains, to be recommended that the student face east and receive the natural illumination that Nature herself is expressing. Yes.

My question is upon acceptance, realizing the merit system and the lessons that we must perceive in this particular incarnation. My question is, Is it just this past incarnation or, I should say, past soul existence, or has it been maybe two or three back?

Thank you very much. As man, this moment, is still affected by the decisions that he made two and twenty years ago and, yea, even more, so it is with our soul and its eternal expression.

Vibration seems very important. And I think that, at times, I understand what vibration is. But when it comes to the words consolidate *and* solidify *my vibrations, I'm not sure I have a grasp of the meaning.*

Thank you very much. And the lady is speaking in reference to and to solidify one's vibration. And that simply means not to scatter your thoughts out into the universe and not to dissipate your energies; to recognize and realize that you are an individualized soul. When a person's mind is concerned with people over there and there and what's happening over there, etc., they start to scatter their forces and their vibrations start dissipating. Then, they experience what is known as a depletion of energy. That's what it is referring to.

Getting back to meditation and turning to the east, may I ask whether, in meditation, you should sit in the dark? And then, how does nature's illumination come into this? I have been taught this and I have been doing this. Am I right or can we sit in light in our meditation, too?

Darkness is only, as we all know, a lesser degree of the light. And one of the main reasons that many students on the spiritual path have chosen to sit in the lesser light is simply to help them from being distracted by the forms—the physical forms, you understand. However, when a person is truly meditating, it is not important whether or not they are in the sunlight of the day or they're in the lesser light of the night, you understand, because we're referring to the divine light that is within our own soul. And also, as we were speaking on facing east, well, that is where the light for this planet is arising: in the east. And so man becomes receptive with those natural forces of Nature herself. Thank you.

Would you, within the context of this understanding, explain the difference between generosity *and* givingness? *I also recall that at one time, I think, you said that givingness is the principle through which the Divine flows. Also, consideration was mentioned as the principle. Could you clarify the difference between this and gratitude as opening the door to supply?*

Thank you. And the lady has asked several questions, including generosity, givingness, gratitude, compassion, and the door to supply. When a person is truly grateful, they emanate a rate of vibration. And that rate of vibration goes out into the atmosphere and brings its kind back. Now, for example, we understand that God, the Divine, is not a master, but is the greatest servant of all. And a servant, in our understanding, is one who serves. And gratitude is an expression for a service rendered. So when a person is truly grateful, they are expressing their recognition and their acceptance for the service that they have received. Therefore, they guarantee a continuity of that service.

Now, what happens when a man is ungrateful? Now one of the easiest ways to recognize ingratitude is complaining. If you have a person that is constantly griping and complaining—that this isn't being done and that isn't being done and why is this being done and why isn't that being done and I can't accept that without a full explanation first. That level of consciousness, whenever we express it—because the level exists in all of us—that level of consciousness is a level of ingratitude. Therefore, you will notice with people who complain and cry the most, they're the ones that seem to have the most difficulty with God's divine, abundant supply, you see. All right. So that is our understanding of gratitude. Now, gratitude isn't something where you say, "Well, now, thank you, God. I'm very grateful," then you complain about something, because, you see, that's contradiction. And a house divided cannot stand. That's our own house: it cannot stand. So doors open through an expression of gratitude.

Now, what does that have to do with givingness and generosity? A man may be generous for many, many varied motivations, but a man in givingness is in God. And that is the basic difference. I do hope that's helped with your question.

I wish to reask a question that was answered in a private class. I believe there was something mentioned in The Living

Light. *The question was, "Where in the center of the body is air located?" Now, I thought it was in* The Living Light, *but I may be mistaken. May I please have some enlightenment?*

Thank you very much. And I think that question was brought up at our last class and I do believe if you would review it on the tape that you would have the answer that you are seeking. It was discussed at either our last class or the one before. Thank you.

Could you give us a little hint as to the relationship between soul faculties and sense functions to the states of consciousness?

You want the relationship between the soul faculties, the sense functions, and the planes of consciousness?

Or, well, the levels of awareness or states of consciousness.

Yes. The first level of awareness or state of consciousness, as I'm sure you already know, is self-preservation. Now, when we spend some time and effort on study and application of what self-preservation truly means to us—you see, my friends, unless we spend the time to give some thought to what self-preservation means to us—for example, to one person, self-preservation guides them to do this. Another person makes a decision, depending on the level of self-preservation, for that, that, and that. These are known as man's values. So first, my friends and students, I recommend that you take stock of what you truly have value for. So you will know what that level of consciousness is doing for you, in this life here and now, before we move on to the next level of consciousness. First, my friends, find out what *is* of value in your life, according to the level of consciousness known as self-preservation. It is amazing. I am sure we all will find, once we take the time to find out what is valuable in our lives and we will really question what that has to do with self-preservation—let us first study that. Thank you very much.

I would like to know the spiritual connotation of repentance. Thank you.

Thank you very much. And the lady would like a sharing of our understanding on the words *repent* or *repentance*. Perhaps you may gain a better understanding if we use the word with that—repent—"to review." Now, a person cannot have a feeling of contrition—or whatever you want to call it—of an act or a thought that they have already expressed, unless they review it. Now, of what benefit, of what benefit is it to review a past event, unless in the reviewing we are able to make necessary changes of thinking so that we do not repeat that experience? Would you not agree? Yes.

Now, we must ask ourselves the question, "Then, of what value is repentance?" Well, many people repent—or think they do—so that they feel better, that is, to help free them from their guilt complex concerning any particular experience. Do you understand? Now, that, of course, would serve of some benefit to the individual. However, my friends, unless we take stock of ourselves this moment and we say, "Where am I going? And what am I here and now? And what is my life really and truly all about? Am I just working to put food into my body and to put a roof on my head and a car to move me around? Is this what I am living for?" If it is, of course, sooner or later, we will guarantee the awakening that it's a very small world that we have been living in. Repentance is of no great value unless the individual truly makes an effort to make the changes necessary. Thank you very much.

In this study, is there such a thing as the law of grace? Do things that you may do here on this planet, or if you have lived before—and the things that you have done and you merit a working out? Is there a law of grace or must you work out everything here and now?

Thank you very much. There is a divine law known as divine grace. Now, that is not an exception to the divine Law of Merit, no. What it means is this: every soul has so much so-called good stocked up in life and so much of its so-called lesser good.

Now, when a person transgresses certain laws and they are about to experience the effect of their error or transgression, if they have what in this understanding we call a spiritual bank account, they may draw upon that substance, which is known as divine grace. Now, that means for the selfless good that they have done in their soul's expression, there is that deposit made in a universal spiritual bank, so to speak. Do you understand? This is why, my friends, we're all given the opportunity to serve God and to do some spiritual good in the world. And when that opportunity is brought to us, according to the natural law of our seeking, and we need to take material substance or supply for our efforts—don't you see?—we're robbing our spiritual bank account. And then, when the time comes that we are in need of divine grace, there's nothing in that bank to draw upon. And so, wisdom herself dictates to do a little something in this old world without seeking a material recompense and a material or mental reward. Because if that's the way we do things, we're going to find ourselves, if we haven't already, spiritually bankrupt.

And when, as it always does, it comes time for our prayers and seeking and beseeching for a divine grace to bring us through a certain experience and disaster that we find ourselves entering, well, we find there is no divine grace because we haven't made any deposit up there. And what deposit was made—how many incarnations ago—has been all used up, you see. There's one thing, my dear friends, I can assure you of: there's no credit in spiritual dimensions. It's all cash on the line. I haven't found a credit system yet in the world of spirit. So be good, students, and build up a substantial spiritual bank account, just for plain old common sense, because you never know when you're going to need to draw a little bit. And that's divine grace.

Thank you very much. Let us go have refreshments. The time has passed.

MAY 29, 1974

CONSCIOUSNESS CLASS 50 ✣

[The recording of Consciousness Class 50 began after the class had begun. The transcription begins in midsentence.]

—by the Law of Repetition. And we will get where we want to go by the Law of Repetition. And so it is that a lesson must be given in many, many different ways, because we are all a part of the human race and we're receptive at different moments to different levels of consciousness. It has been stated that we have ears to hear and hear not; that we have eyes to see and see not. That, of course, depends entirely upon our level of consciousness when we view something, our level of consciousness when we hear something.

Now I'm going to turn the floor over to your discussions and to your questions. And I know that if you sincerely are seeking and thinking, that the question you have to ask will be its own answer. You're free now to ask any questions you have.

I would appreciate some clarification of the difference between the mind of the vital body and the subconscious mind. I believe that you told us at one time that the vital mind is the reactor mind or the vibration mind, and that it acts as a tuning fork. It's my impression that the brain also acts as a tuning fork onto which the subconscious, the conscious, and the superconscious play. I wonder if there is a parallel between the brain in that respect, and also if the vibrational mind is speaking so often for us, should we be talking to it as well as the subconscious?

Thank you very much for your question in reference to the vital body or mind, the subconscious body or mind, and the brain. Now we understand that the brain is merely the vehicle through which these bodies or minds are expressing themselves. The vital body is the vibrational body or the energy body. Now, what depletes this vital body or mind is when there is contradiction in the mental body; that is, there is a contradiction in our thinking. This contradiction causes a short circuiting in the system and our energy is depleted. It is the major cause of what is known as tiredness. Now, whenever we are united in thought in any endeavor, this so-called feeling of tiredness, we do not experience. It is when there is this contradiction, which causes a grounding between our magnetic field and our electric field.

Now, we have discussed before that the conscious mind is the electrical mind; that the subconscious mind is the magnetic mind, which governs our emotions and our feelings. Therefore, that is one of the great reasons for the harmonizing of our conscious–electrical being and our subconscious–magnetic feeling, because when the conscious mind thinks one thing and the subconscious computer has recorded a contradiction or an opposite to that thought, then there is a depletion of energy in what is known as our vital body or, as has been stated, the tuning fork.

Now, when a person wishes to bring about harmony in their body, in their mind, or in their life—which is all one and the same—then they bridge the gap between the conscious and the subconscious mind, between the electric and the magnetic fields with the bridge of what is called kindness. You see, my friends, all things in creation—whether it is a conscious mind, a subconscious mind, whether it is an animal or it is a plant—all things respond to kindness. For kindness is a vehicle through which divine love is expressed. Therefore, it does not behoove us to try to dictate changes to our magnetic field or subconscious.

You reach and make changes with your own inner mind, your subconscious. You make those changes through what is known as the bridge of kindness, which is a soul faculty through which divine love expresses itself. If you try to dictate and order your subconscious mind, you will guarantee a retaliation, because the ordering of the mind is received as a rejection. It has been stated before that our subconscious is like a small child, and when you order it, it reacts. And it reacts in a negative way. I do hope that's helped with your question.

In the evolutionary process—my question is on the merit system of the soul. Well, I know the soul is subject to merit, as what it rightfully deserves. But how does it work in relationship as to what country, as to what color, etc.?

Thank you very much for your question. Thank you. In reference to the soul's eternal journey throughout creation—and the question is asked, How does a soul merit a particular country or a certain race in which to express through? Whatever lessons are necessary for the soul's unfoldment is what is guaranteed by the law that the soul itself has set into motion. For example, if a soul, having not passed the lessons that it had merited in its prior incarnation, it once again guarantees those lessons for its next expression until such a time as it is able to grow through what it, and it alone, has set into motion. Now, if those lessons can best be offered through an expression in a particular country or through a particular race of people, then that is what the soul will express through. Thank you very much.

You say that a soul has to complete the lesson, and then, you also say that one must grow through the laws that one has set into motion. I don't feel that I understand that completely. How does a soul—or how does anyone know when they have completed the lesson or passed what they came here to learn?

Thank you very much. Whenever the lesson has been perceived and that grade of school has been passed, then the lesson, the experience, is no longer entertained in the thought or in the mind. That is one way of knowing that one has passed a particular lesson. It no longer entertains their thought.

Now, the lady has asked the question, Well, how does one know what lessons they have to learn in this life? Each moment, each day, a lesson—a multitude of lessons—are appearing in each soul's universe. One of the easiest ways of knowing whether or not you have done your part, so to speak, in a certain lesson or an experience is to recognize the lesson for what it has to offer. Now many times in our daily acts and activities and experiences, we merit the opportunity to express the soul faculties. Usually, after the experience is over, we say to ourselves, "Well, I didn't express too well on duty and tolerance and gratitude." There's an inner knowing within our own being. The next moment we guarantee another experience and after it's over we have the feeling, "Well, I could have used a bit more patience in that area, a bit more faith, a bit more understanding, a great deal more humility." These are the things that we become aware of.

When we balance those soul faculties with what we call the sense functions, the computer brain, then we have a beautiful life in the here and now. A person may ask themselves, when they arise in the morning—they're aware of a few of the soul faculties. Most of my students are aware of at least six or ten of them. Every day grants us the opportunity to express through those soul faculties. Every moment grants us that opportunity. Are we using consideration and tolerance? Or are we automatically, so to speak, reacting from a patterned level of consciousness? I hope that's helped with your question. Thank you.

I've heard you speak on prior expressions and incarnations, but not reincarnation. And I am a bit confused with teachings as to how to clarify these or separate these, one from the other. Because doesn't reincarnate *actually mean to "incarnate again"?*

Thank you very much for your question. It's a very important question. The lady has asked on the difference, if any, in this understanding between evolutionary incarnation and reincarnation. The present-day theory, and the theory of reincarnation for several centuries, has been and is today that the soul leaves this physical earth realm and returns to this earth realm until such a time as it is completely freed from the cycle of cause and effect. That is the basic teaching of so-called reincarnation.

The teachings we offer are evolutionary incarnation: that man's soul, setting the laws into motion in all incarnations, has evolved to this Earth planet, to this grade of school, and will pass through this grade of school, as it has passed through several planets prior to this one, and will express through another planet in another day. That is the basic difference between what is known as reincarnation and evolutionary incarnation.

We teach that there is a constant, evolving process; that Nature herself teaches us that there is an evolution of form. All we need to do is to look at nature and we will see how it is constantly evolving. We teach that the soul is not the formless, free Spirit, but that it is the covering of the formless, free Spirit and that it does have form. And that the laws that govern form, whether they be on a soul level, a mental level, an astral level, or a physical level, are one and the same law. And that the Law of Evolution of the forms, that we can see with our own physical eyes, is the same law that governs our own soul. I hope that's helped with your question. Yes, thank you very much.

My question is, What—may I say first, my understanding of animal *would be "functioning of the senses." The point is, in what part of this particular incarnation that we're in—how did the animalism begin to play its part in the attachment of the physical body? And if so, getting back to the basics of prior incarnations, has everything stayed pretty much the same, with the exception that as one incarnates there is a refinement? The next dimension would be more of a refinement, but basically everything remains the same. Has this been throughout incarnation in form?*

Thank you very much for your question. And I believe you're referring to what we call the basic animal instinct of the human race or the human being. Well, the so-called basic animal instinct or vibration of the human being is merely a level of consciousness known as self-preservation, for the preservation of the self.

I think perhaps it may be of benefit for us to have a little clarification or a little discussion on the soul's journey through space. Now I know that some people, perhaps they question, "Well, this is a planet in this solar system. And I am in a physical body in what I call a human form. Now, my soul, according to these teachings, has expressed before in a form somewhere and by that expression guarantees its continuity to express in another form somewhere." And so the questions must arise, "Well, did the form that my soul expressed through prior to this form, was it similar? Was it human? Was it something that my mind can conceive? And, if so, when my soul leaves this physical body, is it going to express on another planet in this solar system? And if it does, will the form be something that I recognize as a human form?" No. It definitely and positively will not.

There is life on the planets. But it is not the life of which we, in our minds, conceive. In other words, if you're looking for a life form in this solar system that is similar to what we call the human being, don't waste your time, because you're not going to find it in *this* solar system. I'm talking about the Earth and Mars and the Moon, etc., and Venus, and those different planets. No, my friends, you will not find it, because you are looking for a physical form. No.

It is true that the soul expresses through forms, and many there are in this solar system. Intelligences in physical form exist in the universes. This is not the only planet in all of the billions and trillions—numbers beyond our ability to count—of planets in the universes in outer space. There are many, many, many planets with physical forms and with intelligences much higher than what we call the human race. But it is not—I repeat—in *this* solar system.

Now, we do—our soul—express through the various planets of the solar system in bodies that our physical eyes cannot and do not see. When our other vision is opened, we may, be that in order, according to our own merit system that we set into motion, view those different life forms.

The soul's journey—for example, it has been stated that this is the fifth planet in this solar system and that the souls have entered this particular planet to learn the lessons that faith has to offer. And so this planet offers us a multitude of lessons under the title or heading of so-called faith.

We've stated once before that if man will look at himself, he will see himself, not the way he thinks he is, but the way he really is. Now, of what benefit is it to view yesterday unless we first make the effort to view clearly today? For this is the day and the moment that we can do something about. And remember, today is tomorrow's yesterday. And so if we're doing something about today, then we can view all of our yesterdays in the spirit of joy and gratitude. Don't you see, my friends? And if we're doing something about today, we can view all of our tomorrows the same way. It's known as the law when our hindsight—that that has taken place back there—becomes our foresight: that, my friends, is when we gain insight.

So we're here and we're conscious, of course, of this moment. And I know on a level of awareness, we're also conscious not only how we got here, but where we're headed. Because, you see, we all know, in truth, where we're headed. Our attitudes are telling us that every moment of every day. We all know that a certain attitude sends us along that path; and another attitude sends us along a little better path. Now, we all know that. I am sure we know that life is an effect of our level of consciousness, of our attitude of mind. Now, we all know that. Where we appear to bog down is not in the knowledge. No, no, no. That's not where we appear to fall. It's not in the knowledge. It's in the application. Because, you see, my friends, it will behoove us, before we react and before we speak, to take a moment to pause, that we can become aware of what laws we set into motion. Now we all know that when we open our mouth, we open a door. And we move our tongue; we turn a key. And that sets a law into motion. And that's known as, The spoken word is life-giving energy.

You see, my friends, it's not just the words we speak: it is the level of consciousness from which we speak them. Many people can talk on a multitude of subjects. And one person may talk on a subject that is not popular, and yet they will attract the multitudes, because they're speaking from a level of consciousness that guarantees that experience. Now what is that known as, when we speak our word and express our thought? It's known as our true motive.

When we leave this physical dimension and we've left this physical voice box, we express through thought. In the higher realms, you see, there are no words to speak. There is an expression of thought. And that thought reveals a color. And on those levels of consciousness in the world of spirit, you see, there are no untruths because the color is revealed and there's no way of stopping it. So our motives, you see, are constantly revealed to anyone around and about us. And so it is as we enter those levels of consciousness in the here and now: we emanate a rate of vibration when we speak a word and the listening ear, it senses it, it feels it, it knows it. I hope that's helped with your question. Thank you. Yes.

Is it necessary to understand these lessons of metaphysical questions in order to expand spiritually? I ask—

Absolutely.

Because I feel like in our classes I'm absorbing them as an experience rather than studying them as a lesson and learning them intellectually. Is that all right?

Absolutely and positively. And that's the way things should be perceived. You see, we once had a discussion on study and investigation. And there's quite a difference.

Now, that that we experience records not only in our mind, but in our feelings and in our inner being. That that we intellectualize about and study is recorded—that is true—on certain levels of consciousness. But when we experience something, we become a part of that something. Do you understand?

You see, it isn't something that we can put into words. The purpose of awareness classes is not to give you volumes of words and information, which will not in any way transform your life. But when you put your soul, your feelings, into the experiencing, then the transformation begins to take place. And so it is when man puts a part of his soul, his heart, his feelings, his being into something—no matter what that something may be—he becomes a part of that. And becoming a part of that, the changes take place within. Would you not agree? It isn't important that the mind and the intellect understand a word. It is important that it is receptive to the vibrations and the level of consciousness from which level it was given birth, therefore, having the experience and the transformation. I hope that's helped with your question.

Thank you. I have a question regarding soul faculties. They are triune in expression. Is it delusion for one to say, "I am trying to work with tolerance"? Can we work with one part of it? Or is it necessary—or are we, in truth, working with all three things?

Thank you. And that's your question?

Yes.

Yes. The lady has stated that all soul faculties—our teaching is that they are triune in nature and, indeed, they are. And so whenever a person chooses one of the soul faculties, for example, such as tolerance, to work with, they guarantee duty and gratitude. Now, if you decide to work with the soul faculty, for example, of faith, then you're going to guarantee poise and humility. They are inseparable. Does that help with your question? Yes.

Yes. But with that, why then, if we are working with one particular part of it, do we seem to be having difficulties with the other parts?

That's most understandable. We are the one who has directed our energy and our attention to one of the triune faculties; therefore, you see, we are not directing energy to an understanding and expression of the other two. And we would experience what is known as difficulty with them. For example, if a person says, "Well, now, I'm going to work on duty." And so they put their attention and their energy into unfolding the soul faculty of duty and they forget all about tolerance and gratitude. They guarantee to have an experience with those other two because that, you see, my friends, is an imbalance. Do you understand? Thank you. Does that help with your question? Yes.

Thank you. We've had considerable discussion on divine love. And it's my understanding that divine love is, like, a noun. And yet we are given, "Love all life and know the Light [Discourse 2]*." And there the word is used as a verb. I wonder if we could have some discussion on that.*

Thank you very much. I do hope this will help with that question in reference to nouns and verbs, which, of course, I know we will all agree, is something that man has created. And divine love, not being a creation of man, you see, is not governed, nor is it controlled, in that sense, by what man has created, such as a language. No.

Divine love *is,* as truth *is*. It expresses through all things at all times and in all ways. It is true that man, having what we call choice or self-will, chooses to direct it into perhaps what some may feel are strange areas or areas that do not seem to be very lovable at some times. But, you see, my friends, it's still God. It's still energy. But man has the choice. And so it is that man has the choice to direct his understanding of what he calls divine love, to make it a noun or a verb. But, in truth, it is still one and the same. Does that help with your question?

You see, my friend, divine love *is,* as truth *is*. Whatever man chooses to make of it, does not change truth. It doesn't change divine love. It does not change it to make it a verb or a noun.

It doesn't change truth to give it many garments. It's still the same truth. Yes.

Well, what is meant then by, "Love all life and know the Light"?

Thank you very much. The statement, "to love all life"—to love *all* life—"and know the Light," is the divine will, known as acceptance. Now we cannot love all of life until we can accept all of life. And therefore, until we learn acceptance, we will not love all life. And we will not know the Light, which we understand to be God.

Now, a person says, "Well, that is not lovable." But who made that decision? Who, we must ask ourselves the question, made that decision, which, of course, is choice? Man made that decision. That is man's law. That's not God's law. That is man's law. God's divine natural law is to love all life and know the Light. God's divine natural law is acceptance, which is total consideration. But, of course, we can't love something we can't consider. And we can't consider something that we can't tolerate. And so we have, basically, our first soul faculty of duty, gratitude, and tolerance.

So what is important here in this class—many things are important to many levels of consciousness, but what supersedes all levels of consciousness, it's known as acceptance. Man can only experience what he can accept. He cannot experience any more and he cannot experience any less. And so you see that God is ever equal to our understanding. And wisdom herself is dictating to love all life and to know the Light. You see, my friends, it is acceptance that frees us. It is rejection that binds us. What does rejection do? She binds us to self. She binds us to the so-called computer of our limited acceptances. That is not divine will, nor is it God's will. Thank you. I hope that's helped with your question. Yes, please.

I believe that I've been given an opportunity to reconsider and I'd like to keep my door closed.

Thank you very much.

You've spoken many times about selfless service, and I wonder if that is a soul faculty. And, if so, would you discuss it in relation to givingness and acceptance?

Givingness and acceptance. Thank you very much. Service—what we call selfless service—service is the expression of the soul faculties. Service is an expression of the divine Spirit.

Now, we have stated many times that our understanding that God is the greatest servant of all. And so it behooves man to serve. However, we all serve something or a multitude of things. Now what it is we're usually serving, of course, is whatever the patterns are: what we have accepted in the past. Then, like dutiful, faithful little servants, we serve those patterns. And every time we have an experience—we have great loyalty to those patterns. Now remember, friends, our loyalty is revealed by our reliance. Whatever we depend upon, we're extremely loyal to. What we're trying to bring into your understanding is, Be loyal to that which frees your soul; be loyal to that that never fails you.

Now, when we make an effort or give some thought to service that is not self-motivated, what we're doing, in truth, is we are being a dutiful servant to something that is not a patterned program in our subconscious. And when we start to do that, we start to break the addiction to the patterns of mind. Now, we teach that service—selfless service—is the only path to spiritual illumination. Can you not see why, my students, that it is the only path—the only path—to spiritual illumination? Because we are serving something formless and free that is not a pattern.

We're all serving already. And we're serving the patterns that we're addicted to. And the patterns that we're addicted to have become our gods, because we're dependent upon them and we rely upon them. Do you understand? Now these are the false gods the prophets have spoken of. And these false gods we must consider dethroning, so we can free ourselves.

Now, for example, in the course of our experiences we meet a person and we have an experience, of course, that we've set into motion. And immediately we say that our tolerance is tested. All right, now, what do we mean when we say an individual is a tolerance-tester? Now what do we mean by that statement? I've certainly heard it enough times as a teacher here. What do we *really* mean by the statement? Number one: We mean that the individual that we have classified as a tolerance-tester—number one—we mean that we've made a judgment. Number two: We mean that the judgment that we have made is not compatible to the patterns that we're addicted to. And therefore that individual is a tolerance-tester for us. Now, for someone else they may be what they call a patience-tester. Well, of course, my friends, it's all taking place inside of ourselves.

Now, every day and every moment, we're having some experience and we say that, of course, we're "triggered." Well, what it means—we're "triggered"—we're triggered with certain expressions—perhaps anger, perhaps disappointment, or this and that. What we mean, of course, is that that god that we're addicted to, that level of consciousness, that pattern of mind, has that much control over our soul. Is life worth anything then? Is it really worth anything?

Now think about this world. Just give this Earth world some thought. What is it that man in this day of materialism relies upon? Anytime you want to know how addicted you are to anything, have it removed from your life. Now if you have any emotion concerning it, the degree of emotion reveals, of course, the degree of addiction.

All right, a person may say, "Well, I see no reason why I should let that go." Well, of course, you can't see any reason when you want to let an addicted pattern go: reason doesn't exist. Reason doesn't exist in addiction. Reason doesn't exist in desire. You see, my friends, when we start to go into desire—and everything in form desires, you see. The plant desires some nutrients from the soil. It desires some water from above and it desires a little sunshine to keep it going. So everything desires, you understand. It's the creative principle. When we go into desire, we start a descent. And it's kind of like a shield comes between our reason and our soul, you see; it doesn't express anymore, that soul faculty. And so we get to a point in desire where it's total darkness, can't see at all. Do you see?

Now, what does all this have to do with service? What does it have to do with givingness? We spoke before in one of our classes that givingness is a soul faculty. It is an expression of the Divine. You see, let's learn the principle of that soul faculty known as givingness, because we're all going to have experiences—and many of us already have had—when we pray that we may give something up. We want to get rid of something. Believe me, when we have an experience that we don't appreciate, we would give anything in the world to be able to get rid of it. Well, to get rid of it is the principle of givingness. And so it behooves us to express the principle of givingness.

Now, what controls our soul? We all know what controls our soul. For example, here in this material world, what do we rely upon? Look, we rely upon the medium of exchange to feed our senses. Look, the material world and all that it has to offer cannot feed our soul. It cannot feed the part of us that is eternal. The only thing this material world can offer us for food is to fill our stomachs, which we all know represent our affections. It's amazing how many people are so affectionate in this world. I never realized that there were so many affectionate people! Of course, food is a major thing in the world we live in today. And so are our affections. We're quite bothered by them, it seems, according to how we eat.

Now, it behooves us to express and learn the principle governing the soul faculty of givingness and what we call selfless service. You see, selfless service simply means serving a non-addictable pattern. Now that means we're serving, formless and free, ever ready and willing to change, because, you see, there's no pattern. Do you understand?

Now, please, my students, don't misunderstand that. Don't say, "Well, I'm serving God in this way, but God wants me now to serve in that way." Because so often, my friends, it isn't God's desire at all, because God doesn't desire. It's our receptivity to certain levels of consciousness and sometimes it's questionable how godly it is. Do you understand? You see, let us search our motivations. Go deep inside and say, "All right, now, what's my true motive?" See? "What is my true motive?"

Many people come to the Light they call God with a multitude of motives. Now, what happens? I will agree that these motivations are usually self-oriented: they're for self-help. Life has had some great struggles for them. All right, so we come with the motive to rise out of a certain experience, which is a level of consciousness. Now that's fine, because if we're truly seeking to help ourselves, you understand, we will find what is necessary for us to rise up out of that level of consciousness. However, when we rise up out of that level of consciousness, unless there is a transformation—a change of motivation within our being—we no longer stay. We have received what motivated us to the effort and the experience. And so it is, my friends, a broadening of one's horizons, a constant change of motivations, ever to serve the formless and the free.

Thank you all very much. Our time has passed. Let us go have refreshments.

JUNE 6, 1974

CONSCIOUSNESS CLASS 51

Good evening, class. This evening we will spend a few moments in discussion of the soul faculty of peace, poise, and power.

Now, we have discussed, at many of our classes, how an attitude of mind is a rate of vibration; how thought releases electromagnetic energy from the brain. We've also discussed that peace is our understanding of God, the Intelligence itself; that power is an expression of its energy; and that poise is the perfect balance through which harmony may manifest in our lives. We have also discussed the soul faculties and the sense functions and the importance of bringing these functions and faculties into balance.

And so now we know that it is through the soul faculty of poise that an expression of balance is possible in our lives. When man is poised in his thought, there is an equal distribution of the Divine Intelligence, known as Energy, Love, or God, throughout his entire being. When there is an equal distribution of this energy, known as harmony, then, of course, man does indeed experience his divine birthright of perfect health and expression.

Many parts of the anatomy have already been given to you as representative of a soul faculty and a sense function. When man has a thought, a feeling, he releases energy from that area of his brain. The brain, of course, as we have discussed before, is likened unto a computer that has been programmed. And so it is that our thought does, indeed, by releasing energy through our system, affect our health.

When man is in need of bringing balance or perfect health into his life, it is necessary, of course, to work in the three dimensions on which the soul is expressing: the physical dimension, the mental dimension, and, of course, the spiritual dimension. And so it is that when we have a thought, perhaps of anger, there is a certain part of our anatomy that is affected, because there is an imbalance of energy being expressed from the brain to that part of our anatomy.

And so tonight the discussion is peace, poise, and power. That soul faculty, as spoken in your "Total Consideration" affirmation, is most important. And if you will take the time and make the effort to truly study that affirmation, then you will become aware of how it can truly benefit your life.

We all face, of course, a multitude of experiences in the course of a day or in the course of an hour or a moment. We may, in those experiences, express our consciousness, our godhood, our intelligence through the soul faculty mentioned—or through its opposite sense function.

Now I know that many students have asked for more knowledge concerning what soul faculties are, what numbers, and what are the corresponding sense functions. When much has been given, wisdom dictates, unless application is expressed, more should not be given. We have discussed many times that the purpose of these classes is to help you to think. And so it is the teachings are given to you in bits and in pieces, because that is the way that we grow. We don't grow all of a sudden. It is a very slow, gradual process.

Where we are today is only, of course, an effect of the many years of where we have been. And so it is, my friends, most important to all of us to truly think more deeply and more often, concerning our thoughts and concerning, of course, our feelings.

Now you're free to ask any questions that you have.

During our discussion last week, I got the feeling you were talking about the millions and millions of universes and planets and so on. I began to put some things together. In The Living Light *it says that the purpose of form—or form exists so that Love may become aware of itself. And the question which arose in my mind is, Why does Love ever want to become aware of itself? If this is a perfect void, why would it want to go through all these things?*

Thank you very much for your question. It's a most deep question. And we must consider and think that Love becomes aware through expression. The Divine Intelligence—we've spoken before—to try to define it, of course, is to limit it. It is our understanding it is the great void. But, you see, my friends, the limited cannot know the limitless. It is not possible for the human mind, or any mind, to know that that is beyond the mind, beyond the possibility and the capability of the mind to understand.

Now, each individual, of course, knows their God, equal to their understanding. And our understanding is ever limited by our willingness and our ability to accept. And so it goes back to the principle and to the teaching that acceptance is the divine will. So man must prepare himself to be ever ready and willing to change, if it is man's desire to experience a greater God than he has yet experienced.

Now, the lady has asked the question, Why, if God is the Divine Void, is it necessary for it to express through form? That would take someone much greater than myself, I am sure, to answer a question that only the Divine Intelligence itself could possibly know. It is not man's purpose, to my understanding, to define by the carnal mind the purpose of the Divine Intelligence expressing through form. We can only share with you our limited understanding, as we see it in our present state of evolution. I do hope that's helped with your question.

It has been given what the hands are and what the feet are. Can we know at this time what corresponds to the fingers and the toes? I have trouble with my toes and I've had that trouble for some time.

Thank you very much. I'll be happy to share with you our understanding of what the toes represent, and that's indecision. I hope that has helped you. Thank you.

We have had considerable discussion on the soul faculty of reason. And I wonder if you could speak a bit on how perhaps that might, if it does, relate to the discussion this evening on peace, poise, and power.

Thank you. Yes, we have had much discussion on the soul faculty of reason, the foundation of the soul faculties—understanding and reason. And it is only when man is expressing through the soul faculty of peace, poise, and power and the other soul faculties that he truly is in balance and able to express what we call reason. Because it takes a balanced mind, my students, to consider all things. It takes a balanced mind to understand. It takes a balanced mind to accept all things and know that that, indeed, is the divine will.

So we have stated, "Keep faith with reason, for she will transfigure thee." And so we see, my friends, if we want to express reason, then we must make greater effort to understand our programmed acceptances, in order that we may express through the soul faculties, that we may stand at the summit of poise and express our peace, our godhood, and our power, which is the Divine Energy. I hope that's helped with your question. Remember: Reason does not express without those soul faculties being expressed. There is no reason without total consideration.

You see, a person may look at something and they may say, "Well, it is reason to me that this will serve this purpose." But unless there has been total consideration, then it is not reason that this will serve this purpose, because we have limited ourselves in consideration and acceptance that it may serve a greater purpose than what our mind has already accepted. Therefore, we cannot express reason without consideration, without acceptance. I hope that's helped with your question.

In one of the discourses, you talk about the Law of Indirection and, of course, I assume this to mean the parables that are taught. Why are we taught through indirection, when it takes us so long to understand this indirection? Is indirection the same as an indirect method? Or is it just to teach us to think?

Thank you very much. The lady is asking a question on indirection and its purpose.

The teaching is that if the motive is pure, the method is legal. And so indirection is a method. Now, many times it is not possible to reach a person with an understanding or to help them by directly telling them a way or trying to show them a way. The reason that the direct method is not usually possible, or doesn't usually work, is because man is limited in his acceptances. Man, not expressing the divine will in its fullness, rejects so many things. And this is why it is the teaching in that book, The stone the builder rejects becomes the cornerstone. And so it is, my friends, that indirection is used to help the student to rise to ever higher levels of consciousness.

It would not be necessary to use indirection if man were truly aware of himself. Then, when something is said, man would know that he had a limited acceptance on that particular subject and would not accept—because of his own addiction to what he believes is truth—what is fact. Then, it would not be necessary, because he would know that he had accepted four or five things on a particular subject and nothing else existed but what he had already accepted. Then, he could look at that and say, "Well, I've accepted five things. If I accepted five—I didn't accept them all at once—so there's a possibility that there's a sixth way." But, you see, we haven't made the effort to become aware of what our patterns are. We haven't yet made the effort to become aware of what, so to speak, triggers our emotions. We haven't become aware of why we express anger, why we express hurt feelings. You see, we're not truly aware that this is just a reaction, because it does not fit into the limited acceptances of our past.

Now, one of the most beneficial ways of helping oneself to rise to higher levels of consciousness is not only to become aware of how easily one is upset when certain subjects are discussed, but to take the inward journey when one starts to become emotionally upset on a certain subject or a personal matter. To take the inward journey and find out why they react the way that they do. When we do that, my friends, we'll become aware of ourselves and we will be amazed at the many things that we have become. I hope that's helped with your question. Yes, you have another question.

I do.

Yes, certainly.

We talk about the faculties and the functions, and we're living on the earth plane. Are these faculties expressed differently on different levels as we go on? Is peace of a higher degree on a higher level, or is peace, peace wherever we are or poise, poise or humility, humility?

Thank you very much. Peace is peace wherever we are. Our experiencing of it is ever dependent on our ability to accept its fullness. Does that help with your question? Yes, for example, a person may now say, "Well, I accept peace," but their understanding of peace is limited by their program, by their computer. But they may expand that through acceptance. And then, it means more to that individual and therefore they experience more.

You see, things mean more to us through the divine Law of Acceptance. And this is why we get out of anything what we put into that thing and not one iota more. What is it that we put in? We put in our acceptance: that's what we put in. We're willing and ready and able to make changes inside of ourselves. So by doing that, by expanding our acceptance in anything, we get more out of that thing. This is why in marriages, according to the individuals, how much they accept is how much they're going to get out. And what's most interesting, usually in the very beginning days or weeks or months—sometimes years, hopefully—they accept more. So, of course, the relationship means more. It is when they start to revert to their limited programming that it no longer means so much. You see, this is what happens with relationships, with marriages. It's what happens with friendship, with acquaintances. You see, we're very receptive, which means we're open to more acceptance, usually, in the beginning. And then, we start to narrow down and it isn't as beautiful as it was at first. But that's the way our minds work, unless we're willing to make the necessary changes so that doesn't happen. And when we start to narrow down in our acceptances, we start to broaden in our judgment. And that's where problems really begin. Thank you.

A couple of weeks ago you talked a bit about rejection and retaliation. And I wonder if you would discuss this a little more fully: rejection, resentment, and retaliation. So frequently we see retaliation on a very deep, subconscious level. How can we be helped to bring this to a more conscious awareness?

Thank you. Rejection, retaliation, and resentment is a triune function of the mind. Now, when man is rejected by anything or anyone, there is an automatic resentment, because it is a part of the inseparable triune faculty. This resentment, then, moves to retaliation.

Now, why does it retaliate? Why does the mind retaliate? You see, my friends, try to understand that your sense functions—all triune in manifestation—and your soul faculties—all triune in expression—are inseparable. They are like links on a chain. And so when one is triggered, it triggers the two of the same link, and that link, in turn, is connected to the next one and the next one and the next one.

Now, when we move from the rejection to the resentment to the retaliation, we're at the point of the function of judgment, you see. The links are inseparable. And so we judge, inside of ourselves, that an individual has done us wrong. And having done us wrong, we move to the function known as vengeance. And vengeance expresses herself and we experience, finally, what is known as retaliation.

Now there is a teaching in the Christian Bible that says, "Vengeance is mine, saith the Lord." Our understanding of "the Lord" means the law. And so if man, through divine will of acceptance, will, in truth, accept that it is his own level of consciousness that has attracted the experience into his life, then he will be able, through the soul faculty of forgiveness, to release his energy, his soul consciousness, from the sense functions and express it through the soul faculties. Having expressed through the soul faculty of forgiveness, man is then freed from the experience.

Now I do hope that has helped with your question. And I do hope that it may be in divine order that more students will think about these things because, my friends, you know, we once had a discussion on righteous anger. We had a discussion on judgment. We've had discussions on many, many things. But of what value is the discussion if the application does not follow, through acceptance?

Now, we go to school and we learn many things. We learn about functions and faculties, and how to find the way to the light of peace and freedom within ourselves. We learn all about those things. And perhaps on one level of consciousness we have accepted that. We have accepted it and therefore we now have knowledge. But, you see, it's wisdom when we apply it.

Now why is it difficult for us to apply these teachings? They are teachings that free us, once applied. The reason that it is difficult is because we're not yet truly aware of ourselves. And so this process—the links of the chain of rejection, resentment, retaliation, and judgment and all through that chain—it takes place seemingly beyond our power to control it. It is only seemingly beyond our power to control because we haven't made the effort to control it.

But what is most beneficial to man? Is it not more beneficial to control it through understanding and to experience a more meaningful life? Or is it better to be constantly controlled by other people from what they say, from what they think, from what they do? But remember, my friends, this teaching is not an easy one. It is a very, very simple one. For truth is simple and unconcealed. But it is not easy. And the reason that it isn't easy is because when we truly start applying our true freedom and our liberty, we must be consciously, constantly aware of the divine law that liberty becomes license without that law. And so it is that because we may be finding a bit of liberty or freedom, we don't turn it into license. You see, liberty is a soul expression and license is a sense function. *License* is "to do what you want to do, when you want to do it, and how you want to do it." And license is controlled by desire. And desire has no light. Thank you. I hope that's helped with your question.

I hear so much about the psychic nowadays, more than I ever have. Does the psychic serve any spiritual purpose or does it serve the Divine? What I mean by that is, in all these sitting groups, we study the spiritual. Does this help in any way to get people closer to the source of spiritual studies?

Thank you very much for your question. The psychic can, and ofttimes does, serve a purpose, in stimulating the possibility within the mind of the recipient that there is something greater than they have already accepted from their own brain computer. Therefore, having stimulated that possibility, which is an acceptance, it is possible—and ofttimes does happen—that one will move from the psychic level of consciousness to higher levels of consciousness, known as the spiritual. It is also possible—and has ofttimes happened—that a person being exposed to what is known as the psychic becomes satisfied and does not strive and make greater effort to go to higher levels of consciousness. And this is one of the many reasons we teach that irritation wakes the soul and satisfaction lets it sleep. It can, and ofttimes does, serve a good purpose. It is not what anyone should strive for. Thank you.

I've been watching the solar plexus center of the body for quite some time. In The Living Light, *I came across a statement that said to understand it, but not to concentrate upon it.*

That is correct.

Well, I'd like a discourse on that, please, a little understanding. Because I don't know when I am watching and that slips into concentration. I'd like to know exactly what is meant by that.

Thank you. What is meant by the statement in *The Living Light* to understand the solar plexus and not to concentrate upon it may be likened unto the sun of our particular solar system. A man concentrating upon it with his vision is sure to guarantee blindness. But one viewing the manifestations of the light, in time, will awaken understanding.

The teaching also is that if the light is too bright, 'tis best we see it not now. So the first thing that man strives to view is the manifestation of the Divine, that he may first broaden his acceptance and his understanding, that he may not become imbalanced by viewing directly the Light itself. I hope that's helped with your question. Thank you.

Thank you. Could you give some discourse on the difference, if any, between self-will and self-assertion?

Thank you very much. Self-assertion—to assert oneself—is the effect of one's own will. Now I know that that question is not yet satisfied in your mind. And so let us go just a bit deeper with it. We have taught that divine will is what brings harmony and fulfillment into our life. And we have also taught that self-will, being guided by the accepted programs that exist in the brain computer, brings many problems into our lives and does not free our soul. How is it, then, that one receptive to divine will asserts himself and is expressing divine will and not self-will?

Well, my good friends, it's quite simple. We know—no one has to tell us—when we are expressing divine will or self-will. However, if we still think that we do not know, then all we have to do is to view the work that we're doing. If we are in any way attached or affected by the fruits of our action, by the harvest of our sowing, then we may be rest assured that we are still in self-will, because we are expressing through that level of consciousness that must be glorified by the work that is being done.

Now, each time that we have a magnetic reaction, which is emotional, concerning any work that we have done anywhere, the degree and the extent of that emotional expression concerning its harvest or the effect of its labor—the degree and extent of the emotional reaction reveals to each and every soul whether or not that was the work of the Divinity they understand, the soul faculties, or the sense functions. This, as I said earlier, is known by each individual because there is no soul in any universe that does not, in truth, know its own motivation.

Now, don't be discouraged when you do a job and it turns out well and you are pleased. Do not be discouraged when you do a job and you are not pleased because it does not turn out so well. We have repeatedly emphasized the importance of understanding that our soul is expressing through a sense body, which is known as functions. We have also expressed the thought that our soul is expressing through its many soul faculties. If you deprive completely the pleasure of the senses, if you deprive the senses completely of their expression, then, my friends, you will not long have the self-will for your soul to express in this form. This is revealed to us by untold multitudes of people in so-called hospitals and the doctors say they have lost the will to live. What they are saying, in truth, is that the individual no longer is experiencing pleasure from the harvest from the fruits of their action. And so it is that we teach a balance between the functions and the faculties.

Now, that balance, my friends, isn't that you say, "Well, now, there's twenty-four hours in the day. So I'll spend twelve hours on my functions and twelve hours on my faculties." It doesn't work that way. And the reason—the only reason—it doesn't work that way is because none of us have that much control. So we can't make that decision and apply it.

But we can do this: we can become aware of our motivation. We can become aware and know when we are expressing self-will and when we are expressing divine will. That awareness is possible to all of us. And so, my friends, accept the truth. Accept that we're in a world of creation, that the brain and the ego, in order to survive, must have its expression. Otherwise, it will die and not serve its purpose. But let us be aware when we're expressing the so-called king brain, the crown of our senses. Let us be aware in the moment of its expressing. Then, my friends, you will be able to accept a balance in your life.

There never was, or will there ever be, a soul so illumined, expressing through physical form, that does not express the functions to some extent, that does not express an ego uneducated to some extent. Even the Nazarene himself expressed anger at the money changers in front of the temples in the early days of Christianity. So think, my friends: in history, supposedly one of the most illumined men that ever walked the Earth expressed his temper. Now, if we say that that was just and righteous anger, then we must admit that he was making a judgment. Now, if we accept that he was God and we accept a personal god of judgment, then, for us, of course, that is right. But think, my friends: there has never been a soul, nor will there ever be, so illumined, expressing in form, not to express their functions to some degree. I hope that's helped with your question.

In your last lecture, "Man's Spiritual Search," [Church Lecture 33] *you mentioned—for the first time that I recall—the word or faculty of surrender. And I wonder if you would expand a bit on that, please.*

Thank you very much. In discussing the soul faculty of surrender, my friends, when man decides to surrender the so-called king brain or ego to the divine will, when he truly accepts that, he will, after that acceptance, come into a balance of expression for his functions and his faculties.

Now, why is it necessary, we may ask, to express that soul faculty of surrender? It is simply, my friends, because we have made our programmed patterns the king of our life. This is why it is necessary for anyone to express surrender and move through the soul faculties of acceptance, forgiveness, freedom, illumination.

You see, we have taught that in order to gain, we must give. But it seems we have not yet got out of the thinking that giving is to take something in your hand and put it in the hands of another. That is not the soul faculty of givingness that we have been discussing. We have been discussing the giving, the givingness, the giving up of certain functions in order that you may gain an expression of certain soul faculties.

Now, we may say, "Well, why should we give them up? You just said that we need them." The giving up, my friends, is because they have become so bloated, so overfed with energy, that they need to fast—and some of them for years—in order to bring about a balance in our lives. Now, we can't give and gain unless we surrender the so-called bloated nothingness known as the king brain.

In many ways the truth, the same truth, is repeatedly taught. Knowledge knows much, but wisdom knows better. Because knowledge is not—*is not*—application.

Now, when we decide to give up a certain pattern within our mind that we have decided is right for us—that we will not tolerate an individual talking to us this way or talking to us that way, that we will not tolerate this, that we will not tolerate that, that we will not tolerate something else—what we're saying, my friends, is that we are not willing to surrender the pattern of mind that *we,* and we alone, have made king. And so it is that givingness and poise and peace and power and gratitude and surrender and acceptance and appreciation and all of those soul faculties gradually, but surely, will be brought into balance.

Think, my friends, think about life itself. The very thing that you need in any moment may be the very thing you refuse to accept, because you have accepted at some other time that it has no value. And you have accepted that it has no value because you have listened to another, who has accepted that for himself. Is that, I ask you, initiative thinking? Is it thinking at all? It's not even thinking. Of course, it isn't. So, you see, there again we would need to surrender in order to receive. Thank you very much.

Your definition of surrender *sounds to me like my definition of* repentance. *Is there a difference between repentance and surrender?*

Yes, there is. Thank you very much. The gentleman is asking if there is a difference between repentance and surrender. What happens to man's magnetic field, his emotions, when he repents? Man repents through review. It is not necessary to review to surrender. I hope that's helped with your question. Thank you.

In referring to an earlier question, somehow today this conversation came up about ego and, more or less, finding oneself through, say, the pills that are available. Today, this particular individual was using a hallucinatory drug and he stated that he was able to find himself or to view himself in the hereafter. And yet there were others who weren't able to cope with the situation and, as a result, I think one of them ended up in the hospital. Could you tell me what his responsibility was to that individual? He didn't actually put the pill in his mouth or anything like that, but I felt that it was an obligation on his part, a responsibility.

Thank you very much. And, of course, my friends, it's like in any experience in life. Number one: The individual that was having the experience, his soul's evolution had merited that experience. And the person that was involved with them also—their soul had merited the experience or they wouldn't be there. Now, you go further than that, of course, and then, one has to say, "Well, does the individual that invited the other individual to that experience that was not beneficial for the person invited, do they not have a spiritual responsibility?" Man has a spiritual responsibility unto himself and all his creations. Yes, indeed, that he does.

However, we are not the ones to judge whose responsibility and how much of that responsibility that they should incur, you understand. Because that judgment, my friends, is made by the intelligence flowing through the particular individual, you see. There is—and we've discussed it many times—what is known as a spiritual conscience, a spiritual sensibility with a dual capacity, knowing right from wrong for us. That's, my friends, what judges us. And conscience is very personal to the individual. Thank you. I hope that's helped with your question.

You mentioned the conscience. And is there a difference between the conscience and what we have discussed as the higher self or the other half of ourselves or our guardian angel?

Yes, there most certainly is a difference between the conscience and the higher self, known as, in this understanding, our guardian angel. The higher self or guardian angel is a level of consciousness above form or judgment. Therefore, it is on a higher level of consciousness. But we cannot reach that higher level without the level below it, known as conscious, being brought into balance. I hope that's helped with your question. Thank you.

Throughout The Living Light, *we are asked to become more universal in our thinking. Would you please help us with the principle of universality?*

Thank you very much. The lady is asking in reference to the principle of universality. Yes, I will be happy to share my understanding with you. The teaching is to become more universal in our thought. Now, that is not referring to our thinking about more universes. It's referring to the one universe, the cathedral of the soul, which we are now expressing through. For man *is* the microcosm of the macrocosm; for man *is* the universe. And what that teaching is referring to is that man, through acceptance, consider more parts of his own being.

You see, man is likened unto a tree, and a tree has many branches. And so it is, my friends, that the human being has many aspects. It has many levels of consciousness. And so when man becomes more universal in his thought, he expresses understanding on more levels of consciousness and, in so doing, he is then in a position to bring about a degree of balance in his life. And that's what is meant by the statement to become more universal in your thought, in your act, and in your deed. Thank you very much.

Yes, we have time for one more question.

I would just like a little understanding—help, perhaps—on levels. When I came in tonight, and during class, I feel a quietness and not the enthusiasm that I felt before. I would like to ask you, Is that my level I'm on or am I picking up from everybody? I even picked that up from you. And I want to be very careful to—

Thank you. I do hope that that is your level of consciousness, because you are an individual, as all souls are. Now the lady has stated that here of recent date when she enters the class, she is more peaceful. Is that correct? I believe you used the word *peace*. What did you mean?

I just think it does seem as though the whole class is calmer tonight.

Oh, thank you very much. Well, I'm very happy to hear that. And I do believe that that is your level of consciousness, but I also believe that many others will agree with you, because it's also their level of consciousness. Now, the reference was made, of course, to things being more calm or more peaceful than they were in the earlier classes. Well, my friends, that's truly—according to our own teachings—a mark of spirituality. It was stated in these classes—especially things in your meditation, if they excite your senses, they are not of a higher spiritual realm.

Therefore, if my students are feeling more peaceful and more calm, then, indeed, we all should be pleased, for it means that we are reaching, within our own soul consciousness, higher levels of spirituality. I hope that's helped with your question.

Thank you, friends. We've run past time. Let us go have refreshments.

JUNE 13, 1974

CONSCIOUSNESS CLASS 52

Before getting to the reading of our discourse this evening, we've all had a wonderful opportunity to express through either our soul faculties or our sense functions, while we've had this half-hour wait. And so we've had that blessed opportunity to experience, personally, what it is like to wait for anything. So often in waiting, we don't seem to consider how other people feel when we're late. And so it is a wonderful experience for us to have, at times, what it is like when we have to wait for someone else. And so it is this evening that we have had to wait for this past thirty-five minutes before beginning this class.

Now, it would, of course, be very easy for us to say, "Well, that's because someone forgot something which is a part of our class." Now, the fact is that that is true, but we must go beyond the seeming appearances and facts in life. And we must go inside of ourselves and we must ask ourselves, "Now, why is it that I merited this particular experience at this particular time?" And, of course, it's most interesting, considering there's about twenty-some people here, that we all merited a little lesson in patience, in tolerance, in duty, in gratitude, and the various soul functions [faculties]. I am sure that if you had a little patience with yourself that you'd be able to see a little bit more clearly in this little experience and, in seeing a little bit more clearly, perhaps would be more thoughtful in reference to time—as we do live in an illusion called time here in this material world. And, in so doing, free ourselves from some of these emotional experiences that we seem to encounter so frequently.

This evening we're going to continue on with perhaps a broader discussion of our teaching known as acceptance, the divine will. Now, it is our understanding that, indeed, acceptance is the divine will. And does any student know what the manifestation of acceptance, the divine will, is? If you do have some thought on that, please raise your hand. Yes.

Would that be truth?

Thank you.

Would that be reason?

Thank you.

I believe it would be humility.

Humility. Thank you.

Now let us, for a few moments, spend some time in discussing this. Acceptance, the divine will. What happens when we accept anything in our life? What is its inevitable manifestation? That's the question. *[There is a brief pause, and then the Teacher continues.]* The manifestation of acceptance, the divine will, is desire. Whatever man accepts, man desires. And so that is the divine will in its manifestation. We have taught that all forms desire, for form does not exist without desire. Desire is a function. When man no longer desires, man no longer—his soul—expresses through form. This is why we have taught, When of naught—or nothing—desire is, in vain doth sorrow speak. However, when man does not have desire, which is an inseparable part of the five steps of creation, then man does not have sorrow, nor does he have joy. So what is the balance?

We've also taught that we must learn to separate truth from creation in order to find freedom. Now, acceptance, being the divine will, and its manifestation being desire, it would seem that we are teaching everyone to express their desires. Well, if that happened, you would have total chaos. And the reason that you would have total chaos is simply because man, in his own accepted patterns and programs—there would not be harmony within himself. Now, harmony, of course, is an expression of all things in perfect balance. So we see in life, in our day-to-day activities, that we are accepting different things and therefore we are desiring different things. And these desires—the effects of our acceptances—are not in harmony; and not being in harmony, we find ourselves, of course, out of balance.

Now, we go along in our work and in our experiences, in our meeting with people, in our business, and in our day-to-day activities, and one moment we feel a certain degree of joy and happiness, and the next moment, only to feel its opposite, simply because, my friends, we're not yet consciously aware of these desires, these acceptances, and these different rejections—if you wish to call them that—that we are expressing.

Now, again and again and again, the teaching remains the same, for truth is one. It is individually perceived, according to the individual's own level of consciousness. Again and again the teaching remains the same: that life alone is the mirror and that man alone is the law of his own universe.

You see, my friends, we spoke once in one of our classes here recently about the Law of Repetition. We are where we are because we are the effect of the repeated acceptances and desires of many, many, many years. We drive our car out and we go to the restaurant and we see certain things, and automatically—automatically—we express through patterns that we have not been aware of perhaps for many, many, many years.

Now the teaching is also total consideration, for only through total consideration—to consider all things—can man be in a position to express reason. We've also taught to keep faith with reason, for that is the soul faculty that will transfigure your life, that will transform your being.

How does man know when he is expressing reason? How do we know when we're using reason? What do we judge our expression upon? That's the question we must ask ourselves. For something to us at one moment, we say is reasonable and that we are using reason. But are we really using reason if we are not expressing total consideration? And how can we express total consideration if we are not aware of the levels of consciousness and the patterns of mind that are controlling our lives? And so we have what is known as an awareness class, a spiritual awareness, that we may become aware of these patterns. Because so often when we say that we are expressing reason, what we, in truth, are expressing is a pattern, a programming in our computer, in our brain, that has decided for us, that is reason. That is not reason at all, friends, because any pattern of mind—no matter whose mind it is—does not have total consideration or it would not be a pattern of mind in the first place.

Thank you all very much. Now you're free to ask any questions that you have. If you'll please raise your hands.

I'd like to know where understanding fits in with acceptance. Can you accept without understanding? And if you don't have understanding, are you shirking the responsibility for the decision that you have made to accept?

Thank you very much. And the lady has asked an excellent question: Can you truly accept without understanding? And if you do accept—if that is possible to accept without understanding—are you shirking your responsibility to what you have accepted? Is that basically your question? Yes.

Man accepts every moment of every day without fully understanding. Man accepts according to the patterns of his life of acceptance of many, many, many, many years. Now the soul enters this form, into a child, into a body, of circumstances and conditions of certain basic tendencies of acceptance, according to what that soul has expressed in its prior expression through the evolutionary process of incarnation. And so we might say, in a sense, that we have a few strikes against us when we come here to Earth. However, it's not quite that gloomy, because what we have, in truth—we have before us the lessons that we have failed before. It's just like the lessons of yesterday are guaranteed to reappear until we learn them and free our soul from them.

Now, what does this have to do with acceptance and understanding? In all our getting, understanding is the thing to get, for it is through understanding that our soul is freed. However, the will of the Divine Intelligence itself is total acceptance. So a man says, perhaps, "This seems to me to be very contradictory. Why should I accept something that I don't understand?" No, it's not contradictory at all. Man does not understand the elements contained in the air that he breathes, yet he accepts that air and he breathes that air. However, there is a part of him, his own spirit, that does understand that. Do you follow?

Now, what this means is this: How can you understand what you don't accept? That is not possible, is it? For we first must accept in order to have understanding. But before we can accept, we must consider. Would you not agree? First, a man has to have total consideration to have total acceptance to be granted complete understanding. And so the process is to consider all things, to see the good in all things, and from that consideration, you place your soul and your mind in a position—you understand—to accept all things. Then, having accepted all things, you can go to work inside of yourself and understand all things. So when the prophets have taught, In all your getting, get understanding—it's not possible to get understanding without consideration and acceptance. Does that help with your question?

Thank you.

You're more than welcome. Yes.

Last week we brought up—or rather you did—the law of assumption is the Law of Descent. And I tried to work with this during the week—at least, I thought that's what was said. Perhaps I'm wrong—and I thought, "Well, aren't we always in assumption on this earth plane?" How do we rise from assuming the things that we do assume?

Thank you very much. I believe, if you will listen to that particular class on the recorded tape, you will find that the statement was made that the Law of Ascent is the Law of Descent, not the law of assumption.

I didn't hear it. I'm sorry.

I believe if you will be kind enough to check that particular class tape, you will find the statement was made, "The Law of Ascent is the Law of Descent." Do you have another question?

Yes, I did. I did ask, while you were talking about divine will—and I was a little confused about the manifestation being desire. Is the divine will what we would call, normally, in our everyday language, God's will for us?

Well, thank you very much. We understand in this Association that our God is ever equal to our understanding, that our God is a divine, neutral Infinite Intelligence. What we mean to say by acceptance, the divine will, what we mean by divine, we mean the highest level of consciousness, the Spirit. We do not mean a God that has judgment, for a God that has will, has judgment. Do you understand?

Yes.

Because, you see, if it doesn't have judgment, then it doesn't have will: it follows. Does that help with your question?

Yes.

You're more than welcome. Yes.

I would like to ask a question on opening up our clairsentience. Does that mean to open up to the spiritual world, to know your guides? Or does that mean, as well, to open up as your explanation to her about acceptance and understanding?

Thank you very much. And *clairsentience* does not mean exclusively "to open up to a spiritual dimension." It does mean this: it means "to sense with your senses"—"to sense clearly" is what it means. Now, if your level of consciousness is on a spiritual level of expression at the moment that you are sensing through your clairsentience, then, of course, you will have a spiritual experience. But, you see, in clairsentience, my friends, it is your feeling, and your feeling is the most accurate. But clairsentience does not guarantee that you're going to have a spiritual experience. You see, many people sense, and sense clearly, but their soul consciousness is expressing on a mental level, and so what they are sensing could be interpreted as a thought projection or telepathy. Or they could sense the health of another individual. Or their soul consciousness could be on a spiritual level and they could sense the spirit of those who have left this earth realm. Does that help with your question? Yes. And, of course, without acceptance, you can't even move into clear sensing. Thank you very much.

Thank you. We've had considerable discussion on the soul faculties and the sense functions. This evening you mentioned a soul function. In an earlier class, it was mentioned a sense faculty; and I wonder if perhaps—

Which are you referring to, please?

In the opening discussion tonight there was a mention of soul function.

If there was—I'll be more than happy to check on that—I intended to say "a soul faculty." However, we will check the tape after the class is finished.

May I ask another question then?

Certainly.

We were speaking earlier on responsibility. Could you speak on responsibility with relationship to the sense functions?

Thank you very much. Yes. We understand that this physical body, this mental body, and, hopefully, this spiritual body—which we all hope, of course, is created—is the house in which our soul—our true self—is residing. Man is responsible, of course, to the so-called house or body through which he is expressing at any given moment. So man's responsibility is not only a spiritual responsibility, but it is also a mental and a physical, material responsibility.

Now, of course, I know all of you have heard that, well, God helps those who help themselves. Let us not get out of balance with that teaching. Of course, it is true that as we are receptive to the Divine, then the Divine can express through us. And so it is that we have a physical body, which we are directly responsible for. It is the house that we have merited. We have a mental body that we are directly responsible for. And we have our soul, our spiritual body, and our other bodies that we are directly responsible for. Now, the thing is, that we are trying to teach some degree of balance between your physical, material world, your mental world, and your spiritual world; that these bodies, your soul is, indeed, expressing through. And if we're overbalanced in any of those bodies, then we are certainly not facing our responsibility unto ourselves. Does that help with your question?

Thank you very much.

You're more than welcome.

Two classes ago it was said that this material world and all it has to offer cannot feed our soul.

That is correct.

But I look at the world as God's creation and that it is good. And a beautiful sunset or one of the wonders of the world or man helping his brother can feed my soul. I wonder if I have misunderstood your interpretation or meaning of this material world.

Thank you very much. And perhaps we have a different understanding of the word *material* in that sense. Now by the word *material* that was used in that particular class, we were referring—and are referring—to this mundane material world of business activity. Do you understand? And we were referring to the so-called money race here in this dimension. That does not—and I'm sure you will agree—feed our soul.

Now, when you're looking at a sunset—we're not referring to the sunset or a beautiful tree or nature's expression as the material world. Does that help with your understanding?

Yes. It clarifies—

Does that help clarify? Yes. Because, you see, we're not talking about—we're talking about, my good friends—when we say that this material world does nothing to feed your soul, which, in truth, it doesn't—our race for money, our race for business, our race for security in this material world does not, my good friends, feed our soul. No, it doesn't. But looking at a rainbow, a sunset, or Nature herself, certainly, indeed, it does feed our soul. Or helping a friend. Helping a friend is not interpreted in our understanding as a material expression. You see, that is interpreted in our understanding as we are prompted by our own spirit to help another to help themselves. And that is a soul expression or a soul faculty. Thank you very much.

Would you please explain why it's important to open or unfold the soul faculty of awareness prior to working on clairsentience?

Yes, I'll be more than happy to share with that. And the lady has asked a question on why it is so important to awaken the soul faculty of awareness before experiencing, to any extent, what is known as clairsentience. Now, unless we work on this faculty of awareness—to become aware of the dimensions in which we are, in truth, living, here, this moment—and we open up what we call our clairsensing, well, now, we could sense that a disaster is going to take place with a very close friend of ours. We could sense that through our clairsensing. However, the interpretation may be completely wrong, because we don't have awareness. Now if we had awareness with this clairsensing, we would be aware that that is a projection from that individual's mind, from their own subconscious, because they are presently experiencing something that, through the Law of Association, is associated with a disaster. Now what we must consider, my good friends, is—and not disregard—is that the language of our subconscious is symbology and it is filled with pictures. And it's filled with a multitude of experiences.

Now, for example, when a person has a feeling of anger, when they have that type of a feeling or any type of a feeling, the images expressed from their subconscious are sometimes without number—there are so many. Now how does this really take place? All right, we have taught, and do teach, that the mind is electromagnetic. Fine. A person has a feeling of anger. That feeling of anger is releasing electrical impulses from the brain. Those electrical impulses are all pictures or experiences for that particular individual. And so if a person concentrates simply upon clairsentience and does not work on awareness, then it could be a most difficult path, of course, of unfoldment.

Now, every time we touch an object, we release from our own being electromagnetic impulses and they go onto the object. But all of those electromagnetic impulses that are touching the object—they all carry pictures with them. Because that is a part of ourselves. And under proper psychometric conditions those images can be interpreted. Do you understand? And so it is, my friends, in unfoldment, remember: just because you feel something and just because you hear something and just because you may see something, that is no guarantee, in any sense of the word, that it is from a spiritual dimension. It may or it may not be. And so it is that we work to awaken, to become aware. Aware of what? Aware of ourselves.

Let us make greater effort to awaken our own spirit. And by awakening our own spirit, we will awaken to the Great Spirit of all of the universes. But, you see, my friends, of what good would it be to sense and to feel if there isn't some interpretation, some understanding, and some awakening to what it truly means? You see, I know that sometimes people feel, "Well, it's all in your head. I mean, the departed, they're all upstairs in your head." Well, my friends, of course, they're upstairs in our head! They're in our head and out of our head. Because, you see, it takes our head as a vehicle through which they can express. But they're also there in our thought. We understand that.

But we also understand that they're in a spiritual dimension and that when our soul expresses through a spiritual dimension, then we will have spiritual experiences and we will know the difference. We will have spiritual discernment and we will know. We will not have to be told what is spiritual and what is mental and what is physical and what is astral and what are all those other dimensions.

So the thing is, my friends—and we've said it again and again—it's an inward journey. It is an eternal inward journey. Become aware of your thoughts. Become aware of your feelings. Become aware of what is controlling your life, you see. It's all inside. Then, when you have experiences and you hear a voice, you will know whether it's the voice of your subconscious suppressed desires, because, you see, the voice of the subconscious suppressed desire speaks as clearly as the voice of a departed spirit from this dimension. So it is through here—in the faculty of reason—that we awaken to discernment.

But how can we have this awakening without consideration, without acceptance, without understanding? You see, my friends, if you have experiences, you say, "Well, I don't know if that's out of my subconscious or it really is some other dimension. I don't know." Well, the thing is, if you insist on entertaining that level that you don't know, you'll guarantee that you'll never know. Do you understand? Now a person can go on that cycle forever. It's known as doubt. It won't get him anyplace, because it's a perfect circle.

So what does one do? You say, "Well, now I've had this experience. I'm not going to analyze it while I'm having it, because then I'll no longer have it." Because we're going to a different level of consciousness then. Say, "All right, let the good manifest in my life, for the good to me is God." Now we can say that, but when we say that, we've got to start demonstrating it. It's known as application. Then, we start applying the good that we are seeking. We start applying it. And when we start applying it—the law is impartial—it brings more to us. Does that help with your question?

Thank you very much.

You're more than welcome.

Thank you very much for that. In this teaching of the incarnation and the evolution of the soul, is the filial tie ever broken? I would like to know because I was asked this the other day. What happens when we go on to other planets? What about the mother, the father, the sister? Do we all go our own way?

Not until we're ready. See, man does not leave his attachments until he has outgrown his attachments. Yes. Does that help with your question?

Very much.

But as long as you need them, you will have them. Thank you. Yes.

Is humility represented in the human anatomy in the knees?

I don't believe that has been stated.

Can we say that we have come to the point of meriting that at this point?

Perhaps you would be kind enough to share your understanding with the class of the word *humility*.

Well, I've been doing a lot of thinking on it and I seem to have two definitions. One is a spiritual kind of humility, where I say that I bow to divine will. And the other is the kind of humility that's a debasing kind of thing where a person is humble in the face of some kind of power, physical power.

Thank you very much. Our understanding of humility is not a debasing thing at all. We do understand it to be a soul faculty. And we also understand that an expression of humility is an acceptance of an authority greater than our own brain. Now, for man to accept something greater than himself—you see, every man that has any degree whatsoever of reason or logic, in truth, is accepting some degree—at least a portion—the higher authority than himself. Because there would be only a stupid man that says that he could create all the universes and all of the forms therein. And so, in truth, we must—just for the sake of logic and sanity—accept a greater authority than the brain of man himself. So to some extent, of course, we're all expressing a bit of what we call humility.

Now, at a future time we'll be happy to discuss the location of humility in the human anatomy. At this time I feel it would be in our best interest to gather, perhaps, a little broader understanding of the word *humility*. Now, when man expresses humility, he's in a position, you see, to free himself. Why is man in a position to free himself when he expresses a degree of humility? Well, it's really quite simple. We've stated that humility is an acceptance of an authority greater than ourselves. When we have a problem, if we are humble, we are accepting a greater authority that can help us somehow, some way, because it is a greater authority, to work to a solution. Do you understand? Now, that takes a little humility.

But if you have your soul faculty of humility opened, then when you go through these trials and tribulations—it doesn't mean, my friends, that it's a cop-out, that you can go ahead and transgress natural laws and the laws of creation and say, "Well, I'm expressing my humility. I've given it to the Divine, a higher authority than myself," and not do your part. You see, we're not going to escape the laws that we set into motion. We're not going to do that whether we're using humility or tolerance or duty or anything else. We do understand that there is such a thing as a divine grace. Now that divine grace is simply a so-called spiritual bank account through which our good acts, thoughts, and deeds have built up some substance that can be used when we get into these things. But humility, my friends, seems to be quite a problem or hang-up for many people, because they think that, "Well, if I don't let this go, then I'm not humble. And God has given me a mind to use: I'm supposed to use initiative thinking." You see, we're supposed to do our part in life, and when we have done as much as we feel that we can, there comes a time, there comes a moment, when we release it to a greater intelligence. Would you not agree? And at that moment it takes a little bit of humility to say, "Well, I guess I wasn't smart enough to work it out." Don't you see?

So, my friends, it pays us—it behooves us—to have some degree of humility. Now that doesn't mean that we're supposed to debase ourselves or to feel like an ant crawling upon the ground, because there's nothing worse, you see, than to think badly of oneself. Man must learn to think well of himself. You see, the law states that like attracts like and becomes the Law of Attachment. Well, if you think poorly of yourself, if you're constantly complaining about your aches and pains, if you're constantly crying about your lack and limitation, you can't have anything else for an experience in your life. If you say, "Well, that's all I've got," then God says, "If you're so smart, that's all you'll get." That's understandable, don't you see? So we want to think well of ourselves. But think humble, yet well of ourselves.

Now, what is the danger of thinking well of ourselves? Well, it depends on what level of consciousness we're on. For example, if we're on what is commonly referred to as the ego level of consciousness and we're thinking well of ourselves—and it's known as pride—you may be rest assured, we'll guarantee all experiences necessary to understand what humility is all about, you see. But that is because we have thought well of ourselves in what we call the ego or brain level, known as pride.

Now that's why we teach tolerance is a soul faculty. You see, if you have no tolerance—if you're intolerant—you see, if we're intolerant to someone or something, what we're doing, in truth—the degree of energy we're expressing to the intolerance to the individual—we are guaranteeing all lessons necessary to understand why they're expressing the way that they are. Is that intelligent to you? Therefore, my friends, it doesn't pay to be intolerant. It certainly doesn't. It is self-destructive, you see. And so we want to consider—try, at least, to consider—all of these things. Number one: If we meet an individual, an experience, and it's intolerable to us, pause and say, "Well, what inside of me keeps attracting that experience?" That experience is necessary to free us. And so we guarantee its continuity until we gain understanding and we finally get free.

You know, I know some people, they've been married 6, 8, 10 times. In fact, I have one client—she's been married 12 this year! Fine. Every single husband has the same problem, as far as she's concerned. And I've tried for years to get her to understand that it doesn't matter if she marries 212 times, she will always experience each husband with the same problem, because it's guaranteed. Because the intolerance has reached such a point that, you know—it's like being on a circle: it's going to guarantee itself, not just here in this physical world, but in her next dimension, her next expression. It'll just go on and on and on and on until finally—surely someday in eternity—it gets through the concrete, you see. Now, what does that all have to do with humility? My friends, it has a great deal to do with humility. It takes a little humility to express tolerance and gain understanding.

What is it inside of us that says, "I won't take that. And I won't take that. And I don't have to put up with this. And I don't have to put up with that"? Now what level of consciousness is that, would you say? Would you consider that perhaps it is a level of judgment: that we have judged, we have decided, what we are going to tolerate and what we're not going to tolerate?

You know, it's just like our class here last Thursday. We had some discussion on human relations. Well, just think, friends. Now we discussed earlier this evening about acceptance and its manifestation of desire and all things desire. Well, just think. You know, it's like two people on their honeymoon. Well, everything is beautiful! Well, of course, it's beautiful! They're manifesting desire. They have almost total acceptance. Don't you understand? And so all that total acceptance—they have almost total desire and everything is just beautiful. It's when they start to narrow down the acceptance that the desire starts decreasing and all the problems start expressing themselves. Then, we decide what we're going to tolerate and what we're not going to tolerate. Well, you never heard of such a thing on the honeymoon. Of course not. Because desire is in full expression. Don't you see? And that has to do with acceptance.

But, you see, my friends, if people are going to make it together in life, then they've got to express—even if they don't even know the words of the soul faculties, it's not important. Many people express humility and they don't even know what the word means. But, you see, if people are going to grow in human relations, you may be rest assured—you see, the honeymoon is always over, but it can always be rekindled. It depends on the acceptances of the two individuals involved. Don't you see? But if they're going to make it, sooner or later they've got to open up a few soul faculties, like duty and gratitude and tolerance and faith and poise and humility and all those different things. I do hope that's helped with your question concerning humility. Thank you very much.

Would you be good enough to discuss motive in relation to acceptance, please?

Thank you very much. Indeed, a most important question. The lady has asked, Would we have some discussion on motive and acceptance?

Well, now let us go back to our earlier discussion on acceptance. We discussed that acceptance, its manifestation is desire. Now, when we accept anything, we have a following experience of desire for that which we have accepted. Do you follow me? All right. Now, several things happen within the mind once we accept. Say, perhaps, we accept an ice cream. We're going to go to the store to get it because, you see, the moment we accept it, we have the desire for it. Not just for an ice cream, but for anything else that we have accepted in mind. All right, so we have accepted we'd like to have an ice cream. The moment we accept it, we desire it. All right.

Now, where does motive come in? When we accept, we desire. What motivates us to fulfill it or not to fulfill the desire? Do you understand? Do you follow me so far? We've accepted; we now desire. What motivates us to move, which is the true motive? What motivates us, friends, is the patterns that we're addicted to in our mind.

Now, you see, there are several steps that take place. You accept this, you desire it, you're motivated or you're not motivated. For example, let us say that you accept that you would like to have a new wardrobe, all right? Now you accept a new wardrobe. Following that acceptance, you have a desire for it. Do you understand? However, what happens to the desire? The desire goes through the computer and there's several different priorities. Would you not agree? "Well, I won't have that now because I also desire this over here. And that desire has not yet been fulfilled. And besides that, I've got another desire over here." That's where our motives come in. It depends on our values and our true priorities. Does that help with your question on motive and acceptance?

Yes, thank you.

You're more than welcome. Yes.

The way that I'm understanding acceptance tonight is with the manifestation of desire. Somehow we would have to compute lack. Is that not true?

Thank you very much. Because man has not totally accepted, then man indeed has computed the opposite, known as lack. Do you understand? You see, man could not think lack, feel lack, or be lack if he had total acceptance. Because total acceptance would be total fulfillment. Do you understand? Yes. The reason that man says, "I need this and I need that" is because he's never accepted God. He's accepted a portion, you know, maybe this much. But, you see, God is equal to our understanding and so that's why in all your getting, get understanding. Because in all your getting, get God, because that's what God is: equal to our understanding. That's why we teach, In your getting, get understanding. That's how you get God.

So, you see, if you've accepted that "My life is full. I have no needs," then, don't you see, that would not exist in your mind. But man is not trained that way from childhood on. He's not trained that way. In fact, he's trained just the opposite. Does that help with your question?

Yes.

You're more than welcome.

Tonight, while we were waiting, we had discussion on emotion. And would you please give us your understanding if emotion is a function and does it serve any purpose that is helpful?

Well, sometimes one may say that's questionable. I can assure you it does serve a purpose: it certainly sends adrenaline through our system, depending on the individual and their emotion. Yes, I would say that all things serve a purpose and in all things good does exist. Yes. It's a sense function—indeed, it is—controlled by our magnetic field. What is emotion the effect of? Does anyone know? What is emotion the effect of? Yes.

Is it the ego?

Yes, indeed, it is. Because the ego houses what? *[There is a brief pause, and then the Teacher continues.]* Desire. Think, friends. Emotion—she is the effect of desire. No desire: no emotion. So how do we do without emotions when we can't do without desire? No, what we try to do is bring them into some degree of balance, you see. Now, many times a person may have a feeling, an emotion, you know, that they want to express their love to someone. And they express it by shaking hands or hugging or whatever you wish to call it. But the person that they want to do that with is not programmed that way and they don't appreciate it, period. That's not the way they express their love.

Now, which person is right? The one that wants to do all of the hugging and show their affection? Or the person who does not want to show their affection in that way, but shows it in other ways? Well, of course, they're both right. But if they don't both have consideration, you see, then they've got serious problems, you understand. Because, my friends, emotion—she is the effect of desire. And so now when you suppress desire or when you quash desire, well, what do you have? You have desire expressing in other areas, known as anger, hurt feelings, self-pity, and go right on down the line.

You see, it depends on how we're programmed. Now, if we're programmed that if somebody loves us, then they always send us a dozen roses twice a week or they smile every time they see us or they say, "Oh, how have you been? I haven't seen you for twenty-four hours!" and all of that dripping emotionalism, well, if that's the way we're programmed, then, of course, in this world, you know, we've got a few problems—self-created, now. But, you see, just because somebody else—we must realize—expresses their love by maybe saying, "Well, how are you?"—period—and goes on about their work, then, if we're dripping with that emotionalism, we think the other person doesn't even have a heart. But how can we say such a thing, when God's manifestation is variety? And the person that doesn't express and release all their emotions—which, of course, is the effect of their desires—you know, that doesn't mean that they are right or that the other one is wrong, or that the other one is wrong and they're right. Or vice versa. Or whatever. It doesn't mean that at all, friends.

Total consideration would immediately show to us: This is the way that person's programmed; that's their divine right. That's the way that person's programmed; that's their divine right. And so everyone has a divine right in a world of varied creation. And so, you see, we've got to use a little reason as we move around, because, you know, it's like a chess game. And here's the world, you see, and we're moving and we'd better give some thought to our motion, because we may find ourselves checkmated a thousand times a day. And we won't be very happy because, you know, there's something about the human mind: I wouldn't say that it's particularly a good loser, you know.

You see, we all want to gain and none of us want to lose. And that's contrary to the laws of creation. The Law of Creation is, Every gain is a loss. Did you ever find anything in life that you gained that you didn't lose something else? If you think you have, it means your awareness wasn't looking too clearly. Because every time you gain something, you lose something.

For example, a man gets married. Well, he has a gain. He has someone to cook, someone to sew his socks, someone to take care of the house, etc., maybe share the income, you know, the expenses. But he sure lost something; and that, of course, is very individual to each person. And the same with any woman, when she decides to get married. She's gaining something, all right, and she's giving up a lot, though she may not yet be aware of it.

Now friends, we've run over time. Thank you very much. Let us all go have refreshments. Thank you.

JUNE 20, 1974

CONSCIOUSNESS CLASS 53

Good evening, class. This evening the discourse that was read was discussing the power of the spoken word. And the statement in that discourse, "I am Spirit formless and free; / Whatever I think, that will I be," *[Discourse 54]* is a very important point to consider.

Now, it has been stated that when the lips speak as the heart feels, words become the savior of the wise. And so it is that many exercises have been given to help you, of course, to help yourselves. It has also been stated to think a word thrice before speaking it forth into the atmosphere.

Now, we cannot, in truth, come to a realization of the power of the spoken word until we make some effort in these exercises that have been given. For example, when man speaks forth the word *peace*, if he does not first feel it, then the word does not have that power for him. And so it is that we first feel the word before we speak it, in order for it to go forth into the universe and accomplish that which we send it to do.

Now why is it that man should first feel before he speaks? Well, it is quite simple. Because it has been stated that when the minds are harmonized, then you have the power of God, the power of the universe, behind your spoken word. And so it is that it is our magnetic field, our subconscious, that is the feeling part of our universe. And it is our conscious mind that is the electrical. And so, my friends, when your feeling for the word that you are to speak is equal and harmonized to the spoken word, then it will, indeed, go forth into the universe and it will accomplish what you truly are sending it to do. And so I suggest once again that the students make some effort, and some application, with those exercises, at least for a few moments daily.

Now it is true that some students have tried it for a very short time. But, you see, with the word they are speaking they have not truly felt and, of course, a house divided cannot stand, let alone be the power of the universe itself.

Now you're free to ask any questions that you have. If you will be so kind as to raise your hands, please.

You've spoken many times about freeing the soul. Are you speaking about the soul faculty of freedom? And, if not, would you discuss that a bit, please?

Thank you very much. The lady is asking in reference to the statement of freeing the soul and is that referring to the soul faculty of freedom. Freedom, of course, is a full expression of the soul faculties in perfect harmony or balance, and in that sense we are referring to the soul faculty of freedom. Does that help with your question?

Yes. Thank you.

You're welcome.

I would like for you to share with us your understanding of the word karmic, *especially in the sentence, Through free will man binds himself to the karmic circle of cause and effect.*

Thank you. The lady is referring to the statement in the book [*The Living Light*], Through free will man binds himself to the karmic circle of cause and effect. It is through choice, which is, of course, an effect of free will—it takes a free will to express choice—that man has entered form in the first place. Having entered form, he binds himself, through the Law of Identity, to the form through which he is expressing.

Now, the question may well arise, If that is true, then why has man chosen to enter form in the first place? Well, we have discussed that under our understanding of the formless and free Spirit and its expression, its awareness of expression is only through form.

Now what and how can man, having been bound in form of cause and effect—how can man truly be free and yet still express in form? Well, it may be stated that man must first learn to become objective: to view the part of himself which is governed by the Law of Cause and Effect, which is the creative law and the principle of duality, to be able to see his expression from a vantage point of freedom itself. How is that possible? It is possible when we balance this creation, this conscious awareness, with the subconscious patterns that we have bound ourselves to. When those two levels are balanced—the conscious and the subconscious are in harmony—then we are able, our soul, to view our lives through what is known as the superconscious or the neutral point. Now this happens to people who make the effort to bring about this balance in their life. It is not something that you are going to be able to express through the whole course of a day, for man, his soul consciousness, cannot express through that neutral expression of the superconscious for any long period of time without leaving this physical dimension and leaving form completely.

For example, our soul is expressing in form because we have identified with form. Man cannot experience anything, as we have stated in a multitude of ways, unless he identifies with it. And man does not identify with anything unless he accepts it. And man does not accept anything unless he considers it. So, you see, these laws—although they all are one law, in truth—are all interrelated; they are a variety of expression. And so it is that we choose wisely what it is that we're going to identify with. We first consider it, to see if it would be of value or in our best interest before identifying.

Now, it's just like we've stated in other ways: that all of man's experiences, of course, are taking place within his own mind. They don't take place anywhere else: that's only an illusion. They take place within our own mind. And we have the choice and we have the ability to make the decision whether or not we want to identify, inside of our own head, with a certain level of consciousness. Now this is where man's true freedom comes from: through self-control.

It takes control of oneself, that one may identify with this level of consciousness or with that level of consciousness. The great illusion that we're living in—the great dream—is that the causes are outside of ourselves, that it is something out there that we are experiencing. That, my good students, is not true. The first thing to learn and to accept into your consciousness is that it is not out there. As long as you dream the dream that power over your life is outside of your control, then you are ever the slave and you are the victim of circumstances and conditions. For every time you dream that dream that something outside of you has the power to bring you health, wealth, or happiness, every time you dream that kind of dream, you place yourself into circumstances and conditions where you are the victim of forces outside of yourself. I hope that's helped with your question.

Did I understand you correctly that all effects derive from free will?

Man's choice. Thank you.

Yes, all right. Now, a question I would like to ask is, In other dimensions beyond Earth experiences, do clairvoyance, clairaudience, clairsentience, and all these continue on in a finer degree?

Whereas they are the effect of a spiritual expression, they do continue on, as the spirit continues on, yes.

If we go on to another planetary system, would that continue on in that manner?

The spirit is eternal and is an effect of the eternal Spirit. Yes, in that sense it does.

Sir, I wondered if you could talk a little bit about self-control and when self-control becomes self-punishment and leads to self-destruction.

Thank you very much. The gentleman is asking in reference to self-control and when, and if, it does become self-punishment and lead to self-destruction. Well, of course, if we, in our mind, compute a need to punish ourselves through what is known as a guilt complex, then, of course, it can, and ofttimes does, lead to what is termed a self-destruction. This is why we teach to free yourself from what is known as guilt complexes, because they are, indeed, a form of punishment to the individual who cares to entertain them.

Now, that is a choice with the individual, of course. If you feel that your life has not been, or is, the way that you desire it to be and you entertain thoughts of remorse and regret, then, of course, you are punishing yourself; and that path would, indeed, in time lead to self-destruction. However, that is not necessary if an individual will recognize, realize, and accept that they are, in truth, spirit, formless and free, that, of course, their experiences are the direct effect of their own thoughts. I hope that's helped with your question.

I was wondering if you would please elaborate on the relationship between the soul faculty of humility and the sense function of procreation.

Yes, thank you very much. The gentleman's asked in reference to the teachings of the soul faculty of humility and the sense function of procreation. Now, when the soul is expressing itself through what is known as the soul faculty of humility—humility, my friends, is an expression, recognition, and, of course, an acceptance of an authority, of a power, of an intelligence greater than the form itself. Now, when this same energy is directed through the sense function of procreation, it does not, in that expression, recognize the intelligence, the authority greater than its own form. Do you understand? In other words, my friends, you see, the teaching is to balance these faculties. All faculties recognize a greater authority and express with that type of recognition. Sense functions do not recognize, nor accept, a higher authority than their own being and their own expression. And so it is that we are trying to teach the students not to annihilate, of course, the sense functions, but to bring a degree of balance into their lives, to realize that the functions are temporary, that they are an expression of a temporary body, that your soul faculties are the expression of an eternal Intelligence, an eternal Spirit, expressing itself.

And so in the teaching of the soul faculty of humility and the sense function of procreation—in procreation, you see, man, the form, becomes the king of creation. And when the soul faculty, of course, is balanced, then there is a recognition and there is a greater expression of the true Spirit. Thank you very much.

Could you please explain, "And sees the tides of creation, as a captain sees his ship." I don't understand that.

Thank you very much. The lady is referring to the affirmation of "Total Consideration." "And sees the tides of creation, as a captain sees his ship." *[See the appendix for the complete text of the affirmation.]* A captain sees his ship as a vehicle that he may use to transport himself to any port that he decides to be transported to. He recognizes, realizes, and understands that the ship, in and of itself, is only a vehicle of expression for himself to get where he desires to get. And so it is, "And sees the tides of creation, as a captain sees his ship." And so our soul sees the flux and flow, the duality of creation, as a vehicle through which we may express ourselves to get to the destiny that we have set into motion. Does that help with your question?

Yes. Thank you.

You're more than welcome.

I wonder if you could elaborate a little bit on the law of dreams and how can we change our dreams to be more pleasant. And, also, can you explain the amount of time that we sleep during the night, which might we say a third of our life here on this Earth—what happens to our soul at that particular time?

Thank you very much. There are several questions involved there, beginning with number one: He's referring to dreams. I must first ask the question, Which dream of life are you referring to? The one that we are aware of during our waking state or the so-called dreams during our sleep state? Which dreams are you referring to?

Well, I really don't know, because I'd like to have an elaboration on both of them.

Fine. Thank you very much. Yes. Well, there is so much talk of dreams and dream interpretation of the so-called sleep state. And many people do seem to be a bit interested in those symbols and things that come out during their sleeping state. We have discussed before that dreams during our sleeping state are nothing more, and nothing less, than our own suppressed desires, our own fears, and that energy is being released during what we call the sleep state.

Then, we have what is known as the conscious dream, the dream that we're supposedly aware of here and now. All of Life herself is but a dream, and man, having choice, is dreaming whatever dream that he chooses to dream. Now, a person may say, "Well, this is not a dream that I am here in this class. This is a reality." Well, my friends, what is reality? What is reality? Reality is nothing more, nor less, than a conscious realization of passing events. And so it is that all of us gathered here are consciously realizing that we are here. That is our dream and so we are dreaming it in that way. However, there may be a soul present that is physically here and yet they are dreaming that they are somewhere else. And so all of life is a dream.

Now, in reference to sleep, we've also discussed that. It seems that the mass mind, in our present expression here on Earth, has addicted itself to the necessity, to the need, of a minimum of what they call eight hours of sleep. Well, I'm sure we've all had an experience where on a weekend we've decided that, well, we don't have to get up and go to work and so today we will sleep twelve hours instead of eight. Perhaps we'll even sleep fourteen, because we want to catch up on our rest.

Did you ever know anybody catch up on anything of the past? What is past is gone. That's it. You can do nothing about it but dream about it. This is the eternal moment over which you have power. But many people think they can catch up on their sleep and rest by adding another five or six hours on a Saturday morning or sometimes even a Sunday morning. Well, usually they awaken and they feel miserable. They either have a headache or they're totally exhausted: it seems like they haven't slept at all.

Now what is the process during sleep? What actually happens during sleep? Well, there is a point during sleep at which the soul leaves the physical body. It leaves in what is known as your vital body. And that vital body goes out into the universe and it rejuvenates itself with energy. Now that process takes less than nine minutes. That is the only time that your body is truly being rejuvenated. The remaining seven hours and fifty-one minutes is an expression of your suppressed desires and your fears, and that depletes your energy. And so it is, you see, my friends, it isn't a matter that you are rejuvenated by how many hours you sleep. It is a matter that you are rejuvenated in the *way* that you sleep.

Now, if you have gained some control of yourself, some control of your subconscious, some control of your mind, then you can sit down anywhere—you can even stand—and you can release your vital body to go out into the universe and rejuvenate itself, and you'll feel totally and completely refreshed.

Now, many students have asked me how they can cut down on the length of time that they are sleeping. Well, number one: We have to ask ourselves the question, How many years have you been sleeping that number of hours per night? All right, so some of my students say, "Well, it's been about sixty years now." Well, you don't change, my good students, a sixty-year pattern in six days, weeks, or months. No. Because if you try to, you will have a phenomenal reaction, not only mentally, but physically and chemically. No, that is not the way.

If you want to stop wasting so much of your life, then gradually, slowly, but surely, start reducing five minutes a night. And try that for a few weeks. And if the reaction is not severe, then increase it after a few weeks another five minutes. Then, gradually, slowly, but surely, you will be able to cut down from these long eight-, ten-, and twelve-hour sleep periods—which is a lapse of conscious awareness, of course—until you get to the hours that you feel are best for you, perhaps two or three.

Now, I do hope that's helped with your question in reference to the soul. It is true that sometimes during sleep the soul will go out in its astral body and its spiritual body—if you have one created—to these other dimensions. It will sometimes go to school. Now, we have stated many times the importance of what type of thoughts you are entertaining when you lose conscious awareness in what is called sleep. Because, you see, the level of consciousness that you are on when you lose conscious awareness is more than indicative of where your soul is going to be traveling, in what dimension; for dimensions, my friends, are merely levels of consciousness. Thank you very much.

I've heard it said in this study that our God is not a judge—and I'm glad he isn't—which leads me to the Ten Commandments, which I was taught from the Christian Bible. Does that have a place in this study? And if it does, and they are violated, if God is not a judge, who judges?

Thank you very, very much. Yes, in reference to your question in our teachings that God is not the judge who judges, and also in reference to a teaching of what is called the Ten Commandments, my friends, it is our conscience. Our conscience is a spiritual sensibility with a dual capacity, knows right and wrong for us. It does not have to be told. It is our own conscience that does the judging.

Now, we might say, "Well, how is it that my conscience is different from another person's conscience?" Well, it's most understandable. God's manifestation is variety and our souls are evolving through time and space. You understand? And so it is that some people, they have a greater expression of what we understand to be conscience and others don't seem to have such a great expression.

Now, how does this conscience know right from wrong? The conscience knows. This is a spiritual sensibility with this dual capacity inside of us here and now. It knows where we've been, where we are, and where we're going. It knows our true motivation. And for us it knows what is right or wrong.

Now, many people mistake this spiritual sensibility, known as conscience, with their programmed acceptances of what is right or wrong for themselves. And then, we've got problems, such as we discussed earlier of guilt complexes, which are not beneficial to the human soul. So we must learn to discern for ourselves which is our true spiritual conscience and which is the patterned, programmed acceptances of a lifetime that say what's right or wrong. Does that help with your question?

Thank you.

You're more than welcome.

I've been doing a lot of thinking about the messages that people get in a Sunday morning service. If we are striving to contact the Spirit, which is formless and free, and is total peace, I don't understand the place of spirits—frequently a grandmother or mother or whatever—who have left this earth realm and who, then, come back to give advice or in some ways attempt to—or offer direction for someone's life. That, to me, seems to be depriving. If I were to accept that, this seems to me to be depriving myself of contact directly with the Spirit. It seems that I am choosing to give up my free will to do so and I don't understand that. Would you explain it, please?

Well, I'll be more than happy to share with you our understanding. The lady is referring to communication with other dimensions. And perhaps you are referring to, Why is it necessary to communicate with intermediaries, so to speak, rather than direct with their God?

That's right.

Fine. Thank you so very much for your question. First of all, let us understand what we are really trying to teach here. We're trying to teach that God is ever equal to our understanding. Now, if our understanding is such that we may find a greater peace, a greater purpose in life, and a greater fulfillment by reaching what we call God or Divine Intelligence through communication with other dimensions and that proves itself to be beneficial to us—do you understand?—then that is the way that we have found of expanding our understanding of what we call God.

It is also the teachings of this Association, and its philosophy, that God is not a person, place, or thing, but God is an expression through all things. Therefore, each time you talk to a person, each time you talk to an animal, each time you feel any type of communication with the stars or the sun or the moon or the trees or the blade of grass, you are communicating with your God. Do you understand? Fine. Now, if your understanding of God has expanded and broadened to that expression, then everything you see, hear, touch, or feel, for you, is a communion with God. Is that clear? Yes. And so it is, my friends, that communication with other dimensions does indeed serve a most beneficial purpose in broadening our horizon, expanding our understanding of our acceptance of God or the Divine Intelligence.

Now the question may well arise within the mind, "If a person, having left this physical world and trying to get to higher realms of consciousness—what are they doing by coming back down here to help guide someone's life?" Is that your question?

Yes.

Yes. Well, my friends, you see, we cannot go forward until we've helped another upward.

So many people in life think that, you know, they can put their mind to some particular study or some endeavor. It is contrary to the universal, divine laws that man will find God without helping another along the way. And so it is that those who have crossed the veil—not all of them, but those who are truly trying to find their God—they see the path of service and communication with this earth realm to help those souls that are still here in the physical flesh to rise to higher levels of consciousness, so that man left here on the Earth will not have to *believe* that there is a life eternal, that he will not have to take the word of another, but that he may, through a greater effort and through a communion with higher dimensions of consciousness, may become aware for himself: for that is man's—truly man's—divine birthright. Does that help with your question?

Yes. May I ask—

Yes.

I believe I understand what you're saying. The one thing that puzzles me is I know here, when I try to talk with you interpersonally, we sometimes have great communication difficulties. And you're talking about crossing dimensions and becoming a channel and, say, in the church service, you may offer a message to me which comes through you as a channel, and I take it for what it means to me. And it seems to me the possibilities of getting the message garbled are profound.

Indeed, they are. But is not communication here in the physical world filled with its possibilities of misunderstanding?

Yes, and it causes people a great deal of pain and difficulty.

Now, my friend, think. If communication with anyone in the physical world or with other dimensions causes us pain and difficulty—we have just finished discussing, I think earlier in this class, that all experience takes place within our own mind. Now, if we, you understand, have some need to experience pain and difficulty for our own good and our own benefit, is that not our own divine right?

Is it not true that the political situation of the world today is causing untold multitudes pain and difficulty? Would you not agree? But is it not, my friends, also true that untold multitudes are not experiencing difficulty and pain because of the political situation of the world today? Is that not true? Therefore, do we not see the divine right of each soul to choose whether or not they wish to experience pain and difficulty or its opposite? Is that not true? And so it is, my friends, that no matter what we encounter or experience in life, the choice is ever within our own mind. And, for example, what brings light to one may bring darkness to another: that is entirely dependent upon their level of consciousness and, of course, their receptivity to it. Would you not agree?

Yes.

Does that help with your question?

Thank you.

You're more than welcome.

I wonder if we might return a moment to the faculties and functions. It's my understanding that there is a counterbalancing faculty for each function, and yet there are some parts of the spiritual body that do not exist as they do in the physical. Now what I would like to know is, Do we continue to express some functions in the spiritual physical world? Or what happens?

Thank you very much. And first we'd like to clarify which part of the anatomy are you referring to that is not expressed in the spiritual body as well as the physical? We'd like a clarification on that point, please.

It's my understanding that in the spiritual world you do not eat, so that would be digestive or elimination or reproductive functions.

Thank you very much. As we evolve into the higher realms of light, it is our understanding that there is not the need to partake of food to replenish the body. That is correct. That teaching does not imply or guarantee that man no longer has a digestive system. This, we must first understand.

Now, each part of the body, whether it is physical, mental, or spiritual—for example, the physical body is an effect, as we have taught, of the mental body; and the mental body is an effect of the astral body; and the astral body is an effect of the spiritual body. And so it is, my friends, although the parts of the physical body may be difficult to recognize in higher realms of light, that does not mean the essence of that part of the body is not there, because it is. Does that help with your question?

Thank you very much.

You're more than welcome.

I have a question that a friend of mine asked that I was unable to answer, and I was wondering if I could ask that now. It's my understanding that I'm asking this question of the Wise One through the mediumship of Richard Goodwin. Is that correct?

If that is important to you, yes. Is that important to you?

Yes. OK, this is his question. Given that the law of conservation of energy and mass ensures that an entity's energy will exist into perpetuity, although in an unincorporated state, how is it possible to gain contact with the previous combination of matter and energy?

Thank you very much. Because all things, in truth, are energy and a variety of its expression, there is no separation to the Light itself; it only expresses in lesser degree. Therefore, communion with anything in what we may term past, present, or future is possible if man is able to touch within his own universe the eternal now, which is the Divine Light itself. I hope that's helped with your question.

Thank you.

You're more than welcome.

I have a question that's in another discourse, but I hope you can answer it: "As we give, unto us is given. / I pray each day that my God / Will show me the way to serve today [Discourse 5]." We know that God is the universal law of life. And when we pray to our God, how do we—well, what I want to know is how to serve better. How do I pray to my God that I may know how to serve better today?

Thank you so very much. It's simply by expanding, of course, our understanding. If it is true, my friends, that God is equal to our understanding, then, if we want to have a greater God expressing thorough our universe, then, of course, it follows that we must expand our understanding, we must broaden our horizon.

Well, how does man expand his understanding? Understanding is the very foundation of the soul faculties. Simply by expressing, more often and more fully through the soul faculties. And one of the most important of the soul faculties is tolerance. And so, my friends, what is tolerance equal to, of course, in anything? What we're able to have tolerance with, we have a greater understanding of. If you have an understanding—that being the foundation of the soul faculties—then you have more peace, you have more tolerance, you have more duty, you have more gratitude, you have more patience, you have more perseverance, you have more poise, and on through the entire soul faculties. Does that help you with your question?

Thank you.

You're more than welcome. Yes.

We spoke once here about tolerance-testers. And I'm wondering, Is there ever such a thing as a natural, electromagnetic disharmony between people? Or is there always something that you have caused or merited in this encounter where you can't possibly get along?

Thank you very much. Number one: My friends, I would like it clarified that the word *tolerance-tester* is a word that my students seem to have somehow coined along the way in this understanding. And, of course, I can share with you that it does seem, many times, when we are striving to express tolerance that our self is constantly testing us. And what's testing us, of course, my friends, is our own levels of consciousness and our addiction to those patterns or to those levels of consciousness. And, in that sense, that could, of course, be called a tolerance-tester.

Now, the lady has asked, Are there times when a person meets another individual and there's a discord and disharmony on their electromagnetic vibration? Is that correct? Indeed, there is and it happens all of the time. Now, what is the disharmony? Well, it's very simple: you meet a person and they're expressing on a level of consciousness that you have not, as yet, been able to express a sufficient degree of tolerance to, because perhaps you haven't yet spent enough time and effort in trying to understand that level of consciousness. And consequently, there is a disharmony or there is a discord.

Now, there doesn't have to be, of course. If we spend the time and energy to understand that level, then we will be able to go down there, you see, and experience that level and we can have a harmony.

Now, to help a human soul, you must first be able to go to the level of consciousness on which their soul is expressing. Then, you must be strong enough, when you go down to that level of consciousness, to not only pull yourself up, but to help rise their soul level of consciousness. Do you understand? Then, in so doing, my friend, what you are really doing, you're not only helping yourself, but you are the instrument through which the Divine is able to help another soul and to rise them to a higher level of consciousness.

Now, how does a person learn the technique—if you wish to call it that—to rise or to lower their soul consciousness to a level of another individual and to rise them up to other levels of consciousness? How we learn it, my friend: there is payment for all attainment. We must first experience those levels of consciousness—not only experience them, but awaken and have the strength to grow out of them. And once having done that, then, and then only, are we truly qualified to go to the level of consciousness to help another soul and to bring them back up. Does that help with your question?

Thank you.

You're more than welcome.

Thank you. One question was answered. In fact, two or three were. What we hear so much about in communication, about communicating with astral shells—and I've heard this in my communication work: that I was communicating with somebody in the astral. I would like to have, if you please, an explanation of what the astral is.

Thank you very much. And first off, when a person makes the statement—which was originally coined, I believe, by the late Madame Blavatsky, termed "astral shells"—do they really know what they're talking about? Do they mean by an astral shell a body through which the soul is no longer expressing? Well, if that's what they mean, it's really a rather confusing statement, considering, my friends, when the Divine Spark, known as God, expressing through the soul, expressing through a physical body, when it leaves it, the physical body, of course, returns to the elements from which it was composed. Now, when the soul or the Divine Spark leaves an astral body, the astral body returns to the astral substance of which it was composed, and therefore, in that sense, there is no such thing as astral shells, no more than there is such a thing as physical shells. And how long does a physical body stay a physical shell? It immediately starts into the process of disintegration and returning to the elements of which it was composed. So, in that sense, we do not accept it. It is contrary to the divine law and its revelation that what is composed of a particular element returns to it by the very laws of beginning and ending of form.

Now, what is the astral body? We have stated just a few minutes earlier that the astral body is an effect of our mental body. Now, for example, it is also stated in our teachings that our attitudes of mind are our levels of consciousness, our patterns of mind, that they form and deform our astral body. How do they form and deform our astral body? Well, each part of our anatomy represents a sense function and a soul faculty. If the energy expressing through the body is directed 90 percent to a sense function, that particular part of the body will be deformed. And that is what is referred to in the study book [*The Living Light*] as astral cripples.

Now, how long does the soul express through an astral body? Friends, we're expressing through an astral body here and now, because we have a mental body, and the astral body is an effect of that mental body. Just because we don't see with physical eyes the astral body is no proof that the astral body is not there. It takes astral sight to see astral bodies. It takes spiritual sight to see spiritual bodies. It takes mental sight to see mental bodies. And it takes physical sight to see physical bodies. And so it is, my friends, the importance of balancing these faculties and functions, so that you will not have to experience, when you awaken your astral vision, you will not have to experience a body that is not formed well, sound, and solid. I hope that's helped with your question.

About two or three weeks ago you stated something about the affirmation—to investigate it, to know it a little bit more, so that it can be applied to our daily meditation or when we say our affirmation. But there's a couple of points in the affirmation that I feel are sort of the key to the whole thing: "eternity is my true awareness." And through that eternity, all this knowledge that our soul is aware of through our soul faculties—is this all available to us as we start to meditate or as we say, "I pause to think and claim my divine right?" [See the appendix for the complete text of the "Total Consideration" affirmation.]

All things are available to the true seeker. Now, if a person wants to know of things past or future or present, there is a part of the self, the spirit within, that knows all things. No one has to tell it. Does that help with your question? Yes. Now, how does a person get to that level of consciousness? Well, the paths are varied for the multitudes and the masses. But you can be rest assured, my friends, if you have the patience, the poise, the perseverance, the day will come when it will gradually, slowly, but surely, awaken within your own being.

How does one determine the aspiration of one's soul?

"How does one determine the aspiration of one's soul?" My friends, soul aspirations are not known by what we call a mental body or a mind, because they are of soul substance. Now, for example, the mind—and we have discussed this before—the mind is a dual vehicle: it is in a constant process of accepting and rejecting. It is in a constant process of analyzing. Now, when you take that which is finite to analyze that which is infinite, you're not going to find the essence of truth itself. And this is why the statement has been made that, "When of thy mind thou seekest to know the truth, / On the wheel of delusion thou shalt traverse *[Discourse 1]*."

Now, truth expresses in a multitude of ways. Truth is one. It is constantly and continuously individually perceived. That is why, my friends, when we make the statement that we have truth, what we are stating is that we have accepted the facts, the patterns, that are in our own mind and, to us, of course, that is a truth.

Truth, it is stated, is like a river: it continuously flows. It is not something that you can grasp and you can hold and you can state that it is yours. Because, my friends, in doing that, you've brought it into limitation and stagnation. You see, a wise man is ever open: he is ever ready and willing to change. He is ever ready and willing to accept that what he has accepted in the past is in the process of change, because man is in a constant process of change. All of form is in a constant process of change. And mind is an effect of form. Therefore, things of the mind are not permanent. Things of the mind are not stable. Things of the mind are not eternal. Now truth—I am sure we will all agree—truth, to be truth, is eternal. And so how does man perceive truth? He can only perceive it with the part of him that is eternal, and that we understand to be spirit.

To try to perceive truth with any other part of your being is only to guarantee discouragement and disappointment. Therefore, my friends, let your eternal spirit express itself. Let your mind accept the divine law that governs creation, that governs form, that it will ever change, for it is its very nature.

Thank you very much. I see time has passed. Let us go have refreshments. Thank you.

JUNE 27, 1974

CONSCIOUSNESS CLASS 54

Good evening, class. This evening, in our tenth class of our summer semester, it may be of some benefit to our students to discuss perhaps some of the experiences that we may expect after leaving this physical dimension, whether it's at the time of so-called death, or transition, or it's prior to that time, through our own spiritual awakening and unfoldment. We spend a great deal of time in this philosophy in discussing the importance of peace, the importance of concentration, the importance of self-control, etc. Now, one of the many reasons that we emphasize the importance of these things—of peace and self-control and concentration—is because of the abode: your home that you are building here and now for your own so-called future.

When we have left this physical body, we no longer have a physical dimension in which to express. Not having a physical body, we are in a mental, astral, or spiritual body. And the experiences that we have, of course, and our homes that are built and all of those things are the effect of directed energy through the vehicle known as thought. Now, here in this earth realm, man directs his energy through thought and he moves physical substance with a physical body. Now when you've left this physical body, you don't have it and therefore cannot move physical substance and build a home of physical substance in a spiritual, mental, or astral world. And so it is very important that we learn the process that is necessary to build our home in those dimensions.

So many people, after leaving this physical world, find themselves in realms of confusion and regret simply because they are unable to control the multitude of thoughts and feelings that are expressing through their own mind. Now, if you wish to build a stable home in those dimensions and you have merited that plane of consciousness, then you must be able to entertain in thought—for example, if you wish to build a chair, you have to be able to entertain that in thought long enough for the substance of that dimension to be gathered into the chair that you desire. Now, many people in those dimensions, they try so very hard to build even a flower or a rose. It starts to take on the shape of the rose that they're thinking of and trying to visualize, but it keeps changing, and therefore the days, the weeks, the months, and the years roll by, and still the thing that they desire has not yet manifested itself. And it never will, unless the individual is able to concentrate: to keep their mind pointedly and fixedly upon the object of their choice. And that, my friends, is one of the many reasons that we try to emphasize, here and now, what is known as peace and self-control and concentration.

The experiences, of course, that we encounter here and now are the effects of the inability of ourselves to hold our mind to one thing. Some may call it goal. Call it what you will: it does not matter. But we have not practiced sufficiently what is known as concentration. And so when we take the time, when it means enough to us, we'll not only realize and recognize and accept the great importance of controlling the thoughts of our mind, but they, indeed, are the world in which we are living.

We've spoken a great deal about awareness, self-awareness. So often in a day's experiences we forget that the experiences encountered are ever the effect of our own attitude of mind. This must be spoken again and again and again, until we can rise to the level of consciousness where we can see clearly that life, in truth and indeed, is a mirror. That's all that life is, is the reflector. For creation herself is the effect of directed energy through the vehicle known as thought. This is why we have that little affirmation, "The universe is the Lord's meditation and man is an idea of it. As mind is ever one in substance with the idea and the whole idea, so man and the Lord and the universe are one and the same." And, of course, our understanding of the Lord is the law. And so it is, my friends, the transformation, the rejuvenation of our being, the great awakening, the joy, the peace, and the beauty of our life are ever within our power to control it. But unless we remind ourselves more often that that power is indeed within us, then we will continue in the circumstances and conditions that we find not so beneficial to our lives.

Now you're free to ask whatever questions that you may have.

Would you explain a little more fully the dimensional or energy levels of the soul faculties? For example, in the creative principle, the first soul faculty of duty, gratitude, and tolerance is placed on the triangle so that duty is on the electric side, tolerance the magnetic, and gratitude the odic, regardless of our level of consciousness that we're expressing on at any moment. Does that in any way affect the positioning of these different points on the triangle?

It does, in the sense that there is an imbalance of the energy. Yes, indeed, it does. For example, in the creative principle, as you have stated, that duty is expressed through the electrical, and that tolerance through the magnetic, and gratitude through the odic or the divine neutral. It does have an effect if there is an imbalance. If there's an imbalance in either the magnetic or the electric, then, of course, we are not receptive completely to the odic or to the Divine. You see, so often in expression—or what the lady is referring to, the creative principle, which, of course, is the effect of directed energy through the vehicle known as thought. When our feeling for anything is not in harmony or in balance with our thought and desire for it, then—for example, if you are 60 percent into the magnetic and only 40 percent into the electric, then you are not completely receptive to the power that can bring it into manifestation for you.

This is why so much of this new thought business in your world today does not work for everyone. Because some people who study the power of positive thinking, they bring a balance between their magnetic, their feeling universe, and their electric or thought. Therefore, it is manifested to them, whatever they desire. Do you understand? So it is that a person—whatever it is, of course, that they're desiring—they must not only feel it, but they must think it. And the thought and the feeling must be in balance for it to fully manifest for them. Does that help with your question? Yes.

Could I ask for a little further clarification, please? Tolerance would never be on the electric side.

Tolerance would not be, no. It deals with the magnetic field.

And if tolerance were combined with two other soul faculties in a different triune soul faculty, would it continue to remain a magnetic?

Not necessarily so. It would remain magnetic in the particular triune faculty of duty, gratitude, and tolerance, as gratitude would remain neutral or odic. Does that help with your question?

Yes, it does. Thank you.

You're more than welcome.

When you're on a bummer trip, so to speak, and you're down in the dark places and no matter what you do you can't seem to come up—it's like your spirit is willing but the body is weak. Can you share with us what it is we can do at that time to bring ourselves up out of the dark?

Yes. Thank you very, very much. And the lady has stated it most beautifully: that the spirit is willing but the flesh is weak. Now, we understand by that old statement from that book that the Spirit, the Divine, God, the great Neutrality, is always willing; the flesh, the magnetic, the emotion, the feeling is not yet able. What it means is this: that the soul consciousness—our soul consciousness is expressing 90 percent through our feeling, emotional magnetic field and we do not have the sufficient energy or strength, because we are not expressing a sufficient amount of this energy through the conscious mind or through the reasoning faculty of the conscious or the electrical field. Therefore, we find ourselves what is known as grounded; grounded in the magnetic field of this feeling and emotion.

Now, how does one—how can one, rather, help oneself to come up out of those levels of consciousness? Well, the first thing, my friends, is when you're grounded in the feeling or magnetic field, you are extremely receptive to what is known as visualization. You see, at that time you are able to visualize anything that your mind cares to imagine. Now, some people say that they can't visualize. Well, everything visualizes or it would not express form, for form is the effect of visualization and directed energy.

So it is if you find yourself in despair and discouragement and hurt feelings and all of the other things that are involved in your magnetic field. At that time, visualize. Choose whatever you desire to choose at that moment and close your eyes. You're in the magnetic or feeling dimension. Feel the ocean. Feel whatever it is that you want to feel. Do you understand? And if you will do that, you will find yourself still in the magnetic field, but you'll be expressing through something over which you have control. For example, if you feel discouraged where you are and with the experiences that life seems to be reflecting back to you, then visualize a time and a place when you were happy. Do you understand? Let your mind drift into that experience. Now you have control over that, for you have set that into motion consciously. And this is how you're able to come out of those levels of consciousness.

You see, when we're in those lower levels of consciousness, they are the effect of uncontrolled thoughts expressing through our mind. That's what they are: they're the effect. We have not consciously, you understand, said, "Well, I want to feel terrible now." We can do that. We have the power to do that, but it has happened without our conscious awareness. Now, the reason that it has happened without our conscious awareness is because we're not thinking. The thought has passed through the conscious mind, but because we are not truly self-aware, we cannot see the inward journey that the thought is taking, and the next moment we find ourselves feeling just miserable and full of discouragement, etc. So if you will try the process of visualization—choose whatever it is that you desire to choose—you will find yourself still in the magnetic field, but by your own choice, your conscious choice, and from that you will be able to rise to higher levels. Do you understand?

I do hope that's helped with your question, because it's most important to all students because we're all moving up and down like a barometer through these levels of consciousness. Now, the thing is, friends, you know, every one of us present knows when we're down there, but very few of us are aware when we're on the way, you see. You know, when you start the descent—the moment you start it, you have to make great effort through your soul faculty of reason, through your electrical field, because you're being pulled. That's why it is the magnetic field. You see, you take one step and the next instant you've taken twenty more. And then, you're aware that you're way down in the basement. That's why we teach to nip it in the bud: to become consciously aware of the thoughts that put you on the descent and become consciously aware of the thoughts that help you on the ascent.

Now, that is also one of the great benefits in spiritual studies: to have someone to study with; to have someone to discuss with. Because, you see, the spoken word is life-giving energy. So when you are on a spiritual study and a spiritual path, if you discuss these spiritual things with someone who is harmonious with the understanding, then what you are, in truth, doing is supporting yourself. Because the spoken word is life-giving energy, there is a harmonious exchange of thought. You are not only the instrument through which another individual is being helped, but you are also helping yourself. Because instead of one spoken word from one person, you now have two spoken words from two people. And if the motive is similar or in harmony, then you will not only rise, but the individual with whom you are discussing spiritual matters with, they also shall rise. And this is why it's so very important and the teaching has been given many times: Choose wisely your associates and with whom you spend your life-giving energy. Now, what does that really mean? It seems to be a very clear statement to choose wisely your associates and with whom you spend your life-giving energy. Because if you don't choose them wisely, friends, what happens is, you're talking with someone or they're talking with you and the negative projections are so great, your listening ear becomes triggered, so to speak, and you start on the descent to their level of consciousness.

Now, how can a person expose themselves to the world and not be fluctuating up and down on over eighty levels of consciousness? Well, that takes self-control and self-control takes self-awareness. You know, we're all living in this mundane world and we have jobs to do in the mundane world and we meet many, many people. Well, now, some people seem to be able to go out on their daily work and activities and to stay in a rather harmonious level of consciousness. Some people get up in the morning and they feel wonderful. They go out on their jobs and by the time they come home they're in a terrible condition, terrible shape. Well, it is obvious and it is self-evident that the individual is unable to control himself. They've gone out and exposed themselves to the world and they don't have sufficient self-control to stay up into a higher level of consciousness. Now, it is also true that some people get up in the morning and they're miserable: they're in a terrible level of consciousness. They go out on their job, they go to work, they come home, and they just feel wonderful. Well, it is very evident they've exposed themselves to some people with a positive vibration and they have been lifted up. So, you see, it's working all of the time, friends.

Now this is why we've also stated, choose wisely your thoughts when you lose consciousness and you go off to sleep at night, because whatever your thought and your attitude of mind is, that's where you're expressing during your so-called sleep. Does that help with your question? Thank you very much.

I think a couple of classes ago you stated something about the soul faculty of tolerance—that we must be able to associate with other people who we may think we are intolerant with in order to grow.

That is correct.

Now you say, now choose your friends wisely and carefully.

That—yes, most certainly. May I just say this one thing. If the light is too bright, it is best they see it not now. You may go ahead with your statement.

I think you've answered it.

Well, you see, friends, it's a matter of discernment: to spiritually discern. Do you, as an individual, feel strong enough to help—to be the instrument through which another soul is helped? And if you do, how long do you honestly know you will be able to communicate with that individual while they're on a lower level of consciousness? How long will you be able to be the instrument through which they're being helped—ten minutes or an hour—before you descend yourself? Does that help with your question? Yes. Now some people may be able to communicate with a person for five or six or ten hours, you see, and when they leave that individual, they just feel fine and totally refreshed and the other individual now feels much better. That deals with self-control and concentration. I do hope that's helped you. Thank you.

As we've heard many, many times the expression "to stay in our own vibration," would you give us your understanding, your spiritual understanding, of what that really means? I think I've misunderstood it.

Yes. And that's a wonderful statement that has caused much thought: to stay in your own vibration. Well, my friends, can man stay in what he is not aware of? So the first thing is we must become aware of what our vibration really is. Now, having become aware of what our vibration is—of how we feel, of how we think, of the level of consciousness we're truly on at any given moment—we have the divine right to choose and say unto ourselves, "I'm going to stay in my own vibration." Now, when a person—and what the statement means, "to stay in our own vibration," it does not necessarily mean that we must become a recluse on a mountaintop. However, if that is the only way we're able to stay in our own vibration is to become a recluse on a mountaintop, then, for us, of course, that is necessary.

Now, some people may think that, well, they won't physically associate with anyone, so they can stay in their own rate of vibration. My friends, vibrations are not limited to the physical dimension. Vibrations are not limited to the mental dimension or the astral or the spiritual. So a person can be at home doing their daily acts and activities and find in an instant that they are no longer in what they know is their rate of vibration—because we are all receptive. We may have—a thought flashes through the atmosphere. We're receptive to the thought and all of a sudden we feel not very well. We've gotten onto a level of consciousness within ourselves that is associated with an individual and an experience which is not pleasing to us. So to stay in our own rate of vibration is number one. Self-awareness: to know what your true rate of vibration is at any given moment.

And then, if we find that certain people with whom we have been exposed, or are exposed, trigger a level of consciousness within us that is not beneficial to us, then, if we choose, we may avoid them, if that is the way we have found of staying in our own rate of vibration. However, there is, yea, even a greater way. And the greatest way of all is to be with a thing, person, or place and never be a part of the thing, person, or place. And so our teaching is to be in the world and not a part of the world. Does that help with your question?

Yes. Thank you.

You're more than welcome.

We're taught to become the master of our ship and yet we are also taught the great importance of selfless service. And I wondered if you could speak a bit on the relationship between the master and the servant within us.

Thank you very much. In reference to your question, the teaching is to be master of our ship and the captain of our destiny. And we're also taught to serve selflessly and to be the servant. Now, we teach a divine, neutral, Infinite Intelligence that knows all things, does not have to be told. We also teach that this Divine Servant that sheds its light upon all form without any thought of who or what they are is a servant. We also teach that the crown is greater than the kingdom. We also teach to be the captain of your ship and the master of your destiny. And so the gentleman has brought up a most important point. How can man be the master and the captain of his ship, and his destiny, and at the same time be the willing servant, with whole and complete total consideration and acceptance?

Well, my friends, we must look at the servant and the captain. Servant to the divine, formless, free spirit that is the eternal you. Master and captain of the forms, which is the ship upon which your soul, your spirit, is sailing through so-called time and space. Now, when we come to the point of realization in our consciousness, when we truly accept that we are the great servant, the divine, eternal free Spirit, then, my friends, we will no longer be the victim of created form. But we will be its master, for the father is ever greater than the son, for that that is the power that sustains creation is greater than the created form. That is why man, the creator of machines and things, is greater than the machines and things. It's like a man saying that a great, gigantic, unbelievable computer has been built;

that it can do more things than man can do. My friends, this is not viewing with the light of reason. For whatever man has created, man is greater than the creation, for man is the captain of all of his creations. He is the master of them, but his soul is the servant of the divine, formless, and free Intelligence. I hope that's helped with your question.

Thank you.

You're welcome.

Last week we were told that when a soul or the divine spark leaves the physical body, it returns to the elements from which it was composed, the same as the astral body and so forth. Therefore, by the divine law and its revelation that when a particular element returns to it, does that, then, mean that the destiny of our soul is to return to the Allsoul? And is that what we try to be reaching for?

Thank you very, very much. The discussion is a most important one and a very important question to all of us. The lady has stated, as has been stated in this class, that whatever is composed of any element, in truth, in time, returns to the element of its own composition. And so the physical body returns to the elements of a physical world and the astral body returns to the elements of an astral world and so does the mental body return to the elements of a mental world. And so it is, as above, so below. The law that governs the astral body and the spiritual body and the soul body and the vital body is the same law that governs the physical body.

So we see that our physical body rises up from the elements of a physical world and our eyes look and see that that physical body returns to that physical world. But the Divine Spark, the Intelligence itself, goes on and expresses through other forms, other bodies in other times.

Now, the lady is asking the question, Does the soul individualized return to the Allsoul? For that is our understanding, that it has come from the Allsoul. It is also our understanding, yes, indeed, it does return to the Allsoul. But, my friends, be not disturbed that you're going to be annihilated, your individuality. You see, the soul, the individualized soul that you are now expressing through, is not going to return to a so-called Allsoul until it is no longer individualized. Do you understand?

You see, as man becomes more universal in his thought, he rises into the Law of Principle. Then, his soul expresses less in personality. And this is why it is stated, If the light is too bright, it's best they see it not now. If a person, here in their level of consciousness, feels, "Well, what's the sense? I'm going to be annihilated anyway," and we haven't yet grown through the self, the self-motivation, we haven't yet expanded our consciousness to a greater expression of universality, then we're not yet ready.

But, you see, my friends, that that comes from a thing returns to the thing from whence it came. And so man says he has come from God. Well, man *is* God. Everything *is* God. But go beyond the form. So we come from God, we return to God. That that belongs to the physical returns to the physical, and that that belongs to the Divine returns to the Divine, only to express itself again, again, and again.

We have stated many times that this is not the first time your soul has expressed and it will not be the last time. Don't you see, my friends? You're not new to the world and the world is not new to you. Eternity is our true awareness. This life, this moment, the twenty, fifty, or seventy years that you have been expressing in a physical body at this time is only one page in an endless book. So let us think more about that. Let us think about the eternity through which we have already been expressing and are expressing. That's why, when you have turmoil in your life, stop and think, "This is not even a moment in the great eternity of which I truly am." It's not even a moment. It is stated that wisdom lives in patience. So what is the great rush to the grave? My friends, we have always been. We will always be.

Let us do something with the moment of eternity, this moment, for it is, in truth, the only moment of which we can do anything about. Has that helped with your question?

Thank you.

You're more than welcome. Yes.

I was called last night and asked to pray for someone who is desperately ill. And I would like to know from a spiritual side of life, How do we pray for a mother or a father or someone who has gone to the spirit world with no knowledge of the spirit world at all? How can we help them awaken or to pray for someone who is desperately ill? What is our responsibility and how do we go about it?

Thank you very much. And I would like to ask you a question in reference to being solicited to pray for another individual. Did you understand that the person requesting the prayer wanted you to pray that they had health or that they passed to another world? Which were the specifics? What does a person mean when they request a prayer of that nature?

Well, it was for someone who is on the earth plane, but my thought—

What was the prayer for? That they were to be well?

For healing.

In other words, they were to be freed from the obstruction that the soul was experiencing at that time.

Yes.

Is that correct?

At this time.

I see. Thank you very much. When a person declares divine right action, then divine right action will indeed take place for that individual's soul. Now remember, friends, when we decide with our minds what is best for another individual, we immediately accept the law that is governing that individual. For example, someone will say, "Well, would you pray for me that my finances may improve?" or "Will you pray for me that my health may improve?" If you permit yourself to pray in that nature and form, what you are doing is accepting the law that is governing that individual's life and you will experience whatever is necessary to understand why their soul is expressing through that particular obstruction. This is why we do not teach a type of prayer to pray that a person be freed from this or to be freed from that. We simply declare, prayer is the soul's aspiration to the Oversoul. We simply declare divine right action and peace, which is God, to express itself. You see, one type is an expression on a mental level and an emotional level, and the other is the soul's aspiration on a spiritual level. Does that help with your question?

Yes.

This is why, my friends—you know, I've heard, oh, in this movement and many movements, so many times people say that their guides are watching this for them and watching that. And that their guides and teachers are keeping their house from burning down. And that their guides are taking care of this and that their guides are taking care of that, here in this mundane world. I sincerely pray that I may not slip into that level of consciousness, because I would not want guides and teachers trying to inspire me to do God's work who were still concerned about the mundane things, such as my automobile or my television set.

My friends, let us use reason. Now, how illumined can a soul be in the realms of spirit, or any other realm, who would still be interested in my wardrobe or in my television or my radio or my tape recorder or my house or my automobile? You see, this is such an important thing to remember: If a guide is evolved to realms of light and reason, then they're not concerned with a physical substance. They're concerned with our soul. They are concerned with our spirit. They're not concerned with finding gold mines. They're not concerned with diamonds. They're not concerned with the stock market, but they're concerned with our soul.

And so it is that we try in this philosophy to bring some balance between what is known as the science of communication in Spiritualism with a philosophy of an evolving soul throughout eternity. My friends, it is so important that you not attract unto yourself so-called entities, guides, and teachers that are driving you down the highway when God gave you a faculty of reason, that you may know how to drive down the highway; that you're not attracting entities from the astral realm who are concerned with how many pounds you've taken off or how many pounds you've put on, because God gave you a faculty of reason to use balance so that you may balance your physical body. Let us remember that.

Now I want to strongly impress that on all of my students' minds: that that excites our senses is not of a high spiritual nature. And so remember, if you ask your guides and teachers and helpers from the realms of spirit to take care of your mundane jobs, be rest assured, what you're trying to do is to bring those souls to a lower level of consciousness, out of the light and into the darkness. Now, if they are strong enough, they won't descend down into this dark, mundane realm to do those things. And you will attract some of those good-enough guides from the lower astral realms.

Now, let us not misunderstand the true purpose of communication—and I want to finish this up here, but still it's important to your philosophy, to your class. There are times when those departed, having merited some higher realms of light, see in this mundane world that the only way to reach the soul is to speak a little bit in what their desire is locked into in this material world. But unless they can rise them from that material concern and desire into a higher level of consciousness, you be rest assured, my friends, the communication for that individual does not long continue. This is where we must learn to separate spiritism from Spiritualism; fortune-telling from mediumship.

The purpose of mediumship is not to solve your love affairs. It is not to know when the stock market is going to make you the most money. It is not to get you a job in this mundane world. It is to help you to see that life, in truth, is eternal. That what you do here and now, what you think about, what you feel, and what you desire have a direct effect upon whether or not you're going to rise to realms of the spiritual world of light and understanding or whether or not you're going to remain in the lower levels of consciousness, known as the lower astral world.

Remember, friends, communication with these dimensions is a very serious business. It is indeed the spirit of joy, but we are the instruments through which those souls of the departed are striving to help humanity. Its purpose, my friends, is not to entertain our senses. Its purpose is to serve God, to help man to see the light within himself. A hundred times, again and again, we have spoken about the sincerity of our motive. Let us remember that everyone, in truth, is a medium, for everyone, in truth, is in communion with some level of consciousness.

So let us, friends, look at the job that God has given us in life with the spirit of gratitude and the spirit of joy, the spirit of complete and total acceptance. And let us never forget that whatever the job may be and however mundane it may appear to be, it's God's work and the greatest work, if we will let God move into it through our thought and through our feelings. So let us seek to serve God in whatever job we have merited in this life. There's no such thing as a bad job or a poor job, unless we've made it that way in our thinking. And so it is there's no such thing as a great medium or a poor medium, unless we, with our thinking, choose to make it that way.

So many people, friends, they come into a church of this nature—what is called a Spiritualist church—and they're seeking, we are sad to say, not the light of God and the true spirit of freedom, but they're seeking a way out of the problems that they have placed themselves into. However, it indeed can serve a good purpose if, through this type of work, the individual is able to find the way inside of themselves to get through their problem. Perhaps they will think that what has helped them to get through their particular crisis may help another human soul. And if they think and look at it that way, then they will become the ambassadors of goodwill. They will become the servants of God and the world will be better off for it happening.

Thank you very much. I see our time has passed. Let us go have refreshments. Thank you.

JULY 4, 1974

CONSCIOUSNESS CLASS 55

Good evening, class. We have mentioned, I'm sure, before some of the allegorical statements contained in our study book, *The Living Light*. However, I would like to speak for a few minutes on the statement that was given, "As the wolf howled / And the frog croaked, / The ears of Ego heard not / For the door was locked / By the key of fear [Discourse 5]." Now many students have asked for an understanding of that statement and, of course, according to our level of consciousness is our understanding at any given moment. We all, I'm sure, understand that in this teaching the ears represent in the functions what is known as ego, which, of course, is the house of the functions. Some of us don't seem to be yet aware that on the faculties the ears represent perception.

Now, what does the statement mean, "The ears of Ego heard not / For the door was locked / By the key of fear"? Does anyone know? Well, we've discussed for many weeks and months that man is guided and controlled by the patterns of his own mind. The patterns that he has accepted in the past are the control of his present and, of course, the guidance of his future. These patterns are under the direct control of what is known as our ego, which is the house of the functions. And so it is that the ears of ego hear not anything that is not in harmony or in accord with our own accepted mental patterns.

Now it is also stated that truth is like a river, for it continuously flows. Now if that is a true statement—and we believe, of course, that it is—then whenever we are unable or unwilling to adapt to change, we become the direct obstruction to what is known as truth, for truth is a continuous flow. Therefore, when we accept something today, this moment, as an ultimate truth, what we are doing, in truth, is obstructing the continuous flow of what truth really is. And so it is that we have found with this study course over these many weeks and many months, for many of us, that there is a constant evolutionary process taking place; that each and every one of us are on different levels of consciousness, and according to that level are we receptive to a certain teaching at any given moment.

Now, our purpose has been, and is, to help you to recognize the patterns that you are the victim of; to recognize them and to help to guide you to making what changes are necessary in your thinking to broaden your horizon, that you may be free from these addictable patterns of past acceptance. You see, my friends, the reason that the ears of ego hear not is not only because of the patterns that we are controlled by, but it is because we have found a false security with the things with which we have become familiar. And so it is from fear that man closes the soul faculty of perception. What man fears, he is blinded to, and therefore the soul faculty of understanding is not open and there is no true perception. So we see how advisable it is for us to make, yea, even greater effort to apply an acceptance to change, to remember that yesterday is past and gone, to let those patterns leave when they no longer serve a beneficial purpose to our eternal spirit and the evolution of our own soul.

This is where we find our problems in life, my friends: from this fear, from this insecurity, that there is, in truth, a change taking place. So many of us seem not to be aware that Life herself is a continuing changing process. It has always been and it will always be. And so often we say, "Well, I'm open and receptive to whatever changes that I think will be beneficial in my life." But the sadness of that type of a statement is that we don't think when it means we're going to actually let go of old mental patterns. That, my friends, is where we stop thinking. And therefore the application of the change is not truly made.

Many times it's been said as a student unfolds there is an increase of sensitivity. Well, of course, there's an increase of sensitivity. There's not only an increase of sensitivity to finer vibratory waves in the atmosphere, there is a great increase of sensitivity to the gross vibrations of which most of us are already used to. And so it is that without self-control, we cannot find freedom.

Now you're free to ask whatever questions that you have, if you'll raise your hands, please. Yes.

I was wondering what actually constitutes sympathy and how mankind got associated with it.

Thank you very much. And the gentleman is speaking about the word *sympathy*. And in our understanding, sympathy is an expression of our functions and compassion is an expression of our soul faculties. Now, whatever man has had an experience with, man is sympathetic to. For example, if man has broken his leg at some time in his life, he has suffered the pain and discomfort of it. He is sympathetic to any other person who has broken their leg and is suffering and in pain. Now the question is, Well, why is he sympathetic? Because, my friends, he is sympathetic through the Law of Association. When you have had any experience in life and you view that experience being expressed through anyone at any time, that, through the Law of Association, once again opens up your computer to that experience and therefore a person is sympathetic.

However, my friends, remember, sympathy is a sense function and we do not advise an imbalance between the functions and the faculties. Therefore, a man who has compassion—a man having compassion has understanding. You see, many of us can have an experience and not understand it. We experience many things and we can have sympathy when somebody else is experiencing it. But if we do not have understanding, we cannot express compassion. If we have understanding, we know the law through which we got into the experience and, knowing the way in, we also know the way out. And therefore compassion, of course, would be much more beneficial. I do hope that's helped with your question.

In the statement of principles in the hymnal there's the statement—I don't remember the first part of it—but the part that I'm interested in is, scientifically proven through the phenomena of Spiritualism. [During the church service the congregation read aloud the Declaration of Principles of the National Spiritualist Association of Churches.]

Yes.

Now my understanding of a scientific proof is through a deductive method of logic. And I do not or have not seen this kind of scientific proof in my association with Spiritualism. And I would like to know or understand more what is meant by that in relation to my understanding.

Yes, thank you very much. And the statement in the Declaration of Principles of our national association is, "scientifically proven by the phenomena of Spiritualism." The statement very clearly means that there is a spiritual, scientific evidence for communication with a world known as the world of spirit. That has nothing to do with a scientific, deductive logic of the mental body. You see, the spiritual body cannot be examined or scientifically proven by the mental body: it can and is scientifically demonstrated by the spirit. Now, if you consider, for example—perhaps this may help you best: many times in this work I have had people come to me and say, "If you could only tell me my mother's maiden name, that would prove to me beyond a shadow of any doubt that there is such a thing as a spirit world." That is not proof in any sense of the word, except to that individual's logic and deduction. For example, not knowing the science of spiritual communion, one can easily accept life eternal or the continuity of life by such a request as this person in question. However, the same so-called phenomenon could be easily demonstrated by telepathy or by mind reading. Therefore, we have no proof whatsoever of spirit communication by giving someone's name because they have passed out of this physical world. That is not scientific, spiritual evidence or demonstration. So we must consider, my good students, if you want scientific evidence and demonstration of spiritual communion, then you must awaken your spirit, for it is your spirit that will sense, that will know, that will see, and will hear other spirits on the same level of consciousness. I do hope that's helped with your question.

Could you please give us your understanding of the difference between spiritual healing, magnetic healing, and mental healing, and which is the greatest?

Thank you very much. In reference to your statement on healing, we have discussed this before. The father is greater than the son. And so the Spirit which sustains all life is greater than the life that it sustains. Therefore, spiritual healing, in our understanding, would be the main principle. For example, the Divine Spirit or Intelligence sustains all this form. And the spirit is greater than the component parts, which are the soul, the mental body, the astral body, the vital body, and the physical body. Do you understand? And therefore, in our understanding, spiritual healing would, of course, be the greatest. Thank you.

Yes. Would you distinguish between and clarify more on applying the Law of Continuity and patterns?

Yes. Thank you very much. The lady is asking a question in reference to a difference, if any, between continuity and patterns. Yes, perhaps you would best understand it this way: a pattern is something that we have established by the Law of Continuity but are no longer consciously aware of and is not being directed by the soul faculty of reason. Yes. Continuity is a conscious, directed effort, not addictable by a so-called subconscious pattern. Does that help with your question?

Yes. Thank you.

You're welcome. Yes.

Thank you. We often speak of a person's character. Would you please give us an understanding of what character is?

Thank you very much. The lady is asking in reference to a person's character. Now, there are many differing understandings of what character is and we must be very careful in examining what we call character, because it is the open pit and trapdoor to judgment. For example, a person may say that, "My character does not permit me to do this and to do that. My character wants me to be this way or to be that way." Well, what is it that establishes our character? When we speak of character, my friends, we are speaking on a soul level of total consideration. When a man is expressing character or principle, then he—or she—considers all parts of his own personality, which is the sum total of his mental patterns. Character can be summed up as the principle of the soul faculties in expression, and personality as the sum total of mental, addicted patterns. Does that help with your question?

Thank you very much.

You're welcome. Yes.

I wonder if you would be good enough to discuss, a little more fully, organization, especially in relation to one's personal vibrations or personal life.

Thank you very much. The lady is asking the question on organization in relationship to one's personal life. Now I'm sure that we will all agree we cannot organize what we're not aware of. And so awareness is the first step to organization, because no man can organize something that he has no awareness of. And so it is that we first go to work on the inward journey of awareness: to become aware of our desires, to become aware of our likes, to become aware of our dislikes, to become aware of the causes of those desires, to become aware of the causes of those likes and dislikes. Then, after man has become aware on that inward journey, then he is in a position to organize his life.

Now, organization cannot come about without awareness and self-control, because you cannot organize what you can't control. Therefore, the step is: awareness, control, organization. Now, we've made the statement many times, "When you awaken in the morning, put your house in order before confusion sets in." But, of course, my friends, if we're not in a level of consciousness where we have some awareness, we can't put the house in order, because we can't order things that we cannot see. Would you not agree? And so if we—in our seeking, in our searching for awareness, let us also strive for greater strength, because it takes great strength, once having found the different patterns of our own mind that we're not too happy with, to bring these things into balance and self-control. Does that help with your question?

Thank you.

You're welcome. Yes.

To continue on with that statement, in the collecting, regardless of what it may be—as I understand what you've said—self-control is the essence. In collecting other body or bodies, in the control of a certain thing or things, would the self-control of other things or people or etc., be the control of the color essence within that group that you're trying to control, as to the completion of that circle or whatever it is—money, spiritual things, or what have you?

Thank you very much. And, of course, we all understand that color is vibration and vibration, of course, is sound. And so the gentleman is asking, in reference to control, how, really, to control these vibrations, which we call in life these different experiences, as he referred to one, for example, of money. You see, my friends—and we've spoken that many, many, many, many, many, many times—it is not outside: that is the illusion of life. It is not outside. It is inside. And that is the only place that it exists. We must awaken within our being the truth. Control is not something out there. That is not where it is.

Now let's take the example that the gentleman has brought up in reference, of course, to material supply. Our mind has become addicted to the illusion that it is outside and we must do something about events and circumstances out there. That is the illusion, the great illusion. It is in our thinking; it is in our attitude. Now, a person says, "I always seem to attract in my life these so-called tolerance-testers." Now, you see, it's the same principle at work. The same principle in getting money is the same principle of what some students call tolerance-testers: that "I just can't understand how I'm always attracting to me these tolerance-testers." Well, my friends, it's the same law, you see. It's a magnetic law. The tolerance-tester outside is the testing one is doing to oneself. And the people out there that are attracted to them are the mirror.

So it's the same principle with supply. It's the same principle with what you call money. It's inside, in our attitude. Now, when we change our attitude, then we can come into rapport with what is called money and divine flow. But, you see, the change has to take place in here. Now, we made a statement several classes ago that we don't need money, that money needs us. You see, the moment that your mind says that you need something, you deny your divinity. You take out of your aura energy, and you give it to the thing that you say that you need that's over here. Now, when you do that, you become the victim and the slave of circumstances and conditions.

So, you see—let us put it another way. When man educates his desires, he finds his true wealth, you see. Now, we've also stated in the creative principle in one of these classes—and even made a chart and a diagram for you—"As you believeth, you becometh." If you believe that you need something, what you are saying is, "I deny the truth that I already have it." You see, we already have everything. However, we have permitted ourselves to sin for untold centuries—and by sin, I mean the error of ignorance—saying that we don't have this and we don't have that. Now our God is equal to our understanding and as our understanding has narrowed through the centuries, our God has become more stingy. And so we find ourselves in what is known as lack and limitation. Well, lack and limitation of anything—I don't care if you call it money or you call it health—is a revelation, my good students, of the narrowing of your understanding, you see.

Now, we try to teach here to broaden your horizons, to expand your understanding. And then, these so-called needs will disappear, as you come to the realization that all that you are seeking, you already have. Then, my good students, you'll get off the treadmill of delusion and you will be free. But you will not, and cannot, be free until you dethrone the false gods that you have created in your thinking that tell you that you must chase here, there, and everywhere to get what you're seeking. That's not where it is.

Now, if a person—and a million people seem to be doing it every day—if a person can attract repeatedly so-called tolerance-testers and bummer experiences into their life, the same law—identically the same law—will attract for you all that you think you need. Now, I do hope that that's helped with your question. It's very important. You see, a man says, "Well, I've got to do this in order to get that." As long as man believes that—man is a law unto himself—and so he will have to do this to get that. Someone else believes a different way and he doesn't have to do this to get that. But it depends on what you care to believe in life.

You know, some time ago I had a discussion with some of my students—how interesting it was—the age of the forties. The reason that it is so interesting—it's known as the hindsight years. All of a sudden we awaken to the fact that we haven't done too much with the forty years that we've already spent and we're not too happy. Yes, my friends, the forties and up are known as the hindsight years. But remember, when our hindsight becomes our foresight, we will gain insight.

You know, if we're worried about our old age and we're worried about retirement and we're worried about our pensions and we're worried about a supply, well, where do you think we're going to be when we're sixty? If we worry that much today, we'll worry that much tomorrow, don't you see? Because we already believe the dollar isn't worth but a few cents. So if it's only worth a few cents today, what's it going to be worth ten years from today? My friends, the greatest pension man can have is an awakening in his consciousness that life is only the way that he makes it and it's ever the way he takes it.

What is it that causes all these kinds of thinking, all these negative projections of energy? Well, what is it? We stated it earlier this evening: it is our fear. Can man fear what he understands? Of course, he can't fear what he understands. And so the first thing that we teach is, Let us, in all of our getting, get understanding. Because if we have understanding, we don't have any fear. And if we don't have any fear, we have no problems. They all disappear, you see.

Now, we have stated many times, "Our problems, they are ever companions as long as we love them." Now, how do we know how much love we're giving to our problems? Carry a little tape recorder with you and listen to how many times you express what you call a problem. Then, you'll know how much of your love and your energy is going to that level of consciousness. I seriously suggest and recommend that more of my students carry a pocket tape recorder, so that after the day has finished for them and before retiring, they can listen and they can hear what they are projecting out into the atmosphere. Because if they will do that, be rest assured, very soon they will think before they say another word. Now, you can teach that the spoken word is life-giving energy, that we open our mouth and set a law into motion. But you have to think about it. You have to do something about it. You see, if you carry a little tape recorder with you and every time you start talking, push the button, and you go home at night and you start listening and then you mark down, "I set that law into motion, that law into motion, that law into motion, and that law into motion. What a miserable experience I'm going to have. I'd better start doing something right now!" Friends, that deals with awareness.

How many times do we say what a wonderful world it is? How many times do we stop and think, instead of react, and say, "Well, that soul's on that level of consciousness right now. God help me be strong, because that level exists in me and I don't want to get triggered"? Do you understand? Let's think about it, friends. You know, we're not two years old anymore. We're not nursing from our mothers. We're supposed to be adults and we're supposed to be grown up. Well, let's think! Let's start to think. Think about what you're doing to yourself. Think about what you're doing to your life.

You see, you know you're not twenty or thirty or sixty years old. Our soul for centuries has been expressing. Isn't it about time that we recognize, realize, and accept that we are the law, that we are doing these things to ourselves? Remember, so-called need is a delusion of our mind. God, the Divine Intelligence, has given us everything. Everything is inside of our own head. When we become receptive to the thing that we desire, then it shall manifest in our life. But as long as we tell God that's the way it's to come and that's how it's to be done, then God will let us work along that way, running down the path with blinders on until someday we stumble so many times that we cry out in humility and accept a Divine Authority that knows what it is doing. Thank you.

Thank you. Could you speak a bit on hope with regard to the discussion this evening?

Thank you very much. And in reference to hope and this evening's discussion, we must remember, friends, that hope is eternal, but truth is inevitable. Now let us perhaps share some understanding about hope and truth. So often a man hopes for things. He hopes for a bigger house. He hopes for a pension plan. He hopes for another car. He hopes for things, which are creation and governed by the laws of duality. Now, hoping is not truth, because it's more than hope that brings things into our life. When we accept, truly accept, in our levels of consciousness anything, then it will manifest itself in our life.

Now, for example, a man can hope for a new car. He can hope for thirty years and it will not appear. The reason that it will not appear—man is hoping for it, but he has not changed certain laws that he has set into motion concerning the automobile that he's hoping for. Do you understand? You see, in his brain, in his computer, in his so-called subconscious, he has established certain patterns and certain laws through acceptance. He has accepted that's it's going to cost so many dollars. He has accepted that that is the way that it is to come. Do you understand? And consequently, he can keep right on hoping and it's not going to come, because he is not fulfilling the laws that he and he alone has established. Is that clear to you? Fine. So, my friends, it is good to hope. It does serve a purpose, but it is truth that we are seeking.

Truth reveals that man is a law unto himself. Therefore, understanding is the first thing we work for: to understand

and become aware. Then, when we understand and we become aware, we see the laws that we have already set into motion. We go to work to neutralize those laws and, having neutralized them, they can come through the divine law, which is acceptance. Does that help with your question?

Thank you.

You're welcome.

Yes. I've been thinking for some time, trying to reconcile some of the teachings that I've learned in this class with my understanding of how the organization of the Association works. I would like to know if the only person who communicates with the Spirit Council is Richard Goodwin.

Is that important to you?

Yes, that's important—

Then, that is correct. Your statement is correct.

The teaching that I'm having some difficulty reconciling, then, is the teaching of recognizing an authority higher than oneself. Because I have seen in this organization that the Spirit Council's word is the last word in many things, and I have been wondering about the reliability or the advisability of relying on one person's ability to communicate with a council without any check or balance. And I don't understand how those things are reconciled. It appears to me sometimes that in this organization, rather than relying on the authority of, say, a God or an Infinite Intelligence, we may be relying on the authority of Richard Goodwin. And I don't know if that's true or not, but I don't know how to understand it differently. And I am also recognizing the teaching that says that we ought to recognize our doubts and entertain them and think about them, that they're very important. And I want to bring that up.

Thank you very, very much for bringing up your question. Are you referring to the operation, organization, and authority concerning your church? Or are you referring to the council and your personal life? Which are you referring to?

To the church.

To the church, as an organization, yes. Well, I'm very happy to share with you our understanding and how this church is organized and how it is operated and the final authority is the council, who brought it into manifestation in this world. Now, it appears that, as the lady has stated, there is some question and doubt in reference to the authority that guides the Serenity Spiritualist Association. Now, if there is some doubt in your mind to the authority—all organizations have an authority. Now, usually, that authority—and so it is with this church—it has a president and it has a board of directors. Anyone who has any question or any disharmony or misunderstanding or lack of acceptance of the organization and the authority by which it is guided and operated may appeal to the board of directors of the Association. Now, this is an organization that is controlled and operated by the laws that govern it, and those laws are that it is and does have a five-man board of directors. We do have a department through which any questions concerning the authority of the church—how it is organized, how it is operated—that you may appeal to. And therefore, I might suggest that you make your appeal through the proper channels, that it may reach the board of directors, so that you may be helped with your problem. Do you understand?

You're assuming that I have a problem.

Well, it seems evident that a problem was discussed in reference to your question of doubt of the organization and how it operates.

Well, I don't see that evidence.

What seems to have been the question, then?

My question is that—

Would you rise, please?

Yes. My question is that—and maybe I'm not stating it appropriately—but I'm not suggesting any malice or anything of that type.

No, we did not understand it in that way.

Fine. Everybody has bad days or communicates inaccurately at times and so on. Organizations, for example—now I know it's not working very well at this point, but, for example, the government of this country has a check-and-balance system. Now what I don't understand is, even with a board of directors, as you've just pointed out, how does the body of this church check and balance that one single communication line.

Through a board of directors. The board of directors has the final vote and is subject to the general membership. The board of directors is also subject to the council who brought it into being. Yes.

Well, you mean they're subject to the council, but the only way they can contact the council is through the person of Richard Goodwin.

That is correct.

Well, that still leaves me with my puzzle.

Well, I think perhaps your puzzle is that you feel that the board of directors of your church do not have, and are unable to express initiative, through what governs the church. And that is not correct. We do have a board of directors and whatever is brought before the board of directors must be voted on by the board of directors. Whether the request comes from the council, who organized the Association in the first place or it comes from one of our members, it has to be approved by the board of directors.

Would the board of directors also know at the time of their voting what the opinion of the Spirit Council might be? Would they know it ahead of time?

No.

Thank you.

Does that help with your question?

Yes.

Yes. So therefore, this is the way this Association has always operated and therefore, we do have what, of course, the lady has stated, a check-and-balance system. Now stop and think, friends. We're trying to teach our students to use initiative thinking. But with initiative thinking, let us pray for understanding, so that we may recognize and realize from which level of consciousness we are using our initiative thinking. Now, all of the students and members in this Association, I sincerely hope and pray, are using initiative thinking and seeking a greater understanding. Now, we are very fortunate here in Serenity—and I'm so grateful the student has brought up the question that she has—we are very grateful that we have a peace, a harmony, and a serenity in the Association. I attribute that to the efforts that are made by the members and the students of the Association to recognize the divine right of each individual to express their level of consciousness. That we are all trying, to the best of our ability, to grant consideration to all souls and to take into consideration that each individual, being on different levels of consciousness, are trying to work for the common good of serving what we call God. Therefore, we do have in this Association, members and students with most diverse thinking. However, no organization can long remain organized if it permitted on its podium and in its literature a multitude of diverse philosophies.

Now, we do try to carry as many books as we can on Spiritualism and related subjects. And our students do express their level of consciousness on our students' forum and in our various lectures. Our mediums express their mediumship in many, many varied ways. But in order to remain organized, there must be some type of a system. And we sincerely try to have a system whereby each individual may express their individuality and not destroy the organization, that it may remain an organization and share its teachings and its understanding. Does that help with your question?

So remember, friends—you know, many people—like the lady brought up a very good point in reference to communicating direct with God. My friends, we are communicating direct with God when we speak to the next-door neighbor. It depends on our level of consciousness. God, the divine Infinite Intelligence, is expressing through the dog and cat. Now, if we are on a godly level of consciousness when we're petting the dog, then we're in contact with God. If we're on a godly level of consciousness when we walk in the meadow, then we're in contact with God. So, you see, remember, when we say that we think that we should communicate direct with God, God expresses through form, not to form. So if we want direct contact with God, let us be godly in our feelings and thoughts when we speak to people. Let us be godly in our thoughts, in our acts and treat the other kingdom—the animal kingdom and the plant kingdom—let us treat it kindly. Then, we will be in communication with God. When we walk down the street and we smile as someone passes by, we are in direct contact with God, for it is the God within that is expressing itself. Let us try to remember that, friends. Let us remember that God is everywhere, that God is never absent or away, that all we need to do is to think good and we will be good and that is God. Let us remember that and let us remember the divine right of each and every soul to express themselves. Let us try to bring out the godliness of all form, not just our own.

Thank you all very, very much. Let us go have refreshments. Thank you.

JULY 11, 1974

CONSCIOUSNESS CLASS 56

Good evening, students. We would like to speak for a few moments on what most of us understand to be the unfoldment process.

Many people interested in this philosophy of Spiritualism seem to think that all those who are interested in it are interested in order to become either a medium or a healer or a lecturer or something of that nature. And, of course, we know that is not the purpose, the true purpose, of this philosophy or of this class. We are not the ones to decide with our conscious mind whether or not our natural evolutionary soul talent is to be a medium, a healer, a musician, an artist, or a carpenter. But if we will free our own mind from the interest and concern of what our natural soul spiritual talent really is, then we will indeed unfold it.

When we strive to express our so-called spiritual talents and we use the vehicle of our mind, which is a mental vehicle, to reach decisions whether or not our true talent is unfolding to the satisfaction of our mind, what we, in truth, are doing is building a mental wall in front of the spiritual work that we truly have to do. Therefore, my friends, we have taught and we continue to teach, Seek not the gifts of the spirit, but seek the spirit itself—the spirit of truth, the spirit of freedom, the spirit of divine, eternal love. When you seek the spirit, in and of itself, first, then you will be freed from the concerns of your mind whether or not your so-called spiritual work is satisfactory.

You see, my friends, if the work that we are doing truly is spiritual, then there is no need for concern or interest whether or not it is satisfactory. Because, you see, the mind cannot, in truth, decide whether or not God's work, the divine work, is the best. That decision, my friends, does not lie within the power or the right of the so-called human conscious mind.

So in our unfolding processes, let us not be concerned with how much we are doing, how great we are, or how small we are. Because that type of thinking, my friends, defeats the purpose of our own soul and of our own spirit. Many times we have stated, "Give what you have to give and care less what is done with it." For the minds of men are very fickle, and one moment to the human mind, something is great and beneficial and in the very next moment, it is just the opposite. That is not what we're seeking in these spiritual awareness classes. We're not seeking to be great mediums or great healers or great lecturers or great anything. We're seeking God. And we find God through the soul faculties. And one of the soul faculties that is so important in finding the Divine is the soul faculty of humility, of humbleness: to recognize that there is an Intelligence that knows what is best for us and that will move through our universe if we will make greater effort not to be the obstruction.

We stated in one of our other classes that unfoldment is an inward journey. And the inward journey that we are all on grants us many, many experiences.

This evening, as you heard from the discourse that was read, that when we think of people, places, and things, we come into rapport with the very thing that we are thinking about. For example, when we give thought to a friend or an associate, what happens inside the depths of our mind is all of the experiences associated with that individual rise to the surface in our so-called subconscious in our magnetic field. Not only do we experience the feelings of those experiences of the past associated with that individual, but we also experience the feelings that that particular individual is emanating at that particular moment at which we are thinking of them. Therefore, does it behoove man to give thought to people, to places, and to things when man is not yet aware of what level of consciousness that the particular person they're thinking of is on at that moment?

However, we have also been given a way to free ourselves: to entertain our thought and our minds with peace. Many people have talked about protection or protection of the divine white light or something else. I can assure you, my friends, the only protection that man ever finds in this universe is known as peace. And that peace is known as God.

So each and every day we're always thinking about things, about people, about places, and circumstances. So we are in a constant process of confusion and disturbance. We wonder what this person is doing and what's going to happen to the world that we're in. And then, in that type of thinking, we come into rapport with all of the thoughts related to the situation. That, my friends, is known as selling your divinity, selling your soul.

Many, many times we have spoken—and we speak once again—of the power of our own thought, of maintaining and sustaining our divine right to our own freedom and to our own peace of mind. And so it is on the inward journey of spiritual unfoldment, many, many, many things will distract you and many, many things will tempt you ever to leave the path that you have chosen to trod upon. But to those who have the courage, the character, and the strength to awaken to their own divine right inside of themselves, those are the souls who will make it through the many distractions and temptations that wait on the path.

Remember, my friends, these distractions are not outside of us; they're in our own mind. They're deep inside of our own subconscious. So let us be free by demonstrating the great freedom of peace itself. Let us not be distracted with the changing things of so-called form.

Also, we'd like to speak this evening perhaps and share maybe a broader understanding on evolutionary incarnation. So many students have wondered upon what is based this teaching of evolutionary incarnation. It is not something that man has to blindly accept. It is something that is constantly demonstrable to all souls who open their eyes to look at the world around and about them. For our world, today and every day, demonstrates the eternal truth of evolutionary incarnation.

Look out at the world and see the many forms. All minds who investigate accept as a fact that form itself is evolving. It is demonstrable to every human being that wishes to investigate Nature herself. We have stated, and state again, that the soul individualized is the covering of the formless, free Spirit, known as the Divine Intelligence or God.

Now that that is individualized or a covering, by its very nature, is form. And so we look at our world this moment and we see that the law governing form is the Law of Evolution. And so it is, my friends, that we are passing through many forms and many forms we have already passed through. For the soul, being form, is in the constant process of evolving, as all form is in a constant process of evolution.

When we seek to become more aware, to become more awakened, that means that we are seeking to gain. And the law that governs gain is identically the same law that governs so-called loss. And so it is as we seek to gain, we must be willing to let go or to lose, for we cannot broaden our understanding or gain anything in life unless we can let go of some of the things that we have been holding to. That is why, my friends, that that truth is like a river: it continuously flows. As you move to level upon level of consciousness, you no longer hold to the thoughts and the beliefs of the past. You do not look back and say how ignorant you were a year ago or even ten. But you may look back upon it as a level of consciousness through which your soul, at that point in time, was passing. And so it is that the teaching of acceptance, the divine will, is a teaching that is inseparable from the eternal truth of evolutionary incarnation.

If man does not accept, he does not let go of what he's already holding to. If man becomes satisfied with all the experiences and things that he has at this moment, then he stays on that level of consciousness. My friends, we are not what we were a year ago. And a year from this date we will not be what we are this moment, for we are indeed a part of the evolutionary processes governing form. And so let your mind be free, that it may expand. Open your consciousness that it may broaden to the great truth that change is the law, the inseparable, eternal law that governs form, that thought is form, that all things recognizable by the mind are form.

Thank you very much. Now you're free to ask any questions that you have.

Yes. Would you discuss, please, the relationship or the interrelationship among the teachings of the responsibility of individualized spirit or soul, the assistance of entities who are in spirit form, and what I understand to be the faculty of humility, which would be accepting a power higher than oneself?

Thank you very much. The lady is asking for the relationship between the individualized soul and the assistance or help that a soul attracts or merits from other souls who have passed from this physical realm. Is that correct?

Yes.

And also, of course, this does involve the personal responsibility of each and every individual and the soul faculty of humility, through which acceptance doth flow. Is that correct? Yes.

Now, for example, my friends, let us begin with the question, What is the relationship between a soul encased in the flesh and souls who have been encased in flesh and who are now in another dimension, either their spiritual world, the astral world, or one of the other dimensions not of the physical? Each and every individual attracts unto themselves people on the same level of consciousness that they themselves are on.

Now, there is an old saying that has a great truth in it: that birds of a feather flock together; that man is known by the company that he keeps. And so it is, my friends, when you look at these so-called departed who have left this physical realm, who have merited the experience of helping you to help yourself, remember that the Law of Attraction is impartial, that whatever level of consciousness your guides and teachers are on is, in truth, the basic level of consciousness that you, your soul, is expressing. I hope that will help with that particular question.

Now we come to the question of the soul faculty of humility, the soul faculty through which acceptance flows unobstructed. Now why does acceptance flow through the soul faculty of humility unobstructed? Because when man expresses humbleness, man is expressing his godhood. We have stated that God, the Divine Intelligence, is the greatest servant of all. It has no prejudice. It shines its light upon all form, upon all creation, without thought or concern whether or not the individual will appreciate the light that is shining upon them. And so it is, my friends, that we teach, Acceptance is the divine will.

So the prophets of old have taught to be humble. Now what does *humbleness* really mean? How is it that we have a complete flow of acceptance when we're humble? Because when man is truly expressing through the soul faculty of humbleness, of humility, in that moment he, indeed, accepts a wisdom, a power, an intelligence greater than his own mind.

How is it that man is able to accept that authority when his soul is expressing through humbleness and is unable to accept it, usually, when his soul is expressing through the functions of the mind? It is because, my friends, when our soul is expressing through the functions, we are governed and controlled by the patterns of the past that we have accepted. And patterns, my friends, are limitations, and limitation is not freedom, nor is it light. For example, when man's soul expresses through the functions, through the patterns of the past, he cannot accept what is not already programmed into the particular pattern that he is expressing through at that moment. So let us seek, when we're seeking God, let us seek to express through our soul faculty of humility.

Now what does the mind say? What is the opposite of humility? Do any of my students recall? Surely, someone present knows the function of humility? Yes.

Procreation.

Procreation: the function which is the opposite of the soul faculty of humility. Let us think for a few moments. Does man or woman think that they are, in truth, the father or the mother of the child that they bear? Is there any parent present who does not entertain the thought that they, they indeed, are the father or they indeed are the mother? Think, my friends. Is that, in truth, humility? Is there any man in the universe so intelligent that he can create life? There is no mind expressed through man in any time, in any universe—nor will there ever be—who can, in truth, create life. He may bring about the circumstances and the conditions, known as the negative and the positive poles of nature, in such a way that the divine spark, known as life, will enter. But no man has ever, or will ever, create life.

Did you ever see a parent that wasn't proud of their child? They may or may not approve of what the child does at certain times, because it does not fit into their accepted computer, their patterns of addiction. But be rest assured they are proud, because they have accepted in the functions that they are the mother or they are the father. The truth, my friends, is they are only the instruments that were used by a greater intelligence, that a soul may enter in physical form.

Now many times with this teaching a person says, "Well, I don't want to accept any authority or intelligence greater than myself, because I feel that I will lose my individuality." My friends, we have already lost our individuality when we permit the patterns of acceptance of our own functions to be the authority that we bow to. I do hope that's helped with your question.

Yes. Thank you for laying such a beautiful foundation for it. My question is, there is a teaching, Give what you have to give and care not what someone does with it. And there is also the teaching, Do not cast your pearls before the swine.

That is correct.

And I wondered if perhaps we could have some discussion on it.

Thank you very much for bringing up that most important teaching. The teaching is to give what you have to give, to care less—that is, not to be concerned—what the individual does with what you have given; that is, to free your soul from the fruits of action. And there is also the teaching to cast not your pearls before the swine.

When you are on a level of consciousness that knows what your pearls truly are, then, my friends, you will be able to reach an intelligent decision whether or not you are casting them before swine.

Along with that teaching—and a very important one—is, Unsolicited help is ever to no avail. So, my friends, it means, before we give, we strive to enter the soul faculty of understanding. And from that foundation stone of understanding, we know by giving, we will not be attached if we are not concerned—concern being a function—with what we are giving. We also know from that foundation stone of understanding whether or not wisdom is dictating to give to this one or to that one. I hope that's helped with your question.

Thank you.

You're welcome.

I wonder if you would comment a bit on, Cleanliness is next to godliness with respect to organization and also with respect to outer manifestations revealing inner attitudes.

Thank you so very much. Would you care to share with the class your understanding of the word *cleanliness*?

I really wouldn't because I think that I'm not too clear about this.

That's all right, thank you. Perhaps we might view the word *cleanliness* as something expressing its true nature that is not contaminated with foreign elements or vibrations. Would you agree with that understanding?

You're saying currently.

That is correct. Yes. In other words, it's expressing its true self. It is not polluted with other vibrations. And if you will understand it in that way, then you will understand that cleanliness is next to godliness: that the object, person, place, or thing expressing itself without auric pollution or contamination is revealing its own goodness. Do you understand? Yes.

Now, the lady has asked in reference to cleanliness and next to godliness in reference to organization. Well, if all things in life are revealing their true essence, then we can be rest assured that a process of organization is also expressing itself, because each and every thing is organized to its own true nature and it is not contaminated. Does that help with your question?

Yes.

Now what was your other question, please?

I think that you've answered part of it: cleanliness in relation to outer manifestation simply revealing inner levels or—

Thank you very, very much. Yes. For example, a person may say—and many people have—that it is very easy to see where that particular soul is expressing itself—on what level of consciousness—according to the home that they live in. Now that doesn't mean it can't be very humble. But it is a revelation when you go anyplace in this life, you either see organization or you see chaos.

Now, it is true that if a person lives in their abode where everything is disorganized and just thrown wherever is convenient, it is a revelation of a level of consciousness within their own being. Now, that doesn't mean that we should judge each individual according to whether their particular abode is neat and clean or whether everything is in a chaotic state. What it is revealing is just a level of consciousness. Now you might go someplace where everything is very neat—everything in its place and a place for everything—but the individual on a certain level of consciousness is extremely disorganized. It reveals the level of consciousness associated in that particular area, for example, with one's home. Do you understand?

Now—and perhaps we ought to speak a little further on that, because it's a very important point. Now many times people get married and they're filled with expectations. And the years pass by and their expectations, you see, and their desires are not really fulfilled the way that they thought they should be and consequently there is a degree of rejection that they may experience and retaliation. Especially, for example, if it's a woman and her husband's very particular about how everything is set in the house. Well, she may find a way of expressing her retaliation and revenge by keeping the furniture and everything in it in a total disorganized so-called mess. So, you see, that is only revealing a particular level of consciousness.

Now, if the wife—or if the husband, it could be—gets their desires fulfilled and etc., then the mate may come home that day and everything is just clean and beautiful and the dinner's on the table and etc. and the laundry is all done. So, you see, it reveals a level of consciousness. Does that help with your question?

Yes. Thank you.

You're more than welcome.

When our conscience knows right from wrong, why do we still do the wrong thing?

Thank you so very much. And what a wonderful question the lady has asked. When our consciousness [conscience], being a spiritual sensibility with a dual capacity, knowing right from wrong, not having to be told—why do we still do what seems, for us, to be wrong? That, my good friends, is dependent upon our addiction to our levels of consciousness, to our patterns of mind. This is why, even though we know what is right for us at a given moment—you see, that's the great war that goes on within.

You know, take a look at it this way. Say that a person is driving down the highway and they're in great desire to get to a certain place and they're late. Many people will drive through the caution light or the red light to get where they are going, because the desire is stronger than their soul faculty of reason. And so it is, though our conscience knows right from wrong and does not have to be told, we have to reckon with our desires, which are, of course, the effect of the mental patterns to which we are addicted.

Now, before we do anything, if we would only stop to think. If we'd ask ourselves the question, "From where cometh this thought?" In that instant that we ask ourselves that question, we would know whether it is the effect of our so-called desire or whether it is the whisperings of our soul faculty of reason.

Remember, friends, that reason has total consideration. And so how important it is that we pause to think before we act! Because if we will truly pause to think, we will hear the promptings and the whisperings of the still, small voice within us that is our conscience, that knows what's right for us. And we will be able to reach a wise decision whether to listen to our own inner conscience or to listen to our suppressed desires. Does that help with your question?

Thank you.

You're welcome. Yes.

In my short time of association with this philosophy, I have been brought to the awareness of the soul's progression and a minute understanding of what to expect, due to the Law of Merit. However, there has not been, to my knowledge, any recognition, possibly, of a past. And, of course, the question could arise, As the soul progresses, why be interested in past? But there again, if one is to recognize a foresight, possibly a little hindsight might be in order. May I have some enlightenment, please?

Thank you very much. Of course, my good students, in reference to the student's question about our past experiences, we must ask the question, How far past do we have concern? Are we interested in an hour ago, which is a past experience? A year ago? A century ago? Or fifty centuries ago? Which will be of benefit to us? I try to get my students, in their thinking, to find insight on the inward journey to review not twenty incarnations ago, but to review the last minute or the last hour. You see, my friends, it's not advisable to try to leap with your consciousness from this life moment's experience to twenty incarnations ago when you're not yet ready or willing to leap to an hour ago, to a year ago, to ten years ago, to twenty, or to thirty. So, you see, the inward journey, my friends—wisdom dictates to become aware. But if we are not interested, truly interested, or sufficiently interested with the causes of this moment, then, of course, it would be to no avail or benefit to be interested in the effects of several incarnations ago.

So let us become aware of this moment. Let us become aware of what is controlling our acceptance. Let us become aware of the patterns that we habitually express upon. And in becoming aware of this instant and of this moment over which we can do something, then we can move step by step by step back through the days, the months, and the years, and we will become aware. And through awareness, we'll become organized. And through organization, we will become free. Because, you see, it takes organization to be free, my friends. Organization is control. And you must control ignorance in order to be free to express truth.

So the interest that we have, my friends, is in what is happening to us this moment, this day. Then, we can look to yesterday and the day before and the month before and the year before and we can see the so-called unseen causes. We can see the causes of why we like or why we dislike, of why we're accepting or we are rejecting. This, my friends, is the cure that leads to freedom of our soul. I hope that's helped with your question.

When a person wishes to accomplish a task in this life—maybe it's connected to their natural soul faculty or their life work—what is the proper balance between knowledge, a collection of knowledge in that area—say, in biology, for example—versus, or in relation to, what comes from the inside of a person, what a person already knows in their soul or their gut, however you want to call it? What's the relation or the balance?

Thank you very much. And the lady is referring to a particular work in life, as she referred to, for example, biology. Is that correct?

Yes.

Just for an example. Well, friends, if we have a feeling within our being to express what the lady has referred to as our task in this life through a particular field or profession, we understand, of course, that that particular field or profession is form. Being form, it does have its own limitations, would you not agree? For example, my friends, if your task is to be a biologist, then, of course, you're not going to be a musician or etc. You are, in other words, expressing through that particular vehicle with your task in life or your talent. And so we do have a limitation of what is known as the form of that particular profession.

Now, the lady has asked an important question, of course: What is the relationship to our own inner free spirit and the limitation of the profession through which our soul is expressing? We are limited only by our own acceptance.

Now, say that a person, as the lady has stated, has chosen biology. The laws governing biology have been established over many years. Would you not agree? Now, if we do not express our free spirit, then the particular field or form of biology does not expand and it does not grow. Because the biology of today is not the same biology of a hundred years ago. Consequently, in any form, in any profession, man must wisely use his own inner initiative and feelings and understanding, because that is what expands and helps the profession to grow and to fulfill its purpose. I hope that's helped with your question.

We've heard the expression—and I think you've answered most of this, but I still would like to ask—"Man, know thyself." And, as I think, I wonder sometimes whether I'm parroting others or is this really my soul expressing the words that I use, the feelings that I have. How can I best know myself so that I am free from the thoughts and the expressions of others, be they—and I ask tolerance on this—teachers or be they friends or whoever they are? How can I know myself?

Thank you very much. And the lady has asked an important question: How may man know himself? Man starts on the inward journey to know himself by understanding his own motives, his own motivation. And so it is, in all our getting, we seek to get understanding.

So, my friends, we start on the inward journey to understand our own motivation, to understand our feelings, to understand why we feel happy and joyous over one experience and we feel sad and depressed over another experience. We must first seek to understand why we have those types of feelings. And when we seek to understand them, you see, my friends, we must step outside of ourselves to get inside of ourselves. And the reason that we must step outside of ourselves to get inside of ourselves is because there are eighty-one levels of consciousness. And while the soul is expressing on one of those eighty-one levels, we can't see the other eighty. Do you understand?

So a person, seeking to understand themselves, they strive to become objective. And they look at themselves over here and they say, "Now that's most interesting. I get my feelings hurt almost seven days a week. Sometimes I feel very joyous and very happy. Now, why do I feel this way? And why do I feel that way?" And the first thing that the mind starts going through is, "Well, with certain people I'm very happy. I have a rapport with them"—don't you see? "Now with other people, I don't have a rapport. They're so sharp. They don't have any understanding." Well, that's the first step.

Then, the person says to themselves, "Now I want to work on myself concerning the individual that doesn't have any understanding of me. Because the individual that I have experience with that doesn't have any understanding of my feelings is revealing to me that I am not emanating understanding to that individual. And that individual is a mirror that's reflecting back to me a lack of understanding." Consequently, my friends, you see, we want to work on the things that are distasteful in our life.

You see, my friends, the things that are tasteful and satisfactory, that's a waste of energy to work on those. You see, irritation wakes the soul. It is satisfaction that lets it sleep. So, you see, we want to work on the situations in our life where our feelings are hurt, where it's difficult for us to express the soul faculty of tolerance, where especially in areas where we don't get our own way—and those are the areas, my good students, that we want to work on. Because, you see, we want to work on those struggles, you see. They will reveal to us levels of consciousness that we haven't, before, been consciously aware of.

You know, it's just like a person, they go to work and, you see, they walk in on their job and maybe the boss says hello. Maybe he's not feeling too good and doesn't say hello. How do we feel? Do we feel hurt? If we feel hurt or slighted, don't look at the boss. Look at yourself and ask yourself the question, "What inside of me causes me to experience a hurt feeling? What causes me to feel slighted?" Is it because we have decided that somebody must speak to us, because that is what we desire?

Now, if we have decided that, then we're constantly under the control of all of the people that we have decided should speak to us under certain circumstances and conditions. So when we meet those people and they're in another level of consciousness and maybe they have a lot of thoughts on their mind and they don't speak to us, we take the slight for an injury. And our soul starts to descend.

Don't you see, my friends? It's our own patterns. Remember—and again and again, we got where we are, friends, by the Law of Repetition. So get used to repetition to get you out of where you are, because what gets you into a thing is the same principle that's going to get you out of it. So repetition got us here and repetition's going to rise us higher. So again I say, it doesn't exist out there, my friends: it's in our head. That's the only place it is.

We have made these decisions, for example, like on our job, that our boss must speak to us when we walk in, you see. We have made those decisions, and in making those decisions, we have sold our soul to those levels of consciousness. Don't you see what we're doing to ourselves? It is in our own head. It does not exist outside of our own head. That's where heaven is, friends. And that's where hell is.

But isn't it wonderful that God, the Divine Intelligence, has granted us what is known as choice. We can decide at any moment whether we want to be in heaven, where it is so beautiful and active and progressive, or we want to descend into hell. You know, friends, I know of no greater hell than the hell of self-orientation. I know of no greater hell than the hell known as self-pity. So let us rise to heaven in our own consciousness. Let us not be concerned, when we walk down the street, whether somebody says, "You look so great today," or they don't even recognize us. Let us not be concerned with those things. Those things are the very things that take our soul to hell.

Let us not be concerned whether or not our friends tell us how great we are. Because if they keep telling us how great we are, they're not our friends: they're our worst enemies, because they're helping us to become self-oriented. Be cautious, my friends, when someone tells you how great you are. Be alert and be awake. Be careful. For you can descend into the delusion of your own self-importance. And that's what takes our soul into hell. Think about it. I do hope that's helped with your question. Yes.

Once, in discussing organization, you just mentioned in passing the word clarification, *but I wondered if you would go a bit into that.*

Thank you very much. The lady's interested in the word *clarification*, "to clarify." Now, what does that mean to us in our day-to-day acts and activities? We look at all experiences, of course, from the level that our soul is expressing on at that given moment. And so it is that, though man may experience an identical situation in the course of a day, one time he will have one understanding concerning it and another time he'll have a little different understanding. Because that is how man is viewing it: from different levels of consciousness.

However, there is a level of consciousness where clarification—"to clarify" and "to see clearly"—exists within our being. Now that, my friends, is through what is known as the expression of the superconscious. Now, when we bring into balance—the balance, of course, of our subconscious computer and our conscious mind—concerning any particular person, place, or thing, we free ourselves from the pattern on which the soul is expressing at that moment. Then, we are able to see objectively. We're not controlled by the patterns of the magnetic field, which see it according to what is already in the computer. Do you understand? Consequently, my friends, if you want to see clearly, then make the effort to become aware of your attitudes concerning the subject that you wish to see clearly.

Now when you become aware of those patterns, those attitudes, you bring that into the conscious mind; you bring them into a balance. And when you bring them into a balance—the electric and magnetic field of your own aura—the superconscious sees clearly and you have clarification. I hope that's helped with your question. Yes.

Could we, then, feel that simplicity is related to clarification?

Absolutely. That's why truth is simple and unconcealed. It is not concealed and controlled in the magnetic field. Yes.

Thank you.

You're welcome.

I believe this is on one of the last discourses or one of the seminars. And I read this over and over. And I would love to have your understanding on perceiving the colors of peace and harmony and poise flowing from us to help another. Would you give us your understanding of that?

Yes, would you like to read that section? Perhaps it would help the class.

Well, I have to read a little bit above that. May I?

Certainly.

"Each attitude of mind that you entertain releases from your aura a color and that color blends only with the colors that are harmonious to it. Therefore if your experiences are bitter, go into the silent sanctorium within and change your color. Learn to perceive the colors of peace, of harmony, of poise, and then the power will flow through you to serve all mankind [Seminar 1]."

Thank you very much. And I'm so happy the lady has brought up that question of peace, of power, of poise. It is, as we have said earlier, again and again and again, an inward journey. This is why it is so very important to view objectively all of our experiences in life. For they are the direct effect of the attitude of mind, the level of consciousness on which our soul is expressing at that moment.

Now many times a person, you see, will talk to another individual and consciously they feel a joy, a love, a peace, and they just want to have a sharing with the individual—and the individual immediately rejects them. Now we have to ask the question, Why does that happen? And it's a very important question. And the reason it happens, my friends, is this: the magnetic field of the subconscious is the stronger expression than the electrical field of the conscious mind. And so, though we are aware consciously of what we want to do, of what we're trying to say, we are aware of that, and we do not receive the results that we think we should because what the recipient—the person that we're talking to—is sensing and feeling is not what we're saying. Oh no, they are experiencing what we're emanating from the depths of our magnetic field, because our magnetic field is expressing the stronger vibration.

That is why so often in life a person says, "Well, I try to do good. I try to be pleasant. I try to be kind. And look at the experiences that I have!" You see, my friends? Yes, we're trying on a conscious level, but we're not aware of our true motivation. We're not aware of those subconscious patterns that are emanating the greater degree of energy. And the individual, oh, they *hear* us all right, loud and clear, but they *feel* us even stronger.

And so this is in reference to this teaching here that the lady has brought up on peace and poise—to become aware of our attitudes, you see, to become aware of our desires. Are we truly interested in sharing with the individual we're communicating with or are we just interested in fulfilling an addicted subconscious desire pattern? That is the question we must ask ourselves.

Now Life, she's revealing this to us with our experiences. Again we say that life is a mirror and all things in it are reflecting our level of consciousness. So we go out into life: if we have experience of peace and poise, then, my friends, this is what we are emanating from the depths of our inner being.

A person—now think—a person can talk to another individual about the weather and when the person has finished talking, the individual leaves, he feels just wonderful! Well, the topic of conversation was a very mundane topic of conversation, but there was an emanation of selfless love, emanating from the magnetic field of the individual that was talking.

This is one of the great wonders and beauties of entering the spirit realms. Every attitude emanates a color. The color, you understand, is seen in these other dimensions. And so no matter what we say, the color reveals our motivation. And it's a wonderful, wonderful, wonderful experience. Because, you see, it doesn't matter whether we're talking about politics, mathematics, religion, philosophy, or the weather. The color of our aura—that magnetic field—reveals what we're truly feeling. And so it goes to another teaching here in the book: When the lips speak as the heart feels, words become the expression of the wise. So, my friends, when we talk to people here or hereafter, let us say to ourselves, "What is my motive? What is my true motive?"

What makes a day beautiful for people or makes it miserable? Well, I can tell you honestly what makes it beautiful for most people and what makes it miserable: the fulfillment of desire or its suppression. If the desires are fulfilled, it was a beautiful day. If the desires are suppressed, it was a miserable day. And so we teach, When man educates his desires, he finds his true wealth.

Now what does this have to do with the question that the lady asked? It has everything to do with the question that the lady asked. When we become aware of our true motivation, of the depths of our inner mind in our subconscious, we won't have to ask what color this or that is, because we will feel, sense, see, and hear the color that that level of consciousness is emanating.

You see, my friends, we not only *see* color, we *feel* color and we *hear* color. But until we awaken more of our soul faculties, we won't hear the sound of the color blue or red or orange or pink or yellow. But, you see, color is vibration and vibration is sound. So, you see, when you wear a certain color, it not only vibrates and appeals or doesn't appeal to the eye, but it appeals or doesn't appeal to your hearing, to your sense of hearing, and your sense of feeling. This is why people, they look at a certain color, oh, they feel wonderful when they wear that color or they see that color. They feel wonderful because color *is* sound; it *is* feeling. And you can hear it, you can sense it, and you can see it. And this is why, when you're communicating with people, it's not just your words that they're sensing and they're hearing and they're seeing and feeling. It's your inner attitudes.

So look at life's experiences and say, "Thank you, God. Once again I am awakening to the fact that I'm on a level of consciousness that I do not appreciate." Thank you very much. Yes.

I notice sometimes that there is a distinction made between the words sense *and* feel. *Could you please share with us your understanding of that?*

Yes, thank you very much. Our sense of feeling we understand to be our original sense. Now, the lady has stated that she notes at times there is a distinction between the word *sensing* and the word *feeling*. And I'm sure, if you will listen attentively, that there are times when the word *sense* and the word *feeling* are interchangeable. That is entirely dependent upon the subject matter being discussed at any particular time. Does that help with your question?

Thank you very much.

Or is it—perhaps what you want to know is, What is the definite use and meaning of the word *sense*? And over here, What is the definite meaning of the word *feeling*?

Well, I don't care to limit it.

Thank you very much. That's why at some times you will find them used interchangeably and sometimes they have different meanings. But that is dependent upon the subject matter being discussed. Does that help with your question?

Yes.

You see, my friends, it's very important in understanding your awareness classes that you move with the spirit of the law, for it is the spirit of the law that frees you and it is the letter of the law that killeth. Why does the letter of the law killeth? For the letter of the law is the form of the law, and the form of the law is the limit of the law. And that, my friends, of course, having its beginning, has its ending. And so it is the spirit of the law that we seek to express. For when man speaks, there is a form created. And if we limit ourselves to the creation of that form, then we cannot move onward to broader forms, to greater freedom.

Thank you all very, very much. Let us go have refreshments. Thank you.

JULY 18, 1974

CONSCIOUSNESS CLASS 57

Good evening, students. Now for the benefit of our new students, and as a constant reminder to our regular students, the teachings of Serenity—the Living Light philosophy is the teachings of evolutionary incarnation: that our soul is not new, that it is not born at the moment of conception, but that the soul is evolving through time and space. It is not the teachings of reincarnation, which is an experience on Earth and an immediate return thereto. But it is an evolutionary process. And the circumstances and conditions that the soul enters at birth are a revelation to the soul of the lessons that it must learn in order to free itself from the bondage and the duality of creation. So it is the struggles that we have in life—and we all seem to have them—that are the lessons that need the greatest attention, for those are the things that we did not pass through in a prior expression of life.

Now, the souls do not differ in quality. They do differ, however, in quantity. Some souls have had many expressions in form. And some have learned few lessons, while other souls have learned many. But remember that eternity is the moment of which you are consciously aware. It is the only moment that you can do something with.

So we try to teach in these philosophy classes an awareness of the laws that govern our life. One of those first laws is the

Law of Personal Responsibility. Man, indeed, is a law unto himself. Whenever man entertains a thought in mind, he sets a law into motion. The thought does not dissipate into the nothingness. So it behooves us to become aware of what our thoughts are, what our attitudes are, and how to control them. It is also through our daily process of concentration and meditation—an awakening within ourselves to the depths of our own so-called subconscious mind, which is known as the great computer, the brain computer. Whatever has been accepted in that computer has established a law. And man is governed by these patterns beneath his own conscious level of awareness.

And so, my friends, awareness is the name of our course. And it takes effort on your part. If it means enough to you, then you will awaken and free your soul. No one will tell you how you have to do it, because you will know how to do it, because you will gain self-awareness—awareness of what brings conditions and circumstances into your life, how they work through an electromagnetic field, known as your own aura, and how to change those experiences that seem to be distasteful at times.

Now you're free to ask any questions concerning this philosophy, if you will be so kind as to raise your hands. Yes.

I wonder if you would discuss more deeply the functions of suspicion and credulity and how these relate to acceptance.

Thank you very, very much. And the lady is referring to our teachings of the functions. And, for our new students, we understand and teach that there are eighty-one levels of consciousness, that we have soul faculties and sense functions, that creation or form is the law and expression of duality. And so the lady is asking in reference to one of those teachings, known as the circle of logic, which is balanced by credulity and suspicion, and how these affect, if they do affect, what is known as acceptance.

Now, my friends, we teach that acceptance *is* the divine will, that man's acceptance is dependent upon the acceptances of yesterday and those acceptances of yesterday have become an established law in the depths of our own mind. And so when man is out of balance with either his credulity, which means easily imposed upon, or his suspicion, then the function of logic is not expressing itself fully. Therefore, if we are overly suspicious, we are not expressing logic. And not expressing the function of logic, we are not receptive to accepting what is not already in the computer. Do you understand? Therefore, my friends, balance your credulity with your suspicion. Then, you will be free to broaden your horizons and to accept the possibility of all things.

You see, all things, to the Divine Intelligence, are possible. The reason man does not experience the possibility of all things is because man has limited his acceptance and therefore man is not expressing the fullness of what we call the divine will. I do hope that's helped with your question. Yes.

Would you, please, discuss more fully on Discourse 33, that all color is vibration and if you wish to help another, you must first see and know the color of your so-called aura.

Yes.

If one is not clairvoyant, how can we help another?

Thank you very much, student, for that question. The reference to the word *seeing* is not referring to *clairvoyance*, which we understand is a spiritual talent or seeing beyond the physical senses. It is referring to *seeing* in the respect of awareness. Now when a person becomes aware, they know the vibration of themselves. They know their own aura at any given moment. Knowing their own vibration, they are then in a position to know the vibration of another. Now, it does state that when you're of a pure heart and a sound mind, you are expressing a white aura or an aura or vibration of purity.

Now, a person may say, well, as the lady has spoken, if you're not clairvoyant, then how are you going to know the aura of another? Because you sense it. You see, my friends, everyone is clairsentient. That means "sensing clearly." That's that inner knowing. But few of us pay any attention to it. Now the reason we don't pay attention to our own clairsentience is because of our educated brain. That is what has limited us in this life and all lives. Because of our lack of accepting something that is not already in our program or can be related to a pattern in our brain, we limit ourselves and therefore do not see clearly. I do hope that's helped with your question.

In prior incarnations, have we always had a brain?

The soul has always expressed in form and has always had a brain to some extent, yes.

I'm referring back to your comments about evolutionary incarnation. I've been puzzled about how so many different philosophies or understandings can be present here on this Earth. I want to believe in the evolutionary incarnation theory or statement or reality—whichever it is. And I also find that other people make equally strong statements about reincarnation. And I'm confused about those two. I wonder if you could help me in reconciling how the two can coexist. How does one figure out what, indeed, is the truth, if people are presenting their reality so firmly?

Thank you so very, very much for your question. And the lady appears to be a bit confused in what to accept. When man accepts the possibility of all things and is disturbed by no things, then man is free and is truly expressing what is known as the divine will. For example, my friends, the lady is referring to a particular theory known as reincarnation or the return to this Earth life. If we look at nature, we will have a living demonstration of the process of evolution. Now, if a person is receptive to that teaching at any moment, then that is the teaching for them. If they are not receptive to that teaching at any given moment, then for them that teaching, of course, will be of no value.

Now, we have taught, and we repeat again, that truth is individually perceived. Therefore, my friends, if you will be receptive to your own spirit and your own soul, the seeming contradictions of the world of form, which is duality, will not disturb your mind, your spirit, and your soul. That is what we're trying to teach. We're not trying to put something into your brain. We're trying to show you a way to free yourself from the educated brain, that you may find truth. Because, you see, my friends, only you, as an individual, can find your truth. You can read untold thousands of volumes of books and teachings, but unless you make the effort to go deep inside yourself, you will not find truth and you will not be free.

We have stated earlier that there are eighty-one levels of consciousness. Some of those levels are receptive to certain teachings. And then, our soul is fluctuating through these levels of consciousness throughout the course of a day and throughout the course of a moment. So it depends, my friends. Don't you see? At one time in your life, at one moment, you're receptive to a certain teaching; only in the next day, you're receptive to some other teaching. So where is truth? It's inside, my friends. Remember, the moment you speak, you put the energy of the Divine into creation. You put it into form. It's called words. And that form guarantees its own opposite. This is why we teach that silence is not only golden, it is the divine wisdom expressing itself. All teachings, my friends, are guidelines to help you in your soul's evolution to find yourself. And when you find yourself, your true self, you will no longer be disturbed by God's manifestation, which is known as variety. I do hope that's helped with your question.

Good evening. The question sort of came up in a meditation and I thought I would ask this question. Could you give me your understanding of concentration and awareness? And also, a second question, dealing with us as students. As we are becoming a little bit more aware of ourselves, we realize that as we recognize ourselves that we are becoming—how would you say?—so unaware of our awareness. As we sort of unfold, we sort of tend to become so unaware of things and yet we realize the mistake that we're making. And yet we still continue to be in that particular level of consciousness. Could you give me your understanding?

Yes, certainly. Thank you very much. And the gentleman is speaking first on concentration and awareness. Now we do teach that concentration is the key to all power. Awareness is the effect of that power.

Now the gentleman has also spoken that some of the students are becoming more aware of their unawareness, and yet they continue on with the awareness of their unawareness and the unawareness doesn't seem to become awareness. Well, my friends, think how old we are and how long we've been here just on Earth alone. The Law of Repetition has put us where we are today. And only the Law of Repetition will move us on to another level of consciousness, to another plateau in life. And so do not be discouraged when, in a matter of a few months or a few years, you are becoming aware of how unaware that you have been and that that unawareness continues to express itself in your life. Because, my friends, you cannot compare one year with forty-some years. Would you not agree? And so if you permit yourself to be discouraged because of your awareness of your unawareness, you will only become more unaware because discouragement is self-orientation.

You see, my friends, when we're discouraged, we're not thinking about God. We're not thinking in universal consciousness. We're thinking about ourselves. And [when] we think about ourselves, we're thinking in limitation. Because, after all, I'm sure we'll all admit we're limited. We have a body and we can move it here and there, but it is not the whole universe, although it is an inseparable part thereof. And so, my friends, gratitude opens the door to supply. And when we are grateful for the crumbs, we will guarantee the loaves.

Now if it is true—and it is demonstrably true—that gratitude is the law of abundant, continuous supply in whatever we may be seeking, then it is also true that ingratitude is its opposite and guarantees lack and limitation. And so, my friends, let us stop and think, and let us say, "Thank you, God. At least now I'm aware of how unaware I am. Before that, I wasn't even aware of my unawareness." And so, you see, it is an evolutionary step. And I do hope that's helped with your question. Yes.

Thank you, sir. Are we speaking to the Wise One this evening?

Is it important to you?

Well, it's a story that he related and I wanted to know—

I'm sure we'll be happy to answer it if we can.

All right. In Discourse 2, it says, "You know, oh, so long ago, so many centuries ago, there's an old, old story, a story about a diamond chariot and an old ox wagon. The diamond chariot was drawn by the fastest of animals, and one day a gentleman, burning with enthusiasm, wanted to know all about all things—now. Not tomorrow, but now." And do we go on and know that the gentleman sped and sped, but the ox wagon—I wondered if a story could be told regarding the ox wagon at this time.

Thank you very much for your question in reference to that particular allegorical statement. And I think if you will ponder and study it, that it is referring to the law known as patience. We teach that wisdom lives in patience and that the functions of impatience block the eternal Light from our view. And so it is, my friends, what does patience do for us? Does it help open our soul faculty of faith?

Yes.

Does it open up hope in our heart?

Yes.

Does it increase courage, determination, and continuity?

Yes.

And so it is, my friends, in all your getting, get understanding. But I assure you there is no understanding without patience. There is no understanding without the soul faculty of tolerance, for man cannot understand what he cannot tolerate. And he certainly cannot understand what he does not have the patience to thoroughly investigate. I hope that's helped with your question. Thank you.

Good evening. In tonight's talk or reading dealing with colors and vibrations, there's one portion here that says, if you "open your vision, you will perceive, not necessarily in the way you think, but you will perceive the color of vibration and in doing so you will help many to help themselves [Discourse 33].*" My question is, How do you open your vision and how does a human being perceive in colors?*

Thank you so very much. And I would like to refer to that statement because it's related to a question earlier from the lady in group eight. If you open your vision you will perceive, but not in the way that you think. Is that not part of the statement? Not in the way that you think, you see. The teaching is referring to the soul faculty's awakening. It is referring to the process of humility. When man is truly humble, he accepts the possibility of all things. It is when man is in his educated ego that man decides what's best. Now there's a statement that when man decides what's best, all is hell. When God decides what's best, all is well. Now that statement is not referring to some power outside of us. It is referring to the God, the Divine Spark that is deep within our own being.

You see, my friends, what we want to seek is wisdom. Remember that knowledge knows much, but it is wisdom that knows better. And so let us think for a moment, not on the letter of the law, but on the spirit of the law. For it is the spirit of the law that giveth life; the letter of the law is what killeth.

Now I know that you want to know the process by which you may perceive these auras and these sensations and this awakening. If you will do your part in a daily, simple meditation, never forgetting that truth is simple and unconcealed, always remembering that falsehood is complex and deeply hidden, I assure you the awakening will come from within the depths of your own spirit.

It is not our purpose in these philosophy classes, my friends, to teach you techniques. That is not our purpose. Our purpose here, in these awareness classes, is to share with you our understanding of the universal laws of life that govern all of us, that govern all things, at all times, in all places. And remember that God is the greatest servant of all. And so when we are humble enough to be a servant, then we will express our godliness. I do hope that's helped with your question.

We have been taught about the Law of Continuity and following a thing through to its completion. Can you give us your understanding of the difference between habit and continuity? If we are present in something that is not seemingly—and I use the word seemingly—*good for us, how can we, without putting another law into action that would be just as negative, get out of that situation? I think I have the answer, but I would appreciate it if you would help me with that.*

In reference to the lady's question of habit or habit patterns and continuity and what is their relationship with each other, if any: my friends, habit takes no effort. Continuity does. Habit takes no conscious thought. It has become an established law of the subconscious. Continuity takes constant thought. And so man must choose what it is that he desires in life, what it is that he is truly seeking, and it must mean enough to him to demonstrate the Law of Continuity. Does that help with your question?

Thank you.

You're more than welcome. Yes.

I wonder if you could help me. I have a difficult time trying to understand meditation, contemplation, and concentration.

Thank you. Yes. Our teachings do not refer to contemplation. However, they do refer to concentration and meditation. Now, concentration we understand to be placing the mind pointedly and fixedly upon the object of our choice until only the essence remains. Now we do teach it is advisable for the student to concentrate upon peace. When a person is truly concentrated, they become the thing of their concentration. If it is peace, they become that peace. They no longer think about it, because they become it.

In reference to meditation, meditation, in our understanding, is when the mind is perfectly still. There is no thought that enters it. There is no image. There is no picture. There is no feeling. Does that help to clarify that for you?

Thank you.

You're more than welcome. Yes.

You said earlier that the struggles that you have in life are lessons that you haven't overcome or learned yet. I was wondering, do those lessons come from within us? Because it seems like sometimes we're not quite ready to learn the lesson that was given to us. Because sometimes it feels like the lessons are coming from outside of us. Yet I must have put some law into motion that made them also come to me.

Thank you very, very much. Now remember, friends, the body cannot ever experience what the mind has not first accepted. Do you understand? So all of your experiences in life, this moment and any moment, are the effect of an acceptance on a certain level of consciousness at some time. So often people think that, "Well, I never accepted this situation that I'm experiencing," because, my friends, we forgot the laws that we set into motion yesterday and the years before. Yes, all things take place within our own consciousness. Do you understand? And though we may feel or think that we are not ready for an experience, that is not true. All experiences we encounter, we've set the law into motion and we are well prepared to go through the experience.

Now there is help. There's help within the depths of our own being. Regardless of the experience, look for the good and the benefit that you can gain from it. Because there is no experience in life, here or hereafter, that does not have good in it that's waiting to express itself. The experiences, my friend, are not from out there: they are generated from within our own consciousness. They are attracted to us according to the Law of Magnetism, according to the attraction of our own subconscious mind. Does that help with your question? Thank you very much.

I have a question regarding time and whether or not it's related in some way to the Law of Continuity.

Thank you very, very much. The lady is asking in reference to time and its relationship, if any, to the Law of Continuity. Well, let us stop and ponder for a moment about the word *time*. Time is an illusion. It is a conscious awareness of passing events. Now when a person is interested in anything, their time consciousness is not as accurate as when they are bored with something. Do you understand? Now, if you are referring to time and the Law of Continuity in reference to the effort necessary to attain any particular goal in life, then, yes, there is a direct relationship. Because, you see, my friends, we're living in a realm of illusion. You open your eyes and you see this a certain way. Someone else opens their eyes and they see it a little differently. You see, it's all created in our own consciousness. Does that help with your question?

Yes. And remember, friends, there is no time and space. And we are the eternal moment in that space. And Life, she's just the way we take it and she's ever as we make it. And so if we become interested in how limited our time is, then we may be rest assured we will guarantee the limitation of that time because we have directed energy through the vehicle of thought to that level of consciousness. And we will guarantee all experiences necessary to justify our declaration of time consciousness. Does that help with your question?

Yes. Thank you.

You're more than welcome.

I would appreciate very much having your understanding of the difference between mind *and* brain. *Do we say, "My mind concentrates" or "My brain concentrates"? Perhaps there is no difference, but we hear about this mind so much. Would you tell me what that is?*

Thank you very much. In reference to mind and brain, we understand that brain is merely the physical vehicle through which the mind expresses itself. However, the brain is like— you can liken it, perhaps, unto a phonograph record. Certain patterns have been established and when your mind, your consciousness, gets into the groove, it continues to play that particular pattern or whatever it is. You know, people wake up in the morning and they go through a certain process and the needle goes into the groove. And if something comes up to change their morning routine, they immediately go into frustration and usually express the function known as anger. This is because of their unwillingness to make the effort to adapt, to adapt to change. You see, the Law of Evolution is the Law of Change. And so when you are receptive, through this divine will of acceptance, to change, then you're flowing with the evolution, your soul is rising and evolving, and your horizons become broadened. But, of course, it's up to us, friends. It's not up to anything or anyone outside of us. The only change we're going to make is the change we're willing to accept and then apply. Thank you.

I just opened the book and I turned to Discourse 39. I have heard this expression before, "spiritual arrogance," but I've never heard a question regarding it or the Wise One's answer to this. It says, "Balance in all things, balance in your endeavors." I've noticed it in other philosophies, but rarely have I seen it in this. Could you give me your understanding of it?

In reference to spiritual arrogance? Thank you so very much. Man cannot be arrogant spiritually, but man can be arrogant concerning his knowledge of spiritual matters. Yes. And then, that's referred to as "spiritual arrogance." Now, what happens to some souls, as they begin to awaken in study of spiritual subjects and matters, they start to think how much more they know than anyone else. And then, what happens with that knowledge that they think they have, they guarantee to lose because they dissipate it through what is known as the brain or ego level of consciousness. If we have truly awakened inside of ourselves, then we don't have to say that we're humble: we just are. And we don't have to ever tell anyone we are, because everybody knows that we are, if that's what we've really done.

You see, my friends, when we speak about things on how great we're growing, we set a law into motion and we guarantee all of the experiences necessary to understand what we are declaring as a truth for ourselves. Let me say that once more, perhaps so everyone, hopefully, can understand it. When we speak—the spoken word is life-giving energy. And when we speak, a law goes into motion. And if we say how we're growing, thank God we've grown to the point that we have, we send that law out and it bounces back to us with all of the experiences necessary for us to demonstrate what we've said. Do you understand? So it doesn't behoove us, my friends, to tell the world how great we are, because we'll have whatever is necessary to test and demonstrate our greatness. Do you understand?

Yes.

Now that's how it works, friends. And think! God, the Divine Intelligence, is a great servant, the humblest of the humble. So who is man that he is yet greater?

I would like to ask a question about concentration to obtain peace. I thought you said the first thing we must obtain will be peace.

That is correct.

Let's say that after a certain amount of concentration, we do obtain this peace. Now, my question is, As the course of a day goes by, a month and so on, do you try, after you do obtain this peace, to obtain something better, something more, in other words?

There is nothing greater, sir, than peace.

Now if in the events of the day you become angry, in other words, if you do lose this peace, do you have to start all over again, to concentrate again?

No, you do not.

Are you going to lose anything else going to this peace?

No, you only gain the greater good through peace. Now, if you are concentrating daily, in a daily meditation, upon peace, in the course of a day, when you lose this feeling and awareness of peace, you can, by the law of thought—you understand?—and recall within your own mind, tune into that meditation moment, and instantaneously regain that level of consciousness in time of greater need. Do you understand?

Now, peace, my friends, brings you all good in your life. It is Peace which we call God, the Divine. Peace balances all things in your life in a harmonious way. And your good health is the direct effect of a balanced mind, between your conscious and your subconscious. When the electrical mind of your conscious is in balance with the magnetic mind of your subconscious, you are then, and then only, receptive, through the superconscious, to the Divine Power, known as God or Peace. Does that help with your question?

Thank you.

You're more than welcome.

I'm interested in relating some questions that have come down about time and about making changes in my life. If a person, for example, should get into a level, or levels, which cause him to become ill, say physically ill, or to lose the peace, as you were just describing, and the body becomes ill, then the person moves into the levels of peace again, or can climb to that—I'm interested in the residual. Is it necessary for there to be a time—and I think this can be psychological changes as well as physical changes—is it necessary that a person spend a certain amount of time regaining his physical health or his emotional health once he's taken his mind to another level?

Thank you so very, very much. And it's a very important question. That will depend, of course, upon the individual and how he or she sets the law into motion. For example, it doesn't necessarily deal with so many days, weeks, or months. No. If a person has gone into a certain level of consciousness where there is an inharmony and their body is expressing the effect of this inharmony—do you understand?—what is necessary to bring back the balance is not necessarily a matter of time. If 60 percent of the person's energy has gone to create that particular level of consciousness, then it will take 60 percent to bring it back out of that level of consciousness. Is that understandable? Now, that may take a day, a moment, a week, or years. That depends upon the individual. But it is ever in equal proportion. You see, the way out of a thing is the way that we went into the thing in the first place. So an equal amount of energy must be directed to bring the soul to another level of consciousness, where the transformation will take place. Does that help with your question? Yes.

Thank you very much. When the knowledge exists that something is the truth and there's a desire, or aspire, to seek that, what can be said of asserting the will?

A very good question. Thank you very much. When there is a desire to seek knowledge or awareness, the man is asking the question, What can be said about asserting the will? Now, let us understand that we have the will of the functions, the will of the human brain and mind. We have the will of achievement, the will of accomplishment. We have the will directed into the function of greed, into the function of envy, and into all of the various human functions. Do you understand? So when a man is seeking to awaken his mind to spiritual truths, then man must go into the silence inside himself and find his true motive. Now, my friends, when the motive is pure, the method is legal. And so it is in reference to will. Is the individual receptive to the divine will? The divine will considers all things, respects all creation, seen and unseen—do you understand?—and is free from the limitation and the will of the human brain.

Now in reference to that question, let us clarify our understanding that man has 10 percent free will: that's known as his choice. The other 90 percent is the fulfillment of the law of what he chose yesterday. You see, once having made a choice in anything, we've set the law into motion and we've got 10 percent free will to change that, but no more. Do you understand? And so it is if you are truly seeking to awaken the mind to the spiritual truth that is within your own being, then it will come peacefully. The intellect will not have to tell God which way you're to experience it. Do you understand? And the intellect won't have to tell God how long it's going to take, because you will be in divine will, which is total acceptance. Does that help with your question?

Thank you.

You're more than welcome.

My question is, I think I understood you correctly to say when correcting an illness in the body, in the mind—and if you can detect it in your soul—applying energy to correct it to the proportion that you've used energy to gain it—

That is correct.

Now that would depend upon, let's say, the efficiency of gaining health would depend upon naming the cause correctly. No?

No. It does not. You're working with the mind now, my friend. You're dealing with the human intellect and the educated brain. You see, that's not what does the healing. That's not where the healing takes place. You see, it is not necessary to know whatever a physical or mental condition is in order for it to be healed. Because the Divine Intelligence knows all things. All man needs to do is to be receptive to that Divine Intelligence and to let go. Now when man lets go, that means that his thought, which is the vehicle through which his energy is expressing, is no longer going to that level of consciousness. Do you understand?

You see, this is so important, my friends. Ofttimes we get into a level of consciousness—whether it's lack and limitation, whether we think we need abundance of this or abundance of that—and we think about it. And the more we think about it, the more energy we direct to that level of consciousness. Don't you see? When man forgets about a thing, God goes to work. Does that help with your question? See? Yet that's the hardest thing for the human brain to do. There is nothing more tenacious than the human ego. There is no four-legged creature in all of the universes that has the tenacity of the human brain.

But what does it take to let go, my friends? What does it take to let go? Would you agree that it takes faith? I think, perhaps, we'd agree that it takes faith. But faith in what? Faith in an intelligence that holds all the stars in the universes; that it is capable of moving the planets in space. Think about that. That intelligence, man cannot possibly compete with. And yet man does not want to let go and let God move his life.

We must ask ourselves the question, "Why? Why is this so?" Have we, as men, become so important in the universe that whatever we think is in our best interest, that we and we alone must make the decision? My friends, it takes a little bit of reliance, a little teeny bit. It takes an acceptance to say, "Well, I can't seem to put my finger on this intelligence, yet it moves my body around, it causes me to think, it causes the plants and the trees to grow. I think I'll give it a chance to get me out of the mess that my brain has got me into." Think about that, my good students.

What does worry do? It moves like a rocking chair and gets nowhere. But what does God do? That Intelligence, it moves any and all obstructions if our brain will permit it to do so. Man's only limitation in life, in any life, is his denial of God. Don't you see that, my friends?

Have you not heard the statement a thousand times that God helps those who help themselves? He certainly does, the Divine Intelligence. God helps those who are willing, ready, and able to say, "I recognize your intelligence is greater than my intellect." Then we get help, my friends. That's when we get help. But ofttimes we've got to go to the bottom before we will let go of what is known as the human brain and let that great power go to work in our lives.

It says in the Bible that least ye become as little children, ye shall not enter the kingdom of heaven. We understand that heaven is not a place you're going to. It is a state of consciousness that we're growing to. Now, in order to grow to go to that heaven, to grow to that state of consciousness, the prophets of old have taught us that we must become as little children. Well, let us look around at little children and let us see what little children are really like. They have faith. They have belief. They have acceptance. And all is well in their little world. They don't worry whether or not there's going to be food on the table: they just accept it's just automatic. And because they do accept, they receive. And so, friends, let us grow to heaven. And let us grow to it now. Let us not think about heaven after this so-called thing called transition, which the world calls death. Let us grow to heaven this moment through a change in our attitude, which is the effect of control of our thoughts.

Now we have time, perhaps, for one more question.

I would like to offer for consideration the possibility of finding a more satisfactory word for the human race than the limited word man.

Thank you very much. Have we considered the root meaning of that word *humanity* before we choose to change it? Have we considered the root meaning of the word? *Man* is an abbreviation of *human*. And so let us consider the root meaning of the word *human*. Do you have the root meaning?

No, I don't.

Yes. But I would suggest, my dear student, first to study and bring the root meaning of the word. And perhaps we can have some discussion over it before considering that perhaps we have more wisdom or knowledge than those who have brought it into being, because it has a very great meaning and it has a very spiritual meaning. So I do hope you will consider that.

I see our time is way past. Please join us for refreshments. Thank you.

SEPTEMBER 5, 1974

CONSCIOUSNESS CLASS 58

Good evening, students. I would like to speak for a few moments on something that we are all familiar with and that is commonly referred to as desire. Now we all have experience daily, of course, with what we call desire, but let us think for a few moments about what desire really is. What is it that man desires? We look across in the world and we see there is a limitless variety of things that man desires in a lifetime. Now we must ask ourselves the question, "Why does man desire the untold variety of things that man does desire?" We desire because we believe that what we desire will bring us some satisfaction or some type of benefit.

Now I wanted to speak for a few moments on desire and belief, because our lives are controlled by what is known as the forces of desire and belief. And when we think for a few moments about that, the question must arise, What does that all have to do with faith? For it has been stated, Keep faith with reason, for it is reason that will transfigure you. And so we see that man believes what he desires and he desires because he believes that it will be some good. But what about faith, my friends?

We have faith that what we believe is right for us. And so we must question our own minds of what it is that we choose to believe in life. For we, and we alone, are setting the law into motion. And we, and we alone, are giving the divine power to people, places, and things outside of ourselves. We give power to our employer. We give power to this material world. We give power to our husbands, our wives, our children, and our families and professions. And the degree of power we give to these things, to that degree are we the slave of those things. How does man regain his divine right, the divine right to perfect peace and freedom, the divine right to fulfill the true purpose of his soul's incarnation? He only gains that, my friends, by becoming aware—aware of what he insists upon giving power to. How do we give power? We give power with our mind and with our thought.

And so now you're free to ask any questions concerning the subject matter discussed, anything that is discussed in *The Living Light*, or anything of a spiritual nature that interests you at this time. And remember, my friends, if a question is important enough for you to entertain in mind, then it is indeed important enough for you to speak it forth and consider the answer which may be forthcoming. Thank you.

In tonight's discourse it says, "We understand that it is not advisable to pierce the aura of form without understanding how to properly close it." What is the proper way of closing it?

Yes, thank you very much. And the particular discourse, Discourse 36, is referring to what is known as psychic surgery. Whenever there is a surgery—and I know that some of you are aware or familiar with psychic surgery and some are not. All form exists in what looks like an egg. And that shape, or that egg, is known as its aura. Now when this aura is pierced in psychic surgery, as it is, the surgeon—the psychic surgeon—must have the awareness to know how to close that aura. You're not dealing with physical substance. You're dealing with ethereal substance.

If the physician—the surgeon, psychic surgeon—does not know how to close an aura that he has pierced or opened, then that aura, which is the vibration of that particular form, that individual, is open to any influences to enter directly into their magnetic field.

How do we close the aura once it is pierced? By knowing the science of vibration. And what is the science of vibration? It is an understanding of color. For color is vibration and color is sound. I hope that's helped with your question. Thank you.

In Discourse 51, if I may bring this up tonight, it says, "He who thinks in a universal way shall act accordingly." Would you give us your expression on acting in a universal way?

Thank you very much. And it may simply be stated, he who thinks in a universal way will act accordingly. And a universal way of thinking is known as total consideration. It considers the seen, as well as the unseen. And therefore an individual who is thinking in a universal way will be a person who expresses total consideration in all areas. Thank you very much.

We've been taught that reason has total consideration. And I wonder if you would, perhaps, relate reason to our universe.

Thank you very much. Yes. Man does not, in truth, express reason until he has understanding, for man cannot be reasonable with anything that he does not fully understand. And so it is the teaching is that in all our getting, to get understanding.

Once we have gotten understanding, then we are in a position to use what is known as the soul faculty of reason. Now, understanding is the foundation of all the soul faculties and reason is an expression of total consideration. When man has total consideration in anything, then he can balance whatever it is that he is considering. And it is perfect balance, my good students, that is known as reason. Thank you.

There is a proverb that says, "Physician, heal thyself." Would you give me some in-depth meaning to those words?

Thank you very much. Any person seeking to heal another is not truly qualified to do so until they have first healed themselves.

Now, I know a lot of you will disagree with that statement, because you will say, "Well, I went to the physician. He was very sick himself with the flu, but he gave me what was necessary for me and I'm now perfectly healed." My friends, the only thing—if you call symptom removal healing, then, of course, that statement could be known as true. But symptom removal is not healing. It's only a covering of the effect. It is not a removal of the cause.

Now, a healer, any healer—be a medical doctor or be a spiritual healer or whatever—they themselves are simply, merely the channel through which a balance of electromagnetic energy flows, through them as a channel, into the patient's aura. The healing itself takes place within our own consciousness. You see, my friends, if you go to a doctor, he doesn't heal you. If you go to a spiritual healer, she or he does not heal you. God, the Divine Energy, the Infinite Intelligence, is, in truth, the only healer. Now, according to our receptivity to this balanced energy—which will balance out our own aura, our own being—is the healing made manifest.

Now, if a healer is not themselves balanced, then they are not a clear channel for this healing energy to flow through them. Do you understand? And so the Bible prophets have taught, "O physician, heal thyself." That is a great responsibility.

Remember, my friends, if we want to remove hypocrisy from our world, let us first remove it from ourselves. When we speak a word and make a declaration, let us first make that word and declaration a law for ourselves. Once we have done that, my good students, then we are qualified to share that understanding with another. If the individual is receptive to that understanding, then they themselves may demonstrate the same law. I do hope that's helped with your question.

I would like to check my present understanding with you about understanding. My present understanding of understanding is that it's an ever-changing frame of mind or consciousness. My question is, It seems that understanding has been spoken of in more of a finite term. In other words, perhaps I've gotten the impression that, perhaps, you evolve along your particular understanding until you arrive at the understanding. And I'm wondering if this is a correct interpretation of what I heard tonight. Or is understanding a continuum thing?

Thank you. Thank you very, very much for your question. In reference to *understanding*, it is indeed a continuum. However, we are, and have—and do express on—eighty-one levels of consciousness. Therefore, say, for example, that our soul is expressing on level twenty-seven of consciousness and we have a full understanding on that level of consciousness. We—our soul—may in the next moment move to level twenty-eight of consciousness and therefore the understanding is broadened even further. Does that help with your question?

Yes. Could I ask another question?

You may, certainly. Yes.

Thank you. The question then is, Does the being find himself frequently evolving into a higher state of consciousness and then falling—in other words, getting glimpses of understanding that perhaps are a higher level of consciousness, and then finding himself also back into his previous?

Absolutely. Expressing on another level of consciousness.

Almost at the same time.

Almost. Yes, because it's instantaneous. Level-of-consciousness changes are instantaneous. Now, this is why we teach that as we are in the process of unfolding, we do not make a declaration that we have grown to this point. Because if that declaration is made from the human—what we call—ego or brain, it will set a law into motion, sending our soul consciousness down to another level in order that we may gain more understanding. Do you understand? Yes. Does that help with your question?

Thank you.

You're more than welcome. Yes.

What makes us change levels of consciousness so fast?

So fast? Yes, thank you very much for your question. Because, my good friends, our thoughts, our attitudes change that quickly. Now, for example, you could be on your regular job and these mundane activities and one moment you have a thought and you feel good. And the very next instant, you have another thought and you feel terrible. Is that not your experience in life? Again and again, yes. And so it is because of a lack of self-control, a control of our own mind, we are moving, second by second, into these different levels of consciousness—because of a lack of control of our own being, our own mind. This is why the changes are constant fluctuation. Yes.

Sometimes it seems like my changes of levels of consciousness come from my subconscious.

Yes, my dear, that's where they do come from. Yes. See, this is why we teach divine will. Acceptance is divine will. You see, my friends, we're all governed and controlled by the patterns of our own subconscious of what we accepted yesterday. And so when a new experience comes into our life, it goes through the computer. If the computer doesn't have any reference to that experience, it knocks it out. It doesn't accept it: it rejects it. Do you understand?

Can you expand on that a little teeny bit more?

Well, for example, if you have an accepted pattern—an accepted pattern that you have to do certain things in life in order to have an abundance of material supply—that is a law that you have set into motion. Do you understand? Now, God did not set that law into motion. Man set that law into motion. Fine. Now, if a way is shown to you that you don't have to do those particular things in order to be receptive to God's abundant divine supply, what happens is the thought enters your mind, it goes into the computer, and the computer rejects it, because the computer has accepted a pattern over many years of the past.

Now, why does the computer reject anything that is not already programmed into it? The reason that it rejects new experiences and new thought is simply because it has found a false security in the things—the patterns of mind—with which it is most familiar. Does that help you?

Thank you.

You're more than welcome. Yes.

With reference to your answer to, "Physician, heal thyself," how does the healer get into balance in order to be able to heal?

Thank you. How does the healer get into balance in order to be the vehicle through which the healing power flows? The healer gets into balance by first becoming aware of themselves. You see, my friends, we can't do anything about our patterns until we become aware of those patterns. But once we become aware of those patterns, we can make a conscious effort to bring them into balance with our conscious thought.

You see, when the conscious thought—the conscious mind is the electric mind; the subconscious mind is the magnetic. And when the conscious thoughts are in harmony with the subconscious patterns, then man expresses balance and is, at that point and that point only, receptive, through his superconscious, to the Divine Intelligence, known as God. Does that help with your question?

Thank you.

You're welcome. Yes.

Could you elaborate a little bit more on the word expression, *the spoken word, and also elaborate a little bit more on the original sense of touch? Does this follow the vibration or the ability to sense or the spoken word or vibration?*

Thank you very much. The sense of touch, the sense of feeling came first. And then it evolved to the other senses, such as the sense of sight, the sense of hearing, and the sense of smell, etc. The sense of touch, the sense of feeling is the first and original sense and it is the most accurate sense in the human form.

In reference to the spoken word, we teach that the spoken word is life-giving energy. Now, when we speak any word into the atmosphere, if our mind and our heart are united, it goes out into the universe and it accomplishes that which we send it to do. Now, a person may say many things in life and very few, if any, of them may be accomplished. The reason that they're not accomplished, my friends, is they haven't put their soul consciousness into the words that they are speaking.

But your sense of touch, your sense of feeling is the most accurate. You can see many things with the eyes and you can hear many things with the ears, but there is a sense known as clairsentience—clear sensing—that is absolutely accurate in all forms. Thank you very much.

Would you give us your understanding on love as it is described in The Living Light, *the love of the Divine, the pure love, and belief.*

Thank you. Well, my friends, *love,* as referred to in this book, is not referring to conjugal love. Conjugal love has need, want, and desire. Now, we're referring here in this teaching to what is known as divine love.

Now what is divine love? Divine love is an expression of God, the Infinite Intelligence, and it has the same feeling when it's looking at a sunset or another human being. Now there's a big difference between divine love and conjugal love. Divine love is fulfilled in and of itself. Conjugal love has a need, a need within itself, to share an experience with another. Divine love does not. Divine love is totally impartial. As I say, it loves the trees and the sunsets with the same feeling that it loves another human being. Does that help with your question?

Now what does that have to do with belief? Well, my friends, we believe many things. The truth of the matter is that we have a group of about fifty people here who believe they're here! Well now, they will justify that they are here because their physical bodies are here or at least they believe they are here. But if they did not believe that, then they would not be here. Do you understand?

For example, we *believe* that today was rather a fall day. Well, it wasn't the summer that we've been having for so long. We believe that. I'm sure we will all agree. But the question is, Why do we believe that? Why do we believe it? Because we have accepted it somewhere in our life. And having once accepted it, my friends, we believe it. Because we've already had the experience. And so that's what life is all about. This is what we're talking about, my friends. This is what's controlling our lives. What we believe is what controls our life.

Then, a person will say, "Now, just a moment. Here are the facts." But what are facts? Facts, my good friends, are what we believe and somebody else agrees with. That's fact. But it's not truth.

See, truth will free us. Facts—they will bind us. Because, don't you see, if a man says, "I feel terrible and that's a fact, because my wife agrees with me and everybody else I talk to," is that freedom? No, but it certainly is bondage. But think, my friends. It's not truth. Yes.

I think that we believe what we perceive, not necessarily what we have been told.

Thank you very much.

Are you saying that our perceptions have no validity?

I am not saying that our perceptions have no validity. I am saying that our perceptions are dependent upon our acceptances in our subconscious. For example—think, my good friends. There is no greater blindness than the man who does not wish to see.

Now, let us take, for example, a domestic problem of a man and his wife. The wife says, "I perceive very clearly, my husband, that you have this problem." And he says, "I perceive very clearly that I don't have the problem, but you have the problem, because you're the one that's upset." Now who's right? Where are the facts? That's the great question. Now the wife may say, "All right, my girlfriend's coming over today and she's going to prove to you that you have the problem, not me." Fine. So the wife gets her friend and they both agree. Now we're two to one. So what does the husband do? He says, "This is a bunch of foolishness. I'd better get out of here or have her locked up." Think, my friends. What does that have to do with perception? Our perception is dependent upon what our subconscious has accepted in this lifetime. Think about that.

Now, you can present to anyone certain facts. Each person will look at them, but they will perceive them differently. A person wakes up in the morning. We all perceive the sun. We all perceive the sky. Not everyone feels the same. Now, it doesn't mean, my good friends, that perception has no validity. It does mean that perception is limited by our acceptance. And this is why the teaching is, "The ears of Ego heard not, / For the door was locked / By the key of fear." Think about it.

Yes, perception has validity and it has limited limitation. Does that help with your question, madam?

Yes, it does. What does have validity, then?

What has validity is truth. And truth, my good friends, is deep inside of our very soul. It is not something that you're going to find over there. It's not something you're going to find here. All of this is a sharing of understanding. Now in that sharing and in that exchange of thought—you hear?—depending upon your receptivity, depending upon your willingness to change, will your soul be freed. And that will all take place in the depths of your own being.

Now you may or may not credit some particular philosophy or person with that happening. But the truth of the matter is it only happens one place: it happens in our own consciousness. It doesn't happen anywhere else. Does that help?

Thank you.

You're more than welcome. Thank you for your question.

I have two questions. The first, with regard to talking about the difference between conjugal love and divine love, I wonder whether it's possible or something to aspire to for a person to transcend the want, need, desire that goes along with conjugal love while they are still in form.

Thank you very much. And still be involved in a relationship?

And still be involved in being a human being. I think I'd like to put it that way.

Yes. But you see, we must clarify what we mean by a "human being," "relationship," and "conjugal love," because, you see, we must have some clarification in order to build a solid foundation for understanding.

What I'm trying to deal with—

Yes.

Inside of myself is the idea of balance. As long as I am in form, it appears to me—and this is something that I am trying to understand—it appears to me that there are certain conditions to being in form. For example, I have emotion. I do have desire because I'm in form. Now, I would want to aspire to divine love. Sometimes I may translate that as meaning I must give up being human, meaning giving up the desire, etc.

I understand your question now.

That's what I'm trying to understand.

Yes. Thank you so very much for your question. Now, my friends, there are moments for all of us when, as the lady has stated, that we may transcend what is known as this want, need, and desire of conjugal love. There are moments of that, yes. However, in reference to desire, it is possible for any person not to entertain what is known as desire for conjugal love or companionship. That is definitely possible. Do you understand? But for any human soul to remain in form totally void of desire is a transgression of natural law and is not possible. Does that help with that question of yours? Yes. You see, when man no longer has any desires at all in anything, not even a desire to look at the stars and the sky, man will not long remain in form. Yes.

May I ask another—

Certainly.

It has to do with a question this lady asked about perception. The way I'm understanding the answer that you gave—well, I wonder if what you're saying is—you said that a perception came from our subconscious, the patterns that we've accepted in this lifetime, if I recall correctly.

That is correct. And the soul merited the form in which it incarnated, yes.

What I'm working with is environmental shaping of personality or of the individual. And that sounds like you're giving credence to the fact that environment does indeed shape the personality according to what a person or an individual has merited. They come into a situation—

Oh, there is no question. We are influenced by the environmental mind, the mass mind, etc. Oh yes.

Where is there room for what the person brings into this world? An infant has his parents there from the very beginning, or whoever is going to be caring for him. Where is there space—if the perceptions of the subconscious mind are based on what's coming in, how they're dealing with the material world—where is there space for what the individual has himself or 10 percent free will or whatever you want to call it?

Ten percent free will. Yes. Thank you very much for your question. For example, the soul enters into a newborn child here in this earth realm; it enters into a mold. Now that mold has certain tendencies, do you understand? And that mold is created, of course, by the parents and by the mother during the nine months which she carries this child. Her mind, her attitude, her subconscious molds and forms this little embryo. Do you understand? Fine.

Now the lady wants to know, Where is the so-called space or this 10 percent free will that we all have? It is within us, regardless [of] whether or not we can see it. Now, a child may be programmed by its parents to grow up and become a doctor. And yet right in the midst of his schooling, he changes his mind. Do you understand? There's always this 10 percent free will that we have to work with in everything. We're never left in any life without choice.

Now, it is true, once having made our choices, we set a law into motion. But setting that law into motion—say that we're halfway on the fulfillment of that law. That doesn't mean that we're void of choice. Oh no, we can still make another choice. Now this here remains to be fulfilled. Do you understand? So we're constantly moving through so-called time and space with all these loose ends we're trying to catch up on. Because today's desire is not usually yesterday's desire. Does that help with your question?

So, my friends, this is what we're talking about: to try to find out who you are and what you are. And, of course, then, you're going to know why you are where you are. You see? You won't have to ask God. And you won't have to ask your friends. Because you're going to know. Do you see what I mean? You're going to know what you are and why you are and where you are. Thank you.

I'd like to ask a question to increase my understanding of intuition, or what I consider intuition. When you were talking about clairsensing or touching, I was wondering if you could speak in terms—the word intuition *to me may have a different meaning along those levels. I was wondering if it's a way of—Is that an understanding that you have of somebody else that has to do with clairsensing, in other words, your intuition, your intuitive sensing of a circumstance or a person?*

Absolutely.

And what does it have to do with reading aura or is there a connection?

No. Our intuition or our clairsentience is an inner feeling and an inner knowing. It has nothing to do with seeing the aura of another human being in that sense or of hearing clairaudiently a voice, etc. Do you understand? But it is an inner knowing.

Now, if more of us would pay attention to what we call our intuition, we wouldn't have as many problems in life. However, this is what happens with this feeling known as intuition: we get this inner knowing and this feeling. And then, you see, it comes to the conscious awareness spontaneously. Then, the brain gets a hold of it and the brain says, "Well, now this is just totally ridiculous." Now, you must realize that the brain and the conscious mind is controlled by the accepted patterns of our subconscious. So it doesn't know too much, you know. It thinks it knows a lot more than it really does know. That's the truth of the matter.

Now, we have educated this old mind and brain of ours and we've poured in all kinds of facts, what we call facts. And what is a fact? A fact is something we believe and we've got a friend to support it. And that makes it a fact, don't you see. And so our intuition, which is the guidance from our own inner spirit, it knows—believe me—and it's constantly trying to tell us and to impress us not to do this, to wait on that, etc. But you see, the brain, the conscious mind—its only reference is what it has accepted. Does that help with your question?

Yes, it did.

You're more than welcome.

If fact is not the truth and is not a function, then what is theory? We hear of a theory to a certain rule or law. What makes it truth?

Well, my good students, the lady is referring to theory and fact. Now what is a theory? A theory is something that does not yet have popular support. Now the moment it has popular support, you now have a fact. For example, my friends, just look at history. It was an absolute fact that the Earth was flat. That was a fact. It was first a theory. It became a fact when it was accepted by the masses of people. Do you understand? Fine.

Now an atheist may say, "Well, this business about God and the Divine Power, that's some screwy theory the world's brainwashed to." Well, it's a theory to them because their particular view has not accepted it. Consequently, it's not supported by their group.

So we have a theory, we have a fact, then we have truth. Now what is truth? It is stated that truth is like a river: it continuously flows. It is also stated that truth is individually perceived. Now, we must ask ourselves the question, Does truth have limit? Does it? We all, I am sure, will agree that truth has no limit. Now, let us ask ourselves the question, Do facts have limits? They have limits. And I'm sure we'll all agree that theories have limits.

So, my friends, if you truly want to be free, then broaden your horizons. Be ever ready and willing to change. Then, you'll move in this great continuum. And you be rest assured, your truth will always be individually perceived and your God will ever be equal to your understanding. And this is why, you see, God keeps changing. God, the Divine Intelligence, doesn't change, but our receptivity, our growing understanding, keeps on changing and God is equal to that understanding in here. Does that help you with theory, facts, and truth?

It does. Could I ask another question?

Certainly.

We hear so much about the intellect and spirituality. Can you tell us the best way to spiritualize the intellect, because everything we get we question? Should we stop questioning and accept? Should we spiritualize the intellect in some means or manner? What is the best way to be spiritual?

Thank you. The lady is asking about the possibility—if it is possible to spiritualize the intellect and should we stop questioning. Now let us stop and think, my friends. Knowledge knows much, but wisdom knows better. Now, what is the intellect? What does it do? What is its purpose? What does it serve? It is a computer of facts and knowledge. Would you not all agree? Fine. Should we stop questioning? Certainly not. For remember, the power of the mind to question presupposes and guarantees, no less, its power to answer. But if our soul is expressing on the level known as intellect, then all of the answers that come on that level of consciousness will be based upon the acceptances of the computer of past time—do you understand?—and anything that is in harmony with the patterns that have already been accepted. So is that the place to ask a question? Is it really?

It's the place to ask a question if you want to know about your job and you've got all the facts here. And you open up the book of your mind and you read on page 16: oh yes, that's how it's supposed to be done! And you close the book and you go like the robot and you go do it. But that's not where you ask the eternal question of Life herself. That question, my friends, must be referred upstairs in the silent sanctorium of your own soul. And there you will get the answer. It may come, like we discussed earlier, through intuition. It may come through clairvoyance or clairaudience. It doesn't matter how it comes. But be rest assured, it will come if we are in the level known as humility. Because, you see, the level of humbleness is the God level. It's the level of the servant. For God itself, the Divine Power, is the greatest servant of all. It sheds its rain on the weed and the rose alike. It is not partial. And the sun shines on all of us when it shines. That is the humble servant known as God. And so when we're humble in our questioning, then, my friends, we're on a level of consciousness that is godly, meaning good and right. And then, we will get the right answer for us and for our own growth and understanding. Thank you.

A friend has asked me to present you with this question: If our soul came from the Allsoul and we're now in the process of trying to return to the Allsoul, what caused our initial departure so that we must go through all these levels and stages to get back? It seems that if we were once there, we would have remained there, rather than go through all the darkness and confusion to get back.

Thank you. If that was your question, I'd be more than happy to share our understanding; however, if that is from a friend, I would suggest that the friend consider classes. Thank you. And it's an excellent question.

She got the tape cassette. She would like to—

Oh, she would like—I see. Now the question is, if our soul came from the Allsoul—and whereas you are also interested in the question, then we'll endeavor to share our understanding concerning it—now, if the soul came from the Allsoul, why did it come out in the first place for individualized expression? It is the purpose of the Divine Intelligence to express itself. If you don't have form, the Formless does not become aware of itself. The Formless so-called Divine Spirit or God becomes aware of itself by expressing in form or individualizing. Do you understand?

Now, so the lady has asked the question, Why we come out in the first place and then, after we get out, why do we go back? Is that her basic question?

Why, why all this struggling and confusion to get back? Why do we have to go through all that?

Why all the struggle and the confusion? Because, you see, what happens, my friend—you know, it's like letting a lion out of a cage. Now, while you've got the lion in the cage, it's very placid and it does what it's told. And you feed it and you take care of the lion. And the moment you let the lion out of the cage, it goes wild. So when the soul individualizes into expression, you see, all of a sudden it becomes aware of how great it is. Now before that, it was a part of the Divine whole. And, as we earlier stated, God is humble. Now when this soul, this individualization process took place and we entered into form and we became aware, aware of ourselves, then what is known as ego individualization started to rise.

Now, therefore we have reached the point in time in form where many of us in this world already have decided we know more than God. Many of us, you understand, rely upon our intellect. We don't rely on the Divine Intelligence for what we should be doing about this or doing about that. We rely upon what we call our intellect. We rely upon the facts that are in our brain. Do you understand? Now that, my friends, is what has caused us all of the struggle. Does that help with your question? That's what causes us all of the struggle. Because our brain, our intellect, doesn't know everything. I assure you, my friends, it's not about to. There's not an intellect in the universe, including Albert Einstein, that knows everything. But at least that wonderful soul was smart enough to know it and to say it, as intelligent as he was and such a great intellect that he had. Thank you very much for your question.

What is the Law of Harmony and how does it guarantee unity?

Thank you very much for that question. It's in reference to our "Total Consideration" affirmation. *[See the appendix for the complete text of the "Total Consideration" affirmation.]* It's known as "The Law of Harmony is my thought."

Now, when you have a thought about anything, a conscious thought—do you understand?—there is a subconscious reaction or feeling. Would you not agree? I'm sure you've had thoughts about many things that you thought this and you felt something else. Do you understand? Fine.

The affirmation states, "The Law of Harmony is my thought and guarantees Unity in all of my acts and activities, expressing perfect Rhythm and limitless flow throughout my entire being."

This is the importance of these spiritual self-awareness classes and your daily meditation: to become aware. Now, when you have a thought, something happens back here in your magnetic field. That is the law of the mind and that is how it works. And when your conscious thought is in harmony with your subconscious magnetic computer, then whatever you speak forth shall manifest in the universe. Your universe. That's what it means. The Law of Harmony means our conscious thought—you understand—is in harmony and total acceptance with our subconscious pattern.

Now this is not possible, friends, until you make the effort through your daily silence and meditation—whatever you want to call it—to take the inward journey. It's only the inward journey that's going to free our soul. That's the only one that's going to free it: is the inward journey. When you do that, then you will know why you are experiencing life the way that you are. Does that help with your question?

Thank you.

You're more than welcome. Now, someone else was waiting. Yes, please.

How is Divine Intelligence different than the intellect?

Thank you very, very much. When we refer to Intelligence Divine or Divine Intelligence, we're referring to what the world calls God. How is it different than the human intellect? Vastly different, my good friend, because it knows all things past, present, and future and is the eternal Intelligence of the moment. The human intellect is dependent upon its own accepted patterns.

The Divine Intelligence is not dependent upon any patterns of any kind. Does that help with your question?

Ah, if you—if a being wants to become more intelligent and use less of their intellect, they would become just more open . . .

Through acceptance.

To Divine Intelligence and acceptance.

Yes. Remember, friends, we're seeking wisdom, not knowledge. The libraries are filled with books of knowledge and you've got all kinds of schools for that. It is my sincere hope and prayer that you are all here seeking wisdom, which comes from within the depths of your soul. We are simply sharing a philosophy and an understanding to be a guideline to help you on your inward journey. Yes.

Could you tell me the significance of opening The Living Light *to the same discourse or the same page time after time?*

Yes, thank you very much. Many of my students have *The Living Light* and they do, as a daily practice, open it up for the message that is there for them. Now, if they are sincere with themselves when they open that book, they will receive the message that is important for them at that time.

Now, if I sat each day, time after time, and opened it up to the same page repeatedly, I would certainly give that full study, because there was something there that I needed to learn about to help myself. Does that help you? Yes.

Now, many times, I know, some of my students don't appreciate that they open up to a certain discourse day after day and month after month, but then again, my friends, can we blame the book or the Divine because we're not yet willing to remove that obstruction from our mind? The one that keeps guiding us to that page? Yes, please.

What do you mean when you say, "Take the inward journey"?

What I mean by the statement, "Take the inward journey" is the journey through the mind to find our own soul. No one can do that for you. No one. No counselor, no doctor, no priest, and no minister can take the inward journey for you. Only you can do that. And depending upon your effort to go inward to find your true self, then that's where your freedom lies, because that's where your truth lies.

On page 126 of The Living Light *it says, "The lessons and application are easier while yet in material form and indeed it is true for many reasons [Discourse 46]." Can you tell us why?*

I'll be happy to share our understanding. It is stated that the lessons are easier while here in this physical clay and in this material world. They certainly are easier. You see, we have this dense physical body and we don't see what a thought looks like while we're in this physical—we don't see a thought with our physical eyes. We don't even hear a thought with our physical ears. But when you leave this body and you're expressing in your astral or, hopefully, spiritual body, then, my friends, you see what a thought looks like. Now, for example, you see, when you express a thought, it not only has a certain color and a certain sound, but it has a shape and it has a meaning. Not what you necessarily consciously think that thought should look like, but what has been created back here by that thought, what emotions you have concerning that thought. That is what it looks like. And this is why, my friends, learn about those things and make the effort to unite your being, your mind, and your feelings while you're still in the flesh. Thank you. Yes.

You just spoke of the astral body, the spiritual body, and the physical body. What is the difference between the astral body and the spiritual body? What are their different functions?

Thank you very much. Yes. Of course, a spiritual body is expressing on what is known as a spiritual world and an astral body in an astral world. Now, we all have an astral body. Otherwise, we wouldn't have this piece of clay, this physical body. Because this is an effect of the astral body, which, in turn, is an effect of the mental body—you understand?—and the vital body and on through.

Now, our spiritual body is created out of spiritual substance. Now this body is built and created through an expression of what is known as the soul faculties. Now if you do not have, as yet, a spiritual body created, of course, your soul will not be expressing on a spiritual realm after you leave the physical world. It will, however, be expressing on an astral mental realm, because we do have an astral and mental body. Does that help with your question?

Yes, I understand that much. I don't understand what the function of the astral body is or why it manifests or how it manifests.

Well, without the astral body, you wouldn't have a physical body. Now that you would not have. The astral body, many times, does leave the physical body during sleep and it does express in an astral realm at that time. However, now remember this, friends—and very few people realize it—your consciousness, which is God, cannot express in six different bodies while they're in six different planes of consciousness. Do you understand? For example, if your soul consciousness leaves your physical body with the astral body, then you are not consciously aware of the physical body, in the physical body. You may look at the physical body, but it cannot move. It is the same way if you're out in a mental body. Then, you cannot be expressing in the astral, the physical body, or the other bodies at the time that you are out. Yes.

Now, what purpose does it serve? Because it's the next step, my friends. You see, when you leave the physical body, there's an expression in the astral realm and the mental realm and, then, in the spiritual realm. It serves that purpose, yes. I'm sure you've heard about earth-bound spirits, if you've done any reading. Well, those are the astral bodies. Now don't think that they're all terrible, bad souls just because they are expressing in an astral body, because that's a terrible way to think about ourselves. Because, you see, we're expressing astral bodies, too, you see. And there's no guarantee that we're going to go to some Summer Land and some realms of illumination when we leave this physical clay. But I can assure you, if you are attached to any of this material substance, you will find this astral substance there in the astral realm. And that's known, of course, as the earth-bound realm. Yes.

You see, we don't teach to annihilate all our desires, because we won't long stay in form. But we do teach some kind of a balance. Now, if you have a habit, well, wait five minutes when you have the desire. That gives you a little self-control, doesn't it? And what is five short minutes, you see? If you can't have five minutes of control, my friends, how can you ever hope for five hours of it? See? So give yourself at least five minutes. When you say, "I've got to have this. I've got to have this right now," well, give yourself five minutes and go to work with that slave back there. Don't you see? Who's the boss? That's the question. That's what you want to ask yourself. And give yourself a couple of minutes. Yes.

But remember, now, about habits—you know, there's nothing worse than a reformer. I wish I could say something different, but I've seen so many reformers. And you know, it's like a reformed drinker, a reformed smoker—you know, why do they all of a sudden become so saintly? Now let's ask ourselves. Thank God they all don't do that, but an awful lot do. And, you know, they go out on a great program to convert the world to save their soul or save their body. Now what is it inside of a reformer that causes that? Is it a sense of guilt? Is it anger, because it took them so long to get rid of the habit themselves? I think, my friends, when we look at these reformers who have an insatiable need to convert everybody else—can't stand anybody that has a habit—see, we all have habits. I know a lot of people who have a habit of washing their face in the morning upon awakening and getting out of bed. I know other people, they have a habit of brushing their teeth every morning. Take away their toothbrush and see what happens to them! Everybody's got a habit. No man lives without a habit.

I'm interested in the habits of our own mind. How we think, you see, that's what we want to get into, you know. And remember, let us not judge, that we be not judged ourselves. Let's not knock something we don't understand, you know. Let's think about those things.

So many people, you know, feel they're—I guess we've discussed it before: it's known as spiritual arrogance. They're so pure and holy. They don't smoke, they don't drink, and they don't do several other things that I won't bother to mention. But anyway, my friends, let's give some thought to life itself and live in joy.

It's now way past our time. Let us go have refreshments. Thank you all very much.

SEPTEMBER 12, 1974

CONSCIOUSNESS CLASS 59

Good evening, class. This evening, before our question-and-answer period, I would like to spend a few moments in discussing the first soul faculty of duty, gratitude, and tolerance. It does seem for most of us that tolerance is so difficult to apply in our day-to-day acts and activities. Now, we must analyze our reasons for being intolerant with any circumstance, person, place, or thing. What is it inside of the mind that expresses what man knows as tolerance and intolerance? What is intolerance dependent upon? Does anyone know the cause of intolerance, the expression of intolerance?

Well, my friends, I'm sure we will all—yes.

It's lack of sufficient information.

You would say that it is lack of sufficient information. And anyone else?

Lack of awareness.

Lack of awareness. The lady in the back fourth row, please. Yes.

False expectations.

False expectations. Yes.

Lack of understanding.

Lack of understanding. Yes.

Unfulfilled desires.

Unfulfilled desires. Thank you. Yes. Anyone else?

Well, as we discuss this first soul faculty of duty, gratitude, and tolerance—and we're questioning what the real cause of intolerance is in the mind. I am sure that we will all agree that the expression of intolerance is caused by judgment. Now, whether or not it is a lack of understanding on our part or awareness or insufficient information, you see, it all stems from what we call judgment. Now, we cannot be intolerant of anything until the mind has judged it. Now the mind makes its judgment—the functions, the so-called brain—it makes its judgment upon the information, the experiences that it has accepted in its lifetime. Therefore, if it is accepted that this is the right way to do something and that is the wrong way, then it makes its judgment according to those acceptances.

Now we have spent a great deal of time in our philosophy classes on discussing the word *acceptance*. Acceptance is the divine will. Do we see why acceptance is the divine will? Because, my friends, it frees us from the limitation of our limited mind, which expresses judgment and intolerance.

Now, when we express the soul faculty of tolerance, we are freed from the lack and limitations of our own so-called computer. But this is not something that you can hear or read about, and have the knowledge of it, and not make the daily effort to apply. It has no value without application. And so, my friends, it is interesting, of course, to all of us to pause more often in our day-to-day acts and activities and in our work that we may see clearly how our mind really works. Because, you see, our mind, of course, is the vehicle through which our soul in the Divine Spirit is expressing itself.

We spoke last week on theories: once they're supported, they're known as facts. But surely we will all agree that a fact is not necessarily a truth. Therefore, my friends, your first soul faculty to awaken and to express is duty, gratitude, and tolerance, which are inseparable. All triune faculties or triune functions are inseparable. Because that that you cannot tolerate you have judged and, having judged, you guarantee the experience to befall you sometime during your life in order that you may be granted understanding. Because we cannot understand what we cannot express tolerance towards.

And so remember, friends, every time you feel intolerant, you are building another block, another obstruction in your aura and in your universe to what you truly want to accomplish in life. Because, you see, that energy directed out through that level of intolerance goes out like a great circle and it returns to you. It is doing this all of the time. And until we awaken that soul faculty, we will not be freed from what they call the so-called karmic justice.

This is why, when we have experiences in life that we don't particularly appreciate, all we have to do is to stop and say, "Well, I don't remember when I fed energy to this level of consciousness, but the law is very impartial, for it is a divine law and therefore it is true justice." Somewhere along life's pattern we have, indeed, directed energy, which is returning to us, and we are having the experiences that we do not care to experience. So let us make a daily effort on expressing that soul faculty. Then, my friends, we'll broaden our horizons, we'll be granted greater understanding. And when you have understanding, you understand something, you can free it from your consciousness, because you can forgive it.

You see, once you forgive something, you free it. But you cannot forgive what another human soul is expressing, you can't forgive them until you can forgive that level inside yourself. And you cannot forgive that level of consciousness inside of yourself until you can awaken yourself to it.

There are many things, of course, in life that we do not care to see, let alone, of course, to hear. But why don't we care to hear things unless they're pleasing to our ears and eyes and senses? Well, of course, that's understandable, because we do not, yet, want to grow through that level of consciousness that has been suppressed inside of ourselves. Now let us all remember that we are an inseparable part of the whole, that life is not the way we always want it to be simply because we're not always willing to make the effort to make it the way we want [it] to be.

Now, for several years we've been teaching these classes and we have repeatedly said that man is personally responsible—the Law of Personal Responsibility: that whatever in life happens to us has been caused by us. And yet, again and again and again, the mind seems to have the need to blame somebody else. My good students, you're not going to be freed—you're not going to be free—your soul—until you have the strength of character to say, "This experience that I encounter is a level of consciousness that I have become receptive to and through my magnetic field of attraction I am now experiencing it." It's inside of us, my friends.

Every time that you go anyplace in life, to work or anything else, and you let yourself be upset emotionally because somebody didn't say hello the way you expected them to say hello or the way you wanted them to say hello, you're only destroying yourself. You're only giving power to another human soul, instead of going inside in that moment and saying, "Well, I admit I must have been a bit unaware, because I blamed another person for this experience. I blamed my job. I blamed my employer. I blamed my church and I blamed all my so-called friends and so-called enemies." Think, my friends, we have spent an entire lifetime to this point—and we have spent many lifetimes in evolution prior to this moment—in blaming things outside of ourselves. If that were not true, then we would be free from that trap of personality and we would be expressing at this moment in time, in evolution, in principle.

Now I wanted to share that with you because, my friends, these classes are here for you to think. And when you start thinking, you'll start growing, as anything grows when it starts to think. So think about where you are. Think about *what* you are, so that you can know *who* you are. You see, if we were the accepted patterns of our mind, then we would never evolve. And the Law of Evolution is the process of constant change of form. And so if you're not willing to accept something new this moment, then that simply means that you're not willing to evolve and fulfill the divine law, which is a constant process of progression.

Now, not everything goes our way, as I stated earlier, because there are so many different ways and laws we've set into motion. We're running as fast as we can to get last year's filled while we're in the same process of fifty thousand other desires. So let's stop still for a few moments and think. That's what life is all about.

Whatever—remember—whatever in life we depend upon, that's what we rely upon. And if you rely upon form, you're going to be sadly disappointed some moment in some day, because the form—all form—is in a constant process of change and progression. So if you rely in life upon the gold standard, the gold standard's in a process of change. If you rely upon the government, the government is in a process of change. If you rely upon your job or your business, that's in a process of change. So think where you're going to be, my friends, if you're not in that total acceptance to move with all these changes, because of your reliances.

Now, if you rely upon your father or your mother for your peace and your happiness and your abundance and your supply and your fulfillment, you're going to be sadly disappointed. It's guaranteed. And if the husband relies upon his wife, he's going to have his disappointments and vice versa: she's going to have her disappointments. So, my friends, what does pure logic and common sense tell us to rely upon in life? To rely upon something that never fails. And what is the something that never fails? Well, some people call it God. The Spiritualists call it Infinite Intelligence. You can call it whatever you want. That is not important. But let's rely upon something that has proven itself for eons of time never, but never, to fail.

Anything else you rely upon, you're going to have the experiences of joy and disappointment. They're guaranteed. And you're going to have that constantly throughout your life's expression.

So remember, friends, your reliance is that that controls your life. And the reason that your reliances control your life is because you have given your soul to them. So let's awaken and let our soul express its own divine right, its own godliness, its own goodness. And then, you may be rest assured you will not have to experience what man calls a repetition of failure.

Thank you very much. Now you're free to ask your questions. Yes.

With regard to what you were just speaking of, I'm trying to relate several things. One is the fact that I am in human form and humans are emotional beings, or that's part of what goes into us. Now, last Sunday, as I was listening to people speak, one of the things that was said was that our emotions are the hardest to change. And you're talking about change. Sometimes when I hear you talk about change and I realize how much change I'm already accepting in my life, I kind of get—I just feel myself kind of expanding, thinking, well, if you really accept change, then everything is in change. Always. If you really perceive that and allow it to happen. And what I know about the way people usually behave is when you change into a new thing, you mourn the loss of the old thing: that's an emotional pattern of behavior. What I want to know is, Is it possible, while we're in form, to transcend human emotionality and accept change without going through a mourning?

Thank you very much. And it most certainly is. Now, of course, if emotions are the most difficult level of consciousness to grow through, that simply reveals it's the level that we have become most attached to or relied upon. Now, that does not mean that we are teaching that you should become completely and totally emotionless, because you cannot be while yet expressing in the human form. But it does mean if our reliance is upon the Divine, then the emotions—you understand—they will make a much easier transition and change for us.

It's just like—of course, if we are totally reliant upon this material world and its material supply, then when we experience a decrease in that supply, we are affected emotionally, because, you see, that's where we have put our reliance. Do you understand? And it most certainly is possible to transcend: by bringing the emotional, magnetic field into balance with the conscious, electrical field. Then, your changing of emotion will be a very harmonious transition, instead of such a struggle.

Thank you.

You're more than welcome. Yes.

Would you please give us your understanding of statement in The Living Light, *"the Law of What Can Be Borne?"*

Thank you very much. Yes, I'll be happy to share with you our understanding on the statement, "the Law of What Can Be Borne." Man can accept, and does accept, some things, while rejecting others. And so this is referred to—this acceptance and rejection process—it's known as the Law of What Can Be Borne.

Now, the Law of What Can Be Borne, of course, we all see is very individually expressed. Some people, you understand, can accept certain changes in their life, dependent on the Law of What Can Be Borne. Now, take a look, my friends, in reference to the statement the lady has made about that law. A person can talk to you about making a change and you accept that very joyously. Another person could talk to you about making a change—the same change, you understand—and you totally reject it. In fact, you reject it so forcefully that you express emotionally. Now, we must ask ourselves the question, How does this work with the Law of What Can Be Borne?

Well, my friends, one person asking the other a certain question to do something is appealing to their soul faculty of reason. But first they must have the perception to know that they can reach that soul faculty known as reason. And so reason goes about her job. And she transfigures that individual from within themselves and there is total acceptance. And whatever was requested gets done. Another person, not perceiving the level of consciousness of the person they're speaking with, does not reach that soul faculty of reason, but reaches directly into the subconscious computer bank and there is an emotional reaction. And yet, both people have asked the individual identically the same question.

Now, first, my friends, to perceive before you ask a person something, to perceive whether or not they are on a soul level of consciousness, known as reason, at that moment, we must first perceive whether or not *we* are on that soul level of consciousness known as reason. And if we are, then we are, then, in a position, you understand—through reason and these invisible energies that are emanating—to reach their soul faculty of reason. But if we are on a level of desire, then we are going to have the reaction of desire from the person that we're speaking to. I do hope that's helped with your question. And that's the Law of What Can Be Borne. Yes.

Two weeks ago you said something to the effect that thoughts are things and they do not dissipate. Now, when one is in a relaxed condition, one can be bombarded with ambient thoughts, good and bad. When one is bombarded with a bad thought and that becomes a part of them, how can they change the bad thought, so as to eliminate it from their consciousness of their universe?

Thank you very much. I don't recall the exact statement, but I do not think that the statement reveals that a thought never dissipates. A thought is held in form, as a thought, as long as it's fed energy.

Now, the gentleman, the student, is speaking about receiving certain thoughts that are not beneficial to them, that he may—the student—consider bad thoughts. Is that correct? And how do they protect themselves or transmute that thought, which is a vehicle of energy, to something beneficial? Well, my friends, number one: We have to be on a level of consciousness—you see, if we call it a bad thought, then we have to be on that level of consciousness to become aware of it. Would you not agree?

Yes, sir.

You see, we can't be aware of something that we're not on the level of its expression. Now that's not possible. And I'm sure we'll all agree about that. You know, when a person says, "Well, that person has very bad thoughts directed to me," well, we can be rest assured that we're on that level of consciousness where bad thoughts are experienced. You understand? That's number one.

So how do we transmute this? All right, well, we're all sensitive and we're all receiving thoughts on many levels of consciousness: eighty-one, to be exact. And, of course, what does man do when he has a radio and he doesn't like the station and what they're broadcasting? He turns the dial, doesn't he? Well, in our understanding, that dial on that radio is known as self-control. And then, when man exercises his divine right of self-control, he can turn the dial of that radio to a different radio station that is broadcasting something that he considers pleasing or beneficial unto himself. Do you understand?

Yes, sir.

Yes. So remember, friends, a free soul is one of self-control. Self-control. So when you're experiencing what you call bad thoughts, say, "Lord, let me be at peace. Let me be at peace, that I may control my mind, because I have the power to control my mind." The mind is the vehicle of the Divine Spirit and of your soul. And your soul is greater than your mind. And so you become at peace, because that's godly and in harmony. And then, you turn that dial of your mind, through self-control, to a higher level of consciousness. I do hope that's helped with your question. Yes.

Would you discuss acceptance a little more, please? What happens in the mind that causes us to accept or helps us to accept? Would you discuss this in relation to visualization? And could you tell me, in practicing visualization, should one rely or should one not rely on images that one has physically seen?

Thank you very much. The lady is referring to acceptance and visualization. And of course, number one: My friends, if we're having difficulty with anything such as visualization, concentration, or etc., it is a revelation that we have already determined what it should be like. Do you understand? Now, having determined just what it should be like, then the mind has to go to work in its reference library to see if it has any experience. And if it hasn't had any experience in its reference library, then it's got all kinds of problems, you see. That deals with acceptance.

So the first thing is, you see, that it reveals—we say we want to visualize a fountain. Well, our mind has determined what it's supposed to be like, this process of visualization. And we've determined that. And yet, we are not able to accomplish it, you see.

Now, remember that God, the Divine, disposes, while man continues to propose, you see. So what does it have to do with acceptance? Accept that what you call visualization is taking place. Accept that truth. Do not stand in your own light and tell the Divine, "Well, I had my meditation and I didn't consider that any kind of a visualization process." Well, how silly that is! First of all, the mind doesn't have any reference to what a real visualization process is. So it certainly is not a very good judge to tell us that it wasn't a good visualization. Do you understand? Yes.

Now, when we go out and we talk to the students, and they say, "Well, I guess I visualize. I see a car, a beautiful pink car right there in front of me, all in detail." Then the student says, "Well, that's the way it's supposed to be." But perhaps, my friends, it isn't supposed to be that way for you. Because you're not the same person that everybody else is. Do you understand?

So when our mind insists that there is an obstruction to anything that we are seeking, as long as it insists this obstruction exists, it continues to feed the obstruction. And so the obstruction continues for us.

You see, it's known as RTD: to release it to the Divine. But you see, to release something to the Divine takes acceptance—takes a lot of acceptance to release a desire to the Divine. Oh yes, how many people desire how many things? And how many say, "Well, Lord, I'm going to release this to your Divine Intelligence. You have created all of the universe, including myself. You are the divine spark that keeps me moving and thinking. And I'm going to release this to the greatest possible source in all the universes"? Well, when it comes right down to it, it's a very difficult thing.

Now, why is it difficult for man to release his desire to the Divine? I can understand it. He never credited the Divine with fulfilling it! Any desire. So if he hasn't credited God with fulfilling his desire, then how can he possibly release his desire to God, who is doing the work anyway? But you see, he's credited it to his own brain and to his own computer. He says, "Well, if it weren't for me, I wouldn't have gotten that desire fulfilled. I'm the guy that had to go out there and do this and do that." Well, a hundred thousand million people went out there and did this and did that, and they didn't get their desires fulfilled! Don't you see what I mean?

Now, man has not yet credited God to be God, because man is greater than God in his thinking. See? And that takes humility. And that takes humbleness. And it takes acceptance, friends. It takes acceptance. I can only tell you that it works. But you're going to have to make the effort yourselves in releasing these things that disturb you to the Divine. So that you can have that experience up here. And, once having had the experience, then, for you, it will always work. See? Thank you very much. I hope that's helped with your question. Yes.

Thank you. Is that what is meant by, "May my will be Thy will"?

Absolutely. Absolutely and positively. You see, you release it to the Divine Intelligence, to the Divine Will, and you take it out of the limited form. And then, according to the laws you have set into motion will you be receptive for that to manifest in your life. Man has free will. Pardon?

May I ask another question?

Yes.

Could you speak a bit on gratitude as it relates to what we have been discussing?

I'll be more than happy to. Gratitude that man expresses, of course, unfortunately, until we get into another level of consciousness—I'm sure we're moving in and out of them anyway. But you see, man expresses gratitude the moment his desire is fulfilled. And he expresses it as long as he's in that field of emotion. Now isn't that sad, but isn't it true?

Well, I mean, after all, you know, you go out and you like steak and it's your desire. And you have a good steak and, while you're eating it, you're very grateful. And immediately after. But how long does the gratitude last, you see? So it does reveal, as the man has brought up the soul faculty of gratitude, it does reveal that man is indeed grateful for the fulfillment of his desires. But his desires are in such a process of constant change that it's hard to recognize his gratitude. Don't you see what I mean? Now, I don't mean we don't all have a soul faculty known as duty, gratitude, and tolerance. But I'm just trying to perhaps share a little understanding with you, you see.

When we have a need, friends, when we compute up here that we need something and we're moving over here and it gets fulfilled, we're grateful. But the reason it doesn't last is because we've always got desires for different things. And so while we were grateful at that moment at that time, then the next day or the next minute we're moving over here or we're in another process. And something happens that we were seeking, and then we're grateful again. Don't you see?

So what kind of gratitude are we going to talk about? Let's perhaps think about the soul gratitude: gratitude to the Divine for its expression. Not dependent upon our little desires that are changing all the time.

You know, in this kind of work, they either love you or hate you. But we understand that hate is only love distorted. So what difference does it make? You know, you either work for God to please the Divine or you're in a constant process of trying to please everybody's desires. And if you try to do that, you're in a terrible shape, I can tell you. You know, being one person, you can't please everyone, because there are so many different expressions and desires in the world, you see.

So I do hope that's helped you with gratitude: to shed a little light on how grateful we really are when we get our little desires fulfilled. And, of course, the bigger the desire, the greater the expression of gratitude! You know what I mean? So let's be honest with ourselves and let's recognize in here—you know, we don't have to judge everybody else—but let us at least recognize in here when we say we're grateful. Did that mean, "I just got my desire fulfilled"? or, "God, am I truly grateful for my life expression"? Let's be honest with ourselves and then, we'll get to grow.

What is visualization, please?

Thank you very much. Visualization is a process of the mind in which a thought is accepted and, therefore, created into an image. Do you understand? For example, all of life's experiences are mirrors that are revealing what our own attitude or thought or visualization is. You see, Life herself is a dream and we are the dreamers of that Life. And so when you wake up in the morning, you know, and you have a good day, you're in a process of visualization things inside of your mind that will cause a sensation of goodness to express in your being. Do you understand? That is a visualization process that is taking place not in the conscious mind, but in the subconscious mind.

And so it is very important that the student learn how to visualize. They're already doing it anyway subconsciously and they're experiencing life that way. But let's bring it to the conscious awareness. And, you see, if you want to have a good day, well, you first create that; you create that with your feelings, your magnetic field. And then, that whole process will come out into your conscious awareness. Does that help?

Is that like preplanning?

It's more than preplanning, because the thing that preplans is usually the desires. And you want to go beyond those, because, you see, they're not always fulfilled the way we want them to. It's in a deeper level of consciousness, ma'am. It's on a higher level of consciousness. Yes.

Thank you.

You're more than welcome. Yes.

Yes, sir. In the Bible it says keep the eye single. In The Living Light *it says goal is the lifeline. Now then, if you should perchance achieve your goal, shouldn't you be grateful for it and set new goals?*

Well, thank you very much for your question and your statement. Yes. The gentleman is referring to keeping the eye single, which is in the Judeo-Christian Bible, and that in *The Living Light* the statement is made that your goal in life is your lifeline. Well, I am sure of what the goal reference means. And I do not believe that the Judeo-Christian prophets, who were a part of the composers of that book called the Bible, meant by "keeping thine eye single"—that they meant to confuse our petty desires with life's goal. Now, if you say that, "This is my desire. And I want to get married and have a nice family and children, etc."—now if you confuse that with being your goal, then I can understand your question and your statement. But I do not believe "keeping thine eye single" meant an expression of our multitude of desires, my good friend.

You see, a goal—a true goal—is never completely fulfilled. Now, if you have a desire, you fulfill the desire. But if you call those goals, then you're in a constant process of a multitude of goals. And that's not the teaching. The teaching is oneness, because oneness is God; oneness is the Divine; oneness is the Power itself. So surely would it not behoove us to consider as our goal in life a freedom and an awareness and a fulfillment of the purpose of our soul's journey? I would not confuse those with desires, my good friend. I do hope that's helped with your question.

Thank you.

Thank you.

Could you please tell us whether obedience is a faculty? And if—

Thank you very much—

And if it is, I mean, obedience to what and to whom?

I was just going to say, my good student, that depends on what you're obedient to. Many of us—in fact, I'm sure, most of us—will agree how very obedient we are to our functions. I am sure, my good friends, we will agree upon that. In fact, we're more obedient than most animals. Don't you see? And so it does depend, of course, on what you mean by "obedience."

Now, what man relies upon, he becomes obedient to. And so if man relies on his desires, he's very obedient to those desires. But as far as the word *obedience*—no, my good friend, it is not meant as a soul faculty. It most certainly is not.

But I'm so grateful that you brought up that question, because it surely does reveal to all of us present here this evening how very obedient we are to the patterns that we have already accepted. Oh yes, in fact, my good students, we will go to great lengths with our obedience. I never saw such loyalty in all of my life as the loyalty to desire. I don't believe there's any greater loyalty that does indeed exist. Thank you all very much for that question. Does someone else have a question? Yes.

Yes, I would like to return to the issue that I proposed at the first meeting, that together we might find a better term for humanity than the limited word man. I've given this a great deal of thought and your answer was for me to check the root derivations of the word man and of the word humanity. I have checked and the Latin root is homo, which means "man." I would like to suggest that this was two thousand years ago and in our process of evolution the word man is no longer satisfactory to include women. I feel excluded every time the word man is used, just as if I'm excluded from the men's room and from the men's club.

Yes.

I don't understand how a word can both include me and exclude me.

Thank you so very, very much for your very important question, especially in this day and age and in our evolution here in the twenty-first century. The lady had brought up here earlier at one of our classes a request to change the word *humanity* and to change the word *man*.

I didn't request to change the word humanity.

Well, the word *man* is derived from *humanity*.

But they are not the same word.

Thank you very much. However, as I was saying earlier, the lady had requested that we change the word, let us say, *man* because she felt excluded as a student from this class. Now, whenever the word has been used at any time in our philosophy, it is intended to include both men and women. It has nothing to do with what the world calls sex.

Now, the lady also stated that here in this little log cabin, there are signs on the doors. On one it says Men and on the other it says Women. Well, my friends, I do believe in this day and age, considering the present evolution of the human race, that it would be indeed most difficult to have a rest room that said United Species. However—and this is a serious matter—we must go deep inside of ourselves and we must ask ourselves, "Why do I feel excluded when a certain word is spoken in the universe?"

Now, this is a very individual thing. When the word *man* is used, some women feel, as this lady has stated, excluded. And billions of women feel included. Now where does the process take place? We will all agree it is not taking place out there. It's taking place in our head. Now, if we get someone to agree with us, if we have two women together and they both agree that when the word *man* is used, they feel excluded, the theory—as we stated last week—now becomes a fact, because we have support for it.

However, my good friends, whereas the purpose of these classes is not to entertain controversial subjects, such as sexism, I do not believe that it would be in the best interest of the students present, of the philosophy, and of the purpose of this Association to get into serious debate over a word known as *man*. I do feel, however, that that would be best handled in the political arena, where it is already being handled by many, many people.

Now, man sees inequity, inequality, and injustice according to man's own acceptance. For example, as a Spiritualist minister,

I could very easily feel extremely excluded from the Christian religious body of the world for the simple reason it is not possible for me to become a member of the Ministerial Association of the United States of America unless I accept Jesus Christ as my personal Savior and my only salvation. Now, I could indeed feel very left out. But I do not. Because God has granted us the divine right known as choice.

And I do hope with all of the ladies that we have in our religion and in our church and with all of the work that they do, I do hope that they recognize and realize that equality reigns supreme in the Serenity Association. My good friends, it even reigns supreme in the Spiritualist movement. After all, it was in 1863 that the Spiritualist movement ran the first woman for president of the United States of America. We are the first religious body in the world to ordain women—women!—as ministers, totally contrary to the Christian teachings of the Judeo-Christian Bible when Saint Paul said, "Women, you shall sit in the back of the congregation. Women, you shall cover your heads and wear your hair upon your head that you look not like harlots. And women, you shall speak only when you are asked to speak." So I do believe the Serenity Association, as an auxiliary of our national body, is indeed a great supporter of divine equality for all souls.

Thank you very, very much. Our time has passed. Let us go have refreshments. Thank you.

SEPTEMBER 19, 1974

CONSCIOUSNESS CLASS 60

Good evening, everyone. This evening we will speak for a few moments on something that we're all so very familiar with. And it's commonly known as our security blanket. Now, all of us have security in the things, of course, that we are familiar with. How did this begin with us? We'll have to go back in time to when our soul first entered this earth realm. And it entered what is referred to in these teachings as the womb of satisfaction. Now, our soul enters into form. It's cared for—all of its functions—by whatever mother it is that we have. And so from the very beginning of form on this planet, we see that it is not only receptive to, but it is dependent upon, what is known as satisfaction.

Now, as children we depend and we rely upon those who are caring for us, usually our parents. When we are hungry, which is a sense function, they feed us. When we are cold, they bring us comfort and warmth. And so from very early beginnings on this Earth planet, we become addicted to the things that bring us pleasure, satisfaction, and therefore build up what is known as the chains of reliance, what is known as our security blanket.

Now, as we advance through those young years, we start going out into the world and we see rather quickly that all women are not like our mothers, that all men are not like our fathers. And so there comes a crisis in our life, very early in our life, and we seek something that will represent the security, the pleasure, and the satisfaction that we have, as children, become addicted to. To some of us, this satisfaction and security is accepted in what is known as the material world. We see that in this world if we have a sufficient amount of money, then that is simply a representation of the fulfillment of the patterns of our mind which ever seek what we call a security blanket. To others, they seek many varied things. Some seem to find their security blanket in their employment, in their profession, in their marriage, and, yea, even in their children.

Now, because we are all in human form, we are all blind. That means we do not see with the light of reason, with the soul faculty, when we're in what is known as desire. And what, of course, is desire? It is that need that we have accepted in our minds for security, for fulfillment, for satisfaction, and, of course, for pleasure.

However, as the years pass by and our soul begins to unfold on its evolutionary path, our security blanket ever gets thinner and thinner and thinner. And when we enter what has been referred to in these teachings as the hindsight years, the years of the forties, what it means, my good friends, is our security blanket is getting so thin that we can feel the cold winds of reason entering what is known as our mind.

Now where do we go in life when we reach this point and we find these cold winds of reason sweeping across our minds? And why is reason known to be cold? Because it's cold, my friends, in the sense that it does not satisfy our emotional needs. That that is reason indeed does transfigure us. And *transfiguration* means a perfect balancing between our conscious and our subconscious minds.

So we enter into these years known as the hindsight years with a very thin security blanket. If we have become successful in business and that has been our security blanket, regardless of how successful we have become, there's still something missing. If we have not become, yet, successful in business and that is still our security blanket, it ever seems to escape us because—don't you see, my friends?—what we rely upon, we become. And when the mind relies upon form, known as creation, it becomes that very thing: one moment to be satisfied, the next moment to be dissatisfied. And so a wise man must ask himself the question, "Then, what is the security, the true security, that I am seeking?"

When we become aware of how the vehicle of our soul, known as the mind, truly works, when we become aware of that and accept that truth, then we will find this eternal, everlasting divine security that can look at its losses and look at its gains in the same light. Then, my friends, we have evolved to a point of balance. We no longer will rely and become dependent upon the creation that comes and goes, like the tides of the ocean. We'll rely upon the one and only thing that never, ever fails.

It is indeed interesting to note in life that when we are young—in our twenties, teens, and perhaps even thirties—it is rare that we are concerned with our health. We are more concerned in those years, usually, with what we call success. We're chasing the rainbow of what will represent security to us. But, my friends, that is never where security truly lies. It's in a constant change. It's in a constant process, when you rely upon any form in any dimension.

Many people, I know, do not understand Spiritualism or communication. And one of the first things they're most likely to say is that the Spiritualists rely upon people who once lived on Earth who have evolved to other dimensions. And that, my friends, is indeed the furthest thing from the truth of true Spiritualism.

A person in this philosophy and understanding relies upon the only thing that never fails them and that is their ability to come into tune and in rapport with what man calls Infinite Intelligence or God. But we also understand and accept that God ever expresses *through* man, not *to* man. And so wouldn't it behoove us to listen? For we never know when God is going to speak through man. We never know when he might be speaking, that Divine Intelligence. We never know when it might be speaking in the sunset or in the morning, at dusk or at dawn. We never know when that still, small voice is whispering the very words we need to hear.

So let's not expect in life to sit down in a chair and to come in direct communication with what our mind has conceived as God. Because if we think that that's the only way we're going to experience the Divine Intelligence, the divine security, then we will close all doors of expression for God to speak to us.

Think, my good students. You all know that duty, gratitude, and tolerance is the first soul faculty of this philosophy. And many of you know that the second soul faculty is faith, poise, and humility. Many students have asked, "What about all the other soul faculties?" Well, what does it behoove us to know all eighty-one if we haven't yet demonstrated our ability and willingness of self-control so we can express the first soul faculty?

Now, if we are seeking, truly, to find God, the Divine Light, which is within us and within all things, and if we have considered that duty, gratitude, and tolerance is a soul faculty which unfolds our own soul, our own divinity, then doesn't it stand to reason when we are given the opportunity by the laws we alone have set into motion to express through that soul faculty, to express tolerance and duty and gratitude? My friends, doesn't it stand to reason that God, the Divine that we are seeking, is speaking through the form that is causing us to think and try to express that faculty, a little bit of tolerance?

You know, it is stated in that Good Book that the stone the builder rejected became the cornerstone. So often, my friends, the things we cannot tolerate are the very things needed as the cornerstone for our own fulfillment. The things that we are seeking, my friends, come to us in accord with the laws that we have set into motion. Now, if we have set laws into motion that require an unfoldment of our soul faculty of duty, gratitude, and tolerance, then it only stands to reason that we're going to have the opportunity to express that soul faculty. So when you meet someone in your daily activities and they seem to be testing your tolerance, remember that God is speaking to you, my friends, and that person is not the one that's testing you. You, your functions, are testing yourself. Don't you understand? Think about it.

There are many things in life that we do not agree with; then, there are many things in life we do agree with. And those who express the things that we agree with—we usually call those people friends. Well, I always was under the impression that a friend is one who helped us to help ourselves, whether we liked it or we didn't like it. And so, you see, my friends, what the world has accepted as friendship is a function. But true friendship is a soul faculty. And it clearly states, True friendship respects the rights of difference and will weather any storm.

But is it not true how quickly and frequently we make fair-weather friends in this old earth realm? What does "a fair-weather friend" mean? It means a person that we are in rapport with because they have similar patterns and similar acceptances to our own. And as long as we and our so-called friends are expressing in those levels of consciousness, everything is fair weather: all things are running well. But let one of those so-called friends express on a level of consciousness that the other so-called friend has not yet accepted in their consciousness, and that is the end of what is known as a fair-weather friend.

We don't want those kinds of friends in life. Think, my students. They don't help you grow. They help you stay right where you are. If the person you call a friend always pleases you, then look twice at what's really going on. It means that you're staying where you are and they're helping you stay there. That's just what it means.

Now, we all know that evolution is the divine law. We're not exactly the same that we were last year—and some of us even yesterday. For new things have entered into our consciousness. And, you know, there is the statement, my friends, that when the need is the greatest, the law is fulfilled. Now, why is the law fulfilled when the need is the greatest? When the need is the greatest, my friends, the patterns of mind that are locked into our subconscious, not fulfilling our need, our mind, then, becomes receptive to the possibility of a new thought. And so in these teachings it says, "O suffer senses not in vain, for freedom of your soul is gain." And indeed, freedom of our soul is great gain, because it is our soul that is the eternal expression—not our physical body and not our attitudes of mind.

So let us think. Think, my friends. Are you a friend to yourself? For to have a friend, you must first be a friend—a friend, of course, to yourself. You cannot grant unto another anything in life that you have not first granted unto yourself, for that is the demonstrable law of life. So let us ask ourselves the question, "I have many patterns of mind and many levels of consciousness. To which of those levels am I indeed a true friend?" And let's look out into the world more clearly and all of life's experiences and thank the Divine Intelligence that every emotion and every experience that we have is nothing more, my friends, than the mirror of reflection. You can look at the sunset one way in a positive vein and see its good or you can look at it in another way and see its so-called opposite, known as bad.

We have stated many times that this world, and all worlds, are ever as you make it and they are indeed just the way you take it. So we've made our world the way we are this moment. We might as well take it and in so doing make whatever changes are necessary.

It will do no good to complain, for complaining, my friends, is an expression of ingratitude. And gratitude is the Law of Divine, Abundant Supply. So if you're complaining, it means there's something you desire that you don't have. And so you stay on the wheel of delusion by complaining, because complaining is ingratitude—the opposite of gratitude—and closes the door of eternal supply.

Now, we've taught this same law for many, many years: Be grateful for the crumb; you will guarantee the loaf. Don't you see, my friends, what we do to ourselves? When we complain, we are declaring. We are speaking a word out into the atmosphere. The word is life-giving energy. The word, my friend, is the law. Think about it. Man is a law unto himself. The word is the law.

For untold centuries, humanity has been taught that great truth. And yet, it seems it has not yet got to that level of consciousness where it can accept that great truth. So do yourself a great favor. The thing that you are seeking knows your face and is already on its way to your heart if you do not transgress the divine, natural law.

When you say, "I don't have this and I don't have that," you set that law into motion. You express that ingratitude and you continue on without what you are truly seeking. But if you say, "Thank you, God. I have the crumb of my desire," you will set the Law of Abundant Supply into motion, and it shall go out into the universe and it shall increase and multiply. Some people call that positive thinking. But I assure you, it's a lot more than positive thinking. It's known as acceptance. That is the divine will. If you accept that truth in your consciousness, then you will be in a position to demonstrate its immutable law. Thank you.

Now you're free to ask whatever questions that you have. Yes.

Are faculties lessons that we haven't quite learned yet? When we're expressing a faculty, is that like—well, that's the question.

Thank you very, very much for your question in reference to soul faculties and lessons to be learned. Many people—perhaps it would be best to give an example, as we discussed earlier. And I like to refer often to the first soul faculty of duty, gratitude, and tolerance, because without duty and gratitude, there's no tolerance expressed. Now, if a person is not able to express tolerance, which is a soul faculty, then, of course, what will happen to the individual, having set the Law of Intolerance into motion, they will guarantee a continuity of experiences which is necessary for them to understand. And once having understood, they will be able to express what is known as the faculty of tolerance.

Now there is a statement in our teachings that says clearly, "What today I criticize, tomorrow I shall idolize." And in line with that same teaching is, "Our adversities become our attachments; it is a subtle law." In that sense, yes, they are lessons, because we have made them lessons. Does that help with your question?

Yes. Thank you.

You're welcome. Yes.

Thank you, sir. In today's discourse it was stated, "Is my duty a true responsibility or is it a fabrication of the illusions of my mind?" I wonder if you could clarify that statement.

Well, I'll be happy to share with you our understanding. And the student is referring to Discourse 36, where the question is raised, Is my duty a true responsibility or is it a fabrication of my mind? Now that's a very important statement. And it's very important that we have some discussion with it. Thank you for bringing that up.

Many of us, deluded by what is known as desire, which has no light, justify the expression of that desire by calling it our duty. Now, once we do that, of course—and the reason that we do it is because we're defending our actions. Now, you see, this is very important. Truth, we have always stated, truth needs no defense. Because truth *is*. Anything that needs defense—take a second and third look at it. Do you understand?

Now, we may have a desire that we want to go someplace and we have a spiritual responsibility to be someplace else. Now, the question arises in our minds, "Well, what am I going to do?" This is a very important time with anyone and it happens to us all the time. And our mind says, "Well, now that's my duty and my responsibility." And the other part of us says, "But I have set this law into motion for my own soul unfoldment and *this* is my duty and my responsibility." Now, we're standing right on the razor's edge, so to speak, and depending on whether or not we can maintain what is called perfect peace we will be moved by the strongest influence. And usually, my good students, that influence is known as desire. And so the desire says, "I have this duty and responsibility." And so it goes on and it fulfills itself. And then, there comes the moment when it has to face what it shirked: its true responsibility. And so the mind goes into what is known as the level of justification. And in order to justify it, it must defend it. And so it does defend it and it calls that "duty."

Think, my friends. Every one of us knows, for we have a conscience, which is a spiritual responsibility with a dual capacity: it knows right from wrong. It does not have to be told by anyone. And believe me, friends, it whispers every chance it gets. It knows what we're doing for our soul, for our own godhood, within our own being. And it knows what it is doing for the functions. Does that help with your question?

Yes, sir.

Thank you.

What is meant in tonight's discourse or what is your understanding of what is meant by "lying waiting for your recognition"?

"Lying waiting for your recognition." And in reference to that statement, which, of course, is taken out of the contents of that discourse—"lying waiting for your recognition." Now, let us all think for a moment. We desire many things in life and we seek to attain others. Because our soul faculty of tolerance may not be sufficiently opened, the thing that we are seeking lies waiting to express through the very person we cannot tolerate. Now, it is stated that, "All things I have already given you." The Divine has given us everything. But we have denied our divinity because we refuse to express through what is known as our soul faculties. So all these things that we seek in life—they are all lying waiting for our recognition.

You see, the stone the builder rejected is the cornerstone. And so it is, my friends, whatever your desires of the moment may ever be, they are already waiting, lying there, for your recognition, dependent, of course, upon what is known as acceptance. Does that help with your question?

Thank you.

You're welcome.

We're taught that thoughts are forms and things. Sometimes if there are people around us sending out negative thoughts to us, are we the victim of these thoughts, without control? Or is there a way that we can protect ourselves against them?

Thank you so very much. And indeed we are the victims, without control, if we permit our soul consciousness to express on the level known as the negative. Yes.

Now, this is what happens, friends. You know, it pays to be up, because, you see, if you have any desire or thought and you feel good about it, all of the good thoughts of the universes of the past, the present, and the future are there supporting your thought. For there is nothing new under the sun and to God all things *are*. Time and space is an illusion. So it is that if people are bombarding your aura with negative thoughts, the only time you can be affected by them is when you, as an individual, permit your consciousness to be negative. Therefore, think how important it is to protect ourselves. And we protect ourselves by setting the law into motion. By knowing that all *is* well, all *becomes* well for us. And so it is very important when you're thinking about anyone to think a thought of peace, to see the good in all, because it all returns to you, my friends.

And when you experience what you feel is not good, remember that God gave you choice. You can, in an instant, make a decision within your mind and, making that decision, rise to a level of consciousness where all is good.

You know, there's a very ancient custom that's still a custom in our civilization today. And it's known as blessing the food that you eat. That is man's responsibility. He is the highest-evolved species in the animal kingdom and he's called human. We have a responsibility to all the other kingdoms—the animal, the mineral—all those kingdoms. We have a responsibility. Our responsibility is to express thoughts of peace and love to all of God's creation. And, in so doing, you help those forms to rise to higher levels of consciousness. This is what God's angels do for us. At least, they try to. To inspire our thoughts with godly thoughts, with good things, to know that all is well, that God indeed is at the helm. So, you see, my friends, we have a great responsibility in life.

Personally, myself, I try, to the best of my ability, to release thoughts of peace and love to all God's children, which includes all kingdoms. Because—don't you see, my friends—when you rise to that level of consciousness, you're going to experience the great freedom and truly know the joy of living. Now that depends, of course, on ourselves. It doesn't depend on anybody else. It depends on what we want to accept.

You see, one of the difficulties here in creation is that when we rely upon man and we rely upon whatever position we think that he has in life, what happens to us when they don't do what we think they should? We lose our faith. And isn't that a sad day? But think how often we permit that to happen to us. That means, my friends, we haven't yet raised our soul consciousness to the universal, where to God, all things are possible. So let us choose this moment where we're going to place our faith. And let us place it in a Power, in an Intelligence that never, ever fails. Thank you very much.

Good evening. In our meditations, we have the word peace, *as you were just mentioning. In Sunday's service you were expressing a desire that our Teacher's students use the vibratory word of* peace. *And it touched me in the fact that the recipient of the message was, in expressing the vibratory word of* peace—*that doves, which are the symbol of peace, went out into the atmosphere, going out to where it did the most good. And you expressed the desire that you wished that our students—or your students—would do this more often or on a daily basis. Could you elaborate a little bit more on that?*

Well, I think, if we will recognize, realize, and accept that any thought entertained in the mind does not dissipate into the nothingness—but the thought takes the form. It's like going out into a plastic vibration: it forms according to what the masses of civilization have accepted.

Now peace—the universal symbol of peace is the white dove. It always has been for untold centuries. It's just like the rainbow is the universal symbol, in the mass mind, of promise. Well, it ought to be. After all, it's mentioned in the Bible that God would place a bow into the sky and he made a promise. Well, this has been accepted by untold billions of people and so this creates a vibration, you see. So when a person has thoughts of peace, true peace, there are doves going out from their aura. They take wings and they fly and they go to where peace is truly needed. Now what happens is those doves, which are the symbol of peace, they land in a person's aura. There's a feeling that comes over them, a feeling of peace. Do you understand? You see, thoughts are so very important and yet we're so careless with them.

You know, they say—and we've said a million times—that as you believeth, you becometh. So why not believe in something that truly works? Look at where thought has brought us and then, let us think where we want to go. And remember that it takes thought to take us there. You see, we can't experience anything we haven't accepted and the acceptance is known as thought. So you see, if you want to go from here to New York, you must *think,* "New York." You must accept the possibility.

You see, the vehicle of thought, you understand, is called the mind. And the mind is the vehicle of our soul. And our soul is the vehicle of God, the Divine Intelligence. And our bodies, you see, they are the effect—the direct effect—of accepted thought, which is called patterns of thought or attitudes of mind. This is what our body is, and that's all that it is. It is composed of the elements of nature. And you see, my friends, when you leave this physical body, you go with your mental body. And when you're in your mental body, you can only experience what that mental body has already accepted. So let us use thought more wisely. Let us use it more constructively.

You see, my friends, let's say a person says, "Well, I think about being rich and it doesn't happen." My friends, you don't *think* about being rich. You *become* it in your thought. You've got to feel it. You've got to know it. But let us become rich in wisdom, in understanding. Because, my friends, if you will seek, with greater effort, wisdom; if you will seek, with greater effort, understanding, all of those other things will fall into place. All of the things—you see, a man may say, "Well, I just want to be wealthy so I can have this and have that for myself, my children, and my family." If you'll pray for understanding, once having understanding, you will know the law. You will not have to theorize about the law. You will know the law and have the ability to demonstrate it. And so having understanding, the foundation of all soul faculties, you will speak your word into the atmosphere, knowing that it shall not come back to you void, but accomplish that what you send it to do. So I do hope all of my students will pray each and every moment for understanding. Then, you're in a position to demonstrate the Law of Opulence and divine abundance. Yes.

My question is on psychic surgery. I was wondering, before the aura is pierced on the patient, must the colors blend with those of the doctor who is to pierce the aura—before it is done?

They most certainly should. Thank you very much for your question.

My question has to do with thoughts. Actually, I have two questions. Thoughts are forms. My question is, Lots of times, when you're sitting in your chair or you're meditating, a myriad of thoughts just form out of your—out of somewhere. And I seem to have no conscious control over the nature of these thoughts. And some may be negative and some may be positive. And I'm wondering, is this good or is this bad? In other words, should I be able to gain better control over these thoughts as they flow out of my head? And the other question I have is, How is the spoken word different from the thoughts in terms of the way it manifests or forms, and what kind of power it has in relationship to all of this?

Thank you very, very much. Yes. Now, first of all, we want to realize that we are, in truth, an inseparable part of the whole, whether we like it or not. And everybody we see in the universe, we're a part of them, even though we may not be able to tolerate them.

Now, in reference to your question concerning your receptivity to a multitude of thoughts and forms that enter your mind and with a seeming inability to shut them off, is this beneficial or is it detrimental? Well, it could be either. But because—you see, the first thing we want to try to do is to gain self-control: to control the mind so these thoughts and images will not be floating in them. Do you understand? What it means is this: that we have become receptive to that level of consciousness. And if the thought forms are pleasing to us and they're beautiful, then that is, evidently and obviously, a level of consciousness that's in our best interest, usually. Do you understand?

Now I say "usually"—and I want to bring this point up at this time and it's extremely important: Truth is simple and unconcealed; 'tis falsehood that is complex and deeply hidden. Whenever the mind, the intellect, starts to study a spiritual truth, unless it constantly recognizes and accepts that it is mind, that it is form, that it is fallible and cannot grasp the eternal, it sends itself into what is known as the realm of illusion. And this is why the statement has been made, "When of thy mind thou seekest to know the truth, on the wheel of delusion thou shalt traverse." We cannot comprehend the Infinite with the finite. And therefore it is critically important that we recognize and accept the great truth that the mind is finite and only the Spirit is infinite.

Now, these thought forms—and, of course, in reference to the spoken word, for example, the student is experiencing different thought forms at times during the day. Well, you could be receptive to whatever level of consciousness, you understand, within yourself and that's where you'll have these experiences. We are an inseparable part of the whole. For example, if we think the word *anger*, there is a vibration of the color red emanated from our aura. Now, what we're going to say is, "Well, nobody taught me that red is the color of anger." Do you understand? All right. Now, those things you don't have to be taught, because they have been universally accepted by the mass mind and it's known as the primitive mind.

This is where you might hear, you know, a person was so angry they saw red. Well, the truth of the matter is, they *did* see red. Because that's how angry they got. All right. Now, a person may say, "I've been extremely angry and I didn't see red." That doesn't change the truth. The truth is that it has been accepted for untold eons of time. It is the primitive mind.

Now, what most people seem to forget is that we are a part of the primitive mind, that the primitive mind exists back here in our brain. Because, you see, my friends, that that has been and is yet to be is here this moment. Now, this is the truth about everything. That's the eternal moment: that there is no past, there is no future. There is only the eternal now. How do you think prophecy works? By touching the levels of consciousness of the eternal moment of now and seeing the Law of Cause set into motion and predicting its effect.

All right. Now, what does that have to do with the spoken word? We state that the spoken word is life-giving energy. All right. When you open the mouth and you move the tongue—and we've discussed what that means. Any of my students remember what the mouth means in this class? Pardon?

The door.

What does the tongue mean?

The key.

Fine. So we open the mouth, we open the door, and we turn the key and that's called the spoken word.

We release energy. When we speak a word, we release energy from our aura. And that energy creates a form right here in our universe. Do you understand? Now, that exists dependent upon how much we continue to feed the form, either with the spoken word, which is very potent, or the mental thought. It continues to be fed as long as we do that.

So now what happens is this: We have stated before that man becomes the victim of the games that he plays. Well, what is the game that mankind is always playing? He's playing with his words. He says this and he means that. Of course, it guarantees failure. But anyway, some of us don't think it does. All right. We become the victims of these children that we have created with our spoken word. Do you understand?

Now, the more we speak on those levels of consciousness, the stronger these forms get in our aura. Now, they don't have soul, because man has created them. Do you understand? All right. Now, those forms, if you'd open your clairvoyance and clairaudience, you would see them and you would hear them speaking to you. Now these are our children. We have created them and we are responsible for them. The thing is that they become very unruly sometimes. Now, how do they become unruly? Say that we create, through our spoken word and our desires and thoughts, we create a form of opulence, of abundance. All right? Now, we're creating it by our mind. Now, I'm not talking about the divine Law of Abundance and Opulence. I'm talking about man's mental desire creations. This form gets created. All right, so each time we think about it, the form gets bigger, the form gets stronger. In time, if we keep feeding it energy, the form gets to speak. It now has the spoken word. All right. It starts to influence us. It starts to tell us to do this and to tell us to do that. And if you don't continue to feed the form—the forms of our creation are very greedy. Believe me.

Now why are the forms of our creation very greedy? You want to know why? Because greed created them. Don't you see? What is greed? Greed is an acceptance that we do not have what we think we should have. Do you understand?

All right. So the forms that we have created are known as the greed children. And believe me, there's never enough to satisfy them. I do hope that's helped with your question.

In Discourse 39, there is a reference to the music of the spheres. Could you give us your understanding of that, please?

Thank you. I believe we have discussed that before. We will discuss it again.

All forms are a symphony. They're all expressing a beautiful symphony. Not only the human form, but the lower forms. Now, if you will be perfectly still, in perfect peace, you will hear the symphony of the movement of your own physical body. Now this is an absolute truth.

Now, because we have not practiced peace in our life, it's going to take us a little while to become perfectly peaceful. Then, my friends, you'll have a great awakening: the symphony of the spheres—the symphony of your own body, of the drumbeat of your heart, of the blood going through your veins. If you are peaceful, you will hear that symphony.

Now, sometimes you will hear it and it'll be playing a tune that you don't like at all. It is playing the tune of your own level of consciousness, of your own attitude of mind. So think, my friends. I wish that all people could be so peaceful [as] to hear the symphony of the spheres, because, I assure you, if you did that, you would make great changes, because you would become so weary of hearing the same tune over and over and over again. I do hope that's helped with your question. Thank you.

You discussed earlier a little bit about setting a law into motion. And some of the examples you gave were rather clear. But so frequently in life they seem obscure. And I wonder if you would discuss a little more in depth of how we really set laws into motion.

How you really set a law into motion? Every time your mind has a desire, you set a law into motion. Every time your mind has a thought, you set a law into motion. Now, think of the untold numbers of laws that man is now, at his present age—and I'm sure he will agree—is the victim of.

Well, my friends, now how are we going to neutralize all those thoughts that we've had and all those desires? It behooves us to go to work this moment on a little bit of peace in our life and divine acceptance.

You see, let us go back in time for an example and say that a person desired to get married. All right? Now we have to ask the person, "Why do you desire to be married?" And so the person will say, "Well, I want a family and a home and security." It is rare—it is very rare—that a person will say they want to get married that they leave out the word *security*. Now I've talked to a lot of people and it's very rare that a young girl will say that she wants to get married and security does not exist. No, no. She might say, "No, I don't worry about security." Believe me, she does: she doesn't want to face it yet. Well, anyway, so we set a law into motion—the law to get married. But it's more than just getting married and putting the ring on the finger. It's all those other desires and motivations. They're also a part of that law that we've set into motion.

Now, sometimes it takes twenty or twenty-two years—sometimes even longer—for a law we set into motion to be fulfilled. Do you understand? So, my friends, if you want to be free from this multitude of self-will laws you're setting into motion, pray for a little awareness to find out what your true motive in life is. Not the seeming motivation, but what's that real motive deep down in the depths of our being. Now, if you take moments to pause, you say, "Whoops! I finally see what my motive was thirty years ago. I'm sick and disgusted with myself." Forget it! That's not going to help you. You've got to live with *this* moment. This is the moment—the only moment—you've got any power over. So you've got to be strong in life and you say, "OK, twenty, thirty years ago that was my motivation, but I got a little seasoned from experiences in this life and that hasn't been my motive for at least ten years." But, see, we are fulfilling the law that we set into motion.

Now, this is why it's so very important to cross the bridge to the depths of our patterned mind inside to see what all of those laws are. At least become aware of them so you can do something about them. You know, you can't do anything about anything you're not aware of. That's contrary to even what they call logic. So first we want to become a little bit aware, a little bit aware of what our real motivation is, etc.

Now, there's another law that says every attainment has its payment. Well, of course, it is. You pay for everything. The lungs have to pay for the air that you breathe. You pay for everything in life, friends. Don't ever delude yourself, my good students, to think you get something for nothing. Nobody ever got something for nothing. That's contrary to God's divine, natural, prudent laws—and they're very prudent, because they're very practical. Nature herself, the expression of the Divine, does not waste. She's very practical. And so it is man, a part of nature—he doesn't get something for nothing. If he ever thinks in life he ever got something for nothing, the only person he is deluding is himself and, of course, his friends, because his friends are on the same level of consciousness or they wouldn't be his friends. You understand? Fine. So they are the only ones that are ever deluded about getting something for nothing.

Now, the thing is, you see, that we set these laws into motion and we make certain payments and we have our attainments. Say, for example, for marriage, you know, a woman—she has her husband, etc. But, you see, as life goes on, some of those other motives, at the moment of engagement, start to come to the fore. You know, they took twenty, sometimes forty years to get up there. But that depends on the individual. And those start to come to the fore and the next thing you know, she says, or he says, "This is costing me too much!" And they don't mean money. Usually. But it's just costing too much. Well, my friends, let's stop and think. Let's be cheerful and joyous in life and let's say, "Well, all right, I'm not all bad. But then again, I'm not all good." So let's bring balance in our life and let's say, "Now here this moment I can do something. I can do something with what I've got. I might not be able to change that one, that one, that one, and that one, but I sure can do something inside of me. And that something will change all of my friends, because they're in rapport with me or I wouldn't call them friends, and especially my husband—or wife—and children, because they're in rapport with me."

Don't you see? That's how people change. When you become the living demonstration of truth, the Light herself, those around you will grow or they will go. You won't have to tell them to go. It's not necessary. You see, no husband and no wife need to tell each other one of them has to go: one of them is automatically going to go if you stay where you are and she or he stays where he is. That's how it works, friends. So remember, however you are—and you're strong in your level of consciousness—all things around you shall be in rapport or they shall leave your aura. Does that help with your question? That, my dear, is setting the law into motion. Yes.

Is emotionality inherent in the form or is it a—does it come into being as a result of the patterns of our subconscious mind that develop here once an infant is born, through his patterns of perceiving and the reinforcement?

It is inherent in the form or creation. It is the magnetic pole. And it is inherent in the form.

Is there another way to eliminate emotionality from oneself as long as you are in human form?

Oh yes. Oh yes. You see, you can only experience emotion if your soul consciousness is expressing on the level of emotion, my dear. Otherwise, you cannot experience it. You cannot eliminate it from the very ingredients of the form itself, because the form itself is that magnetic pole. Do you understand?

Now, it is true that the soul in its evolutionary journey has merited that form with strong tendencies in these different areas. Is that clear? However, no, you cannot, in that sense, annihilate the inherent tendencies in the form itself. But you certainly can rise above it and express on another level of consciousness. That you definitely can do. And you're never left without choice to do it at any given moment. Yes.

Could you please discuss the principle of application?

Thank you very much for your question. And the lady is asking for a discussion perhaps on the principle of application. Is that your question? Yes. Well, my friends, we have to ask ourselves another question, "What is it within us that motivates us to apply anything? What is it within us that motivates us?"

Surely all of my students will agree that desire motivates us. I never saw a person in desire yet that didn't get motivated. Would we not all agree that we are motivated by desire? I know that all of my students within the sound of my voice have desire. And I know that they all know that we are motivated by it. Is there anybody to disagree with me? All right, fine. Now we're on a firm foundation to start growing. All right, we all agree that we're motivated with what we call desire.

Now, let us stop and think, and perhaps my student that asked this question may recall the five steps of creation. Would you like to share those with the class? Some of them haven't had it yet. Do you recall them?

Love, belief, desire, will—I don't know that's the correct order—creation.

Action.

Action. Thank you.

All right. Did everyone hear that? Was the word *desire* eliminated? Fine. Those are the five steps of creation, my good students, for those of you who haven't had them before. Desire plays an important part. Now what number—if you want to number from 1 to 5—is desire?

3.

It's number 3. We all know in this understanding that 3 is manifestation, don't we? Now, would you agree that application is a manifestation?

Yes.

Well, I'll tell you, friends, application—the principle of the Law of Application—you know what it is now?

Thank you.

I'm sure you do. All right. Anyone else that doesn't know? Because we just said it. So let's think, friend. "When of naught desire is, / In vain doth sorrow speak [Discourse 2]." When you're out of desire, you're out of duality. And that's how simple it is. Yes.

We just have a chance for a few more questions. We're way past time.

Yes, sir. Would you please elaborate on the difference between motive and goal?

Thank you very much. And the student is asking for a discussion on the word *motive* and the word *goal*. I believe my student asked a question at one of our other classes in reference to goals and desires. And it's most interesting, what we call the chain of events that is coming up again. And this time the question is in reference to motive and goal. Is that correct?

Yes, sir.

Well, the last time I believe we discussed here in reference to a question that was identically the same. Now, I want to bring this point up, my friends. This is very important—with your permission, student, may I bring this up?

Yes, sir.

It's very important, because it helps us to see how the mind works. You see, I happen to know—and I knew when the question was asked concerning goal and desire the last time that my student was not satisfied with the answer. You understand?

Yes, sir.

Now, had my student been satisfied with the answer that was given at that class, then my student would not be asking the same question this moment, only in different form, you see. It's interesting about truth—it's so beautiful. It wears so many garments. And anyway, so I understand that here we are now discussing the very same thing, only now it's called motive and goal instead of desire.

Now, let us think, my friends—all of us—this is how our mind works. Don't you see how our mind works? Look, if one mind works that way, that demonstrates the principle of the law which works in all humanity, because one student is a part of the whole human race, called humanity. And so that only reveals a level of consciousness that one student is expressing on, that some other student may not yet have experienced and, therefore, has no tolerance, because he doesn't have any understanding because he never got to experience that level of consciousness yet.

All right, so here we are—and this is what's important: My student was not satisfied with goal and desire. And here, now, we're going to discuss it under another wording, another form, called motive and desire. I beg your pardon, motive and goal. We're going to get out of desire somehow, believe me, because we're going to get out of this creation. All right. Now we just got through discussing with this lady here on the word *application*, the principle of the Law of Application. And so the statement was brought up about our motive—what motivates us. And so we move from motivation into the Law of Creation, the five steps of creation, into manifestation and into the word *desire*.

Now, let's be at peace a few moments. And let's come out of duality and desire, and let's go back to the teaching that says our goal is our lifeline. Let us not have our goal in life as our desire and motivation. Because, my Lord, man, our desires change so often, so frequently, it's hard to keep up with them. Don't you see? Our desires are way ahead of us. They're sometimes ten, twenty years ahead of us. We're thinking how young we're going to be when we're sixty. And we're taking all kinds of steps with our desires to make sure that we're going to be that young when we are sixty and maybe that's twenty years ahead of us. So let's come back. Let's take the reins on what we call creation and desire. And let's think about this moment. And let's remember, my friends, satisfaction lets us sleep; 'tis irritation that wakes our soul. And the purpose for being in this class, my friends, is waking our soul.

So I'm sorry when you're irritated with the answers that you have merited. But we're not here to please our senses and go to sleep in the womb of satisfaction.

Thank you very much. It's way past time. Let us have refreshments.

SEPTEMBER 26, 1974

CONSCIOUSNESS CLASS 61

Good evening, students. This evening we would like to discuss, for a time, man's most valuable asset. Now, this most valuable asset to humanity is commonly known as health. We understand in this philosophy that health is the direct effect of what is called harmony. And harmony is the direct effect of what is known as peace. And we understand this perfect Peace to be God or the Divine Intelligence.

Now, perhaps it would be of benefit to the class to discuss how this Law of Harmony, which is an effect of perfect peace, is directly related to what is known as our health. We all, I am sure, understand, and will agree, that certain thoughts and thought patterns cause an increase in the body temperature and other thoughts and attitudes of mind cause a decrease in what is known as the body temperature. For example, when man expresses on a level of consciousness known as temper and frustration, there is an increase in the blood pressure and the temperature goes up. Now, what actually takes place in the mind and in the body? We all understand, I'm sure, that the body is a direct effect of our attitude of mind. The body is a direct effect, because of our attitude of mind: our mind uses what is known as a brain for its expression.

Now, when we have certain thought patterns, attitudes of mind, that are like temper and anger and frustration and disappointment and those so-called negative levels of consciousness, we release negative energy from our brain, which goes into our body. This negative energy causes an increase of what is known as negative cells. Now, we all understand that creation is dual: it is both positive and negative. And we are, our bodies, a part of creation and, being a part of creation, being a form, we have what is known as positive cells in our body and we have what is known as negative cells. Now, when this negative energy is released from our brain, there is an increase in the negative cells in our body, which causes what is known as a discord. There's a battle, a war, that starts to go on, because there is an increasing imbalance. This, in turn, is known as poor health.

We all have studied what faith is. We've all studied what fear is. We know that fear is faith in negative expression. For example, when we worry and are concerned about anything, what we, in truth, are doing is expressing faith in something that we desire to accomplish—or to take place—is not going to happen. And that is known as fear. Therefore, my friends, whenever you express negative energy, you are, in truth, expressing fear. Fear, that level of consciousness, attracts its own kind, and man is indeed in discord and disharmony.

Whenever fear is expressing, there is a tension in certain parts of the body that takes place: the muscles contract. Why do they contract? They contract to protect themselves from a negative bombardment of cells in the body. Now, this is how creation, the created body, really works.

And so it is that you have in your world what is known as faith healers. They're not the healers, my friends. They're only the instruments, using whatever methods are legal to stimulate within your mind what is known as faith. Now, we have taught to keep faith with reason, for she will transfigure thee. Now, what do we mean by "reason"? And how does man gain reason? Well, man does not express reason in anything that he does not first understand. And so the teaching, once again, repeats itself throughout eternity: In all your getting, get understanding.

How does man get understanding? By first having the desire to do whatever is necessary to gain it. Man does not gain understanding, however, until he bows the head, known as the human ego, the self-will, to a greater intelligence than his own brain. And it is interesting to note, as all minds, in truth, are a part of the great one mind, that it takes sometimes—ofttimes—great struggle and great suffering for the human will to bow to what is known as the divine will.

Now, we have stated in this course many times that acceptance is the divine will. So if it is understanding that you are seeking—and understanding is the only foundation that is solid, upon which man may build the body known as his own spiritual body—then, my good friends, it certainly behooves you to think about faith, poise, and humility. We have spoken in these classes about what is it we rely upon. We have spoken about our security blanket. And let us face honestly what is known as the tenacity, the undying tenacity of the human will.

We all know that the human will is based upon the patterns of acceptance of yesterday; that it is, therefore, limited; that we are a direct expression of the patterns of mind of our own acceptance. And so if we are not happy with the manifestation and the experiences in our life, then it only stands to reason that we would bow this human will to the divine will, which means acceptance of something greater and something better. However, it takes many paths to get to the Divine, to get to acceptance. But there is one sure way, my good friends, that really works and that way is known as repetition. To repeat over and over and over again, again, and again, until finally the mind says, "I have made my life this way to this point. I'm not happy with the experiences that I am encountering. Therefore, I am now willing to accept a different way, a better way."

In speaking on health and harmony and how this all flows from what we call peace, we all know that heat causes a decaying process in all form. We all know that freezing causes a preserving of the form. Now, not only does a decaying process take place through what is known as heat, but there's an increase in the aging process.

The day is not far off in your earth realm when medical science will recognize the great truth of what is known as temperature and how it affects the body. And the day will come when so-called freezing will serve as one of the many methods for medical treatment of what is called health. Now, think, my friends. Think of what you're doing to your own body. When you go out into the world and you don't like this and you don't like that, stop and think. If you are expressing intolerance and anger and temper, disappointment and frustration, you are literally destroying your human body. And you have a direct spiritual responsibility to your human body, for it is the vehicle through which your soul expresses on this earth realm. My friends, the body is the temple of the Divine, known as your own Spirit. Don't look outside to improve your body. Look inside, because that's the only place you can improve your body. It's only by working with the cause that you make the changes which are necessary.

You know, so often when we're in our youth, we're not concerned about what we're doing to our body. We're not concerned what our thoughts are doing, but we soon become very concerned as the years pass by. But let us remember that we're living in this moment, that yesterday indeed has gone and tomorrow has not yet come. We can have a complete change, a transformation of our body, simply by an acceptance of something greater. But that, my friends, takes a bowing of the human ego. It takes a true acceptance. But, I assure you, it is the only thing that is really worthwhile.

You're now free to ask any questions that you have. Yes.

Let's say a person has a particular fear and they don't quite understand. They don't know what they're afraid of. They keep practicing faith and they say, "Well, if I can only accept this thing, if I could just accept faith." But, then, they have a conflict going, because they have the fear on the other end that's still bothering them. And it's almost like they're suppressing it and they're trying to accept faith. So my question is, How is it that a person would deal with all this going on? I mean, they have this over here and that over there.

Thank you so very much for your question. The lady is speaking on the duality of creation, known as faith and fear. There's one way to bring balance into one's life—and only one way that I know—and it's commonly referred to as self-control. Now, we gain self-control through what is known as concentration, because concentration is that that you place your mind pointedly and fixedly upon until only the essence remains. And so the first step in bringing about a balance between what is known as faith and fear (or faith in the negative, instead of the positive: that's called fear) is to practice, to demonstrate self-control. You are never left without choice. At any given moment, you may choose to express faith (positive) or you may choose to express what is called fear. Does that help with your question?

I have another one. What if you confronted the fear instead?

Fear disappears when understanding is gained. You see, we cannot fear what we understand. Fear is a negative projection of energy. If we make the effort to understand what it seems we fear, then we will no longer fear it. For the father is greater than the son. And man, the creator, is greater than his creations. So, you see, when you are experiencing a fear, you and you alone are the creator of that fear. And being the creator of a thing, you are greater than it. Does that help with your question?

Yes.

It deals with the Law of Personal Responsibility. But, you see, most of us, when we have a fear, we give power to things outside of ourselves, instead of making the effort to understand what it is that we fear. So the first step is to work on understanding. But you can't gain understanding without self-control. It is not possible, no. Can you understand what you cannot control long enough to understand? If you have a moving object and you're unable to control it to stop its movement, can you understand its movement? No. And so it is with the mind. As long as the mind is in motion, through lack of self-control, then you will not understand the mind. And if we cannot understand the mind, we certainly cannot move to the spirit and soul, which is yet even greater. Does that help with your question?

Thank you.

You're welcome. Yes.

In the past, you have told us that if we had a specific ailment, such as a sore throat, or whatever it happens to be, to release it to the Divine.

Yes.

Are we releasing the sore throat or the feeling of that? Or are we releasing the resentment? And does release bring us to the neutral point of peace or balance?

Thank you so very much. In reference to your question, what we're doing, in truth, is forgiving. We have stated before in our classes that to forgive is to free: to free from the bondage of self. And the teaching, Release it to the Divine, means to forgive yourself, to forgive the level, that you may free your soul, that it may rise to another level of consciousness. And that's known as releasing the other level to the Divine. Do you understand?

And the lady is speaking in reference to the throat. It is true that that part of the anatomy is representative of what is known as an attitude of mind called resentment. Now, for anyone to say that they never have resentment is absolutely ridiculous. None of us are so saintly, to my awareness. Of course, I'm not too aware sometimes, but I'm sure my students will agree that we have all experienced what is known as resentment. And if we're honest with ourselves, we can instantly recall when we had that experience. All right, now what does "resentment" really mean? What does it mean? Does it mean "acceptance"? It is an emotional reaction to something that we have chosen not to accept. And yet acceptance is the divine will. So does it behoove a man to have resentment when it is a demonstrable truth that resentment causes negative energies to be directed to what is known as the area in the body called the throat? No, it most certainly does not. Does that help with your question?

Thank you very much.

You're welcome.

In talking on acceptance again, are we to accept all situations that happen to us, I mean, regardless of what the situation is? Is this acceptance of a divine will, as so many religionists say, bowing the head to God?

Well, that, of course, is entirely dependent upon if we choose to be godly. Now, the lady has asked a question, Are we to accept all experiences in life? This is basically the question. Well, we have just earlier stated that acceptance is the divine will. Now, if we choose to express our divinity, which is this perfect peace, then, my friends, we will accept all things in the universe.

Now, it is also stated—and I think there's a bit of confusion in some of the gray areas of the brain with some of my students in reference to acceptance. The teaching is that man cannot experience what he has not first accepted. All right. I know some people will disagree with me, especially if they're experiencing things that they don't like to experience. That's not the point. The law is totally impartial and the law is completely demonstrable. So we can say, "If that's the case, I choose not to experience that level of consciousness because it's so detrimental." My good friends, all levels of consciousness are within us. If we do not accept that, we are going to guarantee all the experiences necessary to understand it. This is why we teach our adversities become our attachments; it is a subtle law. This is why we teach, "What today I criticize, tomorrow I shall idolize." Well, I have yet to find a man that isn't idolizing the level of consciousness that he's expressing at the moment. He certainly doesn't criticize himself while he's expressing it. He criticizes himself just before going into the level or just after coming out of it. While he's in it, he idolizes it. Don't you see? Because if we didn't, we wouldn't remain in it.

Now, let us think clearly. A person may say, "Well, I'm in this level of consciousness and I'm griping and complaining about this level of consciousness." Well, God has not left us without choice, my friends. We may choose in an instant to come out of that level of consciousness. It is within our power known as thought. All right, now we can say, well, we're suffering and we can't get out of a level of consciousness. It doesn't make any difference what level of consciousness that our soul is expressing upon. We have the divine right—and it's demonstrated over and over, again and again—to choose another level of consciousness by changing our thought, which changes our attitude, which redirects the energy, and we experience something different. So think, my friends. The moment in which you are aware is the only moment that you have power over.

Now, when you accept through total consideration—what is total consideration? You have been given an affirmation that is more valuable than the most precious diamonds in your earth realm. It is more valuable than all the gold you can garner up.

And yet many of my students haven't yet reached that state of consciousness to know what that does to their body, what it does to their mind, if they'll use it. Unfortunately, some of us cannot use something that we ourselves personally have not thought of. Well, my friends, that affirmation didn't come from one human being over here or on your earth realm. It came through untold centuries of study and effort and suffering and struggle. I cannot impress any stronger upon your minds what it can do for you and your life.

But, you see, my friends, it's so simple. And this is why truth seems to have great difficulty in entering the human consciousness, because it doesn't fit, perhaps, our patterns of acceptance. You've also been given another great affirmation. The children learn it first and they certainly do a lot better with it than most so-called adults and it simply says, "Thank you, God." It expresses gratitude, the first soul faculty. It recognizes a greater intelligence than the human brain and it declares the truth, "I am at peace." But, don't you see, the intellect hears it, but not the soul and not the heart. And so man doesn't bother with such simple things. Forgetting entirely that a Divine Intelligence spoke forth the word and the word manifested itself and you have the universes. And it all began, my friends, with one word. How simple can it be. Thank you very much.

Does someone else have a question? Yes.

How can a person tell, at the moment of expression, whether he or she is expressing through the soul faculties or the sense functions?

Thank you very, very much. We can very easily tell when we are expressing through the soul faculties or the sense functions. If we are expressing through the sense functions, there is an experience, a feeling, and a stimulation of the senses. If we are expressing through the soul faculties, there is an inner peace, there is no worry, there's no thought, there's no concern. And that is very easy to discern for all of us. Yes.

If, for example, you are aware of expressing through the sense functions, is there a process, or is there some help which you might give us, which would offer us a way to move from being in the sense function or expressing through the sense functions to expressing through the faculties?

There most certainly is. You see, the sense functions are the negative expression of the form and the soul faculties are the positive expression. And we have repeatedly stated that it is not our teaching to annihilate the sense functions, for in so doing you will not long remain in the physical form. We, just a few moments ago, gave a simple affirmation that will help you remain partially aware while going into the darkness, known as desire, to express the sense functions. And that affirmation is, "Thank you, God. I am at peace." If you will use that religiously while you are expressing through what is known as the desire level in the sense functions, you will have a constant inner awareness of where you are. The more you use it, the more it will work for you. Do you understand?

Thank you.

Yes, you're more than welcome. And I'm glad that you did bring that up—on the sense functions—this evening, because we have stated that there are several bodies through which the divine Spirit, known as God, is expressing. There's the soul and there's our spirit body; there's our astral body; there's our mental body; there's our physical body; there's our vital body; there's our desire body. Well, think, my friends. Through the vehicle of thought, energy expresses itself. If we have more desire expressed in our life than we have reason, that simply means that our desire body becomes the strongest body. Would you not agree? Because a body is an effect of directed energy. So when we leave this physical piece of clay, we hope to be in realms of light. If our desire body is the strongest body that we have created, then we find ourselves in what is known as a desire world. Do you understand? Because we have no balance, we have no other body that's as strong as the desire body.

Well, what happens is this—that's known as the realm of satisfaction and regret. You see, my friends, man remains in desire as long as the desire satisfies him. Would you not agree? And when it no longer satisfies us, we soon get out of it. Would you not agree to that also? All right. And so it is that we spoke in another class: desire—one of the five steps of creation.

Ask yourself the question—we're all going to go someday and for some of us, it's much sooner than we realize, of course. But where are we going? Let us ask ourselves the question. Well, where are we this moment? And wherever we are this moment, that's where we're going. We've stated simply that heaven is not a place we go to: it's a state of consciousness, a state of mind that we grow to. So if our desire body is the strongest body, then, of course, we will find ourselves, when we leave the physical body, in what is known as the desire world. Now, we might say that, "Well, that's nice. I like my desires and I wouldn't mind living there." Well, the only thing about that, my good friends, is you don't know all the other people that are there. And their desires, you know, are something else. And we don't approve of all of them, but there we are and we get to see all of that. Well, it's not as pleasant or as satisfying as we think that it's going to be. Then, it dawns in our consciousness, what is known as regret.

Well, how does regret dawn in our consciousness? Through self, through self-concern. You see, first off, we see that those desires, they're not satisfying anymore. We have to tolerate all these other people and their desires and so we start to think about ourselves even more. And the more we think about ourselves, we start to experience regret. We feel badly for what we've done a year ago or ten or twenty or fifty. And so when we go into regret, sadness comes over our soul. And when the sadness is great enough, man calls that suffering. And when the suffering is intense enough, he starts to pray. And if he doesn't pray, he starts to think about something. Anything that will get us out of that level of consciousness and get us out of that world.

This is why we teach, "O suffer senses not in vain, for freedom of your soul is gain." And our soul—don't you see?—it gains in its evolution. If we are imbalanced, you see, then our soul is not evolving as it should and we are here in the descent, known as the functions, because of the imbalance. And sooner or later, you see, the suffering gets so intense we pray to God to lift us up. What happens then—don't you see?—at that moment? At that moment we are experiencing acceptance. We're miserable where we are. So what's going to take us out of it? We have to accept something different. Would you not agree? Because if we don't accept something different, we're going to stay where we are.

Many religionists, for untold centuries, have recognized the value of human suffering. In fact, some of your religionists used to wear what they called hair shirts—some of the monks. So they could suffer, their senses could suffer. I say that is not necessary to go around wearing hair shirts so that your body can suffer. There's plenty of suffering in the world. And when it's intense enough, believe me, my good students, we will turn to God. It doesn't matter what name we call the Divine, we will turn to something greater and that's what we call the Infinite Intelligence. I do hope that's helped with your question. Yes.

In tonight's discourse, at the bottom of the page it says—talking about humility—it says, "You have been given, my children, the various parts of the anatomy. And now think, Where is humility in the body represented? What is it that humbles the mind? What is it that bows the pride? The will [Discourse 41]?" All right, my question is, Could you give me your understanding of exactly what the will is? I have the impression of it—a negative impression—and I'm not quite sure if I understand.

Thank you so very much. Are you speaking of the human will? *The human will.*

Yes, the human will is the expression of the patterns of acceptance of any individual. And it is expressed through what is known as the house of the functions, called the ego. That's the human will. Now, the human will has restricted acceptance. Do you understand? Because it's based upon the subconscious patterns of acceptance of our life. So therefore it takes humility, you see, to open up the door to accept something better. Do you understand that? Did that help with your question?

Thank you.

You're welcome. Yes.

Would you discuss the vital body a bit more, in terms of what role it plays in bringing about a balance in the electromagnetic field, please?

Thank you very much. The vital body, which is also referred to as the energy body, is the direct effect of the balance of the electromagnetic energies. Then, this divine, neutral, odic power moves and builds what is called our vital body. So when man is in harmony, when his conscious thoughts and his subconscious acceptance are in harmony, then he is receptive to the so-called superconscious, through which this balanced energy flows and creates what is known as our vital body. You see, that's called our vitality, our energy, our enthusiasm. You see, my friends, when you're enthused, you literally permeate your entire body with a healing balm. And so it behooves all of us to be more enthusiastic. If you want success in life, you have to express enthusiasm, because that's the power that works. *Enthused* is "in God." And that, my friends, is your vital body. Do you see why it's called vital? Just be without it and see where you land. Yes, I hope that's helped with your question.

Thank you very much.

You're welcome.

On the faculties of faith, poise, and humility—or any other faculties—when we use or express or manifest faith, do the other two come into being automatically or are we expressing all three at one time?

Thank you so very much. And the lady is speaking in reference to the second soul faculty, known as faith, poise, and humility. Now, the soul faculties are triune and inseparable. If you express 2 degrees of faith, then you're expressing 2 degrees of poise and 2 degrees of humility, because the faculty is triune and is inseparable. Yes, does that help with your question?

Thank you.

Yes. You cannot express one without having an effect upon the others. Yes.

Going back to the sense functions again, I think this thought has been in my mind this particular week. But it was brought up last week that old, established patterns—that we can find answers or reasons for the desire. You say that we have an inner voice or something that speaks to us and somehow we don't listen to it, but yet we go ahead with this particular faculty of our senses. What if we do deny and we do say, "Well, this is possibly wrong for me at this particular time"? What happens to our soul if we do deny ourselves? How will we grow?

Man's denials, my good student, are his destinies. And so in reference to your question, How will you grow, you'll grow ever in accord with the law, of course, that you set into motion. You see, we must also realize that man never wants for another what he has first denied himself. And so when we deny, you see, which is totally contrary to acceptance, the divine will, well, what we're doing is shutting ourselves off from the divine Light itself. That's all we're doing.

Now, a man may say, "Well, then, that means I shouldn't deny myself any of my desires." Well, you're not denying yourself any of your desires anyway. Believe me. Man always gets what he really wants. And I never saw a man yet that had a desire that he didn't get it fulfilled one way or another, sooner or later—perhaps to his satisfaction and perhaps not to his satisfaction. But we don't deny our desires, my friend.

See, our teaching is to educate the desire, not to deny the desire; to remember that it's in our own head and not to say, "Well, that person walking down the street caused me to have a desire." That's ridiculous and stupid. I mean, my good friends, if we have gotten to the point of license where we have no control of our mind and we cannot walk down a public thoroughfare without blaming somebody else for triggering our desires, then we're certainly, my goodness' sakes alive, we're back in the womb where we should be nurse fed and taken care of by a guardian called a mother. Well, let's grow up and be men and women. And let's not say, "Well, I saw this movie and I couldn't control myself," or some other foolishness. Let's stop and think, you know.

Our job isn't to go out there and change the world. Our job is to change the world that we have some control over—hopefully, some control. My goodness, look at us, friends. Surely we're evolved in this world. At least, we're two-legged animals and no longer the four-legged kind. Goodness, let us have a little bit of self-control, you know. Why, the dogs and the rabbits don't even act like that. Let's think about it. You know, we say, "What's the matter with my mind? I can't control myself. What's happened to me?" Well, isn't that a sad state of affairs? Isn't that really pathetic? Now, think, my friends. We all have that in levels within us. But goodness' sakes alive, if there wasn't some control—the world is already concerned about the population explosion. What's going to happen if we just go hog wild with all our desires? No. Let's raise to a higher level of consciousness, hopefully. Goodness, otherwise, we'd better consider all going at the age of fourteen for surgical operations, if we have no more control than that. I do hope that's helped with your question. Thank you. Yes.

We have been taught the value of being positive and to hold positive thinking and that, to me, would be faith. Can we sustain and maintain this without negative levels? And are not the negative levels the balance between the positive and the negative? Isn't overconfidence a function?

Thank you very much for your question. And the lady has stated that her understanding of faith is the positive vibration. It's a knowing, of course. And isn't overconfidence a function? Well, I would like to know what the student means by the word "overconfidence." Would you care to share your understanding of the meaning of that word?

I'll try.

Yes.

Well, if I had to go take a driving test, for instance—and I am a very poor driver—and I hadn't studied for that test and I still go ahead and take the test without the application of study, that, to me, would be—or any other type of testing—would be overconfidence.

Thank you. Do you believe that God is ever equal to your understanding?

Yes.

If you believe that God is ever equal to your understanding, do you believe to God all things are possible?

I have said it enough.

Do you believe it?

I—

We say many things, but the question is, do we believe it?

I'm trying to believe it, yes.

Fine. Now, if God, which the lady, the student, believes is ever equal to our understanding—and to us, to God, all things are possible—then, my dear, all things are possible, dependent upon your understanding. I do hope that's helped with your question. Because, you see, your God is as big as your understanding. So if you have a big understanding, you have a big God. And the bigger the God, the more that God is able to do for you. Don't you see? And why, again, we teach, In all of your getting, get understanding. Let's get rid of those miserly little gods. Let's dethrone all those false gods and let's work on our understanding, so that we can let the true God, the Infinite Intelligence, into our mind, into our heart, into our soul. And then, you will speak the word into the universe. You will not rely upon the human brain in its computer. You, I am sure, as a student of many years in the understanding of Spiritualism, are well aware that many, many, many mediums have answered questions that do not exist—the answers—in their brain computer. Would you not agree?

I do.

They have performed many, many, many things in this world that their brain had never, ever experienced. How were they able to do that? Those souls did not rely upon their computer brain for the answer. You know very well, my good student, that a medium ofttimes is able to prophesy events far into the future with great accuracy. Well, how is that possible? How is it possible, if they rely upon a brain computer that doesn't know what's going to happen tomorrow? Some Spiritualists might say, "Well, they rely upon a discarnate spirit that tells them all of that." Well, if their own spirit was not on the level of consciousness with the spirit that has all that information, they could never receive all that information. You see, my friends, the guides and teachers and angels of the prophets are ever equal to the prophets themselves. The guides are no higher, nor are they any lower. So if you are satisfied with the friends, known as the spirits, around and about you, then those are the ones that you will keep. But, you see, it is the Law of Evolution that the soul must rise ever to higher levels of consciousness. And if those around and about you do not rise, as you are personally making the effort, then they shall disappear and they shall leave your universe. I hope that's helped with your question. Yes.

I'm seeking a little clarification. Did I understand you to make a distinction between the desire body and desire world, to distinguish it from the astral body and astral world?

Yes, absolutely. Definitely.

Could you expand?

In what way, my friend?

Well—

What is it that you want to know?

Well, I thought the desires came from the computer of the subconscious, but—

Yes?

Am I understanding you to say that they're coming from a different mind?

No, no, no. We have a mind: it has many compartments. Do you understand? We have feelings and we have emotions. We also have a mind that has thoughts and supposed logic. All right. We have a mental body. You understand we have a mental body. That body goes into a mental world, unless our soul has a stronger body and it goes into another world: a desire world, if it's the desire body; an astral world, if it's the astral body.

Now, I think perhaps where the confusion might exist is that you perhaps think that the subconscious mind creates the astral body and that's all it does create. No, my friends. There is a teaching in this book [*The Living Light*] that says very clearly your soul, all things it can and does create.

So the subconscious mind, it has computed patterns; it has certain feelings and emotions and those create these different bodies. Yes, they most certainly do. And you have a vital body and that's created through a balance between your electromagnetic minds, which is known as the odic and the vital body. Then, you have, hopefully, a spiritual body that is created through the expression of energy through your soul faculties. And you also have a soul body and you have a physical body. You see, it's difficult, I know, for us to say, "Well, here I am. I can touch this and that's the only body I have. Well, what about these thoughts and all these feelings? Where are they? I can't, I don't seem to be touching those." Yes, does that help with your question? Yes.

I understand that there is another class similar to ours on the other side. Is that right? While this one is in session?

That is correct.

Are the questions that come from us, are they from our spirit or are they from the other side's spirit?

Well, that depends on how much control you have, my dear. That depends on how much control you have of yourself. You're asking about where does your question come from?

Yes.

Well, it might either come from you or it might come from someone you've attracted to you, you see. We've discussed before how man is a receiving set—receiving and sending set, you see. He has thoughts and—you know, of course, being grounded for so long in ourselves, we think the thoughts all originate in here. But time and time again, they're originating from somebody over there. And we're receptive to that level of consciousness and so we express it and we think the thought is ours.

Now, have you ever had any experience with how hypnosis works and how a person does things? Well, don't you know they accept that's their own thought, but it's the thought of someone else. Well? We're in those levels of consciousness more times than we would like to realize that we're in them. And so that depends, as I said, on your ability at self-control. Are you able to control your thoughts? Now, you first must control your thoughts before you can discern where they're coming from, you see. Now, a person that's able to control their thoughts and control their mind cannot be hypnotized. Do you understand?

I've not had that—No, I don't—

Well, they cannot be. They cannot be, my dear. So it all goes down to control, to self-control. You see, we do all kinds of things in the course of a day, because we became receptive to a certain level of consciousness and a thought entered our head and we reacted. We don't say, "Why this and why now?" We don't question ourselves: "Where is this thought coming from?" Because, you see, we got so bloated in our self-importance that we credit ourselves with all our thoughts. And anything that doesn't come out of this head, you know, we don't have any value for. Don't you see? It all deals with self-control. Yes.

Now, the question is, "Well, if a thought is coming from outside of me, is that a beneficial thought?" Well, that depends, my dear, if you are on a beneficial level. Do you see that? Sure. When man is negative, then he's the open receiving set for every negative thought vibration in all of the universes. And so what happens when we get negative, we get more negative. And we keep going down and we get more and more negative. Well, it's the same thing when you have a desire: entertain it for a while, the next thing you know, you can't stop and you have to fulfill it, because it starts to drive you crazy. Well, why does it do that? Where does all of that energy directed to that level come from? *You* opened up to all the universes and everybody on that level of consciousness, and you can't control yourself anymore. Would you not agree?

Yes.

Yes, so that's what happens, yes. You want truth, my friends—you see, it's been stated in these classes many times: truth comes to no one without control. That has been stated again and again. Why, you can't experience truth until you can control. You first must control. Yes.

I heard that various literary works have been brought through and composers have brought through music that wasn't completely their own. Is it fair for them to take credit for it?

Well, is it fair for who to take credit?

The one here on the earth plane.

The channel?

To take credit.

Well, thank you so much for that wonderful question. Anyone, anywhere, that takes credit for any job that they do is denying the Divinity. They're denying the true source. Now, he who seeks the praise of man loses sight of God's true plan. When we find it necessary, after doing a job, to search out and to seek glorification for ourselves, there are no spiritual deposits in our eternal spiritual bank account. And we never know when we're going to need to draw on that bank account. And if there's no spiritual deposits there, there's nothing to draw upon. And so it surely behooves man to do the work he has to do not to seek the praise of man, for God's greatest work, my dear, is done in silence. However, if a soul needs to tell the world how good they're doing, because they need—they think they need—encouragement, then that simply means that that soul, on that level of consciousness, has not yet found the true faith and reliance upon what we call God. They're still relying upon the praises of man in order to do God's work. It's known as a mental crutch. But, in time, it shall pass. Does that help with your question?

Yes. May I ask another?

Certainly.

When you submit a work to a publisher, you can't very well say it was written through you, can you?

Well, unless you publish it yourself. That depends, that depends, my dear. If you accept that you cannot submit a book to a publisher without taking personal credit for it, without giving a credit line to the true source, then that's the only way that you can go. But, you see, God's greater than all the publishers. There wouldn't be any publishers if it wasn't for God. So I wouldn't rely upon man. Man guarantees to fail you.

What I was wondering was, just before transition, say, one has a conscious awareness of the physical flesh, and yet, at the same time, maybe they have an awareness of surrounding friends or hearing music, etc. What is it really that stimulates that? And maybe, say, they weren't aware and it wouldn't happen. What is it that really stimulates that coming event?

Yes. Well, coming events, my good student, forecast a shadow for all of us. You see, man is always prepared for anything he is yet to face. Now, the only time that we think we're not prepared is when we are expressing through the magnetic field, known as our emotions. But we're always prepared for all coming events and how fortunate indeed we are for that.

Now, in reference to someone at the time of transition experiencing, sometimes, voices of the departed or their forms or music, etc., that means simply that they have reached that level of consciousness, you understand, and therefore are having the experience on spiritual levels of consciousness—or it could even be astral levels of consciousness.

Now, you know, it's so wonderful when we face a situation where we say, "Well, Lord, I know I have accepted I've only got a few months left to live on this earth realm." It is just wonderful, the experiences that we go through. It really is. You see, man, believe me, doesn't want to think about so-called death or transition. He just pushes that right out of his mind until *[The Teacher knocks on the wooden lectern.]* it knocks. And it knocks according to what we rely upon. For example, if we rely upon a medical doctor and we have faith in the doctor and the doctor says, "Well, Joe, you've got two months left to go," well, of course, we accept that, if that's where we've placed our faith and our reliance. And when we do that, the mind goes through all kinds of changes and processes.

Well, the truth of the matter is, you might go two months and you might go another twenty years: that isn't dependent upon the doctor at all. No. He's not the one who's going to make you go two years, two months, or twenty. No. However, it does ofttimes serve a very good purpose. You know why? We start to think, "Do I really believe, *really* in the continuity of life? Am I pleased with what I've done with my life to this point?" That's where the truth starts rising in our consciousness and we start really to think. Most of us have been brainwashed to a god of wrath, a god of absolute justice. And we start to shudder, because we're not quite sure whether we really believe in the continuity of life or we're going to face this judge, which, in truth, of course, is our own conscience.

And something inside of us starts to go to work. And so it's nice. I think it would help all of my students to sit down and take about eighteen minutes and say to yourself, "Well, in nine minutes I'm going to leave this body for good. How do I feel about it? What have I left unfinished? Who am I going to have to face and what kind of judgment will I be able to accept, because, whether I accept it or not, it's going to be." It behooves you, my friends. Stop and think. Stop and think. Then, you know what will happen? You'll say, "Well, I have nine minutes to go. The train's coming and I'm on my way and I can't turn back. Well, I have a house and I have a couple cars and I have this and that." Well, what value do they have? You're not going to take them with you. What are you going to take with you?

Remember, you take no physical substance into those dimensions, because it doesn't exist in those dimensions. What are you going to take with you, friends? What is going to comfort you on your journey? What is going to encourage you and keep you going? What do you have? What do you have to take with you? The only thing you have is your mind. That's all. What kind of a mind are you going to take? Are you going to be pleased with it? Think about that. Every moment is a death and every moment is a birth, for it is a death and birth in consciousness. So think.

So often we think, "Well, in ten years I'll have this here, in this physical world." Or, "In twenty years I'll have that." Well, my friends, you might not make it ten years. You might not even make it ten days. So is that sensible? Is it reasonable to garner up all of the gold of this material world and put it all into a bank account? Is it logical? Is it even logical to live in that kind of fear? Because, you see, if you live in that kind of fear, if that's where your security is, when you leave your physical body you will not be able to leave the bank doors, because that's where your security is. And so you, your astral body, your desire bodies, will hover at those bank vaults. But all it can do is hover and go through its frustrations. Think, my good students, is that what you want? We're all going to have to face that. And we don't know what hour, what day, or what moment we're going to face it. Prepare yourselves. Somehow you have merited the opportunity to consider it.

Thank you very much. Our time is way past. Let us have refreshments.

OCTOBER 3, 1974

CONSCIOUSNESS CLASS 62

We'll discuss for a while the foundation of all the soul faculties. And many of you, of course, have already been given that foundation. And it is known as understanding.

Now, understanding is composed of a triune faculty, which is known as consideration, acceptance, and expression. We all understand, of course, that God, the Divine, is equal to our understanding and our understanding is equal to our consideration, to our acceptance, and to our expression. Now, consideration is also known as divine love. Acceptance is known as divine will. And expression is known as divine action.

When we broaden our understanding—and it's been taught for untold centuries: In all your getting, get understanding. When man prays for the getting of understanding, he sets into motion the laws: the Law of Consideration, the Law of Acceptance, and the Law of Expression.

We have said before that if man has need, it's not for things: it is for understanding. For when you have understanding in its fullness, you have God in its fullness. And to God, all things are possible.

It seems that consideration is difficult enough for most of us, because we don't seem to want to think about other things and other people. Well, if it is understanding and God that you are seeking—and only through God are your desires fulfilled—then, of course, it behooves us to consider all things, which is the divine love (or the God love) and to accept all things, which is the divine will, and to express those two faculties in order that we may experience the fullness of what we are seeking in life.

Now, that is the foundation upon which all soul faculties are based. And from that we move into the soul faculty of duty, gratitude, and tolerance. Now, you cannot have duty, gratitude, and tolerance until you have some understanding. And you cannot have some understanding until you have consideration, acceptance, and expression. And so we move through these soul faculties—this divine energy does—according to our own willingness and our own effort to consider, to accept, and to express.

When the mind seeks things, it sets laws into motion in order that those things may be experienced in your life. Now, the obstruction to the things that we are seeking is in the foundation of the soul faculties. That obstruction is our unwillingness to understand the divine laws by which things appear in our lives. And so, my friends, again and again the teaching remains ever the same truth: In all your getting, get understanding. So if you are not experiencing what it is you think that you are seeking in life, it is simply because you are obstructing the foundation of your own soul faculties.

Now, many of us, of course, we say we would like to have success in this or success in that. We'd like to find the true being of what we call ourselves. Well, we cannot find ourselves until we find everyone else, because, my friends, we are a part of that one wholeness. And for us to deny ourselves the effort to understand another human soul because we do not want to bother to consider, let alone to accept, is to deny ourselves. We are denying an inseparable part of the level of consciousness that another individual may be expressing.

Now, you have been given an affirmation, which we spoke this evening. It's entitled "Total Consideration." *[See the appendix for the complete text of the affirmation.]* In a way, I suppose, I could be sadly disappointed that after many classes to students, they don't yet seem to find it valuable enough to make the effort, the simple effort, to learn it, to understand it, so they can see for their own personal self what truth it contains and what it will do for you. If you have read it—and many of you have, and few have made the effort to speak it forth—if you have read it and do not understand it, it simply means you have yet to give it sufficient consideration in order to accept it, that you may, in truth, express it.

In life, it seems in this earth realm here, it does seem that suffering is absolutely necessary in order that we may seek the simplicity of Truth herself. So, my friends, when suffering knocks at your door, greet it with a smile, because it is the instrument—if you have suffered sufficiently—it is the instrument through which your soul will seek something better, something on a higher plane of consciousness. And so it is that man—through repetition change for man is made possible.

You're free now to ask any questions that you may have.

Last week you mentioned that there were several bodies created through the subconscious mind. And you talked a bit about the desire body and really made some very sobering comments about where it can take us. I wonder if you would please tell us what the role of a function is of the mind of the astral body itself. And also would you describe to us some of the other bodies created by the subconscious mind?

Well, thank you. I'll be happy to express on some of those questions at this time and namely the one that you have asked concerning the astral body. Now, the astral body, which is created by the subconscious mind, is not the same as the desire body, which is created by—also—our subconscious mind. Our desires, as long as they satisfy us, create what is known as the desire body and take our soul, which is encasing our spirit, to a desire world. Our astral body, however, which is created by our subconscious mind, is the body created by desires that are no longer satisfying to us. That creates our astral shell or astral body.

Now, one might say, "Well, if that's the case, then, of course, it would be better for my soul to go to a desire world, where I will be satisfied, than to an astral world, where I will not be satisfied, because those desires of yesterday no longer interest me." But that, my friends, is not true. It is much more difficult to evolve from a desire world than it is to evolve from an astral world. Because the astral world, you see—the desires that satisfied us at a time have created a pattern and a bondage so strong and so intense, you understand, it is by far—I beg your pardon—to be in an astral, rather than in a desire. There's a correction with that. It's much easier to rise from the astral realm than it is from the desire realm. I hope that's helped with your questions.

And I do feel, though we do have a vital body and several other bodies, we should consider more the bodies of which we are aware. Because it is through our awareness of these bodies that we're able to do something, of course, about it. Yes, thank you so much for your question. Yes.

My question deals with human relations. As long as we're on the earth plane, we have what is known as self or ego. How in communication, both listening and in speaking, can we recognize when that ego or self is getting in the way of a clear communication?

Thank you so very much. And, of course, that definitely comes from self-awareness. And self-awareness is the effect of self-control. Now, I do know that some of my students I have heard—and it does seem most interesting to me, that they seem rather partial to some type of a teaching; it's a bit foreign to me, but I'll try to express on it—on some type of a teaching that ego is only an expression and that a person's expression is their divine right. Well, of course, it is, my friend. And it always is so fascinating to me. Some of you are private students of mine and you are well aware of what is known as the Law of Justification. And I think perhaps this will help with your question concerning ego and self-control.

What is so interesting about the mind [is that] whenever something does not go the way that we desire it to go or whenever someone corrects us or reprimands us—which we alone, of course, have merited by setting laws into motion—that we go into the level of consciousness known as justification. We justify our expression, because we have a need to defend ourselves. Now, we teach in this philosophy that truth needs no defense, because, you see, truth just is. There's nothing to defend when you're speaking truth. Truth *is*.

But it is our ego that has the need to defend whatever position, you understand, that we care to express. It is our ego that demands to defend this by justifying it. It's just like a person that likes to be late, you see. Well, the mind, of course, justifies their constantly being late in order to defend its position, when the truth of the matter is, it is the very same ego that needs to be waited upon. Do you understand? You see, now that's just one thing that we should consider: is how this brain of ours really works. And it's always out to justify why it's done this and it's out to justify why it's done that. It has to justify because, you see, it doesn't have total consideration. If it had total consideration, there'd be nothing to defend and therefore nothing, of course, to justify.

Now, how do we know when we are expressing from the functions, the house of the ego, or when we are expressing from the soul faculties and from the spirit? And this is your basic question, isn't it? Well, learn to listen, my good students. Learn to listen to yourself. When you're speaking, hear what you're saying. So few of us, you see, practice that. We don't even know what we've said five minutes later. And some of my students, you know, when they're corrected on something for their own good, say, "Well, I don't remember saying that." I know they don't remember saying that because, you see, desire has no light and they're not listening.

We've spoken on desire many times in this class. You've been given the greatest affirmation of all. While you're in desire, to [say], "Thank you, God. I am at peace." So you can have a little light when you're in desire, just a little bit perhaps. But don't you see, my friends? It is true that many times we're not even aware that we said something. And it is also true that there are many times we *are* aware, but in order to defend ourselves, we justify it by saying, "Well, I never heard that. I don't recall ever having said that. Well, I didn't mean anything by that." Because, you see, we're not thinking. And if we're not thinking, my friends, then we can't listen. We can't hear what we're saying. Does that help with your question?

Learn to listen. Listen to what you have to say. And I'll tell you, if you do that, you'll start saying less, because it's such an effort to listen to each word. Don't you see? And remember that God, in truth, is silence. Thank you for your question. Yes.

We hear so much about soul unfoldment. Is it the soul that unfolds or is the faculties that unfold? And are the faculties some of the attributes of the soul?

Thank you very much. It is the soul faculties, through expression, that unfold the soul, in the sense that it creates what is known as our spiritual body. Now, we've taught many times that energy is expressed or directed through the vehicle of thought. Now, when you become aware more frequently what your thoughts really are, then you will understand in life your experiences, because they are the effects of the vehicle of thought, through which you have directed all of this energy. The soul unfolds through the soul faculties. The soul faculties are attributes of the soul and they create our spiritual body. Yes.

I wish to express my gratitude for the saying of truth needs no justification: it is. That really rings a bell with me.

Truth needs no defense, my dear, yes. It just is.

Thank you. My question is with regard to internal organization. Can you give me some processes or understanding whereby that occurs?

Well, let me put it this way: of course, whenever we're failing in organization, we're gaining in confusion. Of course, we'll all agree on that, I am sure. Now, it does seem that many students appear to have difficulty in organization, because, my friends, it all deals with self-control.

Now, we have to first learn what has priority in our mind. And when we find out what has priority, we will understand our lack of organization. For example, a person says, "Well, I'd like to be organized so that I can get more accomplished." But, my dear, that is not number one on your priority list. If it were number one, you *would* organize and you would get more accomplished. Don't you see what I mean?

You see, so the first thing to do, through self-control, self-awareness, is to see what your priorities are. When you see your priorities and you understand them, then you can shift them around in such a way as to gain organization through self-control and greater effort. I hope that's helped with your question.

You see, I don't have a magic wand that I can wave to the students who are seeking organization. If I did, the name of that wand would be Greater Effort. Because, my friends, that's where it is. You see, there's nothing I can say or do to organize you. I have all I can do to share with you this philosophy and to give it to you that perhaps someday, in eternity, it will become so meaningful that you will apply it. Don't you see? But I must not be concerned what you do with it, because if I am, I become the obstruction. And that is your divine birthright to do what you—I can only say, in organization, you'll have to check your priorities of desires, because if you do not have organization, there are desire priorities which are the obstruction. Yes. And that's the only thing that is obstructing us is desire priorities.

You see, my friends, it's quite possible, when a person is really striving for organization, that they will continue to think that they're not getting organized, in order to gain the attention, which is energy, necessary for them to stay where they are, because their priorities do not—their desire priorities do not want them to move onward. Do you understand? Yes. And so it is, you see, that only through repetition is the Law of Change made possible. Yes. Thank you.

I'm having trouble apprehending the concept of the fact that our thoughts create matter or create our environment. And I'm wondering if perhaps I am not trying to understand it in a too-literal sense and wonder if perhaps you could share your understanding.

Yes. What seems to be your problem in understanding that thought is the vehicle through which energy expresses itself and through which change is made possible? What seems to be your problem? Are you thinking that man has a thought and a tree is created? Is this what you're thinking about?

Yes. Sometimes I'm confused. I would like that straightened out with me. I wonder if it's a metaphorical thing. In other words, I would gravitate toward an environment that I think myself into. Or if I actually can, through thinking—does manna manifest somehow?

It does. Yes, it manifests through the vehicle of thought. Thank you.

Man, through his error of ignorance, has lost the great power, to a great extent, of the spoken word, which is the physical expression of the vehicle of thought. Man can, through the vehicle of thought, direct his energy—that's what he does with it—through the power of thought and concentration, bringing into his life whatever he chooses to bring into his life.

Now, you seem to be a bit, perhaps, confused by that statement: that man can, through thought (directed energy) create material substance. Of course, he can. Absolutely and positively. The universe is the law's meditation and man is an idea of it. Now, as mind is ever one in substance with the idea and the whole idea, so man and the law and the universe are one and the same.

Now, because it is so rare in this earth realm today that a man may direct his thought and a physical substance materialize—though it still happens, but it is rare. But think of the law and of the principle. If one man, only one in all of humanity, can direct his thought and speak his word and the object is materialized before your physical eyes—the law is totally impartial—then it is possible for all men to do it. Do you understand?

Yes.

Fine. Now, what man has, at this state of evolution, and—as I said earlier, through the error of ignorance, man still directs his thought—oh yes, he still has thought and the energy is still expressed. The experiences come back to him, which are the effect of this directed energy. Now, because we have not practiced concentration and meditation—perhaps, maybe we've done it for a couple of years. But we've gotten so far away from that divine, neutral, impartial power, in the sense of using it correctly, that we now question the possibility of man's speaking forth his word into the universe, knowing that it shall not come back to him void, but accomplish that which he sends it to do. Think, my friends. I mean it literally: that man can—still has the potential to speak his word, direct the energy through his thought, and the creation, whatever it may be, is made manifest for him. Does that help with your question?

Yes, it does. Thank you.

You're more than welcome.

I should like to ask a question regarding attention-getting. Many times when we hear those words, we think that we're trying to get attention from others. Is it possible that we're really, at times, getting attention from ourselves, within ourselves? For example, if the desire body is getting attention from the mental body, where many times we've become too self-concerned—is this actually attention-getting, but attention within ourselves?

Thank you. Thank you very much. That's a very important question. I'm so happy that you brought it up. One of the first things you will notice in life is that people who seek all the attention are the ones most grounded and oriented into self. This reveals the law that man is depleted of energy when he's grounded in self, and his thoughts are in contradiction. So it is made manifest that people grounded in self are constantly seeking attention. What they are truly seeking, my friends, is energy. They're seeking energy because they're so depleted, because of the contradiction in their own thinking, you see. The desires want one thing, the thoughts are speaking something else, and there's no balance. And there's this total depletion of energy. By gaining someone's attention—anyone's attention—they receive this influx of energy. That's the only way they can gain it, because they have not yet made the effort, the true effort, to bring about a balance in their own life and in their own thinking.

Now, it doesn't take a five-year-old child to repeatedly do something wrong to gain attention. Most adults do that. If they feel that charge of energy, then, no matter how many times they're reprimanded, they're going to constantly have an excuse so they can be reprimanded again. Now, they don't want to be reprimanded: they just want to continue to experience this influx of energy. It's just like—you see, you just see it everywhere. You see it with employers. You see it in churches. You just see it everywhere: that people constantly are doing something to gain attention, which, in truth, is energy.

Now, the lady has asked, "Well, doesn't this take place in the self?" Yes, it certainly does. It constantly—all the experience takes place within the self. And, you see, friends, this is why we teach that peace is the power. Well, what do you think power is? Power is energy. We try to teach you a way through which you may be receptive to God's divine energy. So that you don't have to do all of these different things in order to gain this energy. Does that help with your question?

Thank you.

You're more than welcome.

I have a question that has confused me on the difference of judgment and choice. When we make choices in any field, are we not in judgment? And will you share with us your understanding of judgment as is given by the Serenity understanding?

Well, the question—yes, thank you so much for your question concerning choice and judgment. Well, anytime—are you speaking for the choice and judgment inside of yourself or concerning things outside yourself?

Both. But first outside.

First outside. Well, in order to understand things outside, we must first understand things inside, because the outside is an effect of the inside. Now, for example—and this is a wonderful question. You see, my friends, all of our teaching takes you inward, on an inward, eternal journey. Now, this is the nature of the Serenity philosophy—the Living Light philosophy—is to help you go inside to find you. Because you won't find you out there.

You see, we can't find God, the good, outside until we can find God, the good, inside. And so it is a person says to themselves, "Well, I've made a choice to do this." What was it that motivated, that prompted, the choice? A decision had to be made, would you not agree?

Yes.

Some decision had to be made inside of us. Now, what I would like to have clarified: Are you referring to choice and judgment as an experience coming from without? Is this—How are you referring to this judgment and choice?

I was referring to it in the case of going out and having to choose a profession or choose a husband or a wife or choose—if you want to say you have a kind motivation, say you want to adopt a child, and you have to make a choice. And maybe there were two choices. Were you not in judgment of good and evil?

Now, well, that depends on the individual. You might have been, simply, in choice of what you believe, from that level of consciousness, would be satisfying to you and what would not: what would be beneficial and would not be beneficial. That choice, of course, is made inside. And then, in that sense of the word, we could say, yes, we are judging from our level of consciousness. Yes.

I see.

Yes, but, you see, this is taking place inside. Now, that means that what we're doing—we are judging and making choice inside of ourselves that we would prefer this, rather than that. Do you understand?

Yes.

But that's a preference that we're making inside of ourselves. And, of course, when we do that, you see—now this is an important thing: when we make choice, my friends, that implies that we have accepted this and not—and rejected that. Well, that's contrary to the divine will, you understand, which is acceptance.

Now, if you move through the soul faculties, which build the foundation of understanding—that's the foundation for all the soul faculties that we discussed earlier, from consideration to acceptance—do you understand?—to expression to understanding. Now, when you start with consideration—you have two objects and you consider both of them. You consider that you prefer this, knowing that this has come to the world to serve its purpose. If you do not express that total consideration at the moment of choice, then you set a law into motion, you see. You set a law into motion that you have decided on this because this has no value, that this will not be any good for you, you understand? In other words, you have rejected this. So you are not expressing total consideration, nor are you expressing total acceptance, nor total expression, nor full understanding. And God is ever equal to our understanding. Does that help with your question?

It helps to a great degree. I'll have to work on it.

Well, you stop and think, my friends. Man's destinies, man's destinies are his—man's denials are his destinies. Think about that. We've repeated over and over and over, again and again and again that total consideration, total acceptance, and, here you've now been given, total expression *is* understanding. And your God, *your* God, is equal to your understanding. Your God's no bigger—he can't do any more for you, because your understanding is only this big. So the thing is to get more understanding. But you can't get more understanding if you don't have consideration, acceptance, and expression.

See, expression is the divine life principle. That's expression. Now, when you deny, you set a law into motion. That's why your denials become your living destinies. So when you pass judgment, as the lady is speaking on choice and judgment, when you choose, choose what you desire to choose, knowing that that has come to the world to serve its purpose, that it's not left an orphan. Because, my friends, if you don't, you're not expressing much understanding and you are setting the law into motion that guarantees you will gain the understanding necessary in order that you may move up through the soul faculties. I do hope that's helped with your question. Yes.

Is my understanding correct that perhaps my soul—or me—is expressing in many other realities and forms simultaneously to this particular expression that's taking place at this time? And that perhaps because of the power of the senses, say, I am just only aware of this particular expression?

That is correct. That is absolutely correct.

And these other realities are absolutely as valid, as real as—

Absolutely. Yes. Remember, we discussed just a few minutes ago that thought is the vehicle through which energy expresses itself and if we express more of our energy into the mundane world, then we're going to be more aware of it and we're going to have more of it manifest. All right? If we take a little bit of that energy and we express it to these other dimensions, which are already inside of ourselves, then we'll start to have an awareness of those dimensions.

Are all of us in this room, in this form, are we manifestations of the same thought or—not the same thought, but do we originate from the same thinker?

We all originate from the same divine principle, yes. Yes, we do. Now, if you're speaking of the physical bodies, they come from this earth realm and they return. Everything returns to its source. Yes. But the life spark is all one. Whether that life spark is in a blade of grass, a dog, a cat, a human being, or a lion, it makes no difference: it is identically the same life force, the same life principle. There is no difference between the life principle of the plant and the human being. This is why it is possible for man to communicate with all life's forms, when man makes the effort to rise to a level of consciousness where this divine life principle may be realized. Does that help with your question?

Yes. May I ask another question?

Yes.

Does the thought originate from the divine life principle or is the divine life principle expressed here a product of a thought?

The divine life principle expressed here is the *effect* of an idea. The *effect* of an idea. Yes. Remember that ideas are divine, limitless, and eternal. Thoughts are mundane and created by man. There's a vast difference between a thought and an idea. One is perspiration and the other is inspiration. And there *is* a difference. Yes.

I have two questions. The first one is a short one. Talking about the spark of life that you're just now talking about, I was wondering if that spark of life that comes from that principle, that idea, that Divine Intelligence, does that exist also in what we would call inanimate objects, such as stones?

It does. They're only inanimate because of our own awareness. They are not inanimate. They are in motion. Yes.

And the second question—I hope I can make myself clear—deals with color and healing. And I've read in The Living Light *that at certain times specific colors can be used to direct towards certain areas of the body to help heal that area, as opposed to manifesting pure thought, changing your vibration to a white light. And so color can be used for specific things. I was wondering, in aura sensing, if a vibration level of someone's aura seems like it's a darker shade of a color, if it would be more beneficial to just immerse that person in that color; if, let's say, it was a darker green, immerse that person in a green light as opposed to a white or gold light.*

Because it would not be pure. The white light is the pure light. And what you want to do is to lighten the color of the aura of the individual.

And a pure green, let's say, wouldn't raise the vibration of a darker green?

Yes, but think, my good student. Your understanding of a pure green may not be the understanding of the patient. Therefore, where you are on different levels of consciousness, instead of it being beneficial to the patient seeking healing, it could be extremely detrimental. This is why the Bible teaches us, "Thy will, not my will, shall be done."

You see, now you have an understanding and a visualization and thought of what pure green looks like, would you not agree? And I have an understanding, a visualization, of what it looks like. And so does everyone else. Would you not agree that they're quite varied? They might be similar, but varied. So what you want to do is what is taught here in the book [*The Living Light*] is—try to understand that. The pure white, this purity of this pure energy, you understand, will lift the color. You understand it will lighten it to that person's level of consciousness, their higher level of consciousness, though their higher level of consciousness, being similar to everyone else's, is not identically the same. Does that help with your question?

Thank you very much.

You're more than welcome. Yes.

Thank you. In tonight's discourse, imagination is spoken of as the vehicle of expression of the life force and we should image constructively. May I ask, please, regarding the principle?

Yes. We discussed earlier that the expression is the divine life principle. And the lady's brought up the point about imagination. Now, the truth of the matter is, friends, we cannot, we cannot express what is not imagined. Now, a person says, "Well, I just expressed my temper. I didn't give it any thought. I didn't imagine anything." Well, we've expressed it so many times, we're no longer aware of the imagination process taking place in order for the energy to be released into the level of consciousness known as temper. But, you see, the imagination process is taking place all the time.

You see, we imagine that we're here in this log cabin. And through that process of imagination, we believe it. And by believing it, we become it. And so we say, "Well, now, that's reality. I'm sitting here and I am consciously aware of that and that is a reality." Well, some of us are aware of something else and we believe something else and we're someplace else and we're here, too, at the same time. Don't you see what I mean? Because we're more than one person, in truth. But the life principle is expression.

Now I've been—we're close to the finishing of our class here this evening, but I have been a bit amazed that none of my students, after having an understanding given to them at the opening of this class, that none of the review students—and there are many present—have not had some discussion on the creative principle, considering that we just finished here, less than an hour ago, giving you the foundation of the soul faculties. I guess nobody ever thought about it.

Does anyone here remember what the creative principle of life is? I'm sure you remember. Would you like to share that, considering that you're interested in the life principle?

Love, belief . . .

[After a short pause, the Teacher continued.] What do most men do all the time?

Desire. Will in action.

Fine. Thank you. Love, belief, desire, will, in action. Doesn't anyone see any connection whatsoever between consideration—divine love; acceptance—divine will; expression—divine action; understanding, which is God itself? Well, think, my friends. Yes.

Well, there is one question that comes to mind. And that is that if there is divine love and if there is divine will and divine right action, is there, then, a divine desire?

Thank you so very much. And indeed, there is. For without divine desire, there would be no creation anywhere in any universe at any time. My friends, for years we have taught, Do not annihilate desire. Do not suppress desire. Educate it or fulfill it. Yes, there is divine desire. And you know what the divine desire is? Does anyone know what the divine desire is? Anyone? We gave it this evening.

Desire for understanding.

Thank you. Anyone else? Yes.

The desire for love to become aware of itself.

Thank you very much. Anyone else? *[There is a brief pause, and then the Teacher continues.]* My friends, both the ladies had it. It's in the foundation. The divine desire is expression! And look at all of creation. What does all of creation do? It seeks to express itself. And you take expression away from a person and you've sent them on the path downward. You might not agree with their expression. It might call forth your soul faculty of tolerance, duty, and gratitude. But remember, whatever you deny another, you have, in truth, denied yourself. So think about that. Expression is, in truth, the divine desire. If it wasn't divine desire, you certainly wouldn't have the stars in space and all of us wouldn't be sitting here, this very moment. We did not come out of nothing.

So think, my friends. Think about expression. Think how much better you feel when you express whatever level of consciousness you are entertaining. We always feel better when we express a level of consciousness that we are entertaining. The difficulty, of course, is that there are eight-one of those levels and that here in this world of creation not everyone is respecting your divine right to your divine expression. And so there appears to be a few problems. But those problems are simply, my friends, little signposts that say "Total Consideration."

Now, [if] you have total consideration, then you've got divine expression, through total acceptance and complete understanding. So when you want to express, have total consideration not only for all of your own levels, but have total consideration for everyone else's levels that are around and about you. Then, my friends, the seeming problems, they will dissipate into the nothingness. You will feel better. Those around you will feel better. You will gain in understanding and, gaining in understanding, you will not only know the law—you see, there's one thing about understanding. We've stated earlier that knowledge without application is worthless. Well, what do you think understanding is? What is understanding? It's applied knowledge. And applied knowledge, they call wisdom. And surely we're striving to be just a little bit wise.

So let's work on getting understanding. You know how to get it: consideration, acceptance, and expression. You know what it is composed of. So remember, when your consideration is limited, your acceptance is limited, your expression is limited, your understanding is limited, and your God is a mighty, dinky, little-bitty God and he can't do very much.

Thank you very much, friends. Let us go have refreshments.

OCTOBER 10, 1974

CONSCIOUSNESS CLASS 63

This evening we will discuss a couple of those sense functions that correspond to a soul faculty. And one of them for discussion this evening is concern. That seems to be a function that most of us seem to enjoy, in the sense that we seem to entertain it rather frequently. And, of course, we all know that we don't entertain something frequently that we aren't, on some level of consciousness, enjoying. Now, do any of my students, especially the review students, have any thought on what the corresponding soul faculty of the function of concern would be?

Would it be consideration?

Thank you very much. Anyone else? Yes, please.

Strength.

Thank you. Anyone else? Yes.

I believe it's faith.

Faith. Thank you.

The soul faculty which is the balance of the sense function of concern is acceptance. Now, that that we truly accept, the mind no longer is concerned about. But we are concerned about anything that we have not yet truly accepted. Now, we know that acceptance is part of the soul faculty or foundation of understanding. And anytime you understand anything—when you truly understand it—your mind is not concerned about it. Because you cannot be concerned about anything that you truly understand. But you cannot truly understand anything without acceptance, consideration, and expression.

Now let's discuss for a moment that word *expression*. What do we mean by *expression?* What we mean in this class by *expression* is "the application, the application of any thought at any moment in the mind" is its own expression.

And we discussed last week that it is the divine—if you wish to call it the divine desire, that's a good enough term—it *is* the divine desire to express itself. And so, my friends, when you want to know—and many students seem to want to know how much they have grown in a particular soul faculty because, you see, none of us ever completely grow *through* a soul faculty. We may have many experiences which help to expand, for example, our first soul faculty of duty, gratitude, and tolerance, but we never, ever grow, what we might say, through it. The moment that we think we've grown through an experience, whether it's a function or a soul faculty, we set a law into motion that brings to us all the experiences necessary to expand that particular faculty—that we thought we had grown through—to expand it just a little bit more. Now, how does that happen?

You see, the soul knows. Our soul knows that we don't grow through a soul faculty. But our mind, our functions do not know. And so when we say we've grown through something, it is our mind that has made that decision. And our mind has made that decision based upon a number of experiences that it has had. And so the mind decides, "With all of this experience that I have encountered, I certainly have grown through that." And when the mind says that, it sets that law into motion, and a multitude of experiences come back in life that we may expand that faculty that we thought we had grown through.

Now, there is another function that's very important and it's the function of procrastination. Its soul faculty balance is unity. If we are united in our levels of consciousness within ourselves, then there is no expression—or let us say, at least a far lesser expression—of the function of procrastination. Now, what is procrastination? Well, I think it is best described with a very old saying, which is, "Hell is paved with good intentions and broken promises." And so a person has good intention to do something; they just never get around to the point of actually doing it.

Now, we may ask ourselves, "Well, how come I have these good intentions? I have a good intention, for example, of being prompt and being on time, because it's a true mark of my character. And I don't want my character not to be up to the par of my own pride." What is it that we have the intent and we say we want to do something, we say that we're going to do something, and we just never seem to get to it? It's rather embarrassing and humiliating, I would think, for any of us to have all these good intentions and never get them into application.

Well, a person says, "Well, I intended to do that, but all of these other things distracted me." Well, my friends, stop and think. All experience takes place within our own mind. Man is a law unto himself. So man alone is guaranteeing all the experiences and distractions necessary in order to continue on expressing what is known as the function of procrastination.

So the first thing we want to do—and that takes unity inside of ourselves—we want to stop and we want to think, "What am I gaining from this constant and continuous procrastination that I find myself in?" The moment you become aware of what you are gaining, then you're on the first step of bringing unity into your being and you will no longer procrastinate.

Now remember this: there is no mind in any universe that does anything that it does not believe it is gaining from. That is not the way the mind works. So if you have problems with procrastination, find out what it is in your mind that has accepted gain from the experience. And once you find that out—of course, that takes unity—and once you find that out, you will no longer have the need to procrastinate.

It's the same thing as with concern. You know, we say so often that it's so difficult to have faith in life and yet we're using faith all of the time. We're using faith all of the time. When we are concerned about things—which means we are blocking acceptance, which is the foundation stone of understanding—it simply means that we have more faith in ourselves, in our brain, in our computer than we do in an invisible, subtle, divine Power that moves the universes. Now this is what we're truly saying when we say, "I'm concerned about this and I'm concerned about that." What we are, in truth, doing—we are elevating the human mind above and beyond the divine, infinite, eternal Intelligence. That, my friends, is what we're really doing when we are concerned and worry about anything.

Think about that for a few moments. Think about what we're doing to ourselves. And that concern and that worry sets all of the negative laws into motion to guarantee all of the experiences necessary to prove to us, as individuals, that we were right all the time. Think how simple truth is.

If you say, "I'm concerned about the outcome of this situation," to the extent that you direct the divine energy to that, you will guarantee the outcome of that experience yet to be, to be exactly as your concern is, in order that you may justify and defend the self, known as the human ego. Now, that's what really takes place, my good students. And it happens every minute, every day, every place, all of the time.

Which is the best path to follow? Everyone is a follower, and depending on how good of a follower they are will depend upon how good of a leader they are yet to be. But you can't lead anything, my friends, until you can first follow. It's not possible.

So think. Think where we have directed this great universal Power. Think what we have limited it to. We've limited it and guarantee one experience after another. We've stated before that one experience guarantees another experience of like kind, because, you see, we believe what we experience. Think about it. We believe it. That's what we believe, friends, is what we experience. We believe what is in our mind.

This is what our awareness classes are all about: to help you to stop and see what's in your own mind, because whatever is in your own mind, that's what you're going to believe. That's what's controlling your life. If you *believe* you have a problem, you will guarantee the continuity of the problem so that you can justify and say, "You see? I was right all of the time." Look, my friends, nobody's mind wants to be wrong. No. That takes a great deal of humility, to sit down and talk to yourself and say, "Well, I was wrong about that. I was wrong about that. I'm wrong about this." That takes a little bit of humility, a little bit of self-awareness. And so you see what we're doing to ourselves. Now, I don't want to dwell on the seeming negative. I just want to bring a little light over that area of the mind and how it's working.

You know, you can say a thousand words and, be it in divine order, hopefully one or two will be accepted into the computer known as the human mind. Because it only takes one or two words to bring about a complete change and a transformation in our life. That's all it really takes. But let us think a little more often about the laws that we set into motion.

Now, we've said in many classes: The spoken word is lifegiving energy, that it sets the law into motion. But as long as we remain dependent upon the human mind, then we're going to remain limited, because the human mind is limited and it doesn't see very far. The human mind knows many things, but it doesn't see very far.

So we must ask ourselves, "What am I, in truth, relying upon in this life?" If it is your mind, then what you are relying upon are all the accepted experiences of this life. That's the only thing you're relying upon. You're not relying upon God, an Infinite Intelligence. No, you have denied that in practice. You may have accepted it in theory, but denied it in application.

Now, tell me, is there anyone present who believes that the experiences of this life to this point are so worthwhile and infallible that it is wise to rely upon them to guide your life from this moment on? Look where it led you yesterday. Think of how many years it took. Well, I don't think, honestly, my friends, it's a very reliable instrument. And we call that acceptance and consideration and expression. Now, if the human mind were truly reliable, then those who are proficient in the study of the human mind would be reliable counselors and advisers. But time and again, this has proven not to be true.

We said before that knowledge knows much, but wisdom knows better. Now, how are we going to let that little light of wisdom into our consciousness when it's waiting to shine through? It takes acceptance, my friends. It takes acceptance. And when you're in concern and worry, you may be rest assured you're closing the door to acceptance. You are closing the door to the Divine will itself.

It is a known fact that the mind relies upon that with which it is familiar. And because we have not spent the years, the hours, the days, the weeks, and the months to become familiar with the Divine Intelligence, it only stands to reason that we would have this tendency to rely upon our mind, because that is what we are most familiar with. When the mind accepts, truly accepts, there's a harmony that takes place within our being, and things start to run a lot smoother than our intellect has done so far.

Now you're free to ask your questions. Yes.

If you have an attitude of acceptance over a situation in your life, but someone close to you has concern, which would influence that situation?

That would depend entirely on who is the strongest. Now, for example, if you have faith in a situation with another individual and they are having difficulty, let us say, for example, in self-control—you understand?—and you are able to apply and demonstrate self-control in your own life, then the person who was able to demonstrate the self-control would have the strongest power and the strongest influence over the situation. Yes. Because the father is greater than the son. And the stronger are greater than the weak, of course. And so those who are able to control their emotions and to control their feelings and to control their expression are, indeed, the stronger. Yes.

This control over the emotions and feelings, this self-control, is this brought about through the will? Or how is this self-control ...

Thank you very much for your question in reference to, Is it brought about by the will? No, my friend, that's the path to disaster. So many people think, "Well, I'll just use my self-will and I will just control that level of consciousness." Well, what you do, in truth, you don't control that level: you simply suppress it. And someday it comes like a great thunderstorm and it expresses itself, because you have suppressed it for so long a time. That is not the way to gain self-control. Absolutely and positively not. Not through what is known as will or willpower, no.

We gain self-control by understanding. You see, whatever in life you understand, when you understand it, you are in a position to control it. Because understanding grants you—through understanding—the laws by which an experience is operating. Therefore, you pray and work towards understanding. But, you see, we don't get understanding without acceptance, consideration, and expression. Does that help with your question? Yes.

I've only been to four classes and I haven't read much and I don't really understand. But your use of the words acceptance *and* consideration *and* understanding *don't have a lot of meaning for me. Acceptance of what?*

Thank you very much for your question. And when we are speaking of acceptance, we're speaking of acceptance of anything and everything. Total acceptance is the divine will. Now, if you do not accept the divine right of another human soul to express themselves, then you do not have acceptance. If you do not accept the right of an individual to do what is not in harmony with your understanding, then you do not have acceptance. Now, acceptance does not mean that you must experience. Do you understand? It means that you accept the divine right of the expression.

It doesn't mean that you must allow yourself to experience things you don't appreciate.

That's correct. That is correct.

Where is the line?

Where is the line in what way?

Well, acceptance has a passive sound.

Yes. Perhaps it has a passive sound, my dear, to you. To many people, it does not have a passive sound. This depends, of course, on our level of consciousness. Now, perhaps for you at this time, the word *acceptance* is a very passive experience. But it is not necessarily so for all people. Now, do we feel that acceptance is passive because we are permitting ourselves not to be concerned about something?

No. But I wonder if it isn't because we're allowing ourselves to be in situations which are not to our benefit.

But, you see, we cannot be in situations that are not to our benefit if we have not set that law into motion. Because, you see, like attracts like and becomes the Law of Attachment. Now, if we are having an experience that we feel is not beneficial to us, we may be rest assured that the experience, in and of itself, is a mirror reflecting a level of consciousness that we were expressing in order to have the experience in the first place. Yes. Now, consequently, rather than say "I reject that," try to forgive yourself for the level of consciousness which guaranteed the experience, because to forgive is to free: to free from the bondage of the mind. Does that help with your question?

Somewhat. Thank you.

You're more than welcome. Yes.

Thank you. I suppose that we are all seeking wisdom and I wonder if you could speak a bit on how we can move wisdom into our expression.

Yes, thank you very much. Of course, we can't get to wisdom until we've opened up understanding. And we can't get to understanding until we have consideration, acceptance, and expression. And so the first thing that we want to try to work on is to become aware, to become aware of the things that we cannot tolerate in life, to become aware of the things that disturb us, to become aware of our so-called needs and desires. Because, you see, if we're not aware of them, then we certainly are not going to change them. Because man does not change something he's not aware of. No, man first becomes aware of something; then he goes through the process of changing it.

You see, so we want to try to become aware of our own so-called needs and our own desires. And when we become aware of them, we make a decision and we say, "Well, now I don't particularly like this desire that I have and so I'm going to work on educating it. And I don't particularly like this situation that I say that I need in my life."

You see, what the mind does, my friends, it says, "This, that, that, and that—if it will work that way, then I will be happy, I will be free and my life will be fulfilled." Well, when we say that, we set that law into motion and unless those particular things take place in our life, we don't experience happiness. Because we've limited the Divine.

How have we limited the Divine? We've narrowed our understanding. We certainly haven't had much consideration: we only have three things that are going to make us happy. We haven't encompassed the whole universes. And so we become the living obstruction. And that certainly, in my understanding, is not wisdom.

Now, it all takes place inside of ourselves. It takes place—and we say that a million times—it takes place where man doesn't want to look. You see? Now, we don't want to look in here for freedom. We want to look out there for freedom. Because we do not want to face the truth. And the truth, my friends, is it's inside. And there is no God outside that's going to change it for you. There is no God that's done it to us. And therefore, there is no God that can take it from us. That is not the God that this Association and this philosophy understands. There is no God, my friends, that can change your life, that can give you what you want, or take away what you don't want. That type of a God only exists in the illusion of our mind. There's no hero in the sky that can transform our life.

But there is the greatest hero you will ever find: it's in the depths of your own being. And when you follow that path of total consideration, acceptance, and expression, then you will see a great God—and its name is understanding. Thank you. Yes.

This deals in reference to an earlier discussion. And that is, you spoke of forgiving yourself, when you recognize that you're in a situation that is a reflection of yourself. And you might not feel that's a really comfortable situation, but to forgive yourself so you can learn from that. Is it enough just to forgive yourself? Or how can you recognize what were the laws that were set into motion that put you in that place?

Thank you very, very much. The gentleman is asking in reference to the lady's questions, How can you recognize what were the laws that put you into an experience? Right? Well, it's really quite simple: you step back and you look objectively at the experience, for the experience is an effect of directed energy and directed energy is known as the law. All right? That's what law is: directed energy. And this is why we teach that concentration is the key to all power, because it is the law itself. All right? Fine. So you step back and you look at the experience and you look at it objectively. When I say "objectively," that means you do not look at it emotionally, because emotions do not see clearly. But you look at it in the clearer light of reason. Then you will see what that effect is revealing: it is revealing laws that you have set into motion. Then, you go on the inward journey to find out in your own mind what is the need within you that causes you to set those type of laws into motion. One of the most common needs is the need for attention, which is the need for energy. You know, there is nothing more detrimental, in speaking on experiences, there is nothing more detrimental to the human soul than guilt complexes and persecution.

Now, many people feel persecuted. They feel persecuted, perhaps, because of the way they grew up or what their soul merited in this life. And this persecution is known as a persecution complex. It causes us all types of grief. And so we must ask ourselves the question, "Why do we feel guilty in life? Why do we feel persecuted? Why do we feel this way?" Well, the first thing the mind says [is,] "Well, because of the way people treat me." But, you see, my friends, people treat us the way we are. Now, if we have consideration, then people have consideration for us. Do you understand? Now, if we don't have consideration, we're going to be guaranteeing the experiences where they'll have no consideration for us. If we have tolerance, people will have tolerance for us. If we don't have tolerance, they won't have tolerance for us. Do you understand? And so it is that all of Life, she's the mirror. And all of experience is revealing the laws that we're setting into motion.

You know, sometimes I look around and I see so many people and when they want your attention, they say, "You!" And they wave like a flag in the atmosphere, immediately. You understand? They can't wait two seconds. But when somebody calls them, it's maybe ten minutes later. Now, we have to say to ourselves, "What's going on here?" We have to ask ourselves the question. You see, now this is important—we have to say, "Do I go around in life waving my hand and expecting people to jump immediately?" We must ask ourselves that question. "Or do I have more consideration for their needs and for their time?" Do you understand? Then, we'll become more aware of ourselves. Does that help with your question?

Yes. Thank you.

You're welcome.

I have two questions. One is, How does a person educate his or her desire? And the other one is, Could you discuss a little bit on what relation there might be between expression and right action as it appears and manifests?

Thank you very much. Yes. And the first question the lady is speaking about is, How does a person educate their desire? Well, first off, we have to become, naturally, aware of what the desire is that we have. Then, through the process, you understand, the process of analysis—and we go through the desire and we say, "Now what does this desire really do for me? How do I feel? And why do I need it?" Do you understand?

Now, once you start talking to the desire—you see, most people don't talk to their desires. All they do is express them. But, I mean, it's only sensible that we talk to our desires. After all, we're controlled by desire. So why not learn something about the desire? So you take the desire, whatever it is—you know it's directed energy. I'm sure you realize that and I'm sure all my students realize it takes place in our head, here in our mind, you know. That's where it takes place.

And so the truth of the matter is—you see, a person says, "Well, I have this desire." Well, that's fine that you have the desire, but if you don't start educating it, believe me, you soon become its slave, you see, its victim. And anytime that it wants to crop up into your consciousness, it will do so. Well, my friends, if you don't educate the desire, you start losing control—control of yourself, you see. Then, we're in very sad shape. But through analysis and through discussion, through talking with the desire, through finding out what is the need in our own head that we have to do a certain thing in a certain way—and we call that a desire and we have to have that fulfillment. Do you see what I mean? Now that's very important that a person find out what the fulfillment of any particular desire is doing for them.

You see, but you'll always find this about desire: the moment you fulfill it—you hear me?—the law goes into motion, to be fulfilled again, if the fulfillment has been computed in the mind as satisfactory. If it has not been computed as satisfactory, it gets set aside.

Now you also had another question. What was your other question?

May I ask for clarification?

Yes, certainly.

Are you saying, then, that an educated desire is not one that is absent, but one that is under my control, rather than me *being under the control of* it?

That is exactly what I'm saying. When you educate desire, it doesn't mean you annihilate the desire. It means you have it under the light of reason.

You see, we spoke before an awful lot in this semester on desire, to the point that it was even revealed to you the divine desire [is] known as expression. You see, we gave you an affirmation, but it was too simple for most of my students. And it says, "Thank you, God. I am at peace." We have always taught that desire has no light. The greater the desire, the lesser the light. Now, if you get the thought of a desire, you have a little bit of light. You get into the desire, there's no light at all. And there's no light: you can't see. And there's no reason. So we gave you an affirmation to help you on your descent down into what we call the basement, where it's dark, to help you to have a little bit of reason. "Thank you, God. I am at peace."

Because we have discussed for many years the process of educating desire. We have repeatedly taught, never suppress desire, because it's dangerous for your mental balance. Express it, fulfill it, or educate it. When you educate a desire, you know exactly what you're doing during the process of the fulfillment of the desire. You are consciously aware.

Now, I know that most people will disagree with me and they will say, "Well, I'm consciously aware when I'm fulfilling my desires." My dear friends, you're not. You're under the influence of the pattern. You can't see beyond it. Now, you might say, "Well, I'm going to have this desire fulfilled regardless. And I know better." That certainly doesn't mean you got it educated in any sense of the word. I mean exactly that. When you educate desire, you take with you a little light. Yes.

Now your second question?

It was the relationship between expression and right action.

Expression and divine right action? Yes, thank you very much. It is the nature of all form, as we all know, to express: it is their divinity. All form must express, whether it's the plant, the animal, or the human. It must express.

Now, expression does not, in and of itself, mean divine right action. Of course, it does imply your divine right to expression. But, you see, when you have divine right action, you have total consideration. Because if it's divine right action, then it is the divine will, through acceptance and consideration and expression. Now, that is understanding. So there is a difference between just the word *expression* and divine right action, for divine right action considers all things. Do you understand? And considering all things, there's understanding; and understanding is the God or the Divinity. Yes. Thank you very much.

I would like to have your light on—when we see a person, or we are, going through the levels, you know, the bummer levels, how do we express compassion rather than just say, "Well, they're going through a level. They're going through this. This is their merit system," or something? How can we express more spiritually to that condition or that person?

Well, my dear students, I honestly believe when someone is going through what the lady is referring to as a bummer level of consciousness, that if we say, "Yes, they're going through something right now," is expressing compassion under the light of reason. Because it is the divine right of the individual to go through what we may understand to be a bummer level of consciousness.

Now, if we understand compassion to be filled with emotion and to be filled with what we call pity, then we're talking about something entirely different. But we understand compassion to be a soul faculty. And a person may say, "Yes, they're going through something right now. That's just one of their levels."

Why, that person may be expressing the epitome of the soul faculty of compassion.

But we must realize—and I'm sure we all do—that we all have a little different understanding about what compassion is. Now, compassion, to some people, is for someone to put their hand over their shoulder and say, "My dear, I fully sympathize with you. You are going through one of those levels of consciousness. And I know how very difficult it is." Now, let us stop and think. Does that help us come up? Or does that help us stay in that level of consciousness? Now, which does it really do?

If a person has an experience which is truly detrimental to them, but they cannot yet see how detrimental it is, is it better for a friend to say, "You're in that level of consciousness. That's your right, but I don't want it expressed around me," and they go to work? Or is it better to say, "I really pity you and I have compassion for you" in that sense? No. Compassion, my friends, is not pity. And, as I said here, just earlier, that a person, when they're going through a level of consciousness, that is the individual's divine right to go through that level of consciousness. That does not guarantee that it is our divine right to try to get everybody else to join us on that level of consciousness. No. We are all individuals.

You know, we have a saying in this teaching and it is very important: Misery does not love company. No, it is *indispensable* for its own continuity. So when we are in a level of consciousness—now think, students. I'd rather have you have a little light and not be happy with me than to stay asleep in this life eternal and be happy with me. Because you wouldn't know any better anyway, if you were asleep. But think. A level of consciousness that we are entertaining—no matter who is entertaining it—must have support. And so it demands that those around and about us express on the same level. And if they don't express on the same level, then they're not in rapport with us and we may mistake that and feel that they have no compassion. I do hope that's helped with the question, because that's very, very, very important.

And also, I want to continue on with this. When we are in a level of consciousness that's not in our best interest and we are aware of it, but it doesn't yet have enough value to us to make the effort to get out of it, how compassionate another person would be to remind us where we are. What great compassion that is! To have a friend or an acquaintance say, "You're in that level again. Look right where you are." Why, that's the greatest compassion a person could express. Because, you see, we are not yet making sufficient effort to get out of that bummer level of consciousness. That's what we're talking about, friends. That's the benefit of associating with spiritually minded people.

If they're truly spiritually minded, they're not wallowing in sentimental soup. And therefore, they can help us grow. You know, they're not running around saying, "Oh, you pathetic soul. Look what's happened to you." Well, look what's happened to us: we did it to ourselves. And isn't it nice to have somebody remind us what we're doing to ourselves, especially when it's detrimental to us and we don't yet have enough guts or enough energy or enough effort to say, "Now, I've had it. And I'm coming on up." I do hope that's helped all of my students. Yes.

I have a question regarding selfless service. Is it possible for a person to serve selflessly outside of the organization of the church and, if so, how?

Why, absolutely and positively. And selfless service is everywhere in the universe and the universe can always use a lot more of it.

Now, this is a most interesting, most interesting question. I'm so very happy that you have brought it up. That that we receive any help or support from in our lives, we become spiritually indebted to, whether we like it or not. Now, no one has to tell us what the indebtedness is, because, you see, our soul knows. You see, our soul knows what we gain from anything. Do you understand? Yes. And our soul, through our conscience—and our conscience is a spiritual sensibility with a dual capacity, knows right from wrong, no one has to tell it—our conscience will prompt us so that we may know and do something that we're supposed to be doing. Do you understand?

Now, how does our conscience tell us? This is what people seem not to remember. God works *through* man. He does not work—the Divine Intelligence—*to* man. And so you might be walking down the street and someone may say, "Well, have you been doing any selfless service?" or imply, "What are you doing in the world today?" That's your conscience speaking! Do you understand? But it's coming through another human soul.

Now, we can do selfless service anywhere in the universe. Why, we most certainly can. Not necessarily here at this little Serenity Church. We do emphasize that teaching, because we know that it is through selfless service, and selfless service alone, that man walks on the path to illumination and freedom. Why does it take selfless service? Because, you see, my friends, it takes total consideration, and it takes total acceptance for total expression, for total understanding, which is known as God.

And unless we get ourselves active into selfless service, which means we're broadening our horizon a little bit bigger than our little puny universe that we call self, unless we do that, our God remains a little, small God, because our understanding remains small, because our consideration is small, because our acceptance is small, and our application or expression is small. Does that help with your question?

Yes.

Yes, thank you so very much. Yes, please.

My question has to do with emotion. It seems that, at least in my life, emotion occasionally, or quite often, controls the situation over and above what I later think is my reason. And I'm wondering, where does the energy for this emotion come from?

Is this a product of your ego? Or does it come from your soul? Why does it sometimes seem to be out of balance? Where does this energy come from that triggers your emotions?

The energy that is used to express our emotions is the same energy that's used to express our reason. It's a divine neutral energy, known as God. You see, God, the Divine, is expressing in anger as well as in tolerance. But, you see, man, man has accepted—you understand, he has become receptive, through his acceptance, to an emotional expression or outburst. Now, that's simply the patterns of the mind. What is so sad and interesting, most interesting, is that some people can cause us to express great emotion, while others cannot cause us to express any.

But what we want to think about, you know, when we feel upset and have no tolerance and we're angry and discouraged and all those emotions, just stop and say, "Now, let me see, why did I express this emotion?" Then, we say, "Well, because so-and-so said such and such to me." Well, isn't it interesting that we made that individual God. Think about that. We gave that individual power over us. And the moment we give power—to anything we give power—that becomes our God for that time. And so when you're expressing anger or emotion or discouragement or any other emotion, ask yourself the simple question, "Who did I give power to?" Because those are your gods.

You might say, "I don't like that person." Well, you don't like that person? The very moment that you have accepted that you don't like that person, you gave that person power over your emotions. And when you give them power over your emotions, you make them gods. And you destroy your health in the process. Because, you see, our health is our harmony. And how can we have harmony if we give all these people control over us?

But now, there's another step that's very important. First thing the mind gets hold of, you know, and somebody says something to us, we say, "I'm not giving you any power over me!" That expression right there has just given them all the power of the universe. Isn't that beautiful? But that's the first thing the mind does. "That's it. I'm not giving you any power over me!" And they're expressing all this energy and all this temper. You see what I mean? They just made them that much bigger a god.

There is a principle known as ignore: to ignore the expression of an individual; to be with them and not a part of them. Do you understand? Now, that doesn't mean, when you have a responsibility in life—it's like, say, you're an employer and you have employees. There's a responsibility and you have a responsibility. Well, it's like an organization. People, they either fit into an organization or they don't fit into an organization. The organization has a foundation. It has a principle by which it goes by. And those who have merited the position in the organization to see that certain rules and regulations are carried out, they have earned that responsibility. Whether the other people like it or not is immaterial. That's not the point at all. And so that's known as respecting an organization that you're involved in, whatever that organization may be. And when you no longer respect it, you soon find that you're not there too long. Do you understand? Because that's *our* responsibility.

Now, if we don't like the way something runs, then usually what happens, we try to change it. Well, if we're not successful in changing it, then wisdom dictates we should go someplace else. And if we go someplace else and we still can't make it run the way we want to and we're not in a position to change it, then it's only indicative that we should have our own organization. Don't you see? So that's the way things are. Absolutely. Does that help with your question?

Yes. Thank you.

Yes, you're more than welcome.

I'd like to ask a simple question regarding emotion. Many people who have gone through a holocaust or some terrible expression say that after weeping they feel better. If we were not to weep, why was a tear put in the eye?

My dear, if we were not to weep, why was a tear put in the eye? I want to be perfectly clear about this. That seems about the same reasoning as if God wanted a rocket ship on the moon, then why didn't God create a rocket ship? Now, let us be honest. What kind of reasoning, we must ask ourselves, is it that would say that water comes to the eye because God wanted us to weep with emotion. No. God does not want anything.

Now, it's like saying that when we cut our hand the blood flows. Then, we should cut our hand so the blood can flow and be free. No. Absolutely not. Now, I want to be very clear on this, because this is very important, students, to all of us. Because it's justification under the guise of reason. Now think. Number one—and I mean this for all of my students—justification under the guise of reason is called logic. Now remember that. That's what we call logic. When the mind justifies, expresses it as reason, it's called logic.

God does not want us to weep, nor does God want us to laugh. This, my good students, is our divine right: to weep or to express joy. Therefore, God is a divine neutral intelligence. The Divinity expresses itself through form. Man has the divine right to weep when he wants to weep. He has the divine right to laugh when he wants to laugh. That does not please or displease God. But it does please or displease man.

Remember that all things in life can be justified, if we choose to justify them. And let us remember here in the Living Light philosophy that our God *is* our understanding. And if our understanding is to weep at a funeral, then that's our God. And if our understanding is to have a party at a funeral, then that is our God. Because, you see, my friends, that is the limit of our understanding. Thank you so much for your question.

We've had some discussion on law and the meaning of the word law. *I wonder if you could give a little more on the meaning of the word* principle.

Thank you very much. Yes, there's been much discussion on law and we have discussed principle before. The principle of anything is the true essence of the thing itself. However, many of us get principle mixed up—unfortunately or fortunately, depends on how we want to look at it—with what is known as personality. And they're as different as day and night.

Now, we just got through speaking—it's interesting you brought up this word *principle,* because we just spoke on what is known as justification. And that is one of the things that the mind frequently uses—"Well, that's the principle. That's the principle,"—when the truth of the matter is, it may be the furthest thing from the principle, but it certainly is our own justification and we call it that.

So principle is something that we have to truly search for in life—to find the essence of anything. Because that's the only place we're going to find the real principle.

And I think we ought to discuss just for a few moments, for our time has passed, on this business of law and the laws. I mean, we've said a multitude of times that man is a law unto himself. And so if we're a law unto ourselves, what in the world are we doing with the law that we are? That's what we ought to be thinking about. What are we doing, what are we doing with the law that we are?

Now, we understand that law—the law—is directed energy. Now, we've said that, I think, at least a hundred times in these classes. We've only said it in a few different words. We've stated repeatedly, The universe is the Lord's meditation—the *law's* meditation—directed energy, and man is an idea of it. As man is ever one in substance with the idea and the whole idea, so man and the law, or Lord, and the universe are one and the same. So what we are, in truth—we're the idea. And we experience the belief. And that's what we are. So doesn't it behoove us, as students, to become aware of what we're believing?

It's like the lady here asked earlier: If a tear is in the eye, then isn't it meant we're supposed to cry? No. Not unless we want to justify our need for weeping. And if we want to justify our need for weeping, then it is understandable. But that is the student's divine right to justify any level of consciousness, for it is the divine right of a student to be on that level of consciousness. It is our responsibility to try to share with you, hopefully, a little light so that we can find the causes, the causes of justification, you see.

My friends, in this understanding we don't ask God why he's done this or that to us, because we know better. We know that God's not doing it. And when you know that God's not doing it, you're ready to expand your consciousness, the godhood within you, to be receptive to the things that you want done. You see? It's the same energy. The same energy that sends us down is the same energy that sends us up. But it's up to us to make the choice. And we're faced with that choice every moment.

It's like a person saying, "Well, why did I have to come to Earth? Why me?" Well, everybody else can ask the same question. If you didn't earn it, you wouldn't be here. And when you've earned getting out, you'll get out. But you won't get out any sooner, believe me.

Some people think that, you know, they can get out of anything. My friends, let me assure you, there's no escape. There's no escape. You know, there's no escape from this world or this experience or that experience. There's no escape. Let's face it. Because there is no escape. You see, you can get rid of the physical body. That's easy enough. But you can't get rid of the mental one. No. That is, the mind goes right on. And no matter whatever experience you accept in consciousness, that goes right with you, because consciousness goes with us. You see? There's no way out, my friends. Only through acceptance do we grow to higher levels of consciousness here and hereafter.

There is no escape from laws that we, and we alone, have set into motion. You can blame God and you can blame the universe, but it will do nothing more than send you deeper down into self, into more grief, into more misery. You can say that you don't understand until hell freezes over itself, and what you're saying is simply this: "I'm not yet ready to accept."

Thank you, friends. Let us go have refreshments.

OCTOBER 17, 1974

CONSCIOUSNESS CLASS 64

Good evening, class. This evening for our discussion, before our question-and-answer period, we're going to discuss the soul of action. Now, do any of my review students know what is the soul of action? I'm sure you've all read it in our little booklet entitled *Little Lights*. The soul of action. Yes.

I believe it is awareness.

Awareness. Thank you very much. Anyone else? *[There is a brief pause, and then the Teacher continues.]* The soul of action, my friends. Now, in many ways, it's been taught to the world. It has been stated by many people that our actions speak louder than our words and our actions reveal our true self. Well, the soul of action, my friends, is what is commonly referred to in these teachings as motive. And it takes awareness to reveal, of course, our motive.

Now, you have been taught that the mind defends what it desires to defend by what is known as the level of justification. And so it is in life that our actions do, in truth, reveal our true motive. When we find it necessary to defend our actions, what we are, in truth, doing is defending what we have justified, of course, in our own mind.

Now, let us take a few moments on what we call motive. When we become aware of the feelings and the thought patterns that exist beneath our so-called conscious level, we then become aware of our motives. Now, it is stated in this philosophy that if the motive is pure, the method is legal, dependent, of course, upon the purity of our own motive. It is a teaching to be applied, as all of these teachings are, to our own levels of consciousness and to ourselves.

Each day we experience what is known as the level of consciousness called justification. We must express through that level in order to defend the position that we have taken concerning any experience. It is also taught in this philosophy that truth needs no defense. Because, you see, my good students, truth does not need to be justified, for truth *is*. And therefore there is nothing, of course, to defend.

So let us ask ourselves daily, more often perhaps than we have been, "What is my motive in any given situation? What is my true motive?" We cannot find our true motives in anything until we become first aware of the multitude of desires in our lifetime that we have already suppressed. For it could well be, and often is, a suppressed desire that motivates us into action. And because we are not aware of that suppressed desire that has motivated us into action, we find ourselves in a position to defend the action that we are expressing. And so, as one of my students said, as I asked him what was the soul of action, he said, "Awareness." Because it takes, my friends, self-awareness.

Week after week, month after month, and year after year, we teach in this Association that it is inside our own head, that all experience, all freedom, all bondage, all things exist within our own consciousness. This is, for all of us, at least at times, a most difficult teaching and philosophy to accept. But, my good students, until we accept that truth, which is demonstrable, until we stop relying upon things outside of ourselves for freedom, for expression—until we reach that plane of consciousness—we will not, and we cannot, be free.

So let us ask ourselves that question, "What are my reliances in this life? Upon what have I permitted myself, as an individualized free soul, to become dependent?" When you take stock of the people, places, and things that you have become dependent upon, then you will be on the path to removing those dependencies, those reliances, and be free.

But these dependencies, these things and people that we rely upon, they will not disappear from our universe. But *we* will be free. We will be in the world and we will not be a part of the world. We will be with a thing and we will not be a part of the thing. And so let us think and let us think more deeply [about] what we are really doing to ourselves.

Now, as we discussed here, I believe in our last class, about giving power to people, places, and things. And when we say from a level of consciousness of our own mind, "I'm not going to give this one and that one power," from that very expression we just turned the cell lock and put ourselves back into prison. Because we have not declared the truth. We have simply retaliated within our own consciousness.

Now, a person may say, "Well, how can I be free when I don't yet know my own dependencies?" That's why it takes a little daily effort to ask yourself how you feel when someone is near you and how you feel when they're not, how you feel when your desires are fulfilled and how you feel when they're not fulfilled.

It does not mean, my friends, that man was meant to become a hermit, to live on some mountaintop where he had no distractions. Because that's not the purpose of our soul's incarnation on this Earth planet. But man is an individualized soul. That means, he *is* an individual. His spirit is a part of the universal whole. His expression is what is individual. That is what is individualized—is the form. And the soul is form and yet it is formless. It is form because it is expression. And you cannot have expression without having form.

And so think and think again. Upon what are you relying in life? Are you, in truth, relying upon an infinite Divine Intelligence that your physical eyes say they cannot see, your physical senses say it does not know? But your inner being—that part of you they call the perfect peace—that is what knows. And so that, my friends, is what is worth attaining. That is what is worth going back home to. That's when you're home. We call that being in your own universe, in your own vibration.

You see, our reliances in life upon form will bring us joy and bring us sadness. They will bring us all of the duality of creation, because they are creation. And so remember this: Anytime you rely upon form, you guarantee satisfaction and you guarantee regret.

Thank you very much. Now you're free to ask any questions you have.

I would like to go back to motive for a moment. In self-examination, if we should find our motives are not the purest, because of the fact that, as usual, we are in the past, what is it that we can then do?

Thank you very much. And you're referring to self-examination, which—I think you'll find what would be of more benefit is self-awareness. Because, you see, to examine something is to judge it. And therefore, it is not self-examination. That is a mental process. That is not what we're striving for. But self-awareness is to become aware of something and yet be free of judgment. Because the moment that you judge, you attach your consciousness to the very thing that you have judged and therefore you become a part of it.

Now, in reference to a motivation that you may have had a year ago or yesterday or six months ago that motivated you into an action, well, the action has come and gone, has it not?

Yes. And so we want to become aware of the motivations of the now, of the here and the now. Now, we will become aware not through self-examination. You don't want to sit down mentally and intellectually and to say, "I see, that is a desire that I have suppressed," etc., etc., and etc., and examine this and take it all apart, because, you see, you will not be free from judgment if you do that. However, if you sit down in awareness and, like you're viewing a motion picture, and you look at all of these desires, which are the motivations, and all of these suppressions, and you sit back, peacefully viewing this screen of your own being, then, you see, you are at peace. And you will be guided by your own spirit to make whatever changes are necessary. But you will not be trapped by the judgment of the mind. For, you see, my friends, what the mind judges one moment, it endorses the next moment. Because there are these eighty-one levels of consciousness and there are these multitudes of patterns. So it is not judgment that you want. And when you do that—when you view, through awareness, your patterns of the here and now—that's what you can do something about. I hope that's helped with your question.

Thank you very much.

You're welcome. Yes.

Yes. I wonder if you would share your understanding on removing obstructions from your mind and letting go, where you can just turn yourself over to the Divine for a healing or anything like that.

Thank you very, very much. The gentleman's referring to the removal of obstructions, that one may be free to experience what we call perfect health or harmony in our life. It is a very easy thing to say "release something" when the something we're supposed to release we're not yet aware of. And so the first thing that we must do, or should do, is to become aware of what the obstruction really is.

Now say, for example, that a person is seeking an improvement in their health. Well, a person may say, "The obstruction is my own mind and its analysis and its concern over the condition that I am experiencing." However, one just doesn't say, "Well, I set that aside and therefore I now experience perfect health," because that is not the way that it works. We first must become aware—aware of what the seeming obstruction is. And that takes an attitude of peace. Because without an attitude of peace, we cannot, and we do not, see clearly. You see, peace is what balances the conscious and the subconscious minds. It is what balances the electric and the magnetic field. When those are in balance, we can see clearly.

Now, if a person is seeking perfect health—and we're all seeking perfect health, whether we're consciously aware of it or not. Of course, we are seeking it, because we're all seeking to bring ourselves into balance. And so the only thing that I could say to you, in reference to that, is to take more time and say to ourselves, "God, let me be at peace. For I know when I am at peace that I will see clearly. And, once having seen clearly, the obstruction will be removed from my life." You see, what we are interested in, in this course of study, is to become aware. For it is through awareness that perfect balance is brought into our life.

We all have, and are, a computer. And we all play different tapes at different times. The seeming miracle in life is this: it is sometimes the simplest thing in life that brings us happiness. It is sometimes the simplest thing in life that restores our health. It is not important what the thing is. It is only important that it does what we are seeking: to restore ourselves. And so, my friends, remember, it takes constant effort to keep the mind in balance. And only by keeping it in balance are we free, are we restored to perfect health, which is nothing more than the effect of perfect balance. You see, perfect balance permits a rhythmic flow of the divine power, which is known as health. But it is balance that we must seek. And that balance is called peace.

One of the greatest obstructions to this flow of rhythm and balance is the mental concern over any situation that we may encounter in life. Now, it is a very normal thing to be concerned about the outcome of anything that we are interested in. This is a very normal process of the mind. When I say "normal," I mean it is very average. When we permit the mind to be concerned, that is when we become the obstruction to anything that we are seeking in life.

Now, a person may say, "Well, I'd best be concerned or the job won't get done." It doesn't mean that we should sit back and just say, "Well, there's a Divine Intelligence. It will take care of it." No, that's not why we're individualized souls. But there is a fine point. There is a point where the mind does its job. There is a point at which the mind does not, and cannot, go beyond. The mind expresses in a mental level. And it can do many things and does do many things on a mental level. But there is a level of consciousness that is greater, that is far superior than what we call the mind. And when we reach a situation life, whatever it may be—our business, our prosperity, or our health—when we have done all that we feel that we can do to have the situation turn out the way that we desire it to do, there comes a point in time where we must let go. Let go of all concern, because we have done everything that we can do mentally. When we reach that point, there is an inner peace that descends over our vibration. And when that happens, it is amazing: because that which we have tried with such great effort starts to dawn in our consciousness, and it has happened.

What it simply means, my friends, is this—consciously or unconsciously, it does not matter how—it means that we have let go. We have let go of the mental activity concerning the situation and now we will become the living demonstration of what God can do. And that's what happens, my friends.

That's what happens when the mind says, "I've had it. I have tried everything," and it lets go. I hope that's helped with your question. Yes.

Thank you. I believe we've been taught, if I recall it correctly, that that which knows its birth shall also know its death. And I wonder, with regard to that, if you would speak a bit on divine birthright.

Thank you very much. Yes. We teach here—and the student has brought up the point—that that knows birth also knows death. And he has asked that we might discuss perhaps another statement in this philosophy known as divine right. I'd like to clarify that, because it is divine right that we discuss, not divine birthright.

Now, do any of my review students know what is divine right? What is meant when it is stated that is that person's divine right? What is divine right? And we've discussed this before in our classes. Anyone know what is divine right? Yes.

Is it expression?

Thank you very, very much. The divine right is the right of expression. And everything in the universe strives to express its true self.

Now, we may agree or disagree with an individual's expression. But if we are demonstrating total consideration and total acceptance, then we are respecting the right of the expression of the form. And so it is, a divine right is the divine expression. Does that help with your question? Yes, rise please.

Somewhat. What, then, is the meaning of "Peace, Poise, and Power are my birthright"? [See the appendix for the complete text of the "Total Consideration" affirmation.]

Thank you very much. Peace, Poise, and Power are our birthright. Expression is—the true expression of the Divine is peace, poise, and power.

Now, when man decides, of course, regarding this energy, this intelligence, which is expressing itself, which way to direct it, he either directs it in harmony with this Divine Intelligence of perfect peace, poise, and power or he sidetracks it according to his desires. And that's where all of our problems begin. And this is why we teach peace in this study course. Because peace *is* the perfect balance. But man has this divine right of expression. And he has this free will, this choice, to direct this perfect peace, poise, and power into any channel that he so chooses.

Now, when we are concerned over things, what we are doing is sidetracking this perfect peace, this perfect divine energy, and we're limiting it into a negative flow, for we have faith in the negative outcome of the situation in which we are interested. And so this is when we become the obstruction, my friends. It's when we as individuals, when *we* become concerned.

How many jobs—and how many times have we all gone to work, been concerned over something, and when we let go, something happened, and it all worked out just perfect? Well, why did it work out perfect? Because the experience is only an effect of our own level of consciousness. And if we change our level of consciousness, then the experience changes, because the experience is very personal: it's our own.

You see, it's just like a person, you know, they're concerned with somebody else and they're not doing their job. Well, as long as they're concerned with somebody else, that they're not doing their job, you can be rest assured, as long as you're in that level of consciousness, that person over there is never going to do their job, as far as you, as an individual, are concerned, you see.

So we don't change things outside until we change things inside. Because, you see, inside is where the cause of everything is. That's the only place the cause is. And, you see, this is why it's so detrimental to criticize and to complain and to gripe. It's pathetic, because, you see, sooner or later it's going to come like a great thunderstorm and it will drown us.

Now, a person may say, "Well, it's easy not to be concerned, because you're not in the situation." Well, maybe we are and the others can't see that we are. Because we can be in all kinds of situations. You know, unless you're extremely perceptive, you don't know what situation another individual is in unless they tell you or somebody else does.

So, you see, my friends, repetition is the Law of Change. And through repetition will a change take place in your consciousness. You know, it is so interesting, in teaching in these classes, especially in these classes, that I can always tell when a teaching is beginning to get through into the cement. I can always tell, because, you see, there is an emanation from our being. Usually it can be viewed as a resentment or an "I've heard that before." That is the first sign—the very first sign—that the teaching is getting through the concrete.

Now, sometimes a student is able to weather that storm, you know, that crumbling of the concrete, called the human brain, and they have the sincerity of purpose, the motivation, to keep on keeping on. But I assure you, my friends, it's not a negative sign. It's a very positive sign, because what it means is this: the level of consciousness to which the student has become addicted is becoming aware—they're becoming aware inside—that you're not going to feed that level too much longer. And so they start to express and sometimes it's a twitch of the face. Sometimes it's a scowl. Sometimes it's a turning of the head. Sometimes it's an outright statement: "I don't want to have a lecture!" or "I don't want to hear that again!" But that's a good sign.

And so as that's happening to you, my good students, to some of you, be grateful. It means the thing that has kept you where you are—and you're not satisfied with life as it has been going or you wouldn't be here—is beginning to break down. And, of course, humanity calls that the human ego. But it's a very good sign.

And so if you feel angry and frustrated and weary of hearing the same teaching over and over again and if you find yourself falling to sleep while you're in class, be grateful, because what you're trying to do is block out the truth of your own spirit that's trying to speak to you. But, believe me, like a voice in the wilderness, your soul, your spirit, will not long go unheard. Oh no. Thank you very much for your question. Yes.

In line with what you were just saying, would you give us your expression of how we are tempting ourselves to leave the light? And the larger the soul expansion, the greater the effects of creation, I believe, is to hold us back.

Thank you very, very much. The lady wants to know how we're constantly testing ourselves. Yes, you can call it a test. We're testing ourselves. Because we're constantly having to make a choice. We're having to make choices just constantly between desire patterns that we have long addiction to and to reason that keeps striving to shine in our universe.

You know, friends, as we express in this life—and we all express, whether we yawn or we blink our eyes or we snore or whatever it is we decide that we need to do—as long as we are in this life, and in any life, we're going to strive to express our divinity. Because our divinity *is* expression. And so, my friends, the longer we have entertained any desire, any pattern of mind, the more difficult the test is for us. Because what we've done—and we discussed that a few minutes earlier—what we have really done—because the desire, whatever the desire may be that we have entertained for a lifetime—or combination of desires—because they have brought us satisfaction, to some extent, or we wouldn't keep having the desire, of course, then, we've relied upon that. We've relied upon it to satisfy ourselves—do you understand? And so whenever the mind says, "I'm not satisfied. I'm bored. I'm unhappy," it seeks satisfaction. And where does it seek satisfaction? Upon whatever has satisfied it before. And so to those of us who have satisfaction of many years from the fulfillment of our desires, it is more difficult.

Those are the tests. Those are the tests within ourselves. Because, you see, we haven't yet put a new programming in and say, "I don't need to do that to be satisfied. I can go do this over here." But you have to have acceptance first.

Now, the reason that so few of us say, "Well, now, I see that I am totally addicted to this way of living in order to have satisfaction,"—now the reason that it is difficult for us to say, "Well, I can have the same satisfaction by that over there," is not only acceptance—we have no directed faith, you see.

It's very difficult for any of us to have faith in something that we have not yet experienced. This is man's great difficulty in finding God. That's his great difficulty. Because he has not yet, you understand, had what *he* decides is the experience necessary to prove to him that God exists. I do hope that's helped with your question. Yes.

I would like to have the spirit's expression on the faculty of appreciation.

Thank you very much. Upon what is the faculty of appreciation dependent? Does anyone know? Yes.

I believe it's attention and awareness.

Attention and awareness. Do you believe that attention and awareness bring appreciation?

Not always. It's according to what your judgment is on and what you're aware of.

Then, I'm sure you would agree that appreciation cannot, in its fullness, be dependent upon attention and awareness. Because if appreciation were dependent upon attention and awareness, then it would, in truth, express itself, known as appreciation, wherever there was attention or awareness. Would you not agree?

Yes.

And we all agree it does not. We all agree that man does not necessarily appreciate all things that he is aware of or has placed his attention upon. Would you agree? Therefore, we now agree that appreciation is not solely and fully dependent upon attention and awareness. I do believe, however, that that comes from another philosophy, another teaching. But we are discussing here the soul faculty of appreciation. When, how, and why does the soul faculty of appreciation express itself? Does anybody know? Yes.

With understanding.

Understanding. Understanding. Thank you very much. That is when the soul faculty expresses itself. I'm very pleased. You're a new student to this philosophy and I'm very happy that a student only once in one semester—in eight classes—has perceived what has been given for years in this philosophy. All soul faculties are dependent upon their foundation. And we all know that the foundation stone of all soul faculties is understanding. You cannot appreciate what you do not understand. I do hope that's helped with your question. Thank you very much.

Going back a couple of questions, when you were speaking of letting go, in terms of circumstances bothering you, what I was wondering is, before this letting go of concern takes place, my understanding, from what you said before, was that it is a prerequisite to exhaust every effort you can to the solving of this problem. And at that point, does the letting go take place, more or less automatically, outside of the mind?

No. It doesn't let go in the sense that there is, then, an acceptance—to the full acceptance—to the Divine Intelligence or the divine healing power. No. That depends entirely upon the individual. Now, for example, some people may be extremely concerned over a situation for their lifetime here on Earth. And it plagues them for fifty, sixty, seventy, eighty, ninety years. Do you understand? That depends on the individual's mind.

Now, some people may be plagued with a situation they're extremely concerned about and they reach a point and they let go, in the sense they just take off to the other dimension. Because that's a way out for them.

It does not mean that we automatically, being concerned over any situation in our lives, automatically, after we have exhausted all the mental, conscious activity, let go and accept the Divine. No, it does not mean that. That's very individual. Yes.

Is there a technique by which you can rid yourself of concern?

Oh, absolutely. There most certainly is. There most certainly is. Now, first off, we all know from this philosophy that acceptance is the divine will. Acceptance is the divine will. Now, when we have full acceptance, you see, what happens with the mind in any situation—whether it's on a job or whatever it is—first thing the mind tries is this: it goes along; it doesn't work. The mind, then, tries that. And that doesn't work. The mind tries something else and it doesn't work. The mind tries again; it doesn't work. First thing that has happened: it accepts all the tapes, the programs, of its own mind—you hear me?—and any new tapes that are introduced, if they fit into the tapes that we already find ourselves addicted to. All right? Then, there is a chance that it happens, in the sense that we say, "Well," to ourselves, "I've tried everything. I now see that I had my faith in this path: it didn't work. I had my faith in that path: it didn't work. And I had my faith in that path and it didn't work." Because, you see, if we didn't have our faith in a path, then we wouldn't walk upon the path. Right? All right. So what is the key? What is the real key?

Faith, my friends. It takes faith. Directed faith. We've all got faith. We have faith in trying this mental way and that mental way and twenty, thirty other mental ways. And when they all finally collapse—because it takes longer or shorter time. People are all people and individual. And finally we say, whether we say it consciously or subconsciously, finally the dawn comes and we say, "That's it!" And we direct that faith that we have been directing in other mental paths to the divine will. And that's called acceptance. Does that help with your question?

I guess.

Well, you see, my friend, we all have faith. And we're using faith every moment of our life. What we're trying to teach here is to direct that faith with some reason, to direct it wisely, not to permit it to be directed by the patterns of our mind, of experiences that we have had for a lifetime. This is what we're trying to teach here. Direct it to an Intelligence that never will fail you.

You see, God doesn't fail us. God never did fail us. This is in our head, you see. You see, man said, "Well, I prayed for this and I didn't receive it. Therefore God failed me." Well, this is ridiculous. This is not the God that we're trying to share with you. The only one that fails is ourselves. God is our understanding. And, as that understanding broadens, we can see all these tapes that we have, all these patterns we have. The light is cast over them. Then, we can direct our energy, our faith where it will free us. I do hope that's helped with your question. Yes.

There is no magic wand, however, that you can wave and it's going to happen. It doesn't work that way. I haven't found that way yet. It would be nice, of course, if we could, you know, just wave the wand and the transformation has taken place. Just that quick. But I fear that man does not change that quickly. You see, the magic wand is change. Change of attitude, which is change of pattern. But, see, we don't change that that easily. We'd like to. It doesn't happen that way. Just doesn't happen that way, my friend. Yes.

In the application of the laws that we're learning in this philosophy, if we direct them in, say, a proper or a negative way and other people who, say, do not know this particular philosophy—are we more responsible, as students of Serenity, who are more aware of these laws? And do they have a greater effect on us if we abuse these laws?

Thank you very much. Yes, man is responsible unto himself. And he is responsible for his own transgressions. Now, you cannot say that because a man is now consciously aware of some of the universal laws of life that he has a greater responsibility and he will pay a greater price than those who have not yet learned them. Do you understand? Because it doesn't work like that, my friends. I mean, if you cross the street against the red light, whether you are aware of what the red light is for or you are not aware what the red light is for, it's still a transgression and you're still going to pay the price. Would you not agree? Because it is man's own responsibility to become aware. It's his own responsibility.

Now, because his soul may have merited some understanding that perhaps is not bringing as much awareness as you may think or we may think that we have—this is a very personal thing, of course, but he is still responsible. Oh yes. Absolutely and positively. We're responsible when we came to this Earth planet. And we're responsible for all of the things that we set into motion. I hope that's helped with your question.

Thank you.

You're welcome. Yes.

I will ask this question because it's come up so many times. Would you give us the understanding—Serenity's understanding—of the difference between concepts and spiritual precepts?

Thank you very much. We have discussed before, that the mind conceives and the spirit perceives. So man has many concepts in his life and, usually, few perceptions.

Now ofttimes we say, "Oh, I perceive that. I perceive that very clearly." Well, what we mean to say is that we conceive that in our own consciousness and, "What you are expressing is in harmony with my own conception." And then, we call that perception. Well, that's not perception at all. That simply means that somebody agreed with you, you see. That's all that that is.

So when we're speaking, you know, about mental conceptions and spiritual perceptions, if it's a spiritual perception—I'll tell you something, my friends: it's something that comes into your consciousness that is so sacred to you, so personal, you keep it to yourself. Then, you know you've got yourself a perception. Because it comes with that vibratory wave.

Now, you may express your understanding of something you have spiritually perceived, but that's not a spiritual perception. That is your conception of that perception. So when we say, you know, "I perceive the level of consciousness you're on," well, usually it means, "You and I are in harmony because we're both on the same level and we're conceiving jointly. And therefore we feel great." I do hope that that's helped you with spiritual perception and mental conception.

Thank you.

You're welcome. But it is a frailty, of course, of our own mind to feel that we perceive so much, especially when we can find enough people to agree with us, you see. Yes.

In this understanding, is sympathy the same thing as pity?

Thank you very much. The gentleman is speaking in reference to sympathy and pity. There is a fine line of distinction between sympathy and pity. Now pity, you understand, pity is expressed sympathy. And I'm sure you understand that. You see, you sympathize, but the moment you express that, you have pity. And the moment you have that pity, whatever you are pitying, you're denying their divine right and you're helping them to go down.

This is why we teach, No pity, my friends. No sympathy. Compassion, for that has the light of understanding; that respects and considers their whole being, not just one of the tapes that they're playing at some moment. So let us pray for compassion. It has light and it has understanding. And that's a soul faculty. And with that, we can do something.

But, you know, when we're in a situation, all of us, you know, and that tape—well, we're sensitive. We have keen feelings. And we want those around us to understand how we feel. And we think, when we're sensitive like that and going through a situation, that they don't understand us unless they can say, "You poor, pathetic soul." You see? Well, the greatest way, if they are our true friend, they'll say, "Well, now you know this is one of the tapes. And we've got to do whatever is necessary to get our consciousness onto another plane of consciousness, as hard as it is." That's a true friend. But one that pats you on the back and says, "You poor thing, you'll probably be this way the rest of your life," well, I wouldn't call that a friend. I certainly wouldn't. I'd rather have somebody hit me over the head and wake me up than pat me on the back and let me sleep.

Thank you, friends. Let's awaken and go have refreshments. Thank you very much.

OCTOBER 24, 1974

CONSCIOUSNESS CLASS 65

Good evening, class. This evening for discussion we'd like to share, for a few moments, our understanding of what is known as experience. Now, we have a little statement in this philosophy that says one experience calls forth another experience of like kind, unless we take the essence from the experience, which is the indispensable ingredient for the reeducation of the senses. We also know that the essence of a thing is its principle.

And so it is that man experiences the effect of whatever tape he permits to be played in his own computer mind. When we recognize and accept that experience itself is the effect of other experiences that we have had at some other time and that that particular tape is playing at that moment, then we will take the essence out of an experience. For example, if we had an experience when we were three and we reacted in a certain way and the reaction—the effect of the reaction was satisfactory to us, then that tape, that experience, is well computed in our computer mind.

We guarantee the continuity of the experience until such time as we view its principle, the essence of it, until such time as we recognize and accept that this is the way we reacted as a child under similar circumstances, that it brought us satisfaction and we, therefore, became attached to that particular tape in our own mind. And so we find in life here today, as adults, that as we set—and we're always setting—these laws into motion that we call experience, that we are still, forty and fifty years later, reacting as we did when we were children three, four, and five years old.

Now, when we are honest with ourselves, we become aware and we can see—this is the importance of the teaching and the application of self-control. You see, my friends, there is no freedom in life until we apply, until we demonstrate, what is called self-control: to control ourselves from the tape banks—the tapes in our mind—that bring us disturbance and rob us from what is known as peace, serenity, and freedom.

When we look at ourselves honestly and objectively, we can see in the course of any day the number of times that we are acting in ways that we did as little children. This is why we teach that satisfaction in anything guarantees its own attachment. When we were little children, many of us were pampered in certain ways because our guardians or our parents did not want to be bothered or were too busy doing something else. So they did whatever they thought was best to pamper our multitude of desires and to let so many things go by, so they would not have to take the time to correct and to guide us. And here we are as adults, the effect of those circumstances and conditions.

Now, of course, we cannot blame our parents, for our soul merited our parents. But we can, today, stop and think. Stop and think where we are and what we are continuing to do to ourselves. Isn't it really a bit sad, in a way, to become aware that we are, in truth, emotionally, most of the time, acting like two- and three-year-old children when our desires are not fulfilled?

So often in life we blame the world and people and things outside of us, because of our hurts, because of our joys. If you rely upon things outside for your joy, then it is only evident and natural and normal that you're going to rely on things outside for your hurts and, of course, your displeasures. That's not the path, my good students, to peace. And it certainly isn't the path to freedom.

Now, this is our ninth class here of this semester. And I know that many of the students came to this course—who hadn't been in this course before—with certain preconceived ideas or thoughts of what it was going to be like. That, of course, is the individual's right. But ofttimes when we decide what something is going to be like, ofttimes we are disappointed in life, because, you see, my friends, expectation has no light. And so it is in life that we expect many things. But expectation does not see the principle of things. It just hopes. And we know that hope is eternal, but we also know that truth is inevitable.

Now, many students in this Association have asked me—especially new students—"Just what is the process of unfoldment? How does one go about being a medium or a healer?" First of all, of course, we didn't all come to Earth to be a minister, a lecturer, a healer, or a medium. But I can assure you of this: The number one requirement of leadership, if you wish to call it that, is self-control. For if we cannot control ourselves, our emotions, and our own tapes in our own consciousness, then we certainly will not be qualified to try to lead another human soul. And so in this Association the number one requirement for spiritual unfoldment is self-control. And self-control cannot come to any of us until we accept the truth that it is all inside our own head; that it's nowhere outside. It never was and it never will be.

I know that that, to many, is a very difficult teaching to accept. But you cannot accept it when you're feeling great and deny it when you're feeling bad. Because if you do, that's not truth. That's only our own justification and defense of the way we want to be.

Now, you know, when we're dissatisfied with ourselves, we start to think. And when we start to think, things start to happen. And so it is the divine discontent exists in the depths of our own soul, because the purpose of the soul is evolutionary incarnation. And whether we like it or not, we, in truth, indeed are evolving. We may look around the world and think that some other soul is not evolving. They're evolving. It just takes some of us many centuries and others a few years. But that's the way life is. Creation has all its variety. So let's give a little more thought, my friends, give a little more thought that everything is inside us.

You know, I heard a man once say that he was very sick for a number of years. And he said, "You know, it's not because I transgressed any law. I didn't do a thing. It's because of a certain woman I knew. She directed thought force at me and I was deathly ill." My friends, I want to assure all of you students in Serenity that that is not, nor has it ever been, nor will it ever be, the teachings of the Serenity Association. Our teachings are very simple and they are very clear. And because they are very simple, we must get into simplicity in order to see them and to benefit by them. Our teachings are: all experience in life—*all* experience—takes place within ourselves. All experience are laws that we alone have set into motion. And it doesn't matter what experience that we're having.

But along with that teaching is the teaching of the freedom of choice: that your eternity is the moment of which you are consciously aware. And so you can choose in a second, in a split second, to make whatever change is necessary to experience a new life. As long as we have within our mind the need to blame people and things for our life, as long as we insist upon entertaining that level of consciousness, we are going to be bound to the fluctuations, the changes, of emotion. And that's just the way it is, my friends. You don't have to believe it. All you have to do is to pause long enough to see it.

Thank you very much. Now you're free to ask the questions that you have.

Yes. I noticed that you equated in your discussion mediumship with leadership, and I'm interested in your understanding of that. It's my impression that none of us free ourselves from our subconscious tapes totally while we're still in form. Is that incorrect according to your understanding?

There are moments of freedom. But you do not free yourself completely from that computer. You can always reprogram it. And the equation with mediumship is also an equal equation with any position, such as lecturing or healing or any other position. Yes.

I don't understand the equation of leadership to mediumship to unfoldment. It seems to me that each of us will have some tapes, subconscious tapes, that are going on. And, like, I may have fifteen and you may have twenty-three and somebody else may have two. And I want to know, how is it ever determined when a person has got enough self-control over their subconscious tapes—or what your understanding of that—to be called a medium or to be a leader while still in form?

Thank you very much. First off, I think we'd best have a little clearing and understanding, perhaps a little clarification, on what we mean when we equated leadership with mediumship or healing or lecturing.

And unfoldment.

And unfoldment. First, my friends, everyone, in truth, is a medium. They are a medium of expression of their own spirit. So in that sense of the word, this is what we are discussing—and unfoldment.

Now, the lady is speaking in reference to when does a person become a leader. Well, we're all leaders and we are all followers, because at the present moment we are being led by our own experiences, which are from our own tapes of our own computer. And so in that respect, we are all leaders. And we're all followers, because we are following the dictates of those tapes of our own subconscious.

Now, the lady, I believe, is referring to unfoldment and, like she stated, mediumship. What does it mean to unfold? Would the class agree that unfoldment means to open or to free? Because this is what unfoldment means in this philosophy. It means to open. And when you open, you free. It means to free your own soul and your own divinity. You see, this is what spiritual unfoldment truly means. It means to free your spirit from the bondage of the experiences that have been accepted, that are dictating our life at this very moment.

Now, I know that many people, entering a Spiritualist church and organization, seem to think that spiritual unfoldment means to become a medium, to become a healer, to become a minister, or etc. That is not what spiritual unfoldment means in our understanding. It means to free your own divinity by accepting the truth of its freedom in the first place, you see. Now, when man says, "Well, this is the way life is. This is what I have and this is my condition," well, the condition of this moment is not the condition of a moment before, necessarily, or of a moment yet to be. And so we are teaching, for spiritual unfoldment, that a person first must gain some self-control over the patterns of mind that are dictating their life.

Now, you know, these tapes or patterns of mind of acceptance of the past, they're not annihilated. We just don't let them play when we have self-control. And thereby, we free our soul. I do hope that's helped with your question.

May I ask another?

Yes, certainly.

Does that mean, say, you are performing as a medium, delivering a message or healing somebody, does that mean at least during that time you are exercising control over your tapes?

No. Absolutely and positively not. That entirely depends upon the healer or the medium. You see—

It's back and forth.

Oh, absolutely! Because, you see, first of all, we must become aware of this. The medium, the healer, or the individual—whatever you're doing, even if you're digging a ditch or running a jackhammer—unless we become aware, then we do not know which tape is controlling our life. We do not know. You see, this is why we have these awareness classes, you see: is to become aware; to become aware of your feelings and then become aware of what's causing your feelings, you see.

Definitely. Now a person may be in communication—and there is such a thing in our understanding, in this church anyway, of what we call subconscious colorization: the coloring of any communication by our subconscious tapes. That can happen to any medium or any psychic. It can happen to any healer. Yes, certainly.

When that person is referred to as a clear channel, then, and you hear people say, "Well, he's really a clear channel" or "She's really a clear channel," are they, then, making a statement that that person is not subconsciously colorizing things to their understanding?

That is what they usually mean. But, you see, the sadness of these people that say, "Well, this one's a clear channel and that one's a clear channel," what they mean to say is, "I got the message I wanted," you see. So we can't really, you know, base a solid foundation on someone's experience that that person's a clear channel and that person's not a clear channel. Unless they, themselves, are a clear channel, that decision and judgment is based upon their own tapes. Do you see what I mean? Yes. So the only thing we can do is to speak for ourselves when we become aware of what our tapes are. You understand? Now, that's what it's really all about.

Now, of course, there's the statement that you judge the tree by the fruit that it bears. But, yes, usually that's what they mean when they say a person's a clear channel. It's supposed to mean that they're free from personality and subconscious colorization of the communication. But, as I stated earlier, it usually means that they were satisfied with the message that they received at that given moment. Therefore, that does not necessarily guarantee that that individual, in truth, is a clear channel. Does that help with your question?

Thank you.

You're more than welcome.

I have a few questions. My first is—you just spoke of self-control, as far as controlling our tapes and controlling our thought patterns. In meditation I find it's hard for me to control those tapes and control the myriad of thought patterns that are happening. And I seem to keep coming back to those patterns. And I would like to hear your comment on ways of being aware of that.

Thank you very much, yes.

And . . .

Go ahead.

My second question is—last week we were talking about repetition producing changes. And I'd like you to speak of your understanding of a mantra as causing physiological effects, which will, in turn, cause spiritual, mental changes.

Thank you. The first thing the gentleman is speaking of is the controlling of the myriad of thoughts that pass through the mind while we're trying to concentrate, trying to meditate. Well, we must consider and be honest with ourselves that we haven't spent a lifetime trying to concentrate or meditate. Would you not agree? But isn't it wonderful, in our efforts to concentrate and to meditate, that we are now becoming aware of what our mind is doing all the time. Wouldn't you agree?

Now, isn't it a seeming miracle that we are able somehow to sustain the health that we have with the way that our mind is working? Wouldn't you agree? With a multitude of thoughts that you experience during your process of concentration and meditation—so distracting and so disjointed and certainly not harmonious or united—wouldn't you agree that it is a seeming miracle the health we have? If we accept that the physical body is an effect of the mental body, it's a miracle it holds together at all, my friends. This is what I'm talking about.

You see, we have an affirmation that declares the Law of Harmony, which brings an effect known as unity, you see. And so our body is composed of many parts and if they're not harmonized to some extent, we're not going to experience good health. So, number one: We are becoming aware that we, in truth, have lost control of our mind. Wouldn't you agree to that? Now, that's what's happening, friends, in this awareness process. You see, we've all lost control of our mind. Well, just stop and try to be at peace. This is what we're supposed to be doing. Look at all of the images and the feelings that pass through the mind. Would any of my students call that control? I wouldn't call it control.

Well, anyway, that's the state we're at in our process of evolution. But we don't have to remain there. Through greater effort—greater effort—and greater application of the laws that you already know as students, you can begin to control the multitudes of images and thoughts that pass through your mind. At least we are now aware that the process is taking place.

All right. Now, the gentleman is speaking of one of our teachings, known as repetition, the Law of Change. Now, it doesn't seem like repetition is change. The word *repetition* means "to repeat," doesn't it? But there's a subtleness about the human mind that escapes most of us. When you try to repeat anything in the mind, it makes absolutely sure that there's a slight change each time. Would you not agree? Spend a year thinking of the word *peace*. If it stays in the mental level, each peace will be a little bit different. You understand? Because it's still in the mental. And that's the way our mind—the human mind—works.

Now, why does it work that way? Because it is its nature—it is its very nature—to create. And therefore it always adds and subtracts a little bit from whatever is repeated into it. Now, that's known as a part of what we call the superego. And we all have one. We all have a superego. We have an ego and we have a superego.

And because of what we call society and its different laws, we've suppressed an awful lot of our desires. We suppress them—you know why we've suppressed them? We've suppressed them out of fear. How does society enforce the laws that it chooses to enforce? How does it do that? I ask you the question. By instilling fear into the people. And what is fear? Faith in the negative outcome of any given situation. Now, we might not like to agree that this is how laws are enforced, but just go out there and drive through the red light and you'll very soon find out how society enforces its laws: through negative faith, which is called fear.

Now, we want to get to this question the gentleman asked about the mantra. Mantras can be of great benefit or they can be of great detriment. That depends upon the individual. Mantra is repetition and it causes changes to take place, not only within the mind, but within the physical body and its chemistry. For all thoughts, attitudes cause chemical changes in our body and this is an absolute scientific fact.

When a mantra is used daily, it can either send us into a type of self-hypnotic trance or it can literally drive our soul out of the mental consciousness into the spiritual consciousness. Do you understand? Therefore, we do not teach to our public classes the uses of any particular mantras, because I strongly advise the use of mantras should be under the guidance of some teacher somewhere who has already walked the path, who is already aware of the pitfalls that await the student on the path by their use. Does that help with your question?

Yes. Thank you.

You're welcome. Yes.

Would you give your understanding, please, of forgetting or forgetfulness? And what has the ego to gain from this practice?

And how does it relate to suppressed desires or desire priorities and unawareness and justification and so forth?

Well, of course, first, in reference to your question about forget and forgetting and how does it relate to the human ego, etc., first, I would like to state—as we all already know, I'm sure—that it is very human to forget and it's very divine to forgive. But we're discussing forget.

We all have a priority list in our consciousness: it's called a priority list. And so we go by those priorities—unfortunately, not very consciously. You know, it's like a lady who goes to a shopping store. She writes down the list and she has so much money and she has priorities on the list: that's the thing she desires the most and when the money runs out, the other things go. All right? And if she's smart, she forgets the things she couldn't get and keeps her attention on the things that she could get, because those are her priorities, all right? And so it is when we say, "I forgot." What it simply reveals is that was pretty low on our priority list in the first place, you see.

Now, a person might say, "Well, I *really* did want to do that." Well, the truth of the matter is when they first accepted doing something, that tape that they were playing at that moment really did want to do it. And when the moment came—or the day—for them to do it, it got pushed down on the priority list, because other tapes were now playing. Do you understand? And so it's known as our priority list.

Now, I would like to mention here—and I think this will help along with your question—a very old statement of the prophets: You are your brother's keeper. Now, a lot of people have a lot of different understanding about what those prophets meant, that you are your brother's keeper. Well, just look around. The people in life that you become in rapport with—husbands, wives, friends, etc.—they become your brothers. Because you are in rapport with them, you have an influence on their lives and that makes you brothers. And therefore you take on a responsibility and you become your brother's keeper. And so our teaching is to choose very wisely in life who you come into rapport with, because that rapport establishes a bond—whether you like it or not. And that bond, that chain, is what influence passes over to that individual, wherever they are in life, and you become responsible for certain things, according to the rapport that you have established.

Now, in this science here of Spiritualism, when you think of a person, and you start on the path of unfoldment, you'll ofttimes experience a level of consciousness that they're either on at that moment or whatever the strongest tape that is playing with that individual. And you experience it to the extent and to the degree of your rapport with that person. So, can't you see, my students, what a brother's keeper we really and truly are? But we can't blame our brothers for our experiences, because we made them our brothers by getting in rapport with them in the first place. Does that help with your question?

Thank you very much.

And remember, my dear, it's all priority. And so when you make a decision, you know—you see, our spirit is willing, but our flesh is weak. Our spirit makes a decision and a commitment and then all these other tapes start playing and we forget. But—don't you see?—by forgetting, we protect our senses. We protect our pride. It's a defense mechanism from the mental level, known as justification. A person usually doesn't blame a soul because they forgot. And so the truth of the matter is, it's a good cop-out. And this is the way that it is, you know. But that, of course, deals with awareness for all of us. Yes. Thank you.

Would you please give us your understanding of how compassion is the key that locks the door of pride, as given in the Little Lights?

Yes. Would you like to read that verbatim?

My book is off to the side.

That's quite all right. You may get it.

Thank you. "Compassion is the key which locks the door of pride and frees our soul, that it may soar to heaven's heights."

Thank you. Because there's quite a difference. Compassion is the key which locks the door to pride and frees our soul to heaven's heights. Now, think, my friends, we discussed compassion before. We've stated, many times, not to have pity or sympathy—that pity is the effect of sympathy—but to have compassion. When we have compassion, we have understanding and its effect is called compassion.

Now, when we have understanding and compassion, then what is known as pride—the door to pride is locked. Because the self is not in the way when we have understanding. Therefore, pride—the self, the individual self—is not what is viewing the situation. It is our soul, and therefore it is freed, because there is no obstruction for its expression. Does that help with your question?

Thank you.

You're more than welcome. *[There is a brief pause, and then the Teacher continues.]* Now it's a nice, quiet class this evening. I don't know if it means everyone wants to go out, because it's Halloween or what. Thank you.

It's my understanding that when we come into the world as infants, we begin to develop a perception about ourselves, based on the feedback that we get from significant other people, especially our parents. Some theorists say that that's all the self is, in fact: a mirror image of the feedback that we've gotten from the time we were born until now. This is what I'm understanding as our subconscious tapes that you've been discussing this evening. What I'm interested in knowing is, is it possible, while in form, ever, to free ourselves from being the self that we see reflected from other people? Can we ever see ourselves free?

Absolutely and positively, we can see ourselves free, but that takes acceptance of what we already are. You see, most of us are not yet willing to accept what we already are. We're not willing to do that. We do accept what we think pleases certain people. Now, that we accept, because that is a fulfillment of our own desires. But first, we must accept what we really are. You see, what we're accepting is the image that we think we are presenting to people, you know. Just stop and think, my friends: to one person who we like, we are Dr. Jekyll; to somebody we don't like, we're Mr. Hyde. Do you understand?

So we're locked into that level. We've already accepted that, you know. The worst of us comes out with a person we don't like. And the best of us, usually, comes out with the ones that we do like. Would you not agree? Usually. All right. And so it is that we keep going on this merry-go-round.

We are more than the subconscious tape bank. We are an evolving soul. And it is not true that a newborn child is the effect of the feedback of those who are caring for it, because that totally denies the evolution of the soul and the experiences the soul has already gone through. And out of the mouths of babes comes great wisdom. And, I assure you, the wisdom usually has not proven to be the feedback of the parents or guardians, because ofttimes out of the mouths of babes will come true wisdom that the parents haven't even yet accepted. No. So I do not, in that sense, agree 100 percent that a child, an infant, is only the feedback of those who are caring for it, who are meaningful to it. That's only one part of the child's personality, of the child's expression.

Now, I don't mean to imply that infants and little babes do not need some care and guidance in this world. Because, you see, we are an animal form. We are an animal form called human. And we have animal instincts. And we must, in this physical form, learn about the need for some degree of restraint or otherwise, anything we desire, we will just go take without consideration of anything around and about us. Does that help with your question?

Thank you.

You're more than welcome. Yes.

Thank you. It's given in one of the earlier classes, I believe, regarding when the soul leaves the flesh, that there is a period termed reflections—I don't recall the exact terminology—that it passes through. And I would like to ask regarding our daily activities and also, at that time, if we move past these things or if we must eventually, in time, move through them, if we must accept them and educate them as a part of ourselves.

In other words, are you asking, can they be bypassed? Or must we grow through them?

I guess that's what I'm asking. I guess I already know the answer.

We grow through all things that we set into motion. That does not mean that we can't go back and experience them. Do you understand? But we must grow through all of these experiences.

You see, a person may say, "Well, do I have to grow through this here in a physical dimension?" No. You can grow through them mentally. If you have not yet established the law on a physical level, then you will only have to grow through it on the mental level, upon which it has been established in the first place. Does that help with your question?

You see, it's just like forgiving a person. Now, you don't have to forgive a person by walking up to them physically and saying, "I forgive you." You can forgive them in your consciousness, if that's where the law has been established and has not yet got into the physical, you see.

But you have to follow through as far as it has gone?

Oh yes, you have to follow it through as far as it has gone. If it's gone on through the mental and down into the physical, then you must follow it on through. Oh yes, absolutely.

May I ask—

Certainly.

One brief question. It's regarding a continuity of control. I think that all of us, perhaps, have moments of control and moments when we're a little out of control. And there seem to be like gaps, dark areas, that we pass through as we're going through a normal day of going from level to level And I would very much appreciate some method, exercise, or way that would help to fill these gaps, to carry control through those.

Thank you very much. First, we want to consider the truth that we're always under control, because we always are. Even during the "gap" periods, there's another level of consciousness controlling our soul.

Now, what we're trying to do is to get self-control—what we mean is a conscious awareness and direction of the levels that are controlling our soul at any moment. This is self-control: that you consciously are dictating—you understand?—which tape, which level, is going to control you at any given moment. Because all of us at all times are being controlled. We're controlled by one of our levels of consciousness, one of the taped experiences, that is playing. What we are trying to work towards, hopefully, the students, through their daily application and their daily effort, is to be able under all circumstances and conditions to say, "I choose to have this level express at this moment." So that people around and about us won't be pushing our buttons of our little tape machine up here in our head and have our soul expressing on the levels that it is experiencing around and about it. Do you understand that?

Now this is very important. This is what self-control really means: that *you* consciously make the choice and the decision of the experience that you wish to have at any given moment. Now, how many of us are doing that? This is what the classes are all about. This is what this church is all about. This is what this whole Association is all about. You see?

How many times in the course of a single day are we saying, "I choose to play tape number 54, because I know how I enjoy the experiences which are the effect of that tape?" This is what we're trying to get you to grow to: to get all your tapes out here and lay them down and say, "Oh yes, I like that tape very much. Now what number is that?" And then, when you want to play that tape, push the button. And not walk down the street or go home and let your husband or your wife push it, when they want to push it. Because they're usually not even aware that they're doing it in the first place.

Now, this is what we're talking about, friends. We're all controlled all the time. And we sure don't like that. None of us like to think that we are the victim and the slave of something that we're not consciously aware of, but that's the truth of the matter. We've all permitted ourselves to be victimized. But, you see, we did it to ourselves. Only we did that. And because only we victimized ourselves, only we can free ourselves. Nobody else can do it. Does that help with your question?

Yes, somewhat.

Then, please ask further.

I suppose this somewhat relates back to the first problem. What I'm wondering is, in these times, if it is perhaps better to push another button at that time or if it is better to try to wade through it at that time. And, if so, how can we wade through it?

Well, the question must arise then, Are you aware of what that tape is?

Not entirely, no.

Then, I would suggest and recommend, before permitting it to go on the reel to play, that you become objective and listen to it and see if that is desirable for you at this time. That would be the most advisable thing to do.

Now, a person may say, "Well, now how do I sit back and become objective and let one of my subconscious tapes play?" Well, we do that through control of our emotions, which is the magnetic field, and we make that conscious choice, which is the electrical field. And we say, "Now, here's a tape here. It gives me a strange feeling. All right now, I'm going to step myself back consciously"—you've got to have control to do that, conscious control. And then, you push the button of your subconscious and you let the tape play, and then you say, "Oops! I don't like that tape at all," or "I do like it." And then, you control it, you see.

We're being controlled all the time. What we are trying to do is to reverse the process and let you go back into the driver's seat, which is your divine right. That's your divine right, you see. Choice is your divine right. So let's choose which tapes we want to play and, then, not pick up the telephone, have somebody say something, and all of a sudden burst out in tears. I certainly wouldn't call that control. Unless we consciously said, "I want to burst out in tears now. So let me get into a tape where the phone will ring, where a person will talk to me, give me hell, so I can burst out in tears." But, don't you see, my good students, that's what we're doing anyway—but we're not doing it consciously.

Look, you can't have a phone call and have an experience until you've set a law into motion. But, you see, this limited brain says, "Well, I didn't tell her to call me at this time and dump that garbage can on my head!" But we set that law into motion. But because we're not consciously aware that we set that law into motion, that doesn't deny the truth. Truth needs no defense. You see?

Now this is what we're talking about in these classes. Look, there are no accidents in the universe. There are no accidents. All right? I'm sure we all agree on that. It's just our unawareness of the laws involved and we call them coincidences and we call them accidents. All right. Now, if there are no accidents in the universe and there are no coincidences in the universe and all experiences are the effect of laws that have been set into motion—if your telephone rings and somebody gives you hell and you break down and you weep and cry and wail, then you set that law into motion. It went out along the ethereal waves, it registered, and the experience happened to you. That's the way it works, friends.

But you know what the mind says: "I have such good intentions. I would never do that to a human soul. I wouldn't call up anybody and bawl them out and cause them to cry." Well, that's a bunch of holy wash! That's all that is. That's a refusal to face the truth. Don't you see that, my friends? Please try to think and think more deeply.

All experience is an effect of a law we set into motion. So when your phone rings, it's an effect of a law you set into motion. And because you're not consciously aware, that's not denial of the truth, that's just plain old pathetic.

Thank you, friends. Let's awaken and go have refreshments. Thank you very much.

OCTOBER 31, 1974

CONSCIOUSNESS CLASS 66

Good evening, students. Before getting to our regular format of questions and answers, I would like to speak for a few moments, perhaps, on a law that has been stated many times and that it seems we so frequently forget. The teaching of this philosophy is that like attracts like and becomes the Law of Attachment. Now, because the very nature of our philosophy is a continuous expansion and constant revelation, based upon communication with other dimensions, it behooves us to constantly bear in mind the law that like attracts like and becomes the Law of Attachment.

I know that many people in the Spiritualist movement, perhaps, may feel that it is a little out of balance between its science and philosophy and therefore do not truly find the religion of Spiritualism. Unless we maintain and sustain a balance between philosophy and science, we do not have any balanced religion or way of life for us. Therefore, it is the purpose of this philosophy to share its understanding of the laws that govern its science of communication. So when we think we are in contact, so to speak, with guides and teachers and helpers and mentors and friends that have passed through this physical world, let us use reason, by reminding ourselves of the basic law of the philosophy, which is like attracts like.

For example, if we are a proficient engineer, then we attract from other dimensions people interested and of like mind. If we are a procrastinator in our mundane activities and that is our predominant attitude of mind or vibration, then the guides that are trying to guide us, most of the time, are procrastinators. And if they are procrastinators, then they're not from very high realms of light, let alone reason. Now, if we ourselves, in trying to do our daily work, are sincere and make the effort and try to do the job as well as we possibly can and the job that we try to do for others is what we would want done for ourselves, then that's the type of guides and teachers that are inspiring us. So, my friends, I do want to stress here, in our tenth class of this semester, the importance of using reason, especially in the science of Spiritualism.

Now, it is true that there is such a thing as communication and great teachings or awareness—and knowledge about certain subjects is not within the mind of the medium or the communicant. But we're talking about basic principles. We're talking about our character and our priority values. If, for example, you want help, a guide and a teacher that is genuine, that knows what they're talking about, that is accurate, then you must become those things. You can't be tardy and expect a guide that is prompt, because, my friends, that is contrary to the law that like attracts like.

Now, let's stop and think. I have always stated, and I will state again, I have always been skeptical and dubious of so-called spirits that come to me to tell me how grateful they are for how great I am. I always look at myself and ask myself, "What level of consciousness have I descended into to attract unto me such illusion, delusion, and deception?"

Now, my good friends, as Richard P. Goodwin, I grew up in what the world calls séances. I have seen many, many, many demonstrations of materializations of so-called physical phenomena. But let us be honest and let us view all dimensions. Let us become more aware of thought forms, desire forms, and mental forms—and spiritual truths.

For example, in physical séances, it is true—and I have witnessed it many times—that a form may materialize in a séance room from what is known as the ectoplasm of the medium, if that is the type of mediumship they have. The form may materialize, move, walk, speak, and have all the physical substance of a physical form. That does not mean, in any sense of the word, that that is a discarnate spirit. It means that it could be. It does not mean that it is.

Now, what could it be? It could be a subconscious desire projection from one of the sitters. It could also be a subconscious desire projection from the medium themselves. Now, this is what I want you to understand and to give some thought to. Because it is possible, under the proper conditions, for the ectoplasm of a medium to be cloaked in a thought form or desire form, does not deny the truth of a spiritual entity—a discarnate entity—also clothing themselves in what we call ectoplasm and materialization. But it does mean before we go on the path too far in what we call Spiritualism, let us first know ourselves.

The only protection—if you wish to call it protection—from these experiences is the daily effort by the student to become more aware of their own mind.

We talked here at this class before about clear channels. Well, let's talk about *free* channels. What is a free channel? I assure you, it's better to be a free channel than to be a clear channel. Because if you're a free channel, if you are truly free from the taped experiences of the subconscious mind, then you can truly become an instrument through which the divine intelligence may flow freely.

I do hope and pray that it is within the divine merit system of all the students of this Association to think more deeply, to become aware of not only what is known as a spiritual dimension, but to become more aware that the dimensions exist within the consciousness of each and every individual. That's very important, my friends.

Too often clear, so-called, communication with dimensions is based upon the desire of the recipient. That, surely, is a poor way to seriously investigate the deepest and greatest science ever known to the world. And believe me, it is.

So let us understand the laws that govern the science of Spiritualism. And, in understanding the laws that govern it, we will not be trapped into a multitude of mental dimensions that we are not even yet aware of. So think, my students. Because something requires a lifetime study does not mean it is not valid, beneficial, and worthwhile.

The Spiritualist movement in the world today is a very small movement. But let it remain the smallest in the world and have quality, rather than a quantity that degenerates it into what is known as spiritism. And spiritism is an overbalance of interest in the psychic sciences.

And remember, when you go into your meditations or you go for counseling or you go for healing, remember, my good students, if you are emanating principle and quality, that's the only thing that you can receive. Because you can only receive in life what you are giving. And if you are giving peace and joy and sincerity and quality and principle, then that's the only thing you're going to get back. And if you get back anything different, go inside and be at peace, and you will see the light. And you will find that it is good and it will show you the way.

Many times in this life people are concerned, it seems, about abundance. And the minute you mention the word *abundance*, all it seems the mind can think about is the bank account. And I do hope that, when it thinks about the bank account, that it thinks about the *health* bank account. You see, there's not only a *wealth* account, there's a *health* account. And there are all other kinds of accounts. So when we think "abundance," let's free our mind and let it be all-inclusive.

Now, we all know if we don't have abundance of something, that it is simply a transgression of a natural law. Now that's all that it is, my friends. And it's nothing more and it's nothing less. But the first abundance to seek is the abundance of understanding. And then, you will have the abundance of peace. And then, when you have the abundance of understanding and peace, you'll have the abundance of consideration and you'll have the abundance of acceptance, you'll have the abundance of principle, and you will have all things that you seek. So that's what we want to seek, is the abundance of understanding.

You see, all the other abundances are down low here. They're microscopic. When you're standing up there and you have the abundance of understanding, you look down there and say, "Well, I didn't want that anyway. It caused me too much grief. But I couldn't see it before, because I was down there, instead of up there where I could see."

Let's look at life's experiences with a joyous heart. Let's look at the things that we don't like the way that we look at the things that we do like. Because when we look at life that way, we see its true duality and we remain in peace.

It's like a person who says, "I had a miserable day." Someone says, "Well, why did you have a miserable day?" And she says, "Well, it's been raining all day. Can't you see?" Well, it's all in the eye of the beholder. And so it's all in the mind of the individual.

You know, friends, you can speak a hundred million thousand words. And that's important, because one of the hundred million thousand words may be the very word you needed to hear to make the slightest change.

Thank you very much. You're free to ask your questions. Yes. *Would you speak on magnetic healing, the process of it, please?*

Thank you very much. And though we have had some discussion on healing before, we'll be happy to discuss a bit on magnetic healing. One of the usual systems in the world, called magnetic healing, is when a group of people get together and they decide that they're acting as energy batteries so that the person sitting in the center of the group is receiving some type of energy or magnetic healing. The sadness with that type of a system is usually most of the people sitting in the circle don't seem to have enough energy for themselves, because they're not too healthy. Usually. Now, the reason that is so is because—and I'll be perfectly honest here with my class—number one: They think that they are batteries, instead of just being them. You see, that's the thing about life. We think we're this and we think we're that. But we don't do it. And it's important.

Now, magnetic healing—yes, it serves some benefit in the sense that it can bring a balance in the magnetic field of the recipient. But that balance is not lasting or enduring.

Now, you see, we've discussed before that health is the effect of harmony and that harmony is a balance between this electric and magnetic field. All right. Now, you just take anyone that is experiencing what we call poor health—all right, there are times when we feel not too bad. In fact, we feel pretty good. And then, just out of the blue, we descend and we're not feeling so good anymore. Because, my good friends, we're not thinking. We're not aware of what tapes are being pushed back here at any given moment.

Look, a person sits in conversation with another individual and they may be talking about the weather, and, in the process—because we are asleep, because we have eyes to see and see not and ears to hear and hear not, we're asleep. We're talking about the weather. All of a sudden, one of the two people starts feeling badly. They leave. A couple hours later, they feel horrible. In fact, they descend right down into the depths. Well, what happened? One of the tapes in the subconscious computer bank got pushed. It got triggered. We must learn and apply, a little more, the Law of Association. We must learn a little more about ourselves to find out what's happening with ourselves.

Now we discussed in this class—and I do hope this is helping my student who's asked the question on magnetic healing. I answered the question: it is a balancing of the magnetic field of the subconscious. Now, what happens is this—we discussed it before—freedom is the effect of self-control. All right, we can say we're all seeking freedom. So freedom is the effect of self-control. You see, the thing is, my friends, we're seeking freedom, which is an effect of something, but how many of us will raise our hands to say we're seeking self-control? You see?

No, we got ourselves into bondage and we say, "Well, God, give me freedom. I've got to get out of here." But how many of us say, while we're in the prison, "God, give me the strength to control myself." You see, freedom is the effect of self-control.

All right, we've got to that point now. But what is self-control? Well, self-control is a conscious choice—a conscious choice—of *all* your experiences. Now, think about that. Isn't it better to say, "I choose this here today. I choose to feel good. I choose to enjoy life. I choose to have this for dinner. I choose not to have that for dinner." Well, my friends, that's the effect of self-control. And that's what freedom is. That's what it is.

Now, the truth of the matter is that every one of us—every one of us, without exception—is choosing our experiences. Would you believe it? Every one of us. Every single one of us is choosing our experiences.

Now, a person may say, "Well, I'm suffering. I didn't choose that. I didn't ask God for me to suffer." Well, you didn't have to. You transgressed natural laws and that's what you chose to do and now you suffer. However, God, the Divine Intelligence, did not leave you without choice. In the midst of your suffering, you may choose something different.

Look, the father is greater than the son, and man is greater than his own children, called creations. Man chose to create them. Man can choose to de-create them. Now, let's think. You have the divine right this moment to change your life. You have the divine right to look at the sky and say it's beautiful or look at the sky and say, "It doesn't fit in with what I like." You have that right and you're doing it every second of every minute of every hour.

If we look at life and say, "Here I am, God. This is the effect and now this is what I'm experiencing," and you accept that you're trapped and you can't move on, then you've had it. But if you look at this experience and you say, "Here I am. All right. I accept that I am a law unto myself. Nothing out there has done this to me, but I have choice. And I choose a different experience than the one I am having." Then, if you choose that different experience, you make that decision on all levels of consciousness—and you have the right, the divine right, and the power to make that choice on all levels of consciousness—then, my friends, you will have a different experience. I do hope that's helped with your question. Yes.

In Sunday's lecture you gave us a faculty of patience, acceptance, and total consideration. And I wonder if you would give your understanding of that and its relationship to patience, perseverance, and promise.

Well, thank you very much. We have stated many times that all soul faculties are triune and they are all inseparable and one has an effect upon the other. For example, faith, poise, and humility—if you have a bit of faith, you have an equal amount of poise and humility, as we have discussed before.

Now, the lady is asking in reference to patience, perseverance, and promise and patience, total consideration, and acceptance. Well, when you're moving through the soul faculty of patience, perseverance, and promise, that is a movement from the soul faculty of patience, total consideration, and acceptance.

Now, perhaps I should have brought the blackboard for your question, but I'm sure you can all get a mental image of the diagram. For example, all things expand. It is the principle of the universe: expansion and contraction. Now, that divine principle does not change because we now name the soul faculties. For example, patience, total consideration, and acceptance, we're now moving, let us say, through patience. And so that moves—patience now moves into patience, perseverance, and promise. And so it is throughout all your soul faculties, throughout all your sense functions. I do hope that's helped with your question. Yes.

You see, my friends, life is a journey. It never began. So it will never end. Spiritualism needs not to prove anything about life continuous to anyone, because anyone with any common sense knows that they never had a beginning, so they'll never have an ending, unless they are blinded by the form through which their true self is now expressing. Yes. I hope that's helped with your question.

Thank you.

You're welcome.

Just a moment ago, you spoke on exercising self-control on all levels of consciousness. Could you help us, please, in how we would do this on all levels of consciousness?

Yes, thank you very much for your question. How would we exercise self-control on all levels of consciousness? Number one: By becoming aware of all levels of consciousness, because we can't control what we're not aware of. Right? So we go back to our original teaching, to our foundation of understanding. In all your getting, get understanding. And let it be gotten within, because that's the only place where it exists.

So it behooves the student to make daily effort on getting a little awareness, a little understanding, so they may become aware of all of their levels of consciousness. And now, once having become aware of those levels of consciousness, they now work to understand them. Because, you see, my friends, you cannot truly control what you cannot truly understand. Would you not agree?

You know, if you step into an automobile and you do not understand that you must take a key and turn the ignition and put your foot on the accelerator, etc., if you don't have that understanding—now you may have the awareness and you may say, "Oh, that's a little keyhole there. The key must go in there. But what are those pedals on the floor?"—you don't have control. Do you understand? And so it is with this little vehicle, this automobile that's inside of us, you see.

And so we first make the effort to become aware that these levels exist, from personal experience, personal conscious experience, because we're already having the personal experience. But, you see, we don't understand how this tape plays and we don't want that tape to play, but it's playing. So we first must understand that tape. We must understand how it got there in the first place. And when we understand how it got there, we will know how to get it out. Does that help with your question?

So first, you see, become aware, truly aware, that you're playing different taped experiences every day, every minute. After you become aware, if you decide you don't like that tape or you decide that you do like it—you might decide that you do like that tape and you want to be able to play that tape at your choice. Or you might decide you don't like that taped experience and you don't want to play it. So you first become aware. Then, you strive to understand it, because there are times in your life when you want it to play and there are times in your life when you don't want it to play. You see what I mean?

You know, a long time ago, my little friend there, Crystal, said, "You know, it's known as the robotical vibration." That was the first time I'd heard that word. And I said, "Well, what do you mean, 'the robotical vibration'?" "Well," she said, "you know, we're all robots until we free ourselves." And I said, "Robots?" She said, "Yes, of course, you're all victims of your tapes. The sadness is, you don't know how to push the button."

You see, this is called a spiritual awareness class. See? Spiritual awareness. You know what that means? To become aware spiritually. Because, you see, then you're aware of the power that can move in any direction that you choose. And so this is what the classes every semester are all about—is becoming aware. You see what I mean?

You know, nobody likes to walk down the street or go on their job or go home and—feeling great—and all of a sudden something says, "Grrr!" and they feel horrible. Well, now you certainly wouldn't call that self-control, would you? No. If we have self-control, then if somebody smiles, we feel good; if somebody grunts, we still feel good. That's self-control. Goodness' sakes alive, friends!

You know, we haven't even sold our divinity: we gave it away for nothing! Pretty sad. Well, think about that. You go on your job. You're feeling good. The worker next to you, you know, they say this or they say that and you change your feeling? Well, they didn't pay you for feeling lousy: you gave it to them free. You know what I mean?

You know, self-preservation is the first law of the universe. Now that's the first law of the universe of form, is self-preservation. Every dog on the street knows that. And so do all the other animals. Self-preservation. See? Now, what does that really mean? It means preserving your individuality. Preserving your identity. Preserving your peace, your joy, your love, etc. Well, how do you preserve that? Well, for pity's sake, you preserve that by not letting somebody else steal it! Do you see what I mean?

Well, isn't it true? Look out there and then say, "Well, I don't like the way she looked at me. Well, I don't like her attitude. Well, I don't like his temper. And I don't like the way he grunts at me when I say good morning." Well, isn't that beautiful? Isn't that really beautiful? And you call that self-preservation? I call it a word and it isn't sanity. Now, thank you. Let's go on with our questions. Yes.

In Discourse 47 there is a little item here on love, to be the channel in which it freely flows. My question is how to direct it. It says, "Learn to direct it to all life." How do we direct it to all life?

Thank you very much. Thank you. In reference to love, there is a little statement that says, "He who loves himself more than he loves me shall lose himself to find me. But he who loves me more than he loves himself has found the truth: eternity [Discourse 26]." Now let us think about that. It's published in one of your little books. Let us think about that.

What do we mean by, "He who loves himself more than he loves me shall lose himself to find me"? That means your divinity. When you love the tape banks of your computer, desire world more than you love the freedom and joy and peace of your divinity, which is called your spirit, then you must lose yourself, your tape banks, to reclaim your birthright, your own divinity.

Now when you do that, what you have given up, you have gained. So how do we love all life and know the Light? We love all life and know the Light when we are freed from the prejudices of our own taped experiences.

For example, a person says, "Well, this is my husband and I love him. And when he's in a bad mood, I'm miserable, because I love him." What kind of sense is that? That means, "I love him on a limited, predetermined basis, whenever he acts the way that I expect him to act, which is my tape." That is not the love we're talking about. That's self-love.

You see, my friends, the teaching is to "love all life and know the Light [Discourse 2]." But most of us seem to misunderstand that and we compute, "Love all life and know the Light" to be self-love. Well, you see—look, it's like a person that buys their wife a new car. Well, a man buys his wife a new car. What kind of a new car does he get her? Well, he gets the car that he desires, of course, because he's not getting it because he loves his wife. He's getting it because he loves his own tape of the kind of car that he wants. You call that love? I call that selfishness. It happens all the time everywhere.

Then it's like the wife goes to the grocery store. She decides, "Well, let's see, tonight we're going to have beef stew, because I bought that thing that I wanted at the jewelry store and I'm going to have to get it out of the grocery money, because he's so tight he won't give it to me. And that's how we'll do it." Well, you call that selfless love? Well, of course not. That's the love of our desires. That's the love of our desires.

Then a person says, "Well, I can't understand all the experiences I have. I just love everybody. I've really tried to be good to everyone. I have so much love." Ha! Well, what they mean—they have so much love when a person responds to what they call love, which, in truth, is a fulfillment of one of their desire tapes. That's not, "Love all life and know the Light." And that's how come many people love and few see the Light. Do you see what I mean, friends? There's nothing wrong with love, but love does not necessarily mean the fulfillment of your taped desires. Love means love.

Now, let's have an example of love. Well, when a person loves another human being and they have all those wonderful feelings—at least they say they're wonderful—and they look up at the sky and they see the sunrise, and they have the same feeling, now they're getting there. That's love. And they look at the tree and the cat and the dog and the weed and the snake that crawls on the ground and they have the same feeling. That's love.

All the other things, my friends, are fulfillment of our desire tapes. And that's why love seems to come and go in this old world. Because, you see, there's something wrong with the language. It wasn't love in the first place. And I think we ought to check our dictionaries and change them where they have the word *love* and put *desire fulfillment*. I do hope that's helped with your question. Thank you. Let us go on to the next person.

Is there any correlation between dreams and our soul's expression? And, if so, would you expound on that?

Thank you very much. We have discussed dreams before and we're discussing them in the context, "Is there any correlation between dreams and our soul's expression?" Well, our soul is constantly striving to express, either in the daylight dream or the midnight dream, either in the dream of what we are here now—this is our dream; this is an expression of our soul and is a creation. Or—I do believe you're probably referring to the dreams when you're not consciously aware.

Yes.

Yes, I felt that. All right. Well, there are times when a person takes what we call a soul flight during their sleep and they do have a recorded experience in their mind that they are, at times, able to bring to the conscious mind. And that is an awareness of the experience they had in their spiritual flight or soul experience.

However, most dreams—not all, but most dreams, like about 81 percent—are caused from our functions. Now that's what most dreams are. Now, what do I mean by that? Well, I mean several things. I mean that you may be sleeping in a certain position. You've curled up in that position. It's not too comfortable. The window's open, a breeze comes over your face, you have part of your blanket or something, you get cold, and, oh, you have a dream. That's the effect of the functions and it has nothing to do with a soul flight or a spiritual experience.

But over 80 percent of all dreams are repressions. We've repressed certain feelings into our subconscious. We haven't spoken out, you see, or we haven't worked on ourselves in regard to some emotion and they come out in a variety of strange dreams. I hope that's helped with your question.

I hope I can express this the way I mean it. Are there cycles in our lives at which times it is better to direct our attention in a certain direction, making certain decisions or doing certain things that we feel have to be done? And, if so, how do we differentiate between tuning in to these cycles and procrastination?

Thank you very much. And, of course, when a person says they do hope they can express something the way they mean it, the judgment, of course, is always in the effect. So we hope we have a good effect in reference to your question.

The lady is asking about cycles. Are there cycles? Why, yes, there are cycles for all things, you see. This is a world of rhythm. And there *is* a rhythm and there *is* a cycle. Now, the thing is that we are supposed to be self-conscious, self-aware. Think of that: self-conscious, self-aware two-legged animals. Now that means that we have the potential, the possibility of what we call self-control.

Now, I want to make this very, very clear. All of creation, including the animal called man, is influenced to some extent by cycles. Now, for example, I'm sure we've all had a house pet called a dog or we've seen dogs. They're controlled by a cycle for their procreation purposes. Would you not agree? We're all adults. They're controlled by a cycle for the purpose of procreating their particular species.

Now, man has self-conscious awareness. Man can choose. Even though he is not in the cycle at the time, he can choose to do what he wants to do when he wants to do it. Are you following me? What I want you to know—yes, there are cycles. There are cycles for all forms. But man is supposed to be the crown of the animal kingdom. That means he is supposed to be able to have self-control through any cycle, anytime, at any place. Now, I would rather have you have the full awareness of the true position of man on Earth than to be bound by creation's rhythmic cycle.

It is true that these cycles exist for all forms—the trees, the animals, the rocks, all kingdoms. But we're greater than those cycles. You see what I mean? Now a person may say, "Well, I'm an artist. And I can only do my art as it really should be done—and, of course, I'm the one that's making the decision—when I'm in the flow, when I have the inspiration." Well, God doesn't stand there and say, "Oops! It's two o'clock. Time for inspiration!" No! The inspiration is always constant. Now the form, you understand, may be on the descent of that cycle and it is more difficult to tap the inspiration channel. But it is still possible. I do hope that's helped with your question.

Thank you.

You're more than welcome.

Would you please speak again on the relationship between the electrical and magnetic aspects of our being and that relationship to healing?

And its relationship to what?

To healing.

Oh, in its relationship to healing. Yes, I'll be more than happy to. In reference to the electric field and the magnetic field of all form—all form—not just man—and please, friends, don't get your egos hurt because I refer to man as the two-legged animal, because that's what we are. God didn't choose to call us human. Man chose that, to rise himself above the animals. Now let's be honest with ourselves. We have all these animal instincts and we practice them more often than we are aware of, believe me.

And now, in reference to healing—this is very important, you see—it deals with humility, you know. The electric field and the magnetic field, of course, exist in all form. When this electric and magnetic field are brought into a perfect balance—now, what I mean is that equal energy goes into the magnetic and equal energy—50–50—goes into the electric—you have this perfect balance, which creates a receptivity to the divine, neutral power. And that is what truly does the healing.

You see, this is why we teach peace. Again and again and again, we teach peace. "Be at peace, my child, and I will work my wonders" does not mean "Try to be at peace and I will *see* if I can work my wonders." That's not what the statement means. It means, do it! It means, stop trying, stop rapping, and just do it. And so that's what we're talking about in healing. See? Stop thinking about it. Just go do it.

You see, you've got a ditch to dig over there. Go get your shovel, walk over, and bring it back and dig the ditch. Don't think, "Let's see, my shovel is six feet away. Now that's six feet. Do I have enough energy to make that much movement?" That very thought dissipated seven runs of six feet back and forth to get the shovel and dig the ditch. Now, you see, this is what I'm talking about. Be doers in the world. Do! Stop dreaming about it. Stop thinking about it. And if it's healing you're seeking—anything you're seeking—just do it!

You see, what happens to the mind, it says, "What do you mean 'Just do it'? What do you mean 'Just do it'?" See? It starts whirling, you know, like a little old helicopter taking off at the airport. It starts whirling and whirling and whirling. And you know how much those blades whirl before the poor helicopter gets up off the ground. See, and it makes a lot of noise. Now this is important. You're asking about healing. And, you know, I'm talking to you about healing and I'm sure you can see it.

The thing is, my friends, just do it. See? Just do it. Don't theorize, "Maybe it'll work and maybe it won't work. Maybe it'll take six months and maybe it'll take six days. And maybe it won't work at all." Because in that level of consciousness, you are dissipating all of the energy necessary to bring you into perfect balance and perfect health. Now that's what I'm talking about.

But the mind is so conditioned. It runs here and it comes back. It runs there and it runs there and it runs there and it keeps on running. And all of the energy expended in all of the running is the energy that is necessary to bring us the perfect peace and the perfect health.

Now, it is true if we do not have a tape that says, "This is what works. I've already accepted that," then it's easier for those who have already had an experience. Would you not agree? And so it is in healing, if you have had an experience, then it's easier for you to be healed. But if you haven't had an experience, it's more difficult. Well, it's the same thing as driving a car. If you've driven a car, it's easier to drive it. Right? If you've never driven a car, it's much more difficult. But, you see, we've all got to learn something sometime. So let's just be about the learning process and be about the doing process.

See, this is what we're talking about. And I'm so happy you brought up that question. This is what we're talking about, is self-control. You see? And this is our teaching: to nip it in the bud. We teach the longer you play a tape bank out of your computer, the more difficult it is to change it. Do you see what I mean? So when one starts playing that you don't like, all you need to do is to say, "Just a minute. I don't like that tape. I've experienced it before. God, let me direct my thought, which is the vehicle through which this divine energy flows, to something that I desire." And if you will truly do that, you know what happens? The energy moves from this channel over to this channel and a new tape starts playing. And you feel fantastic.

You know, a person can feel miserable and all you've got to do is let some form pass in front of them that they strongly desire, and all of a sudden they feel fantastic! And if you say, "What's the matter with you? You got up out of bed. What's the matter with you? I thought you couldn't move," all of a sudden they collapse. Well now, my good friends, isn't that a living demonstration of our own mind? And I know that you've all had experiences of feeling puny. And I know that you've all experienced, while you are feeling puny, desiring something very strongly. And while you're in that moment of desire, why, you feel fantastic. Would you not agree? Yes.

Why, many people I know, they've had what they call the flu and everything else. And you let some old dear friend, associate of theirs, you know, perhaps one of the girlfriends or something they haven't seen in a long time they're very fond of, why, she just came into town, why, my gosh, flu, pneumonia, it doesn't matter what it is, they're right there at the airport. Well, what happened to the flu in the process? That's what I want to know. Well, I already do know. I know what happened to the flu. It no longer existed, because they no longer played that tape. Does that help? That's very important about healing. It's very, very important.

You know, it isn't just one or two of us. The law works for all of us. You know, it even works for the animals. You see, I have a little dog at home. You know, if he's not feeling too well—he loves rocks—all I've got to do is get a rock. All of a sudden, he feels fantastic. All of a sudden. Now that's the way everybody is. And we all do it and we do it all the time.

You know, when we're having experiences in life that are distasteful, you know, all we've got to do is sit down and say, "Well, what am I getting out of this experience? Number one: I don't like the experience. But what is it I'm really getting? Because I wouldn't stay in this experience, even though I don't like it, unless I was getting something." You see, there's one thing about the human mind: it's always got to be getting. And it's always getting something. Now I mean that. Just look at the human mind. It's always in the getting vibration. And that's why—you know, the prophets knew that. They knew that all men were in the getting vibration—get, get, get, get, get, get, get—they're like jackhammers, they get so much. So they said, "In all your getting, get understanding." Because they knew they couldn't change mankind from his "getting" vibration. They knew that. They had that much wisdom. And so they simply said, "Well, we can't change him from his getting, but let's direct his getting to the one thing in life that's going to free him," and so they said— they didn't say in the Bible, "Get understanding." They said, "In all your getting, get understanding," because they knew the human being.

And so we're all getting all the time. Some of us get things we don't like and some of us get things we do like. And the process goes on. But, you see, because the principle of getting is the same for all of us, then we've got to say, "All right, this experience I'm getting is miserable and I don't like it. But what am I getting out of this miserable experience?" Because, you be rest assured, we're getting something. Now we might be getting more love. We might be getting more attention. We might be getting pneumonia. We might be getting anything. But we're getting something.

God bless you and may you get to the true light of understanding. Thank you.

NOVEMBER 7, 1974

CONSCIOUSNESS CLASS 67

Good evening, students.

Now, I know that for many classes we have discussed so much about self-control and the mind and a tape computer bank, etc., and, as you all know, as students who carry on with this philosophy, who return week after week, semester after semester, that it is a gradual, evolving process. These types of classes, though beneficial for one semester, are something that is designed to help you each moment of each day through your continued efforts, through your continued study, and through your continuing application of the laws that you are learning.

Life is the expression of a planted seed. And it's like a seed that you put in the soil: all things are born in what is known as the lesser light or darkness and they must struggle up through that soil—some of the soil is hard and crusty—in order that they may become a sprout, ever reaching upward to the light. And so it is with the soul and its evolutionary path. If it means enough to you, if it is high on your priority list of desires, then you, as an individualized soul, will make the effort to continue in your study and application.

We're very grateful that we have been given the opportunity to have this philosophy as a continuum for the students who are attracted to it. It does not mean, however, that you have not already benefited or will not continue to benefit from what you have already received. It does mean, my good students, that if you are learning anything in life, you don't start learning it for a month or two or three and you set it aside and go off into other levels of consciousness, when the seed has hardly had a chance to germinate. And so it is that this Association—for those students who are unable, for some reason or another, to continue on with their philosophy classes here at this church have the great benefit of these taped classes. So no matter where they are, they can listen over and over and over again for the word that they need. If they are sincere, they will hear in the right time and at the right moment.

It is most important in learning anything in life that you make the effort to carry on with your efforts. Then, the day will come and it will dawn in your consciousness and serve you in time of great need.

It is perhaps, for many, difficult to understand the ancient teaching that many, indeed, are called, but few are chosen. It is not, as we all know in this class, anyone or anything outside of us that chooses whether we stay in the Light and in our efforts to understand ourselves. It is a decision that is reached according to the desire priorities in our own consciousness.

Now there is a just teaching, a true teaching, that states, On the path to illumination, many, many, many things will distract you. That not only takes place here every moment of your day, but it is, indeed, what takes place when you leave this physical body. And we have discussed in our classes before what so-called death is really all about. We're dying each moment of each day, because we're dying to certain levels of consciousness and patterns of mind, as gradually, slowly but surely, new attitudes, new patterns of mind are being recorded in our consciousness. And so it is when you leave this physical body that many things, as your soul is going on through space, to the Light, to its true home, many things will distract you. But those things, my friends, are taped experiences in your own consciousness—the good, the bad, and the indifferent.

It is true in any endeavor that most people quit just before the victory. And so I do hope and pray that it may be in divine order for those present this evening to give serious thought in making their decisions to continue or not to continue, to give sincere, serious thought to whether or not you are on the threshold of victory. Because, my friends, that will be a strong determining factor in what you do in your efforts.

We all know in life that when we seek something, we are easily distracted by the great variety of creation that constantly tempts us to move in one direction or the other. But that reveals—that temptation to variety—it reveals our own lack of control, of concentration.

It takes energy, which is power, to move our soul from one level to another. And that energy, properly directed, is known as concentration. Now, we may think, when we're in the midst of any struggle in life, that it is just too much to bear. That feeling, that experience—that the cross is too heavy—is the threshold itself, which your own individualized soul is passing through to the next level of consciousness. We experience it as a great cross, a great burden, because the level that has bound our soul is not willing to let the soul be free and leave that level of consciousness. Because a level of consciousness is an attitude of mind, which is the effect of directed energy and creates what is known as an entity.

Now, we all have these so-called entities, because we all have these different levels of consciousness. And so that is when we experience that the cross is too heavy to bear. Those are the entities within our own consciousness in the depths of our own mind that say that it isn't worth it. And that, my friends—become aware of it. So you know where you really are.

You can always move out of a level, if your desire is great enough to do so. For all experience, we know, is the effect of what we, and we alone, have created. But we have a divine Power that flows through us, that is ever at our disposal, if we choose to be receptive to it.

There is no experience in life, in all of the universes, that the Divine within you is not greater than those experiences. So let us remember that. And let us direct our energies through the soul faculties of encouragement and enthusiasm. There is no greater expression of the Divine than enthusiasm. But how does a person become enthusiastic? They become enthusiastic from the effects of a soul faculty known as encouragement. So when you make the little extra effort known as care, when you do that, you will encourage your soul to make a greater effort and you will experience enthusiasm. For *enthusiasm* means "to be in God." So let us spend a little time in our days to encourage ourselves.

You know, it's a known truth that all creation responds to encouragement. The animals respond to encouragement. The plants respond to encouragement. And so man responds to encouragement. So if you want enthusiasm in your lives, if you want to attract it, you must demonstrate it. And remember that enthusiasm in God is the effect of encouragement.

So whatever you are seeking—and may it ever be the Light, for it is the only thing that will free your soul. Remember this: that service is the only path to spiritual illumination. And there is no other type of illumination that is enduring, eternal, or worthwhile seeking. So let us be encouraging to our levels of consciousness, to the ones that we wish to continue to express. And then we will emanate enthusiasm and we will attract enthusiasm from other people.

So often I have heard students say, "This one doesn't want to do this" and "That one doesn't want to do that" and "Somebody else is negative about this or that." That, my friends, is an experience that only we have attracted. The people that we're talking to—they don't want to do this or that—are the mirrors revealing the level of consciousness that we are emanating. So let us be aware of that inside of ourselves. If you want someone to do something in life, then first pray for understanding. Have the acceptance of considering *their* responsibilities and *their* levels of consciousness. But, of course, that takes duty, gratitude, and tolerance.

People are not the way that we are. They are similar, but they are individuals. Their priorities are not the same. Their desires are not the same, though they may be similar. So let us respect the rights of difference and let us use consideration, acceptance, and understanding when we want somebody to do something.

You see, my friends, it's not an automatic function that I should ask a student or a member to do something and they automatically do it. I am not that stupid, I hope. I first must consider and pray for understanding and acceptance and duty, gratitude, and tolerance, that I may strike a responsive note in the person that I am making the request of, ever recognizing that I am not asking their mind. I am asking the divine Power, known as God, that is flowing through them.

So when you want something in life, don't forget who you're speaking to, and then you will not be so disturbed when they tell you no. You know, so many people think that the word *no* is negative. Well, I assure you, wisely used, it's very positive. I mean, after all, we all experience levels of consciousness and we all have different attitudes, and there is a time in life to say no. Self-preservation of the form is the first law of the form.

But remember, my friends, when you say no, you're not saying no to someone else. You are saying no to yourself. And you don't perhaps know, *k-n-o-w*, what door you have just closed. And having closed a door, you don't know whether or not you will be able to open it again.

So in all of these experiences, let us ever remember that opportunity is like the hands of the clock: it meets every so often. And man does not know when those hands will meet.

Thank you, my good friends. You're now free to ask your questions. Yes.

We are taught that we attract everything to ourselves, such as illness. When I discussed this recently with a friend of mine outside of Spiritualism, she said, "Well, how about animals? What happens when they get ill? Do they attract it?"

Yes, thank you so very much for your question. They most certainly do. And so do plants and all other creation. They attract it unto themselves.

You see, very few people have yet done the study necessary to realize—let alone to accept—that animals have personalities. They have egos. And they have frustrations. They have desires, they have likes, and they have dislikes. And plants have the very same thing. Oh yes, some plants will not grow next to other plants: they don't like them. Now, of course, our botanists say that, well, some require different nutrients in the soil. That is true. But a plant can be very selective. It attracts out of the soil the nutrients it needs for its own health. Then, we can say, well, one plant requires a lot of water and another plant requires a little bit of water. One likes the sun and one doesn't like the sun. Well, you can put two plants—they both like shade—next to each other and they may not be in harmony. They may not be in rapport. Their personalities may clash. And one of them will wilt and die. And so it is with human beings, you see. Some people bring out the best in us. And some people bring out the worst. Now they don't do it to us. We let them, you see.

And so it is, of course, with our health, with our wealth, and with all other experiences in life. But if we are in a health situation, we do not feed attention to what is known as the level of consciousness called guilt. For nothing is more destructive to the form than a guilt complex. And so what we want to do is to feed energy to the level of consciousness where encouragement is. Because, you know, we all know that when we're encouraged, we feel better. And when we're discouraged, we feel terrible. So you see, encouragement is the way up out of any experience. And discouragement is the way down. Does that help with your question?

Thank you.

You're welcome. Yes.

In speaking of encouragement, when we see someone in a down level of consciousness and we, at the moment, are enthusiastic, are we to encourage others? Or is encouragement just to encourage ourselves, to rise our own soul?

Yes, thank you so very, very much. And it's a wonderful question. We really appreciate that student.

The lady has stated, when you see another one in a down level and you are encouraged and in an up level, is the effort to be made on ourselves? Well, number one—you see, there is a very clear law that states, What we are speaks so loud we cannot see where we are. Now, what that means, my friends, is this: It takes one to know one. Therefore, if we see a person on a low level of consciousness, that simply means in that split instant, you see, we have dropped from our high level of consciousness to that level of consciousness in order that we may register that that individual is on a low level of consciousness.

Now this is very important because it is an impartial law. And it is a basic law of this philosophy, of this Living Light teaching: Like attracts like and becomes the Law of Attachment. If we are truly on a high level of consciousness, what is attracted to us will be on an equal level of consciousness, a high level, for like attracts like and becomes the Law of Attachment.

Now, it deals, in truth, with awareness. All right. We walk into a building and we say, "Well, I'm feeling just great, just fantastic." What happens? We say hello to someone and they just look the other way. Then we say, "They're on a low level of consciousness." The truth of the matter is, we walked in the door on a high level of consciousness. We said hello, expecting a certain reaction: a desire fulfillment. We did not get the reaction, which is the desire fulfillment, and in a split second we dropped to a low level of consciousness. And when they said, "Ugh!" we said, "I came in on a high level of consciousness. And look at that person there!"

See, my friends, we must think, and we must think very deeply. And we must learn to accept the truth that all experience is a direct effect of our own level of consciousness. So when we say to ourselves, "I'm on a high level of consciousness," we feel that we're on a high level of consciousness and we experience in an instant someone who we decide, then, is on a low level of consciousness, it means that we're not yet aware that we have instantaneously dropped to a level where their reaction was not fulfilling to our desires. I do hope that's helped with the question. It's very important. Yes.

Could you please give us your understanding on—we hear so much about reflections from within.

Yes, certainly. All experience—all experience—is a reflection from within. Now, what do we mean in this teaching—and we'll expand that a little further. Now, ofttimes a person will say things about another individual to the individual. They may say, "Well, you're in a very low level of consciousness." Well, that isn't necessarily a true statement. It may be true. But it may not be true. It may be what is known as reflections from within. Now, the reflections—this is a very important question that follows and expands what we just discussed—now, the reflection from within is this, as I just explained: [We] walk in, we say, "I feel great. I'm in a high level of consciousness. I speak to a person. They do not react the way my desire wants them to react. Consequently, they're in a low level of consciousness." No. That could easily also be a reflection from within.

We are now reflecting—the mirror is reflecting back to us that we are on a low level of consciousness because we did not get our desire fulfilled. They did not react the way that was in harmony with our level of consciousness at the moment. Absolutely. And so we have the teaching known as reflections from within, you see.

And this is what is so important, my good students, that we really think more deeply, really and truly, that we say to ourselves, "What is my desire? I felt so good and here I've been here ten minutes and I just feel terrible." Well, you see, we're not selling our divinity: we're giving it away to the world for nothing. Think. The most precious thing we have—our divinity—more precious than diamonds or gold. The only thing worth striving for, the only thing worth living for is our divinity. And yet we don't sell it. We give it away for nothing.

Now, why do we give away our divinity in life? Because of our unawareness. That's why we give it away. We're not aware. And you can't value what you're not aware of. But we become aware of our divinity in times of great strife and struggle. Then, my friends, once becoming aware of your divinity, you will never again cast those pearls, known as your divinity, to the swine. You will ever be conscious of the peace that passeth all understanding You will ever be conscious of the heaven that is within your own mind. And you will guide it and guard it and treasure it. And then life will become worthwhile for you. I do hope that helps with your question. Yes.

I'm interested in understanding your understanding of the meanings of the soul faculties, which you gave to us this evening. First of all, I'd like a fuller definition of both enthusiasm *and* encouragement. *I would like to know what would be your understanding of the difference between* joy, happiness, *and* encouragement—no, enthusiasm. *Excuse me. And with regard to* encouragement, *when I look at the word, I understand it to mean "to give courage to." And I'm interested in the teaching that states that unsolicited help is ever to no avail. And I'm wondering whether one can give encouragement to someone else if it is not asked for.*

Thank you very, very much. One can only encourage oneself. And that encouragement can only be experienced by any soul that is on a level of receptivity to it.

Now, that may seem to be a bit confusing to the mind at first. But let us think of it in a different way. When we're speaking of encouragement, we're not speaking in the sense that a person meets another individual and they say, "You know, you're really doing great." That's not what we're talking about. First, the individual that speaks those words must first be doing great themselves. Otherwise, the spoken word goes into the atmosphere and returns void. First, my friends, you must become the thing you express or it will not have any effect upon that that you are expressing it to.

Now, there's one thing about animals: you don't have to ask them where they are. They are so humble and innocent, they *reveal* where they are. You see, an animal doesn't have deception. It hasn't evolved to the so-called civilization yet. So this is what we mean: an encouragement within your own consciousness. Then, you will encourage those who are attracted to you. That's a spiritual responsibility.

Now enthusiasm—what does *enthusiasm* mean besides "being in God; to be enthused?" When a person is expressing enthusiasm, all the desire priorities descend into the nothingness at that moment. All of the energy that flows through your consciousness is now channeled into a oneness known as concentration. And concentration is the key to all power. So when you are *en*thused, you are indeed in God, because no other priorities exist in your consciousness during that time. This is why the human form, when enthusiastic, is able to accomplish more work, to do it better, to do it with a greater feeling, a greater effect, a greater experience, when it is doing it under the vibratory wave of enthusiasm. And so if you want a job well done in life, then get into the flow called enthusiasm.

Now, you can't get into the flow called enthusiasm until you can get the consciousness directed through what is known as encouragement. Now, you see, when a person is doing a job, if you are encouraged in yourself, you can share that encouragement, that vibration, with the individual that is doing the job, if they are in rapport and receptive to you. Do you understand? Now then, what happens, this encouragement starts directing the energy into a particular channel. Do you understand?

Say, for example, somebody is a carpenter and they're making a box for you. All right, this is what happens. They're in the process of making the box and you'd like to have it a little bit better quality: you'd like to have it more even, etc. Well, if you are wise, you will encourage yourself, knowing that that is how it's coming out. Do you understand? Then, you will first be aware, so you can be receptive to their level of consciousness. Otherwise, you can trigger their r and r's. And those aren't too pleasant. I'm sure we all understand that. And so you encourage them to bring about the best possible job that they can do.

Then, what happens, those other desire priorities start dropping. And the next step is they get enthused. And then all those other desire priorities disappear at that time and the greatest effect and the most beautiful effect comes to pass. That's what we mean about enthusiasm and encouragement. I do hope that's helped with your question. Yes.

Sometimes people will be in a very good frame of mind and will make a promise or they may be in the opposite and express a burst of anger or so forth and then shift to another level of consciousness and it's all blotted out. How does one suppress these experiences? And doesn't it take a lot of energy?

Thank you very much. Now, of course, in reference to what you are speaking about, that the different levels of consciousness—we make commitments on one level; then we move to another level of consciousness, and it just disappears from our mind—is commonly referred to in psychiatry and psychology as schizophrenia, you see. However, in this understanding, we refer to it as unawareness or an error of ignorance.

Now, does it take—the question is asked—does it take a great deal of energy to be schizophrenic or what we prefer to call unaware? My good friends, it takes more energy to be ignorant and unaware than it takes to be illumined. That's the great sadness. It doesn't take much energy to be aware. It takes an awful lot of energy to play the same desire tape over and over and over again so you can't hear, see, or think, or know what you did yesterday. Oh yes, that takes a lot of energy. And that's why you'll find in life that people who are unaware, why, they're exhausted all the time. Well, of course, they're exhausted all the time, because the tape's been playing over and over and over again and it takes energy to play a tape. It takes energy.

You see, it doesn't take nowhere near as much energy to sit back in a chair, say "Thank you, God. I am at peace," and be at peace. But it takes a lot of energy to play one of the tapes. Yes, it really does. So you see, it really does behoove us—you know, thinking of the conservation of energy and our own good health. It dissipates less energy to be at peace than it does to play all these tapes that are in our head. Oh yes.

So this is why we pray for awareness. But, you know, awareness doesn't come without acceptance of something broader. You know, one of my students said, "My greatest problem is acceptance." And I said, "Well, I don't think your problem is acceptance. I think you've accepted extremely well all of your tapes that you have, to this point in life." Acceptance is not our problem. We've already accepted all those desire tapes: we express them all the time. Our problem may be an expansion of our acceptance. But acceptance, no, that is not our problem. We've limited acceptance. That's our problem. So you see, our teaching is, Let us broaden our horizons. And, you know, also our teaching is, Hell is paved with good intentions and broken promises. And all the broken promises, you know, are paving the path on which we have to trod: that's called hell.

Now, what is hell? Something that man does not consciously choose: that's called hell. And what man consciously chooses, he calls heaven. But just take a look around the world. We're paving the highway of hell every minute, because we're having experiences in life and we say, "I didn't choose that experience." But, of course, there's a part of us that did or we wouldn't have it, you see.

Now that's what we're talking about. We're not talking about way over there in the hereafter. We're talking about here and now. See? So let's have heaven. It's so much more enjoyable and agreeable to us. But then again, you know, it's just like day and night. If you didn't have a little bit of hell, you sure couldn't enjoy a lot of heaven. Now just think about it. So let's be grateful, you see.

What do the opposites of life do for the human mind? Well, if we didn't have opposites, could we have value? Couldn't have comparison. Couldn't have decision. Couldn't have choice, because there wouldn't be anything to choose. Everything would be the same. Well, that's how it is in life.

We can say, "You know, I had a wonderful day yesterday." And then, if we're really honest with ourselves, we can say, "You know something? I chose that wonderful day. But I'm grateful that I made that choice, because it was a beautiful day." Next day, we can say, "I had a miserable day." But you don't think that the mind says, when we have a miserable day, that it says, "Well, I chose that." Well, of course not. But this is what these classes are all about. They deal with awareness, you see.

But awareness, my friends, is getting to the root and getting to the cause of things. You know, not feeling bad or guilty or saying, "Look how unaware I am." That takes energy. It takes energy to think about how unaware you are. It takes only one tenth of that to say, "God, help me be at peace and control my desires, that I can be free."

You know, we teach control. We don't teach annihilation. So, you know, you people that have desires, we're not teaching you to annihilate them. So you shouldn't get all upset when we talk about desire and control. It just means, choose when you want to express on those levels of consciousness, you know. Choose the right vibration for you. Don't be the little donkey behind the cart, so to speak. Yes. Thank you very much. I hope that's helped with your question.

In Seminar 1, it talks about lack and limitation and poverty. It says poverty is not only limited to the material dimension, but also to the other dimensions.

Oh yes.

Would you enlarge on that, please?

Certainly. Poverty is not limited. You know, when you speak of poverty, people usually think of the dollar bill. That isn't what we're talking about in "poverty." That's just one of the multitudes of things. A person could be in poverty for the fulfillment of any of their desire tapes. A lot of people feel that they're in poverty in not having their desires fulfilled. You can be in poverty with your health. You can be in poverty with your wealth. You can be in poverty with any desire that you have. You can be in poverty of work—you don't have the work that you desire. So poverty deals with all levels of consciousness.

And a lot of people, you know, they're in poverty, but, you see, they enjoy the attention that they get while they entertain that level. Do you understand? Now, we're not saying that poverty is something that is beneficial to man or detrimental. Poverty could be very beneficial. If poverty is what is necessary to raise our soul consciousness, then poverty is serving a good purpose. Do you see what I mean? It's serving a good purpose. But that's up to the individual.

Now some people can raise their soul consciousness with wealth. I just myself prefer the latter. But I do not deny the divine right to any soul who chooses poverty as a path for their evolving soul. I simply state that it is not necessary for the evolving process. Do you understand? Yes.

I hope I'm not getting into it, but with this world condition of poverty—"in the stingy vibration", as you put it once—is this not mass thinking which will bring it about, rather than changing the consciousness?

Well, thank you very, very much. Of course, we must also think, if we choose to look upon a level of consciousness which reveals to our understanding that the world is in mass poverty, that, of course, means that we are on that level within ourselves and don't know it, but that's how we're seeing it. Now, we can do more good for ourselves and for the world by seeing the divine abundance of all things good within ourselves, and then that's the way we'll see the world and the world will change. Do you understand?

Now, a person may say, "How does that work? I can't change the world." The truth of the matter is that you are changing the world every minute of every hour. Because you are a part of the world. And the more little worlds control the big world. So let us stop and think more often of our responsibility to ourselves.

Now, personally I see a great prosperity in the universe. I don't see any of this so-called mass poverty. I cannot see it because I do not permit my soul consciousness to express on that level. You see, our teaching is, As you believeth, you becometh. So if you believe abundantly, then you will become abundantly. And so if you see the divine abundance of the universe—you see, what we're doing, in truth—when we see mass poverty in the universe, what are we doing, my friends? We're denying our divinity. And when we deny our divinity—and we are an inseparable part of the world—then we are instrumental in guaranteeing that the world will deny its divinity.

There is no lack in God's universe. And when you're in God's universe in your consciousness, you will see and be aware of that divine abundance. And what you become aware of, if you have gratitude, you become. Now remember that, friends. What you become aware of, you become, through the first soul faculty: duty, gratitude, and tolerance. So let's be aware of the Divine in its infinite, limitless, eternal abundance. Because we spoke earlier: poverty of our health, poverty of our wealth, poverty of our desire fulfillments. Well, you cannot think "poverty" and manifest its opposite. Man cannot think anything and manifest its opposite without guaranteeing failure. So, you see, whatever our job in life, we all have a responsibility—a responsibility to one world, which is called ourselves, which is an inseparable part of all worlds. And so let's look out and let's see and experience the divine, limitless abundance of health and wealth and peace. And then that's all we're going to experience, because that's all we're letting our soul view.

They say that the eyes are the looking glass of the soul and indeed they are, because they tell in an instant where man's soul consciousness really is. It tells right away where we are. The world is ever as we are within. And so if we are limited within, then that's the way the world is.

You know, think, my friends. If we are concerned about depression and if we are concerned about a shortage of food—and there are many businesses making a fortune on that fear today. Buy up all this special food and put it in your cellar. You know, it's just like the same big businesses that made a fortune on these so-called bomb shelters. You see, business in your material world thrives on negative faith, and it's called fear. The moment man has fear—just look at today. People are getting into this fear vibration—negative faith—because there's not too much sugar left at the grocery store. And so what does everybody do? They go out and buy sugar. They buy more sugar than they can use in a year. Or ten years. Well, see what we're doing to ourselves. And that's all fear. That's all that it is, is fear.

And so we say, "Well, that's what everybody's talking about. There might be a depression and there *is* a sugar shortage." Well, there's only a depression and a sugar shortage in our own consciousness. And when we are in that level, that's the kind of people we attract and that's the type of conversations they feed back to us. So let's be awakened and let's enjoy this world. And let's live in the peace and the beauty, the love and the abundance that's our divine right.

Why do we choose to suffer when we can be free?

What comes back to us is ever what is going out from us. So let's not be worried about the sugar so-called shortage, about the toilet paper shortage, and about all other kinds of shortages. And let us declare our divinity, which is an abundant flow of all good in our lives forever.

Thank you very much, friends.

NOVEMBER 14, 1974

CONSCIOUSNESS CLASS 68

Good evening, students.

[Students have an opportunity to ask personal questions relating to their spiritual growth.]

Group number one.

I will pass. [The first student declines the opportunity for guidance.]

I'll pass. [The second student also declines.]

Last week, you gave me three soul faculties, which were acceptance, freedom, and awareness. And I would like you to explain a little more fully to me exactly where I am in my soul faculties.

Thank you very much. In reference to the soul faculties that were given to you—acceptance, awareness, and freedom—that means that at this time your soul is evolving through those particular faculties. It does not mean that it is not expressing through other soul faculties, but it does mean the lessons that are being learned, the strongest, most important lessons at this time, are in those soul faculties.

Now, if you will consider what acceptance really means to you—what you have already accepted in consciousness is revealed in the present experiences that you are having. Do you understand?

Yes.

Your soul is seeking freedom from a level of consciousness. The way to that freedom at this particular time is through an awareness of the accepted patterns that have placed your soul into the bondage that it is now experiencing. Is that intelligent to you?

Yes, it is.

Yes. Now, if you will recognize that the past experiences are past and will not permit them, through self-control, to be the guidance for your present and future experiences—you understand?

Yes.

Then you will move, through awareness and acceptance, into the freedom that you are truly seeking. Does that help with your question?

Yes. Thank you very much.

You're more than welcome. Next group, please.

Could you give me some help with my meditation and if I'm doing the right thing?

Your present meditation is a matter of control of what is known as impatience. You hear?

Yes.

Because the interest in broadening your horizons is so strong, it is expressing through what is known as a degree of impatience. Now, impatience is not only a sense function, it is a denial of the truth. For example, when man is impatient in reference to anything that he is seeking—be it spiritual, mental, or material—it simply means that man, in truth, is denying his divinity by declaring that he is now under the control of time consciousness. Now, time is an illusion. It is an illusion that is created by mind stuff. So if you will work through the soul faculty, the second soul faculty, in reference to your meditation—which is faith, poise, and humility—you will be freed from the impatience, which creates an anxiety vibration—do you understand?

Yes.

And blocks the very thing that you are seeking. Did that help you?

Yes. Thank you.

You're welcome.

You told me at one time in a reading that my efforts would be fulfilled, I believe you said, in three years—that I had opened a door. And I wonder if you could tell me now if that could be my spiritual efforts and if that fulfillment could be my spiritual growth.

Yes, indeed, it is. Now, what the spirit is referring to is this: you've already stepped upon the path to the fulfillment of what your soul came to this earth realm seeking. You understand?

Yes.

Now, although it has already gone through many paths to reach this point in so-called time, it does mean that you, for many years, have had difficulty in attachment. Is that clear?

Yes.

Emotional attachment. Attachment to people, places, and things. So that when you were forced to leave them, it gnawed at your very soul. Is that intelligent?

Yes.

That means—and what is meant by the fulfillment—is that within that length of time, through a greater understanding, you will be freed from the magnetic pull called attachment.

Thank you.

You're welcome.

As a result of these classes, I feel I am more aware of where I am at the moment. And I was wondering, how can I be forgiven my feelings toward my mother when she was alive?

Yes, thank you very, very much. We all understand, as students, I am sure, that a guilt complex is one of the most destructive forces known to the human mind. Now, the lady is asking a question in reference to being freed from an experience. The experience is recorded on a tape in the subconscious. Whenever the eyes view or the senses become aware of any experience that in any way is associated with that tape—do you follow me?

Yes.

Then this tape starts playing in the subconscious and this feeling of guilt starts to rise. Is that intelligent to you?

Yes.

Now, it is known as self-control. Now, for example, number one is to become aware and to recognize that there is a taped experience, recognizing that it is an experience of the past, that it has no control over your present or future unless you permit it to have that. First, you must forgive yourself for what you think were your actions and thoughts that caused this need for forgiveness. Is that intelligent?

Yes, it is.

Yes. Now, once recognizing, becoming aware, and forgiving yourself for the expression at that time—because of your level of consciousness—then you will be in a position to forgive the situation. But first you must forgive your own soul. Do you understand?

Yes.

Because without forgiveness, there is no freedom. You must give to the Divine an experience that you have taken as your own. That's what forgiveness is all about. Does that help with your question?

Yes. Thank you.

You're welcome.

I'll pass. And thank you very much for these classes. [Another student declines this opportunity and the next student speaks.]

I would like to know, based on my current unfoldment, your understanding of the single most—or the one piece of wisdom which would help me to unfold and become a clear channel in all aspects of my life.

Thank you very much. The greatest single vibration, in order for your soul to continue to evolve harmoniously, is to make the effort to free your mind from what is called concern in anything. For to be concerned is to deny acceptance. Do you understand?

Yes.

When you free the mind from concern, your soul—all souls—flow in the vibratory divine will called acceptance. When the mind is concerned, we deny our true divinity and attempt to take on the work of the Divinity itself. Therefore, if you will make consistent, daily effort to free the mind from concern, you will flow in the divine will called acceptance and peace will be guaranteed in your life. I hope that's helped with your question.

You told me that I was being watched by the eye of eternity. I'd like to understand what that means.

Thank you so very much. And it is a phrase that is used rather frequently, sometimes, in our philosophy: that the eye of eternity is down our neck. Now, we all understand, as students, that our neck represents will. You understand?

Yes.

And the eye represents awareness. And that statement means that awareness—there is an awareness that is watching our will. And that is called conscience. And conscience is a sensibility, a spiritual sensibility that knows right from wrong, that does not have to be told. Therefore, my good friend, I am sure you will understand that when the statement is made, "The eye of eternity is down our neck," it means the part of us that knows all things—that's called the conscience—is never asleep and it never goes away. That will help you in a level of consciousness to accept that you are not alone, you have never been alone, and you never will be alone. Because there was a time in your life when you accepted a man on an isle by himself. Do you understand that?

Yes.

And because you had accepted that in consciousness and because it was deeply rooted in your subconscious, that message was given to you to help to free you, that your soul may progress ever onward and ever upward. I hope that's helped with your question.

In my meditation and just prior to it, I experience something that I call dizziness, for lack of a better term. Can you tell me if that has anything to do with this philosophy and, if so, what?

In reference to the particular experience of dizziness that you have been having, I am informed that there is an effect that is taking place in reference to your breathing. Do you hear?
Yes.
And it is recommended that you become more relaxed during and before your meditation time. If you will do that, then you will find that this condition of dizziness that you have been experiencing will disappear into the nothingness.
Thank you very much.
Now because—and I'm sure you will understand that there has been a slight nerve condition between the area of your left side of your neck and your shoulder—you hear?—the left side of your neck and your shoulder, there is a nerve that is creating a tense condition. And when you attempt to meditate, this nerve affects not only your breathing cycle, but it has an effect which is called dizziness. Do you understand?
Thank you.
You're welcome. And so if you will make the effort to go into a type of relaxation prior to going into your meditation, within a very short time that condition will disappear. Thank you.
How can I become stronger spiritually?
My dear friend, we all will become stronger spiritually when the desire rises like a barometer to the top of the list. So often, my dear friend, we do not realize that our desire priorities are not what our conscious mind thinks that they are. Do you understand?
Yes.
Now, we move in so-called time, the great illusion, and we have many experiences. And the day comes that we are grateful we have touched the light of eternal truth. And yet that tape must become strongly rooted in the depths of our mind. And it must, in time, override all the desire tapes of the years prior. Do you follow me?

Yes, I do.

Now, when that happens, then great strength—the strength of the Divine, the eternity itself—will be ours and guaranteed for our expression. At the present time, the priority—it was number five two years ago. It has risen to third place in the subconscious. You hear me?

Yes, sir.

When it rises to number one, the strength that you are seeking will be yours. I know that you know the other two priorities and therefore they need not be discussed. Does that help with your question?

Thank you.

You're more than welcome.

When we have desire priorities, I wish we could all say that God was on the top of the list. Yes, the next person please.

I would like your understanding on the experiences that I have been experiencing within the last week or two weeks.

And you accepted them?

I'm trying.

That is a revelation. Because had you accepted them, you would not be concerned. Do you understand?

Yes.

You see, my good students, the experiences, the things that we accept—then concern disappears, for that is the law. And so it is that if you will accept those experiences and not be concerned from which source they are coming at this time, then your soul will rise. Do not take them as the ultimate, for the ultimate they are not. They are creations. Do you understand?

Yes.

And creation comes and creation goes. But it is the formless and the free, the divine Peace, that is the only eternity. And so it is. Seek the divine Peace. Be not concerned about the panorama that is passing as your soul is rising to that divine Peace. If you will do that, the experiences necessary for harmonious life will ever be yours. Thank you. Next, please.

When I meditate, I feel a definite gravity pull, as I reach my subconscious, as I reach almost a level of no thought. Just before I do, I just feel myself drawn.

Do you feel the gravity pull of the physical body downward?

No. Upward.

You feel the pull of it upward.

Yes.

What is actually happening—there is a process—I'm sure you are aware, or have heard of, what is commonly referred to as astral projection?

Yes.

Yes. Well, there is a process that is taking place. It is nothing to fear. It is a very common experience with some people when they go into a type of trance or a type of meditation. And what is really happening is that the astral body—and the consciousness—is rising out of the physical. That's what's really taking place. But it is nothing to fear. Go forward with peace and you will not have any problems concerning that whatsoever.

Thank you.

You're welcome.

Can you explain the change in attitude I've had this last week and a half concerning my work?

It is the effect of the past six months, you hear? It is not a spontaneous situation, but it is an effect of the past six months. You will find it in your best interest to be not concerned about it, for within the coming four weeks it will change once again. It's like a pendulum that is swinging on a clock: it has moved from out of balance one way and it is moving the other. It will come into its balance within the coming four weeks. Do you understand? Pardon?

Yes.

And so if you'll remember that—four weeks is indeed a very short time. Thank you. The next, please.

Thank you very much.

[The next student speaks.] *If you could impart to me a word or so of your wisdom for my life.*

For your life? My dear friend, as you spoke the word, unity encompassed your entire universe. And so it is that as you make great effort—for great effort indeed it will take to unite your thought. Unity is the only thing for you at this time that will bring this great peace and this joy into your life and its fulfillment. You understand? Unity. Not unity of things outside, but a unity of things deep inside. For there are certain experiences—experiences extremely, strongly, severely recorded fifteen years ago—that need the healing balm of unity. You will find it in the depths of your consciousness. And when you bring unity over that, your soul will come together in a perfect harmony and joy and peace. Thank you. Next, please.

Could you perhaps enlighten me as to what obstruction that I may be experiencing at this time that I may not be aware of? How may I be more receptive to Spirit?

Yes, indeed, my good student. Encouragement is the thing that will bring you through. It will grant you the necessary patience. You see, patience is the path upon which your feet are now treading, but in order to keep you upon that path, that you may reach the goal—the spiritual goal—that your soul is seeking, you need consistent, continuous encouragement. The reason that you need that is because your soul is on this path at this time, this path of patience. And because the experiences of incarnations prior to this one guarantee the continuity until the lesson is learned.

Have you not noticed already in the short time on Earth that from the lack of encouragement you became impatient and left the path that you were seeking? Have you not already noticed that?

Yes, sir.

And therefore let encouragement flow into your soul consciousness, for that is the only thing that will keep you on the path of patience. And you will attain what you came to Earth to attain. Thank you. Next, please.

I would like to express my deep thanks for the teachings given by you. Since I have been attending these classes, I have been trying to apply everything in my daily life. Now, when it comes to meditation, I have certain problems. And it's like a kind of a fear. Sometimes I'm not so sure if it's right or not. And then I can never really experience real meditation. And I would like to have your opinion on how to overcome this fear, which may have something to do with my upbringing.

Indeed, it has.

I was raised Catholic, in the very strict Catholic religion.

My dear, it has to do with your fifth year. At the age of five, you had an experience that almost shattered your emotional magnetic field. And it was a fear that grabbed hold of your soul. If you will peacefully drift off into the universe through the years to that year in time—do you understand?

Yes.

For it is well recorded in your consciousness. If you will peacefully drift to that—not try drifting to that during your daily meditation. Take a few moments, just a few moments—perhaps nine minutes is sufficient. And do it in a soft, comfortable chair, but do it daily. Do you understand?

Yes.

In time, your spirit will guide you to that experience that is so strongly recorded in the depths of your consciousness. And once you have brought that to the fore of your conscious mind, you will be freed from that fear. Do you understand?

Yes, I do.

And I assure you within the coming eight months you will wonder why you ever feared at all. Thank you.

Thank you.

You're welcome.

Thank you very much.

The last time you gave us our soul faculties, mine was belief, intuition, and acceptance. As of late, I've been experiencing certain feelings through service to spirit, or in my service to spirit, and I feel that they are correct. As a matter of fact, I know that they're correct. Would you confirm my feelings of this sensing within myself or a conscience that it knows what is right and what is wrong? Thank you.

Oh, definitely. Remember, my friends, especially through the soul faculty of belief, intuition, and acceptance, in that soul faculty—because soul faculties are triune, and that is, different ones of the triune faculties—belief, intuition, and acceptance. A great battle rages in those soul faculties: the battle between the accepted patterns of experience and the belief in the intuition that one is receiving. Because what happens in life, we find a contradiction; we find a duality. We have an inspiration; through our intuition, we're inspired. And what happens is, we believe that inspiration in the moment. But when it comes to the point of acceptance and application, we become divided over the magnetic pull of the subconscious tape computer and the conscious mind and its acceptance of a new thought. Do you understand? Therefore, be grateful, my good student, for that is one of the crises soul faculties to go through. And in that soul faculty, we either go left—backward—or we go right, ever onward and ever upward.

Your soul entered this earth realm and those are three of the major lessons that it has to learn. And I assure you, those you will learn. And then your soul indeed will be freed. Thank you.

Thank you for these teachings. And I would like to ask how I might be a clearer channel for inspirational writing.

Thank you so very much. And your key word indeed throughout this entire life incarnation is organization—you hear?

Yes.

To be a free or so-called clear channel, one must have what is known as control. And control does not come until one has what is known as organization. My dear, ever since you were born, many things have distracted you when you tried to make a step in any direction. Do you understand?

Yes, I do.

The reason these seeming outward things seem to be the distraction—they are not the distraction. The distraction is because of what is called the sense function of fascination. Do you not recall how fascinated you used to be as a little girl with so many things?

Yes.

Do you not recall that tendency?

Yes.

Do you not even recall at this day and in this moment how things fascinate your mind?

Yes, they do.

They always have, my dear. Your soul entered this earth realm with one of the great purposes: to know that fascination, though entertaining, is not beneficial to control or organization. So if you will work on a balance of what is called the function of fascination, you will gain greater control. And in gaining greater control, your life will become organized. And in being organized, your spirit, your being, will be more open to the Divine Spirit, and you will indeed become a free channel. I hope that's helped you.

Thank you.

Yes, the next person, please.

I would like to express deep gratitude to friends on both sides of the veil for allowing me to be here and allowing me to express. The experiences that have befallen me up to date—are they preparing me for my true purpose? And if so, what is my true purpose?

Experiences to this point in so-called time are a revelation of the levels of consciousness through which your soul is fluctuating. Because of an experience many, many, many years ago, because when you completed—and you did complete, I am sure—a college education and degree—is that not correct?

Yes, it is.

Because you completed that, you accepted, at that time and during the end of that completion, a certain path in life. Do you understand?

Yes.

You accepted that you were going to be such and such and such and such. Do you understand?

Yes, I do.

Because that was so strongly embedded in the depths of the magnetic field—

Sir?

Yes?

I do not know what I accepted at this time.

Let me put it another way to you. You completed college.

Yes, sir.

You had a suggestion, an influence, given to you of what you were going to do on the completion of that college.

Yes.

Do you understand now?

Not entirely.

In order that we may go on with the rest of the class, I will try to make it a bit more clear.

Yes, sir.

You were informed by someone you had respect for that you were to complete college and go into a certain work. Do you understand that?

Oh yes.

Thank you very much. Because you did not, in truth, accept that, it recorded deeply in the magnetic field of your subconscious as an experience.

Yes.

Because it was distasteful to you, that experience, so well recorded, has dictated from that point onward until this point in so-called time a great difficulty in accepting any advice, in accepting any way concerning work or employment or a profession. Do you understand now?

Yes, sir.

Because of that tape, you find yourself here presently in this past year and a half with severe difficulties and problems. Is that intelligent to you?

Yes, sir.

If you will push the button that's connected to that particular tape upon the time of your college education and degree and completion, if you will accept in consciousness that that is a taped experience of many, many, many years ago, and stop that tape from playing, you will open up new doors and you will be freed from the struggle and the problems that have plagued you ever since those days. Do you understand?

Yes, sir.

That's known as broadening one's acceptance. Thank you. Next, please.

When would be the best time for me to give birth to my children?

The month of September. You hear?

Yes.

The reason for this is a balance. And I assure you—now, be patient a moment, because there is some conflict within the depths of your being in reference to that month. You hear me? It is in your best interest and the best interest of a family for your first child to be born in the latter part of the September month. You hear?

Yes.

Are you not aware that you are, let us say, not adverse, but are most uncomfortable in climate that is hot? Are you aware of that?

Yes, I am aware of that.

What we're trying to do is to reveal to you the most proper time in reference to what your tapes of your subconscious are, because it is very important that—you see, the desire, there is a very strong desire for a girl to be born. Do you understand?

Yes.

And if you will free that desire to the Divine Intelligence, then the soul that is meant to come through will come through peacefully, without a struggle. Now, I don't know if you're aware or not, but, you see, you're extremely programmed subconsciously in your acceptance into natural, natural childbirth. Is that intelligent to you?

Yes.

Well, that will be most harmonious and beneficial along about the twenty-fifth day of the September month. I do hope that's helped with your question.

I would like to know if the directions I'm headed in are the ones that are right for me. And I know patience is an important part of that. I would like to know what is influencing me from the past or present that is either blocking that or will be opening me to those aims.

Thank you so very much. In reference to what is perhaps an obstruction or blocking it or affecting the aims that you are seeking, number one is what is called a security fear. Do you understand?

Yes.

That you will have the security necessary to fulfill your desires and to attain your goals. Is that intelligent to you?

Yes.

If you will work on removing the fear of security, then your consciousness and your energies will be free to move to the fulfillment and the attainment of your goals. The fear security mechanism of your subconscious is the only obstruction to the attainment of what you are seeking. Will you remember that?

Yes. Thank you very much.

The only thing that is blocking your path.

Thank you.

You're welcome.

I express my gratitude at this time for the use of the faculty of expression in these classes, particularly between teacher and student. And I would like to know—I have been given the faculty of duty, tolerance, and unity, which was explained. Can you tell me what my duty is with this expression of life?

Yes. Your duty, as your soul entered this earth realm, is to free your soul. That is your principal duty in this life's expression. You hear?

Yes.

To free your soul from the magnetic pull and influences that distract all souls. Because of your great desire and love for life itself, you have guaranteed an experience in this incarnation that calls forth duty. Duty to the soul is your number one responsibility; duty to free it, not duty to accepted patterns. You hear?

Yes.

This is very important that you understand: duty not to accepted patterns, duty to free your soul. And the soul is freed through selfless service. And so it is, as you serve the spirit within you selflessly, without thought of effect, without thought of concern, as you serve for the principle of service, your soul will be freed, and the lesson will never be repeated. I hope that helps with your question.

It does indeed.

[The next student speaks.] *I would like to express at this time my gratitude for these lessons and the peace that they've helped me to attain. My question is this: A couple of Sundays ago, you told me that I would be going on a journey, that, in fact, it was already at my door and I was going. And that by the fifth day of the October month that I would realize the fulfillment of all my wishes. What is that journey and what is the fulfillment?*

It is the freedom from dependence. You hear?

Yes.

That is the journey. The fulfillment is the spirit of joy to brighten your soul. And so it is that the experiences to this point in time—you have what may be, to you, a normal or natural tendency to rely upon someone, anyone, that you respect: to depend—do you understand?

Yes.

Because, as a little child, you, very early, were programmed into the dependence vibration. You hear?

Yes.

And so it is that the mind—your mind—is computed to a dependence and to a respect. And therefore, whatever you respect in life, you have always depended upon. Is that intelligent to you?

Yes.

And so it is that you are going on a journey freed from the dependence, because you're going on the inward journey—the inward journey to find *you* for the first time in this Earth life. Do you understand?

Yes.

And as you are already on that inward journey, its fulfillment is the guarantee of the spirit of joy. I hope that's helped with your question.

Thank you.

You're welcome.

I would like to know anything about my physical well-being at this time.

There is an imbalance between the acid alkaline vibration in your chemistry. You hear? *[The student hesitates to speak.]* Speak to me.

Yes.

However, that is having some effect upon the blood and especially in the area of the abdomen. You understand?

Yes.

You could benefit greatly from a slight change of diet and daily spiritual healing, because the imbalance is an effect of a frustration over the past two years. Do you understand? Let me put it another way. The frustration is that you have not been getting what your mind has computed as fulfillment or, let us better say, accomplishment. Is that intelligent to you?

It isn't.

Well, if it isn't, then I would suggest that you give it some thought. Thank you very much.

Now, does our chairman have a question?

Yes, sir. What could I do to broaden my horizons and to maintain continuity at these period times of peace, harmony, and divine flow?

Thank you so very much. In reference to your question, it is—number one in importance: Keep faith with reason; she will transfigure you. Now reason is the primary faculty for you. Therefore, anything that interferes with your understanding and your reason, you must use great control not to permit it to entertain your thought. Do you understand?

Yes, sir.

Reason is the faculty through which your soul is making great effort—great effort—to express itself.

Now, how does one attain and then sustain reason? Only from a direction of the will and not to permit oneself to remain in any level of consciousness too long. Your soul has wandered in many directions for many centuries. It has come to find a foundation and stability, for it must find its own home. And so it is that great, great, great effort must be made, that it remain in the foundation that it is beginning to build, and that is known as the home of your soul. Do you understand?

Yes, sir.

Thank you very much.

Thank you very much.

Now, we have another worker in the kitchen. I know he can hear me. So let him speak forth his question.

What are the main obstructions to my present unfoldment and how may I harmoniously work through them?

Thank you very much. If I give you too long a list, you'll be discouraged and then the obstruction will become greater. So let us go to the core and the cause. That's it! Reliance on the divine within you—not arrogance—is the freedom that you are seeking. You hear?

Yes, sir.

Now, how do we have reliance and not arrogance? We have reliance upon the divine within us through the second soul faculty of faith, poise, and humility. We have arrogance of the functions when the mind thinks it knows and it doesn't think to think that it knows. Do you understand?

Yes, sir.

So it's commonly referred to in your world as second thought. So in all of your thoughts, acts, and activities, do not think once, my friend. Do not even think twice. Think at least thrice. Think on the mental level. Think on the material level. And think on the spiritual level. Therefore, with total consideration—and total consideration means total, total consideration of your own levels of consciousness before a thought becomes expressed. And with that total consideration, you will remove the obstruction that stands in your path and you will rise not only to higher levels of consciousness, but you are passing through life's experiences learning the lesson of lessons: If man has need, it is for understanding, not people or things. Thank you.

Thank you, my good students. Now, if you'll be patient just a few moments. I know that if you have been receptive to what has been asked and what has been spoken, though personal to each individual soul, it will be of great benefit to you, for all of us are an inseparable part of the whole.

Now, you may shield your eyes, please. And turn on the lights.

I know that perhaps much time has been taken with this special class, which is the last class of this year, as you know, but if you do have any questions in reference to the philosophy and the understanding, you may feel free to raise your hands. And if you don't, we can go have refreshments. Yes, the lady, please, in group seven.

When a person has contributed something to a project and at the same time is critical of what they feel that others should be doing, in a selfless service project, then could you give me your understanding of the level of consciousness of the person that is doing the criticizing?

Thank you so very much. Number one: If we have contributed, truly contributed, anything to any project and we are critical of the project to which we have contributed, the truth of the matter is we never contributed in the first place. To contribute is to give. To give is to free. And so if we have contributed to anything, then we are not critical of what is being done with it, because we are no longer attached. It is no longer ours. And so how can we be critical of something that is no longer ours? We gave it away. Do you understand?

So that means that the level of consciousness is the level which dictates, "I have loaned this. I never contributed it." Does that help you with your question?

Yes.

My good student, it is a loan when we are critical of something that we consider that we have contributed. We have not freed it from our soul. And therefore we are affected by what happens to it. For example, if I have a bushel of apples and I decide to give them to twenty children passing down the street and one of the children throws the apple in the gutter, the other one eats it and spits it out, if I have any emotional feeling, I never gave the apple at all. I loaned them the apple to do with the apple what I thought was best. That, my good friends, is not a contribution, let alone a donation. Thank you. Does that help with your question?

Yes. Thank you.

You're welcome. Did you have another question?

Well, I still don't understand what level of consciousness—

Well, I didn't want to have to say it, but I will be happy to say it now that you are pressing the issue. It's known as the level of self. That's the level of consciousness: *s-e-l-f*. Self.

Thank you.

You're welcome. Yes, please. The gentleman in group eight.

Yes, sir. Could you please tell us the difference between appreciation and gratitude? When we appreciate something or are grateful for it, it seems to me that they are synonymous.

No, my good friend, it isn't. Thank you so much. Not in our understanding. Applied appreciation is called gratitude. Now many people appreciate many things. When they apply that appreciation, it is an expression of gratitude. Do you see the difference?

Yes. Thank you, sir.

Thank you. Gratitude is a soul faculty. So is application. Yes. The lady in group nine, please.

May I ask a question that might help others that is not particularly a philosophy question? When one awakens in the morning or during the day and is filled with music—music that one hasn't heard before—is this from the spiritual realms or from the subconscious?

Because we may hear music that we are not consciously aware that we have ever heard before does not, in and of itself, of course, guarantee that it is coming from spiritual realms. It could or it could not.

Man is an inseparable part of the whole. There is a level of consciousness within all form on which all things, in that level of consciousness, are known, whether those things are past, present, or future. That level of consciousness is possible for all forms to attain. I hope that's helped with your question.

Thank you.

You're welcome. Yes, the lady, please, in group five.

How could we be sure that we've worked through an experience so that we don't have to experience the same thing again?

When it no longer entertains our thought, we are free. If it entertains our thought, then we are guaranteeing its own continuity. For thought is the vehicle through which energy expresses itself. Whenever we permit ourselves to say, "Oh, thank God I got through that experience," then what we have done—we have directed energy—you understand?—to the experience, guaranteeing its own continuity.

You see, my friends, to forgive is human; to forget is divine. And it is divinity that we are seeking. So if you want to be free from experiences, learn control. And control will direct the will and you will forget the experience and you will express your divinity. And having once expressed your divinity, all things for your greater good will be harmoniously manifested about you. Does that help with your question?

Thank you.

You're welcome. Well, I guess—yes, the gentleman, please, in group six.

Excuse me. I believe you just stated the exact reverse of what you stated in a previous class. And I wonder if you could—

Please bring up the point.

You stated in a previous class, I believe, to forget is human, to forgive is divine. It was just stated to forgive is human, to forget is divine.

That is very true. Very true. Is there any place the Divinity does not express? Therefore, what is divine in one level of consciousness could be human in another level of consciousness. And the lady asked a question in order to be free, not to be human. Does that help with your question?

You see, my friends, contradiction only exists in a level of consciousness within our own being. And so it is in a world called creation or duality, we can constantly see contradiction. But we are trying to help you to go beyond duality, which is called creation, which is positive and negative, and to help you to think. For once having thought inward, you will find the truth that will set you free.

All expression guarantees duality. And this is why our teaching is that truth is silence and silence is golden and golden is divine wisdom. From the level of consciousness from which the question is asked is the answer forthcoming, for that, indeed, is the law: Like attracts like and becomes the Law of Attachment. The method is ever legal in all of life if the motive is ever pure. And so it is that words are an expression of a level of consciousness which is, indeed, individual. And that is why what is truth for one is not truth for another. That doesn't change truth. Truth is individually perceived. That doesn't mean that truth is individual. But it means the perception—the perception—of truth is individual.

And so our purpose in these classes and this philosophy is to help you to help yourself to find the truth. And the only place that truth exists is in the depths of your own consciousness. And so it is that the teachings are ever evolving as the students are ever evolving. Here, we stated years ago, these teachings are given to you in bits and pieces, because that's how man grows. He doesn't grow in leaps and bounds. I never did see an overnight reformer that had first reformed himself. That's not how we grow.

And so it is, my friends, if you have no more questions, let us go and have refreshments. But before we do that, let us never forget: The letter of the law killeth; the spirit of the law giveth life. Then, you will ever be free. Let not the letter be your guideline in life. But let the spirit—your spirit—be ever your guidance. Then, you will be able to evolve. To evolve is to change. To progress is to change. And if you let the letter of the law be your guidance, then you will not change and you will not see the Light. You will only hear about it. But you will only see the reflection of the Light and not the Light itself.

Thank you so very much, good students. Thank you.

NOVEMBER 21, 1974

APPENDIX

The Divine Healing Prayer

I accept that the Divine Healing Power
Is removing all obstructions
From my mind and body
And is restoring me
To perfect health, wealth, and happiness.
My heart is filled with gratitude
For the Divine Law of Acceptance
That is healing both present and absent ones
Who are in need of help.
Peace, the power that healeth,
Is guiding my thoughts, acts, and deeds
As God and I go hand in hand
Living a life of joyful abundance.

The Total Consideration Affirmation

I am the manifestation of Divine Intelligence. Formless and free. Whole and complete. Peace, Poise, and Power are my birthright.

The Law of Harmony is my thought and guarantees Unity in all my acts and activities, expressing perfect Rhythm and limitless flow throughout my entire being.

Without beginning or ending, eternity is my true awareness and sees the tides of creation, as a captain sees his ship.

As the Light of Truth is sustained by the faculty of Reason, I pause to think and claim my Divine right.

Right Thought. Right Action. Total Consideration.

Amen.   Amen.   Amen.

Divine Abundance

Thank
(Gratitude)

You
(Principle)

God
(Divine Intelligence)

I'm
(Individualizing)

Moving
(Rhythm)

In
(Unity)

Your
(Realization)

Divine
(Total)

Flow
(Consideration)

www.ingramcontent.com/pod-product-compliance
Lightning Source LLC
Chambersburg PA
CBHW020054020526
44112CB00031B/107